THE
BROKEN HEART
OF AMERICA

ALSO BY WALTER JOHNSON

River of Dark Dreams: Slavery and Empire in the Cotton Kingdom

Soul by Soul: Life Inside the Antebellum Slave Market

THE BROKEN HEART OF AMERICA

St. Louis and the Violent History of the United States

Walter Johnson

BASIC BOOKS

New York

Basic Books
Hachette Book Group
1290 Avenue of the Americas, New York, NY 10104
www.basicbooks.com

Printed in the United States of America
Originally published in hardcover and ebook by Basic Books in April 2020
First Trade Paperback Edition: July 2021

Published by Basic Books, an imprint of Perseus Books, LLC, a subsidiary of Hachette Book Group, Inc. The Basic Books name and logo is a trademark of the Hachette Book Group.

The Hachette Speakers Bureau provides a wide range of authors for speaking events. To find out more, go to www.hachettespeakersbureau.com or call (866) 376-6591.

The publisher is not responsible for websites (or their content) that are not owned by the publisher.

Maps created by Kate Blackmer.

Print book interior design by Linda Mark.

Library of Congress Cataloging-in-Publication Data

Names: Johnson, Walter, author.
Title: The broken heart of America : St. Louis and the violent history
  of the United States / Walter Johnson.
Description: First edition. | New York : Basic Books, 2020. | Includes
  bibliographical references and index.
Identifiers: LCCN 2019057353 | ISBN 9780465064267 (hardcover) |
  ISBN 9781541646063 (ebook)
Subjects: LCSH: Saint Louis (Mo.)—History. | African Americans—
  Missouri—Saint Louis—History. | Saint Louis (Mo.)—Race relations—
  History. | BISAC: HISTORY / United States / 19th Century
Classification: LCC F474.S257 J65 2020 | DDC 977.8/66—dc23
LC record available at https://lccn.loc.gov/2019057353

ISBNs: 978-0-465-06426-7 (hardcover), 978-1-5416-4606-3 (ebook),
978-1-5416-1958-6 (paperback)

LSC-C

Printing 3, 2023

For my children
And Alison—always

O Lord, how long shall I cry, and thou wilt not hear!
Even cry out unto thee of violence, and thou wilt not save!

—Habakkuk 1

CONTENTS

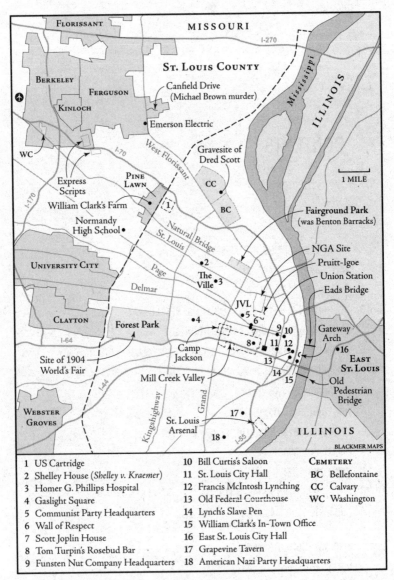

City of St. Louis, showing locations mentioned in this book.

PROLOGUE: MAPPING THE LOSS

They have torn down every house you've ever lived in. The house
on Kennerly gone. Aunt Jennie's house on St. Ferdinand gone.
The flat over Mrs. Scales's bar gone. The house on McMillan
gone. And all the others mushed in a new riddle of one-way
streets leading to vacant lots. Not one damn map familiar
and comfortable.

—COLLEEN MCELROY, *A Long Way from St. Louie:*
  A Travel Memoir

THE ARCHITECTURAL HISTORY OF A ONCE-GREAT CITY LIES
packed into crates in a warehouse near Cahokia, Illinois. Molded ce-
ment pediments, stained and structural glass, ornamental cast iron,
wrought iron, and mild steel; stone columns, friezes, reliefs, and fig-
ural sculptures; doors, window frames, and full wooden staircases.
Remnants of banks and breweries; churches and courthouses; dairies,
department stores, and foundries; greenhouses, hotels, and hospitals;
libraries, mortuaries, and museums; pavilions, post offices, and poor-
houses; schools, stadiums, and steel mills; all of the row houses that
lined one side of a downtown square. The red-brick Gothic classicism

1

of the Little Sisters of the Poor and the beaux arts Lindell Department Store; the Ralston Checkerboard Company's grain elevator and
the fortresslike First District Police Station. The nineteenth-century
skyscrapers that once lined Real Estate Row. The city of St. Louis torn
down, pieced out into elements, cataloged, and packed into crates. The
archaeological remainder of a city that once harbored the ambition of
being among the world's greatest, carefully curated by a visionary demo
man, perhaps awaiting the city's second coming.[1]

Across the Mississippi River, back in the city of St. Louis itself,
the pieces of the past lie jumbled together and scattered around the
foundations of the city's thirty thousand vacant houses, their windows
boarded up and roofs collapsed upon themselves. Many of these houses
have been repossessed by the city and delegated to the St. Louis Land
Clearance for Redevelopment Authority for resale; some can be bought
for as little as a single dollar. Thousands of poorly maintained parcels
of property on the city's Northside have been bought up by neighbors
or speculators.[2]

The population of the city today is just over 300,000—roughly the
same number as in 1870, and around one-third of the total in 1950.
The city has been left behind by its population. Middle-class whites
(and some of their Black neighbors) moved to the suburbs. Meanwhile,
the neighborhoods of poor African Americans (and some whites)
have been torn down around them. It is a truism that the struggles of
American cities in the second half of the twentieth century were due
to "white flight"—and there is no doubt that St. Louis whites moved
out of the city in droves in the years following the Second World War.
But the story of the human geography of St. Louis is as much a story
of "Black removal"—the serial destruction of Black neighborhoods
and the transfer of their population according to the reigning model of
profit and policing at any given moment—as of white flight.

Of the city's abandoned houses, it is perhaps fair to say that they
are worth more dead than alive. The deep burgundy bricks, so smooth
they seem almost glazed, molded out of the clay from pits on the city's

Southside and fired in the kilns of its famous brickworks around the turn of the century, sell for fifty cents apiece today in cities like New Orleans and Houston. For many years, there was little regulation of the demolition business, and rowhouses and brownstones containing anywhere between twenty thousand and forty thousand bricks were easy money for anyone with a pry bar and a pickup. Even today, when demolition companies must be licensed and teardowns authorized, there are rogue demo men, "brick rustlers," who break into abandoned houses to steal the copper wiring, the iron plumbing, and the lead counterweights out of the window frames. Some will set an old house on fire, knowing that the water from the firemen's hoses will soften the mortar, making the bricks easier to salvage and scrape clean for sale. So many of the houses in North St. Louis have been torn down that some of the neighborhoods look like rural farmsteads—clusters of houses here and there surrounded by open space.[3]

St. Louis today has the highest murder rate in the nation (65.8 per 100,000, around four times the rate in Chicago, and thirteenth-highest in the world) and the highest rate of police shootings in the nation (around 5 per 100,000). There is an eighteen-year difference in life expectancy between a child born to a family living in the almost completely Black Jeff-Vander-Lou neighborhood in North St. Louis and a child born to a family living in the majority-white suburb of Clayton, which sits less than ten miles to the west. Indeed, significant differences in virtually any marker of social well-being in the city of St. Louis—rates of adult diabetes or childhood asthma, levels of lead in the bloodstream, internet access—can be charted down a single line: Delmar Avenue, which bisects the city between north and south, between Black and white. Just over the city line, St. Louis County boasts three of the twenty-five wealthiest suburbs in the United States (Town and Country, Ladue, and Frontenac).[4]

Back in the city, standing on streets that, depending on the block, contend to lead the nation in the density of accidents involving pedestrians, gun murders, and payday loan stores, it is hard not to wonder: what happened here?

From the Lewis and Clark expedition to the police killing of Michael Brown in 2014 and the launching of Black Lives Matter, many of the events that we consider central to the history of the United States occurred in St. Louis. Much of this history is so well known that its midwestern origins have often seemed to historians to be beside the point. The Missouri Compromise, the *Dred Scott* case, and the western Indian wars; the East St. Louis Massacre in 1917, the Supreme Court decisions in the landmark civil rights cases *Shelley v. Kraemer* and *Jones v. Mayer* (housing), *Gaines v. Canada* (education), and *McDonnell-Douglas Corp. v. Green* (employment); the symbiosis of urban "redevelopment" by bulldozer, the sequestration of poor Black people in housing projects (Pruitt-Igoe was the nation's most notorious), and white-flight suburbanization in the postwar period; the 1960s synthesis of anticommunism, COINTELPRO, and white nationalism into the Nixonian New Right and the militarization of policing: all of these events, and many others that are treated in this book, are aspects of the history of the United States that cannot be truly understood apart from their St. Louis roots.[5]

Looking behind the curve of the received history, one finds the often forgotten radical history of St. Louis. The history of the city turns out to be less a matter of timeless midwestern conservatism than of reaction: to the consequential efforts of conquered, stigmatized, poor, and radical people to transform their lives and their society into the image of a fuller humanity. The first general emancipation of the Civil War occurred in St. Louis, where Joseph Weydemeyer, confidant and publisher of Karl Marx, was in charge of organizing the city's defense. The first general strike in the history of the United States, which briefly united Black and white workers in what historians have termed "the St. Louis Commune," occurred in the city in 1877. Through the 1930s and well into the Second World War, St. Louis was one of the most radical cities in the United States, and the Communist Party in St. Louis was an important site of radical interracial organizing. Indeed, through both the period of the civil rights movement and after, the Black freedom struggle in St. Louis was distinguished by its focus on economic issues—jobs, housing, and a just social wage. From the successful strike at Funsten Nut and sit-ins at city hall in 1933 to one of the nation's first rent strikes in Pruitt-Igoe in 1969, Black women from St. Louis have been at the leading edge of the radical history of the United States. Seen in the light of this history, there is nothing uncanny about the fact that the uprising that touched off the most recent wave of Black radical organizing—the Michael Brown moment in American history—happened in St. Louis.

Historians have traditionally treated St. Louis as a representative city, a city that is, at once, east and west, north and south. The place where the various regional histories of the United States come together. The "gateway" to the West, the "American confluence," a "northern city with a southern exposure," and so on. This book makes a more pointed claim: that St. Louis has been the crucible of American history—that much of American history has unfolded from the juncture of empire and anti-Blackness in the city of St. Louis.[6]

The city of St. Louis rose as the morning star of US imperialism. It was from St. Louis, itself a city built on stolen land, that Meriwether Lewis and William Clark departed on the journey to survey the commercial potential of the vast Louisiana Purchase Territory, the homeland of dozens of nations that had not been party to the bargain. It was from there that Clark later supervised the forcible relocation—the ethnic cleansing—of the tribes of the Upper Midwest. And it was from St. Louis that the genocidal Indian wars of the late nineteenth century were staged and supervised. For most of the period before the Civil War, the US Army's Department of the West was headquartered at Jefferson Barracks; for a time after, the entire Department of War was relocated to St. Louis. By 1870, St. Louis was the fourth-largest city in the United States, and there was talk of moving the nation's capital to the world-making confluence of the Missouri and Mississippi Rivers. Although the US military footprint in St. Louis lightened over the course of the twentieth century, military contracting remained integral to the economy of both city and county through most of that century. It is not possible to tell the story of St. Louis without including the US Cartridge Company, McDonnell-Douglas, Monsanto, and Mallinckrodt. Behind the story of the rise and demise of the city of St. Louis lies a much more complicated history of continental and even global distributions of violence.

The imperium of St. Louis (and thus of the United States) is centrally framed by the history of genocide, removal, and the expropriation and control of land—all justified in the name of white supremacy. In his 1920 essay "The Souls of White Folk," written in the years following his visit to East St. Louis in the immediate aftermath of the 1917 massacre, W.E.B. Du Bois provided the outline that I have followed in this book. Racism, he argued, was as old as humanity: "Ever have men striven to conceive of their victims as different from the victors, endlessly different, in soul and blood, strength and cunning, race and lineage." The exploitation of one group by another, too, was "quite as old as the world." *But their combination in the conquest of the Americas and the slave trade was something new, something unprecedented, something world-making.* "The imperial width of the thing,—the heaven-defying audacity—makes its modern newness." Using a term I draw from the work of the political philosopher and social theorist Cedric Robinson, I present the history that follows—all the way from the slave trade and the Indian wars down to the murder of Michael Brown and the uprising in Ferguson—as part of the history of "racial capitalism": the intertwined history of white supremacist ideology and the practices of empire, extraction, and exploitation. Dynamic, unstable, ever-changing, and world-making.[7]

At bottom, the history of racial capitalism has been one in which white supremacy justified the terms of imperial dispossession and capitalist exploitation. Thus has it been possible to expropriate Native American lands on the grounds that they were empty—*terra nullius*. Thus has it been possible to justify slavery in a republic founded under the rubric of equality. Thus has it been possible to maintain a distinction between the deserving and the undeserving poor; between the victims of economic downturns and those who lack the personal responsibility to keep up; and between the "real Americans" and "our traditions" and the people who don't respect the country, its past, and the flag. And importantly, thus has it been possible to make poor and working-class white people believe that their interests lie in making common cause with their political leaders and economic betters. Common cause in whiteness: the idea that they might eventually share in the spoils, and the understanding that the discomforts and anxieties of their own precarious lives were due to—are due to—those below them rather than those above them. As the historian Robin D. G. Kelley suggests, guns and tanks and tear gas are sufficient to control the Black people (or, for that matter, the Indians and immigrants); white supremacy is necessary to control the white people.[8]

Critical analysis of capitalism often centers on the ways in which profits are generated, distributed, and concentrated in the form of intergenerational wealth. But can the same be said for this analysis's understanding of "spoils," which must also be generated, but far more widely distributed in order to socially and politically maintain the system? An important strand of the argument in this book traces the promises made to poor and working-class white people—some kept, some broken—in order to keep them committed to social order, that is, to history in the service of empire and capital: to war in the name of white homesteads; to low wages subsidized by segregation; and to social isolation and cultural monotony understood as suburban exclusivity.

Beyond even the function of white supremacy in underwriting expropriation and exploitation, however, the notion of racism and capitalism as organically related *but not identical* helps us understand the excessive pleasures of white supremacy: the joyful mob in East St. Louis in 1917 (it was "like Mardi Gras," one observer remembered); the dumb grins on the faces of the lynch mobs, mugging for the camera in front of the body of the lynched man; the rage of the five thousand St. Louis whites who rioted after some Black kids jumped into the pool on the first day of the summer season in Fairground Park in 1949; the masculine fellowship of the St. Louis police in the 1960s as they traded stories about beating up Sonny Liston, the onetime heavyweight champion of the world; and all the torture and violation by which white people have historically drawn pleasure from the suffering of Black people.

On the other hand, analysis through the lens of racial capitalism helps us understand that the disciplinary tools and predatory takings originally justified by imperial and racial entitlement come eventually to be deployed against the working class as a whole; the insistent generalization of the tools of empire and anti-Blackness, what Achille Mbembe calls the paradoxical "Negrofication" of the white world. Tracing the United States' centuries-long history of imperial dispossession and relating it to the foreclosure crisis of our own times, the legal historian and theorist K-Sue Park suggests that the forms of military, social, and financial control pioneered in empire and slavery (and justified by racialization) were eventually adapted and absorbed, in race-neutral form, into general practice.[9]

"Labor cannot emancipate itself in the white skin where in the Black it is branded," Karl Marx wrote in *Capital*. Beneath their skin privilege, poor and working-class whites have often found (although not always recognized) that the very tools the wealthy rely upon to ensure class rule—the police, the prison, the reduction of the social wage, and the derogation of public education—come eventually to foreshorten dreams of everyone, not just the racialized, the marginalized, and the imperialized. In the fall of 1966, following the previous year's fury in the Black neighborhoods in St. Louis over the police murder of Melvin Cravens, a seventeen-year-old boy shot to death while handcuffed in a police station, the Black activists Macler Shepard and Ivory Perry organized a march in solidarity with Southside whites mourning the death of Timothy Walsh, a young white shot in the back while in police custody. The license to kill, they were saying, has been issued in our neighborhood, but it can be carried into yours. The cover of whiteness, it turns out, offers incomplete protection from the violence unleashed in its own name.[10]

This book traces the history of empire and racial capitalism through a series of stages, beginning with the fur trade in the early nineteenth century and following all the way down to payday lending, tax abatement, for-profit policing, and mass incarceration in our own times. These stages should not be understood as pure forms, nor as having unfolded according to a strict sequential historical logic. These improvised solutions to imperial problems and commercial imperatives have been mixed up with one another and with other ideas about identity and economy. They each have characteristic spatial and environmental aspects. And the stages of empire and racial capitalism were repeatedly interrupted and confronted, and occasionally even overthrown, by the people whom they so insistently dispossessed, ravaged, and repurposed in the service of empire, whiteness, and wealth.

And yet, beneath all the change, an insistent racial capitalist cleansing—forced migrations and racial removal, reservations and segregated neighborhoods, genocidal wars, police violence, and mass incarceration—is evident in the history of the city at the heart of American history. Viewed from St. Louis, the history of capitalism in the United States seems to have as much to do with eviction and extraction as with exploitation and production. History in St. Louis unfolded at the juncture of racism and real estate, of the violent management of population and the speculative valuation of property. The first to be forced out were Native Americans, who were pushed west and killed off by settlers and the US military. But in St. Louis the practices of removal and containment that developed out of the history of empire in the West were generalized into mechanisms for the dispossession and management of Black people within the city limits. And because removal is fundamentally about controlling the future, about determining what sorts of people will be allowed to live in what sorts of places, it is always concerned with the control of gender, sexuality, and reproduction; often women and children are singled out for particular sanction and targeted violence.[11]

From the time of the Missouri Compromise through the decision in the *Dred Scott* case, whites in St. Louis used Indian removal as much as slavery as the model for dealing with their Black neighbors. And from that time on, Black St. Louisans have been repeatedly driven out: from East St. Louis in 1917; from the riverfront, Deep Morgan, Chestnut Valley, and Mill Creek Valley in the middle years of the century; from Pruitt-Igoe in 1972; and from whatever neighborhoods were wanted for "economic development" down to the present day. To be sure, eviction (like extraction and even exploitation) has meant different things at various historical moments. And yet the continuity between St. Louis's role as the gateway to empire and the twenty-first-century project of enclosing Black communities in the hope of a final round of extraction only underscores the point that in St. Louis empire, slavery, and segregation have been distinct aspects of a single common history. The red thread that runs through this entire book is the historical relationship between imperialism and anti-Blackness.[12]

In the aftermath of the murder of Michael Brown on August 9, 2014, and the uprising that followed, the term "structural racism" gained renewed currency as a way to understand the depth of the history that was exploding into plain view across the nation. Part of the work of this book is to try to lend meaning to that phrase—to take us beyond using it to mean simply really bad or really persistent racism and begin to understand the ways in which racism has been built into the material fabric of daily life in the United States—into our roads and neighborhoods and schools and universities. The point of identifying racism as structural is not to just say it is really bad (or still less to say that it is so bad that we can't really do anything about it anyway and so should just go on doing whatever we're doing). The point is to search out the material history of white supremacy and the alibis in which it has been cloaked in order to understand something about structural racism that isn't otherwise visible: the way the racial character of our everyday lives has become inexorable, even as its origins have been insistently obscured. Any program intending to address economic inequality in our society—whether revolutionary or reformist—that fails to grapple with the racialized character of our material lives will likely intensify rather than ameliorating it.[13]

For the sake of example, one might point to various sorts of racism evident in the social postmortem that followed the uprising in Ferguson in the fall of 2014. Most telling for many was the discovery of the persistent *attitudinal* racism of the white police and court clerks in Ferguson, who were shown to have had a particular fondness for hackneyed racial humor. That attitudinal racism shaded imperceptibly into the *institutional* racism of the police department as a whole, manifested in the disproportionate targeting of Black motorists and street-level harassment of Black pedestrians; shoddy record-keeping and routinely ignored training protocols; and the systematic levy, through excessive tickets and exorbitant fines, whereby the subsistence of the government of Ferguson was extracted from its mostly Black population by its almost entirely white police force. All of this was amply documented in the US Department of Justice's report on the Ferguson Police Department.[14]

What the report passed over, however, was the *structural* aspect of the racism: Why was the police department revenue-farming poor Black motorists when there was a Fortune 500 company, doing $25 billion of business a year, headquartered just a quarter-mile to the south of the spot where Officer Darren Wilson shot Michael Brown? And how could that seem so natural that the corporate headquarters of Emerson Electric on West Florissant Avenue, right there where the demonstrators first sat down in the street and the militarized police rioted through the month of August, would go almost unremarked upon in the thousands of pages and millions of words written in the aftermath?

The twelve shots fired by Officer Wilson on Canfield Drive ended the life of an eighteen-year-old child and touched off a new period in the history of the United States—the era of Black Lives Matter. This book explores the two-hundred-year history of removal, racism, and resistance that flowed through the two minutes of confrontation on August 9, 2014.[15]

I began writing this book in the months after that event. In the days after the shooting, activists in St. Louis took to the streets of Ferguson demanding that Officer Wilson (whose name was initially withheld) be held accountable. Police in St. Louis County and then the Missouri Highway Patrol and eventually the Missouri National Guard responded on a scale and with a ferocity that many observers found wildly disproportionate. Armored personnel carriers patrolled the streets of Ferguson. Police armed with automatic weapons occupied the city. Peaceful protesters were repeatedly dispersed with tear gas—a chemical weapon banned under the Geneva Convention. By the end of November, when the now-notorious prosecutor Robert McCulloch announced his decision not to bring charges against Officer Wilson, the protests exploded into violence and "Ferguson" had become a byword for both police violence and the origins of what would come to be called the Black Lives Matter movement.

Having grown up just two hours to the west, I had been to St. Louis countless times to visit family, to go to the universities or the museums, even to do historical research for other books I have written. I came to this book less as a professional historian than as a citizen taking the measure of a history that I had lived through but not yet fully understood. This is a history that I have resisted, but also a history from which I have benefited, as a white man and a Missourian. I offer the result, not in the spirit of academics' too-common conceit that injustice is everywhere but in their own biographical backyards, but rather in the hope that we may all seek to do better—to walk humbly, to act justly, to love mercy.

1 | WILLIAM CLARK'S MAP

However our present interests may restrain us within our own limits, it is impossible not to look forward to distant times, when our rapid multiplication will expand itself beyond those limits, & cover the whole northern, if not the southern continent, with a people speaking the same language, governed in similar forms, & by similar laws; nor can we contemplate with satisfaction either blot or mixture on that surface.

—THOMAS JEFFERSON to James Monroe, November 24, 1801

IT IS A COMMONPLACE TODAY TO REFER TO ST. LOUIS AS THE "Gateway to the West." But there was a time when the land that sits today in the shadow of the Gateway Arch was neither part of the West nor just east of the West, nor the gateway to anything. It was just the world—indeed, the center of the world. Of course, it was not St. Louis then either, but the ancient city of Cahokia, the metropolis of the Mississippian Mound Builders and the largest city in North America during the eleventh century. Cahokia was in what is known today as the American Bottom, on the east side of the river with satellites near what is today East St. Louis and across the river, on the west side, in St. Louis, known in the nineteenth century as the "Mound City."[1]

Over the course of the nineteenth century, many of the mounds for which the city was known were deliberately leveled, so that streets could pass through, or bucketed out and used as backfill to support the rising foundation of the growing city. As many as forty-five mounds were dismantled in East St. Louis and another twenty-five or so in St. Louis in the years before the Civil War. Today only one mound remains in the city of St. Louis. Across the river, around the center of the once-great city of Cahokia, about fifty of the original approximately one hundred twenty mounds, some of them once forty or fifty feet high and hundreds of feet across, remain. Some of them rise out of the floodplain of the Mississippi River in uncanny echo of their ancient grandeur, and some are so worn away by erosion and foot traffic as to seem only small bumps in the otherwise level bottomland. They stand today as a weary reminder of the history before the empire that unfolded from St. Louis over the course of the nineteenth century, beginning in the century's first decade with the upriver journey of Meriwether Lewis and William Clark, an initial reconnaissance mission for a set of increasingly greedy and increasingly deadly military and economic forays launched from St. Louis.[2]

At its peak, Cahokia had a population of around ten thousand (larger than London at the same time) and a hinterland almost fifty miles in radius populated with another twenty thousand or thirty thousand people. It was connected by networks of travel and trade northward to present-day Minnesota and Wisconsin and southward to Louisiana, and possibly beyond to Mexico and Central America. The city consisted of as many as fifteen hundred structures, including one hundred earthen monuments, spread over thirty-two hundred acres. Some speculate that it grew suddenly, over the course of several years, as a sacred site spurred by the deep-space detonation of a supernova that brightened the skies around the globe in 1054. Cahokia was apparently laid out in advance of being inhabited. At its center was a massive plaza (sixteen hundred by nine hundred feet, about six times the size of Red Square in Moscow) headed by the largest of the mounds, the so-called Monks Mound—about one hundred feet high and almost nine hundred feet at the base, as broad as the pyramid at Giza and wider than the Pyramid of the Sun at Teotihuacán in Mexico. Recent archaeological work suggests that the mounds were built out of blocks of cut sod, laid in alternating bands of light and dark, and pounded firm underneath the feet of the builders.[3]

Most of the mounds were leveled at the summit. Topped with buildings, they provided a platform for celestial observations—the entire city was laid out in observation of the movement of the sun, the moon, and the stars—and for sacred rituals. Cahokia seems to have been the site of tremendous festivals; one, archaeologists estimate, involved the simultaneous butchering and preparation of almost four thousand deer. The residents of the city lived in thousands of densely clustered thatched-roof houses, their floors dug down into the earth to keep them cooler in the summer. They made small clay sculptures and copper jewelry and chiseled arrowheads and knives out of river rocks.[4]

And then, for reasons that are lost to history, the Mound Builders seem to have walked away. Perhaps they had overhunted or overplanted their hinterland, maybe the city was riven by political conflict or social unrest, maybe they received the same type of celestial message that had caused them to move to Cahokia in the first place. Archaeologists speculate that, as the rulers of Cahokia gradually lost authority over their hinterland, their civilization dissolved into a welter of smaller polities and internecine wars. By around 1350, Cahokia was abandoned, the houses gone, and the mounds covered with grass, some of the largest falling in on themselves. The descendants of Cahokia spread across the plains and along the rivers, where they became the Arikara, the Hidatsa, and the Mandan, whom Lewis and Clark encountered on their way up the Missouri. For hundreds of years, the remains of what

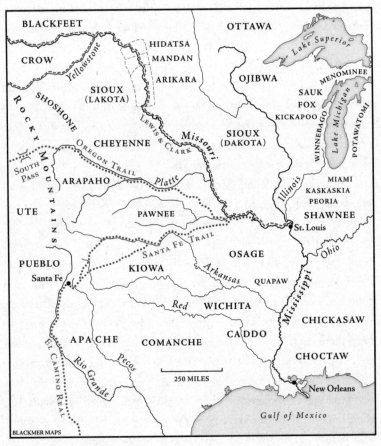

Missouri River Valley, c. 1803.

was once the largest city on the continent must have registered as only a distant reminder or even an eerie anachronism to the Indian hunters and traders who passed through the American Bottom.[5]

In February 1764, a small company of armed speculators led by Auguste Chouteau landed their boats on the west bank of the Mississippi River, across from Cahokia, and began to build a fort. They were employees of Pierre Laclède, a New Orleans trader, and they had traveled more than twelve hundred miles upriver to set up a trading post near the confluence of the Mississippi and the Missouri—the first outpost in what became an empire in what became the West. They came to see the mounds around them as relics of an ancient civilization, one prior to that of the actual Indians in whose midst they had settled, and they concluded that the Indians, too, were interlopers, strangers in a strange land, and colonizers like themselves. They turned the mounds into a self-serving justification for empire.[6]

When Napoleon, sitting over four thousand miles away in Paris, sold the stake originally claimed by Chouteau to Thomas Jefferson in 1803, he did so without regard for the vast majority of the existing inhabitants of the Louisiana Territory—the nations of the Osage, the Mandan, the Arikara, the Sioux, and the Quapaw. Jefferson, of course, knew better. He was a student of Indians and of empire. He imagined the Louisiana Purchase as an "empire for liberty," as a huge deposit of landed wealth upon which the future of white freedom might be based, but he did not think of the territory as empty. He knew that the Indians would have to be dealt with. In 1804, he sent Meriwether Lewis and William Clark to make a survey of the practical challenges and possibilities of empire-building in the West: to search out the long-rumored Northwest Passage to the Pacific; to catalog the flora and fauna; and to enumerate the Indians, announce to them the subordination of their nations to the United States of America, and gauge the economic potential of their lands. The expedition was carried out by a military reconnaissance force called the Corps of Discovery, a name that paradoxically and ideologically erased the people upon whose land they would be traveling and upon whose hospitality and knowledge they would depend—as if they were the first people to navigate the rivers and walk the paths about which they would learn from Indians. They left from St. Louis, which was at that time little more than an imperial outpost—a handful of buildings and warehouses along the riverbank with a population of around 1,200 people, most of whom were connected in one way or another with the fur trade. An 1805 visitor to the city referred to it as "cantonment St. Louis"—an isolated, surrounded, embattled outpost on the verge of a menacing future.[7]

The white men who carried the American flag and the news of conquest up the Missouri River knew better than even Jefferson that the lands through which they traveled were not simply sitting there like so much empty space on a map, waiting to be discovered. They were soldiers and frontier traders, men who were accustomed to seeing the land over which they traveled as contested ground—as a patchwork of claims and counterclaims and a place thick with possible allies and potential enemies. More than as explorers, we should see them as special forces—a military reconnaissance operation operating well beyond the line of effective US control, empowered to make friends among the Indians wherever they could find them, but enjoined always to remember that they were operating in hostile territory.

Meriwether Lewis was born in 1774 to a settler family in Georgia in the midst of a long-running, medium-intensity war with the Cherokee. As a young man, he moved to Virginia, where he became a leader in the new state's militia—a force created to maintain sovereign order among the slaves, the Indians, and even insurrectionary whites—and where he caught the attention of Thomas Jefferson. After the Corps of Discovery returned to St. Louis in 1806, Jefferson appointed Lewis military governor of the Louisiana Territory, but plagued by drink, the famous explorer was dead by 1809, shot to death in a Tennessee roadhouse, whether or not by his own hand no one has ever finally established.[8]

Born in Virginia in 1770, William Clark was the younger brother of the Revolutionary War hero and famous Indian killer George Rogers Clark. He too was a Jefferson protégé; though not as fluent a writer as Lewis, he was a talented cartographer. Everywhere he stopped during his travels across the western half of the North American continent—at night in campsites on the banks of the Missouri; during the snowed-in winter of 1804 at Fort Mandan; near the nineteenth-century Indian villages of Mitutanka and Ruptare and present-day Bismarck,

North Dakota; over the course of the miserable, starving, icy winter that followed at Fort Clatsop, near the Pacific coast—Clark recorded the information and observations he would use to entirely recast the geographic knowledge of the day: knowledge in the service of empire. William Clark's map was arguably the most important and most enduring artifact of the Corps of Discovery's reconnaissance mission: it was both imperial in its ambition to codify and control and ambivalent in its incompleteness and dependence upon Indian knowledge. It was a map of imperial ambition produced by a man who would not have survived his first winter (still less the other winters of the journey) without the help of the Indians over whom the president of the United States would soon give him sovereign dominion. For many years to come, and in many places, that dominion would be nothing more than science fiction waiting to be redeemed in blood. Over the next three decades, Clark would preside over several interlinked dimensions of the US imperial and Indian policy: the removal of most of the Indians who remained on the eastern side of the Mississippi River at the time of the Louisiana Purchase; the negotiation of removal treaties with the Indians of Missouri (among whom were some of his closest allies in the War of 1812) and surrounding territories; and the military reconnaissance, imperial regulation, and eventual invasion of the Missouri Valley. Apart from Andrew Jackson, it would be hard to argue that any white man had a greater influence on the US Indian policy in the first half of the nineteenth century than William Clark.[9]

As well as pen and ink, the men of the Corps of Discovery carried with them fifteen rifles issued by the US Army, several sidearms of their own, and a rare repeating rifle that belonged to Lewis and could fire as many as twenty shots in succession without reloading. They also had a cannon mounted on a swivel on the bow of one of their boats and two large, smooth-bored guns on the others. As they traveled upriver in the fall of 1804, they failed to observe frontier protocol by paying a toll to pass through Lakota territory near the big bend of the Missouri. When they were waylaid by the Indians, Lewis and Clark refused to negotiate, took the Lakota headman Black Buffalo hostage, and held him until they had passed out of Lakota territory. The Lakota, Clark recorded in his journal, were "the vilest miscreants of the savage race, and . . . the pirates of the Missouri," an assessment that proved to be both foundational to the subsequent history of white settler attitudes toward the Lakota and monumentally ironic in light of the kidnapping and the events of the next two centuries.[10]

The Corps of Discovery spent its first winter on the Missouri at Fort Mandan—later renamed Fort Clark—a small stockade built near Mandan villages where as many as fifteen hundred people lived within and outside the walls. For the Mandans, the arrival of the Corps of Discovery was a peculiar, if not unprecedented, event. The Mandans had a history of trade with Europeans that dated to the seventeenth century; their most recent and frequent contact was with British traders who traveled down from Hudson's Bay. As discordant as the assertion of white sovereignty may have seemed when delivered by a ragtag band of fifty men to a powerful settlement with four or five hundred soldiers, the Mandans were especially puzzled and irritated by the Americans' refusal to trade with them. Indian diplomacy on the Great Plains depended upon an ethos of openhanded generosity and reciprocity. The hospitality shown by the Mandans was neither naive nor altruistic—it was their half of a relationship of the exchange portended, they assumed, by the expedition's heavy-laden keelboat. But the white men of Fort Mandan seemed unusually stingy; they were obsessed with storing up their goods for other winters and other Indians farther up the river. When they tried to over-awe the Indians by firing off their cannon, they seemed to prefer "throwing [their ammunition] away idly rather than sparing a shot of it to a poor Mandane," in words attributed to one of the Indians. Only when the expedition's blacksmith finished setting up shop did the Corps of Discovery have something to give in return. "If we eat, you Shall eat," the Mandan leader Sheheke promised the whites.[11]

For the Mandans, the arrival of Lewis and Clark was an odd but by no means unprecedented event: they were familiar with white men and commercial prospectors, especially fur traders. Their main concerns about the future involved their relations with their Indian neighbors, especially the Arikara to the south and the Sioux to the west. Lewis and Clark, by contrast, believed that they were on a pathbreaking mission and had limitless confidence in their ability to find and claim new territory, even believing that they were destined to do so. But they also knew that by the time they had reached the Mandan villages they had also reached the outer limits of their maps. There were European trappers and traders who lived in and traveled the Missouri River Valley, but they navigated according to memory and word of mouth. Based on the information they gleaned from these sources and on their incomplete and speculative maps (some of which were indeed more fanciful than speculative), Lewis and Clark had set out for the Pacific working on the hypothesis that the western half of the continent was a straight-up mirror image of the world east of the Mississippi.[12]

Over the course of the winter, the Mandans and their visitors provided Lewis and Clark with the maps that would guide the Corps of Discovery to the front range of the Rockies and beyond. They were initially drawn out on the packed dirt floors of Mandan lodges and then translated into notes and maps in Clark's journal. When the American expeditionary force set out for the Pacific in the spring of 1805, the landmarks they sought and the decisions they made were based "altogether," in Lewis's words, on "Indian information . . . obtained on this subject, in the course of the winter, from a number of individuals, questioned separately and at different times." After the winter of 1804, every single critical decision Lewis and Clark made was based upon what they had learned from Indians. After spring had turned to summer, months later and hundreds of miles upriver, Lewis and Clark faced what the historians have identified as the defining moment in the expedition. At a seeming fork in the Missouri

River, a difference of opinion about which way to proceed threatened to grow into a violent conflict between the expedition's leaders and their men—a backcountry mutiny that would surely have cost Lewis and Clark their lives. The embattled officers resolved the argument and settled on the south fork only after sending out an exploratory party in search of the landscape they had been told by the Mandans to expect. As Clark put it, "The [buffaloes] and the Indians always have the best route."[13]

It was also at Fort Mandan, in the winter of 1804–1805, that Lewis and Clark met Sacagawea. Soon after the Corps of Discovery landed at the Mandan villages, a French fur trader named Toussaint Charbonneau and two Indian women arrived for the winter. No one knows when or how exactly Charbonneau had met either of the women with whom he traveled and whom he called his "wives," but Clark believed that their relationship with him was something more akin to enslavement than marriage. Having grown up Shoshone in present-day Idaho, the women had been captured and enslaved by the Hidatsa, who lived on the Great Plains, upriver from the Mandans, toward the mountains. Women like Sacagawea and Otter Woman were trafficked—like furs, beads, horses, and guns—among European traders and those who trucked with them. Because property on the plains was passed matrilineally from generation to generation, marrying—buying, taking, raping—Indian women was a primary mode of both sexual and capital accumulation for Europeans.[14]

What Lewis and Clark took from Sacagawea was knowledge. This appropriation, too, was in accordance with the standard operating procedures of Indian slavery on the plains, where far-flung geographies of trade and the diversity of languages made those who could point the way across the landscape and translate among its inhabitants valuable. Indeed, it was in anticipation of their need for translators that Lewis and Clark engaged Charbonneau, who spoke Hidatsa, and his Shoshone wives. Otter Woman, who was seven months pregnant when the expeditionary force set out in the spring of 1805, stayed with the Mandans. Sacagawea went along with Charbonneau, carrying with her the couple's two-month-old son, whom they had christened Jean-Baptiste.[15]

Sacagawea's story bears repeating: it is as amazing as it is familiar. Carrying her son, she walked overland with William Clark and taught him about the flora and fauna of the Missouri Valley. She plunged into the freezing Missouri to rescue the expedition's journals and maps when one of the expedition's pirogues overturned on launching. (Charbonneau, who could not swim, had to be dragged out of the water along with the baggage.) She recognized the meadow where she had been captured, pointed the way to the Shoshone, and then astonished the Corps of Discovery as she rushed forward to embrace the leader of the Shoshone party, who had ridden out to meet the white travelers. He was, they soon learned, her brother. And shortly before the expedition started eastward to return to St. Louis, she insisted on riding out from the winter camping ground at Fort Clatsop so that she could see the Pacific Ocean with her own eyes.[16]

And yet, alongside the anything-you-can-do-I-can-do-better terms in which her story has been assimilated into the mainstream of American history, Sacagawea's years with the Corps of Discovery also provide a set of data points that convey the unstable hierarchies and violent intimacies that shaped life between the borders of worlds. In August 1805, Sacagawea was beaten in camp by her husband, who was then publicly reprimanded by Clark. Clark may have felt protective, possessive even, of Sacagawea, whom he referred to as Janey. His affection for Jean-Baptiste was openly proprietary. His habit of calling the boy Pompey reflected not only the affection of a pet name but also southern slaveholders' habit of amusing themselves by bestowing names drawn from the classical world upon their property. By the time the expedition returned to St. Louis, Clark wrote to Charbonneau and Sacagawea asking them to send the little boy to live with him. "Anxious expectations of seeing my little dancing boy Baptiest" led Clark to promise Charbonneau a fully furnished farm, if only the woodsman would "leave your little *Son Pomp* with me." Jean-Baptiste was educated at Clark's expense after his parents returned to the Hidatsas in 1809. He graduated from what is today St. Louis University High School as a member of one of the first classes after its 1808 foundation.[17]

Historians know Sacagawea, this most famous of Indian women, mostly through the words and deeds of the men who controlled and exploited her, and finally dispossessed her of both her property and her progeny.

In the years immediately following his return to St. Louis, William Clark continued to work on his map. Appointed superintendent of Indian affairs for the Louisiana Territory by Thomas Jefferson in 1807 (the office overseeing the United States' Indian relations, and Indian wars, remained in St. Louis through the 1840s), Clark was responsible for licensing white explorers, traders, and trappers who planned to travel beyond St. Louis into Indian country. His office stood near the levee in downtown St. Louis, on a lot paid for by selling one of his family's slaves. William Clark's office became the epicenter for the expansion of the United States: the literal gateway to the empire, the trailhead of the pathways along which white men were converting Indian country into the West and existing trade networks and animal skins into capital. White men heading west stopped in to get their licenses and to look at Clark's map before setting out. White men returning from the West brought with them their own observations and manuscript maps, which Clark incorporated into the master map he kept in his office. More than any published map, the map in Clark's office provided an up-to-the-minute account of imperial knowledge during these years.[18]

The map itself captured the transformation of empirical into abstract knowledge—the conversion of the immediate, three-dimensional knowledge one gains from walking down a path into reproducible knowledge that can be communicated in two dimensions on a printed page. Upon its publication in 1814, Clark's map would enable viewers in Washington or New York or St. Louis to imagine a western itinerary

After the Corps of Discovery returned to St. Louis in 1806, William Clark settled in the city, where he served as the nation's superintendent of Indian affairs. He continued to work on his map of the West, sharing it with outbound imperial adventurers on their way out of town and adding to it based on the information they provided upon their return. (Beinecke Rare Book and Manuscript Library, Yale University)

in the comfort of their own offices or sitting rooms. With Clark's map, they could trace with a fingertip the course of the Missouri past the Mandan villages and into the mountains; imagine portaging across and following the downward course of the Columbia River toward the Pacific; foresee the day when the arduous journey from St. Louis to Santa Fe would be easy; or divine the purpose of God as it had been encoded in the geography of the continent. Moreover, Clark's manuscript map provided an embedded record of the circumstances of its own creation—the rough, material, empirical process by which this imperial knowledge was created: "Mandan Village, 1500"; "The wintering fort of the party sent out by the government of the U.S. for discovery in the winter of 1804–5"; "Here was found the first Ogalala"; and so on. A final version of the map, stripped of the traces of its own creation, was finally published in 1814, along with the journals of the expedition. Clark's manuscript map today hangs framed in the Beinecke Library at Yale University, a documentary record of the expropriation of Indian knowledge along the westward course of empire—of the translation of knowledge about the land from one kind of vision to another.

The world over which Clark presided from his office in St. Louis—the world represented on his map—was increasingly shaped by the fur trade, most notably by the American Fur Company and its St. Louis principal, Pierre Chouteau, the brother of Auguste, the founder of the imperial city. Among the directives given the Corps of Discovery by Thomas Jefferson was to "decide whether the furs of [the Pacific Northwest] may not be collected advantageously at the head of the Missouri." Beaver pelts especially were valued in the markets of the eastern United States and Europe for the animal's fibrous undercoat, which was pounded into felt. Felted beaver fur was pliable enough to be shaped and yet resilient enough to make warm, waterproof hats that held their form. By the time of the Lewis and Clark expedition, beaver hats had been a standard accoutrement of metropolitan elites and military men across the Atlantic world for over a century. When they returned, Lewis and Clark reported that the headwaters of the Missouri were "richer in beaver and otter than any country on earth."[19]

By the first decades of the nineteenth century, the fur trade linked cities like London, Paris, Vienna, and New York to St. Louis and thence to the deepest reaches of the North American interior. Fur trading in these years was one of the largest sectors of the global economy, and worth over $200,000 a year in the city of St. Louis, one of its principal hubs. The Indians of the Great Plains and Rocky Mountains were its primary producers. Beyond St. Louis in the first decades of the nineteenth century, the global economy followed the centuries-old pathways of Indian trade and operated on "native ground": the trapping was done by Indians who set the terms for the trading that followed.[20]

In these years, as a historian of the fur trade, David Wishart, has shown, white traders in the Missouri Valley worked "within the framework of the existing Indian system." Beaver pelts were prepared according to Indian methods, and bargaining over the exchange rate—between beaver pelts and beads, for instance—began only after the whites had provided gifts denoting their respect. "The Indians are good judges of the articles in which they deal," wrote one St. Louis trader, "and have always given a very decided preference for those of English manufacture." St. Louis traders, particularly Pierre Chouteau and his extended network of family members and associates, maintained a presence all over the West, but the initial locations of their forts were determined as much by Indian needs as European ones—and sometimes they were moved according to specifications of the trade's Indian producers.[21]

Pierre Chouteau embodied what the historian Anne Hyde has termed the *métis* world of the fur trade. Chouteau had grown up in present-day Missouri and along the Arkansas River among the Osage, to whom he maintained a connection through an Osage wife. He spent most of his time, however, in St. Louis, where he lived with another wife, a French Creole woman. Chouteau's brother, A.P., who spoke

Osage and Pawnee as well as English, French, and Spanish, took the opposite course and left St. Louis to live with his Osage wife. St. Louis's first family, able to move between the Indian and European worlds at the heart of the continent, embodied the tactical alliances, restless mixtures, and practical in-betweenness of the fur trade world. Scratched out on paper, the organizational chart of the American Fur Company bore a striking resemblance to the Chouteau family tree. Unlike a family tree, however, the American Fur Trade Company transmitted wealth backwards rather than forwards: the levy followed the bloodlines backwards toward St. Louis.[22]

The *métis* practices of the borderlands were framed by imperial frontiers. Just as the Osage relied on their relationship with the United States to help them hold off their rivals in Missouri and along the Arkansas River, the Quapaw and the Delaware, the United States relied on its relationship with the Osage to help them hold off the Spanish in the Southwest. Likewise, and of even greater concern to William Clark, the Indians of the Upper Missouri Valley had to be kept in alignment with the economic and diplomatic purposes of the United States. Throughout his career, Clark manifested an almost obsessive concern that the Indians of the Upper Midwest not be drawn into the orbit of the British by traders based north of the border. "Whoever enjoys the Trade of the Indians will have the control of their affection and power," Clark explained in a letter to his brother. Clark conceived of the fur trade as an aspect of the realpolitik of the plains, a mode of imperial maneuver as much as a method of accumulation, but the fur trade was, at its heart, a trade, and eventually the imperatives of racial capitalism came fully to define its pathways and practices.[23]

The world that Clark worked so hard to maintain—the world of the fur trade and the shifting military alliance between imperialists and Indians—was built, as it had been intended, upon impermanent premises. According to Thomas Jefferson, the power-balanced reciprocities that defined the world of the fur trade—the choreography of gift-giving and bargaining, of rhetorical dominance and practical dependence—

were never intended to last forever. In February 1803, as he worked to arrange a secret congressional appropriation to fund the expedition of the Corps of Discovery, Jefferson outlined his vision of the future in a letter to William Henry Harrison, then the governor of the Indiana Territory: "We shall push our trading uses, and be glad to see the good and influential Indians . . . run into debt, because we observe when these debts get beyond what the individual can pay, they become willing to lop them off by a cession of land." Jefferson imagined a long game: the Louisiana Purchase lands would be used for the resettlement of eastern Indians driven out by white settlement along a westward-moving debt frontier (imperial racial capitalism) that might take several generations to reach and cross the Mississippi. Indeed, as long as the western Indians remained valuable to the United States, men like William Clark might encourage men like Pierre Chouteau to roll Indian debts over for another year and keep doing business: the competing imperatives of the United States to expand, the American Fur Company to make money, and the Osage or the Mandan to benefit from their relations with whites and defend their position from Indian challengers might be rebalanced by the deferral of any final accounting. But once the parameters that framed those common interests began to change, so too did the choices and the incentives facing William Clark.[24]

The War of 1812 changed the ground beneath Clark's feet. While Francis Scott Key was busy writing "The Star-Spangled Banner" in Baltimore, much of the war was fought in the Upper Midwest. The city of St. Louis spent 1813 and 1814 on high alert in anticipation of attack by those Indians allied with the British. Indeed, in St. Louis, as in the Midwest generally, the War of 1812 was less a war with the British than a war between Indians in which American settlers were allied with one side and British settlers with the other. In the summer of 1813, there were rumors in the city that as many as a thousand hostile Indians were gathered in St. Charles County preparing for an assault on St. Louis. Clark, who had been appointed governor of the Missouri Territory by President James Madison in 1813, and Pierre Chouteau arranged with the Osage to establish a garrison above the city, and for the duration of the war St. Louis was defended by 260 Osage soldiers as well as its own historically unreliable white militia.[25]

The War of 1812 was a multilateral conflict: both the British and the Americans had Indian allies, and the Indian parties to the conflict tried to use it as a way to advance their position against Indian as well as imperial rivals. But the Treaty of Ghent, signed in December 1814, restaged the war as if the only combatants had been the white ones. It reestablished the imperial boundaries between the United States and Great Britain along the lines said to prevail *status quo ante* while ignoring the claims of the Indians who had fought to be included in the negotiation of the "peace." As a corollary, it undermined the ability of the Indians of the Missouri Valley to play the Americans against the British. Henceforth, men like William Clark and Pierre Chouteau would worry less that dissatisfied plains Indians would pursue trade and diplomatic alliances with their British rivals.

The fur trade world had been built not only on an evanescent political foundation but also on finite resources. The American empire in the West was extractive rather than productive, and it soon destroyed the ecological conditions that had enabled the fur trade in the first place. Almost as quickly as it took shape, the unstable order of the fur trade world was upset by European demand for beaver hats. Western Indians refused to trap in the numbers that the fur companies wished, and so the companies tried to establish their own upriver operations, shifting the center of gravity in the political economy of the trade from Indian to white trappers. The immediate result was war. When the St. Louis trader Manuel Lisa tried to establish an upriver fort in 1810, it was attacked and destroyed by Blackfeet. Twenty of the thirty-two men in Lisa's employ died in the failed venture; shortly after, Lisa's Missouri Fur Company was dissolved.[26]

In 1822, the fur trader William Ashley advertised in the *Missouri Gazette and Public Advertiser* for "one Hundred Men to ascend the river Missouri to its source, there to be employed for one, two or three years." His intention was to conquer the fur trade—to replace the existing supply chain and its complicated reliance upon Indian suppliers and diplomacy with a more directly commercial set of linkages to the west, that is, with an alternative racial capitalism. In the summer of 1823, Ashley's trappers were attacked on the Upper Missouri, between the Grand and Cannonball Rivers in what is today South Dakota. Twelve of Ashley's men died, and Ashley immediately wrote to nearby Fort Atkinson to seek the aid of the US Army in supporting his commercial venture. By August, the US Army had defeated the Arikara. But further upriver the Blackfeet continued to defend their control over the river and the trade, forcing the St. Louis traders to look for another route. In the second half of the 1820s, the St. Louis trade began to run from the Lower Missouri Valley westward to South Pass in the Rockies. Gradually, the St. Louis traders succeeded in transforming the fur trade on the east side of the Rockies into a more thoroughly capitalist business: longtime trade and diplomatic relationships with Indians were thrown into disarray and replaced with frequent skirmishes and periodic war; hunters were transformed from traders into workers, and the limits that the Indians had placed on trapping were undermined in a frenzy of profit-taking. By 1840, the western beaver had been pushed to the margin of extinction.[27]

As the fur companies pushed upriver, propelled by global demand and fueled by racial entitlement, and the Indians pushed back, it was left to William Clark to contain the disorder unleashed from St. Louis and keep the racial capitalism of the trade under the control of the United States. As superintendent of Indian affairs, Clark oversaw the relationships of white traders and Indians. Up until 1822, he controlled trade through a network of Indian Agency "factories," which had sole license to trade with Indians. When a white man killed an Indian or an Indian stole a white man's horse, Clark (or, more accurately, his network of agents) was responsible for trying to broker a resolution, often through the provision of gifts. He held regular councils to negotiate boundaries and hunting rights among the western Indians under his charge. At his downtown office, on his farm eight miles outside the city, on Beaver Pond, and at Portage des Sioux, thirty miles north of the city near the confluence of the Missouri and Mississippi Rivers, Clark's councils were a normal aspect of life in St. Louis in the decades after his return from the West.[28]

As early as 1814, when he had to be defended by his Indian guard against a mob of land-hungry white settlers, Clark must have realized that his roles as superintendent of Indian affairs and as territorial governor (of the white settlers) of Missouri were ineluctably at odds. As white migration to Missouri, especially from Virginia, increased in the years after the War of 1812, Clark's constituents demanded that he renounce the traditional practices of Indian-agent diplomacy and the fur trade and let white men go wherever they wanted and do whatever they wanted, at least as far as Indians were concerned. In 1816, white settlers were outraged at Clark's decision to order the removal of two hundred white settler families along the Arkansas River because the farms they were building were located on Indian lands. When the whites refused to move, Clark was forced to admit that his order was "impracticable." Settlers interested only in Indian lands were outraged by the costs of Indian diplomacy. They had no interest in paying for the standard-issue tools of frontier reconciliation and pacification in which Clark put so much stock—medals embossed with the face of the president, vermillion from China, wool blankets from the British Isles, glass beads from Venice, and calico in a variety of prints. For these settlers, firearms were to be used to kill Indians, not as trade goods to secure alliances with them. When Clark ran for reelection as governor in 1820, he was painted by his opponents as a tool of the Chouteau family and their "Junto" of has-been French aristocrats, and as a race traitor who would rather pamper Indians than recognize the soundness of Alexis de Tocqueville's description of what the Frenchman took to be the animating spirit of settler whiteness in the United States: "This world here belongs to us, they tell themselves every day: the Indian race is destined for final destruction which one cannot prevent and which it is not desirable to delay. Heaven has not made them to become civilized; it is necessary that they die." Clark lost the election by a margin of two-to-one.[29]

Though Clark was never as bloodthirsty as his political opponents, as superintendent of Indian affairs up until the time of his death in 1838, he negotiated increasingly harsh land cessions and removal treaties with the Indians of the Midwest. Many of the thirty-seven land cession treaties he negotiated—imposed—in these years were signed in the council grove on his farm by Beaver Pond in today's Pine Lawn, just to the northwest of the present-day city limits of the city of St. Louis. As early as 1808, he began negotiating the removal of the Osage from Missouri. In 1815, he presided over a treaty with the Kansas; in 1816 with the Sauk, Sioux, Winnebago, Ottawa, the Ojibwa, and the Potawatomi; in 1817 with the Menominee; in 1818 with the various factions of the Pawnee, the Quapaw, and most of the remaining Osage; in 1825 with the Shawnee and the final Missouri Osage; in 1832 with the Kickapoo; in 1835 with the remaining Shawnee, the Delaware, the Kaskaskia, and the Peoria, and with the Sauk and the Fox in the so-called Platte Purchase, which added the tiny flange of territory east of the Missouri to the northeast corner of the state. Taken all together, Clark's treaties added some 419 million acres to the domain of the United States and removed over 81,000 Indians from their homelands. Many of these treaties were with Indians who were being dispossessed for the second time, the white settlers having caught them from behind even after their first forced westward move.[30]

The 1825 treaty with the Osage was perhaps the most notorious; the stench of its self-dealing delayed its passage through Congress for months. Hundreds of thousands of acres belonging to the Osage—to whom Clark had entrusted the defense of the city of St. Louis during the War of 1812—were transferred directly to his friend Pierre Chouteau, earmarked as payment for the debts supposedly accrued by the Osage in their years of business with the American Fur Company. Indeed, as the margins tightened in the fur trade, the Chouteau family began to diversify its holdings by opening up a side business in Indian removal: contracting to transport and provide for the Indians with whom they had once negotiated and intermarried.[31]

During the first third of the nineteenth century, the city that had once been the economic center of the fur trade was transformed into the administrative center of midwestern Indian removal—the largest forced relocation camp on the continent. By the time Clark died in 1838, the protocols of Indian trade and diplomacy, the type of calico favored by the Osages, or the different personalities of the various Mandan chiefs, were of no more interest to most white men in St. Louis than the best method of trapping the last of the rapidly dwindling beaver population (for which there was no longer any market in any case). It mattered a good deal less how much a white man in St. Louis knew about Indians than it did how much he hated them.[32]

During these years of unceasing extraction, overhunting, and ethnic cleansing, great fortunes were made in St. Louis, most notably by the Chouteau family, but also by the Ashleys, the Sublettes, the Herefords, and the Bents. The wealth that was drained from the Missouri Valley and its inhabitants pooled along the levee in St. Louis and then spread westward toward the suburbs that began to grow on the surrounding prairie in the 1830s. Between 1810 and 1820, the population of the city grew by more than 200 percent (to a total of 4,598), and the population of the surrounding county increased by around 75 percent during the same period, reaching almost 10,000 in 1820. As the population of the city grew, real estate speculation emerged as a significant sector of the local economy. Both Pierre Chouteau and his commercial rival J.B.C. Lucas subdivided and sold large lots of what had once been the city's common field (about thirty square blocks behind the built-up area on the riverfront, including the site of Busch Stadium today). Lucas had turned a 1,000 percent profit before he sold even half of his lots. Between 1815 and 1821, the number of wood-framed buildings in the city grew by 50 percent, and the cost of pine lumber in St. Louis in these boom-time years was eight times what was being asked in Pittsburgh.[33]

By 1821, the city had forty-six mercantile houses, fifty-seven groceries, three large hotels, three newspapers, twenty-seven lawyers, four hairdressers, twelve tailors, thirteen physicians, and three midwives, as well as a portrait painter, a handful of blacksmiths, and "several musicians." In 1822, the city government adopted a new policy for naming streets. Instead of the names based on existing landmarks (Rue D'Eglise), the city began to employ a system based on tree names and numbered cross-streets—a system that, because it corresponded to nothing specific about the city, was susceptible of infinite expansion. As the fur trade declined through the 1830s under the pressure of first overhunting and then changing demand—silk hats, another imperial good, but this time from Asia, not America, were now the rage—the capitalists of St. Louis began to turn the capital they had accumulated on the plains to other sectors of the economy: to real estate speculation, to the processing and distribution of agricultural goods, and to manufacturing, especially of military hardware.

In the aftermath of Mexican independence (from Spain) in 1821, St. Louis merchants developed increasing commercial ties to Santa Fe, and through the following decades it was the Santa Fe Trail as much as the Missouri Valley that shaped the economy of the city. Furs, woven wool from the interior of Mexico, silver, horses, and the mules that came to be identified nationally as "Missouri mules" all made their way to St. Louis in exchange for cotton fabrics, linens, silks, and manufactured tools like axes and knives. The "Gateway to the West" had once been the passageway through which Indian goods traveled on their way east, to the Atlantic seaboard or farther on to Europe. It increasingly became instead the point of embarkation for white settlers (heading to Texas in the 1830s, to Oregon in the 1840s, and to California in the 1850s) and the Indian fighters of the US military who followed in their wake for the balance of the century: the epicenter of the nation's nineteenth-century empire. And the Louisiana Purchase Territory, once the site of the type of complex and volatile diplomatic and economic interchange that had framed the career of William Clark and the arc of the fur trade, came increasingly to be viewed, at least among white people, as a vast open space into which they could drive the Indians who lived on the eastern half of the continent—the geographical precondition for the idea of the "white man's country."[34]

On September 13, 1832, Washington Irving set out from the levee in downtown St. Louis to visit the famous explorer William Clark. Intent on writing a book about the West for readers curious about the nation's emergent empire, Irving began in St. Louis with a visit to the most famous living symbol of "discovery." The morning was cool and clear, although the city was overhung by the smoke of the tanneries, brickworks, and smelters built up along the levee. The life of the man Irving had come to meet encapsulated the history that had transformed the city of St. Louis from frontier post into the metropolis of the nation's western empire. In a way, the visit marked the end of an era.[35]

Clark's farm was about eight miles from the bustling St. Louis levee, on a little pond known then as Marais Castor (Beaver Pond). To get there, Irving rode though the "scrub oak and marshy weeds" that marked the boundary of the riparian ecosystem and out onto the flowering prairie beyond the city limit. As he traveled, Irving passed a circle of ancient Indian mounds. At the summit of one of them, the fur trader William Ashley had built a mansion with a fountain in the front.[36]

The famous explorer was not at home when Irving arrived. Unlike Clark, who wrote reluctantly and spelled chaotically, Irving encountered the world through words, and while he waited he jotted down notes about Clark's surroundings and his possessions: the embers on the hearth; the long gun and game bag in the corner; the Indian calumet on the mantle; the trees bending under the weight of their fruit in the orchard; a grove of walnut trees in the back, a dovecote, and a beehive; "little Negroes whispering and laughing"; "Negroes with tables under trees preparing meal"; a "civil Negro major domo" spreading a tablecloth for dinner outside.

The man himself arrived "on horseback with dogs," "a gun on his shoulder," his grandson beside him "on a calico pony, hallowing and laughing." Clark was, as Irving recorded him, a "fine, healthy, robust man—tall—about 50—perhaps more—his hair, originally light now grey—falling on his shoulders." Over a "hut rustic" meal of fried chicken, bacon and grouse, roast beef, and potatoes, the two men sat in the grove where Clark had held countless councils with the Indians of the West, beneath the trees under which the delicate balance of reciprocity and extraction that had governed the world of the fur trade had been dismantled over the past two decades. Irving recorded little that Clark said about Indians, no more than a notation that "Gov. C. gives much excellent information concerning Indians." Like the calumet in the corner, the codes of the frontier must have struck Irving as nostalgic reminders of a distant past. He recorded instead the story of how Clark came to emancipate his slave York, whom Clark sarcastically called "the hero of the Missouri expedition and adviser of the Indians."[37]

Historians know more about York's life than they do about most of the millions of other men, women, and children who lived as slaves in the United States. York had belonged to Clark's father on the Virginia plantation where the two boys—the one a slave, the other the youngest son in a famous family—grew up together. York had accompanied Clark through his young adulthood, his career as an Indian fighter in Indiana, and famously on the expedition with Meriwether Lewis up the Missouri to the Rockies, across the Continental Divide, and down the Columbia River to the Pacific. Throughout the expedition that accounted for Clark's renown, York had walked along the riverbanks with Clark and his native guide, Sacagawea, and her infant son, Jean-Baptiste. He had suffered the heat and mosquitoes of the Upper Midwest summer; the freezing, hungry winter at Fort Mandan; and the torturous, uncertain passage over the mountains. He had rowed a boat upstream against the current of the river and portaged the expedition's goods around the Great Falls of the Missouri. He had cared for his owner when Clark was disabled for days on end by the irritable bowel that left him not only physically incapacitated but also unable to control the crew of mountain men allegedly under his command. York had seen his owner utterly dependent upon Indians for food and for the directions that guided him along the trail that today bears the white man's name. York had been celebrated by Indians, who had never seen a man with skin so dark as his, who wondered at it, caressed it, and understood it as a sign of his vitality and his potency.[38]

Two years after the expedition, when William Clark traveled to Virginia to court his first wife and bring her back to St. Louis, York went with him. On the way back, the newlyweds stopped in Louisville, where Clark's family had settled and kept York's wife enslaved. When Clark began to prepare for the final leg of his homeward journey, York told his owner that he wanted to stay behind in Louisville with his own wife. Upon Clark's departure for St. Louis to set up housekeeping, however, York and nine other Clark family slaves were forced to leave their own families behind. Many were hired out on their arrival in St. Louis. One, Scipio, was traded for a lot on the corner of Main and Spruce (near the riverfront) on which Clark built his in-town house. Their tears were stanched with violence. "I have been obliged [to] whip almost all my people," Clark wrote to his brother shortly after his return to St. Louis, "and they are now beginning to think that it is best to do better and not Cry." The few traces of York's life in Clark's correspondence after 1808 express mostly Clark's bitterness toward and resentment of his onetime companion. In November 1808, he wrote that he was planning to sell York down the river to New Orleans or "hire [him] out to Some Severe Master," if he did not "provorm his duty as a Slave." A month later he wrote that Meriwether Lewis had convinced him to hire York out in Kentucky rather than selling him in Louisiana, and he advised his brother to find the slave a "severe master" who would make him grateful to return to Missouri and "give over that wife of his."[39]

Although historians have disputed Clark's veracity, the story he told Irving that afternoon was that he had emancipated York and provided him with "a large wagon and team of six horses to ply between Nashville and Richmond." According to Clark, York had been too lazy and too stupid to be free. "He could not get up early enough in the morning—his horses were ill kept—two died—the others grew poor. He sold them and was cheated." "'Damn this Freedom,'" said York, according to Clark, "'I have never had a happy day since I got it.'" The old man continued, talking about his former slave and the perils of Black freedom: "He determined to go back to his old master—set off for St. Louis, but was taken with the cholera in Tennessee and died." Indeed, Clark declared, he had emancipated several slaves, and always the story had the same moral: "They all repented and wanted to come back." They could not live without him.[40]

The story Clark told in the orchard that afternoon was not about his own dependence upon his slaves and his outsized pique when they did not "provorm" as he wished. Still less was it about the way the famous frontiersman had depended upon the kindness of strangers as he and his ragtag reconnaissance unit struggled across the mountains.[41] It was instead a parable about personal responsibility—the life lessons drawn by a man oblivious to the way his own success had depended upon the actions of others. It was a white man's moral, one of a kind increasingly likely to be drawn by white men who lived in the place St. Louis was becoming: a place—on the plains, in the Upper Midwest, and in the city itself—where the complicated web of cross-cutting relationships (familial, para-familial, parasitical; commercial, diplomatic, imperial) that had supported Clark's famous journey west and his early career was subordinated to a racially fundamentalist understanding of the world (red, white, and black) and the politics of white settler imperialism and ethnic cleansing.[42]

2 | WAR TO THE ROPE

> Armed occupation was the true way of settling a conquered
> country. The children of Israel entered the promised land
> with implements of husbandry in one hand and the weapons
> of war in the other.
>
> —THOMAS HART BENTON, "On the Armed Occupation of Florida"

AMONG THE THOUSANDS OF WHITE MEN WHO ARRIVED IN ST. Louis in the years after the War of 1812 was one who would later become one of the most famous imperialists of the nineteenth century. This man envisioned the transcontinental railroad decades before the first rail was laid; proposed simply giving away large portions of the West to white men; came to view the conflict over slavery as a distraction from the real business of empire; and considered dead Indians simply an afterthought, an acceptable cost of doing business in the West. Under the stewardship of Thomas Hart Benton, the western empire of the United States took shape. In the second quarter of the nineteenth century, St. Louis became the military headquarters of the Western Department of the US Army and the staging post for the Indian wars. White settlers—backed by that St. Louis–based US Army but often operating well in advance of its lines—violently removed Native Americans from lands all over the Upper Midwest. During Benton's career, we can see the process by which genocidal settler wars replaced the volatile reciprocity of the fur trade world and then finally became the (made in St. Louis) official policy of the United States in the West.

In later years, Benton would be known for his speeches. For hours at a time, he would pound out one well-turned phrase after another. Whether he was on the floor of the US Senate or on a stump at some backwoods crossroads in central Missouri, he always sounded the same—like an angry god in love with the sound of his own voice. Benton would become one of the most renowned orators of an age that cherished words and admired speech, and the acknowledged equal (and persistent antagonist) of Daniel Webster, Henry Clay, and John C. Calhoun. But in 1815, Benton's only claim to fame was among those who thought him a thief, a liar, and a bully. Like so many others, he had come to Missouri as a wounded white man seeking a second chance. As a young man, he had been expelled from the University of North Carolina for pulling a gun in an argument with a school-aged child and repeatedly stealing money from his roommates' trunks. Disgraced, he had moved with his widowed mother across the mountains to Nashville, where he trained in law. He was finally beginning to establish himself when he was drawn into an affair of honor that would pit him against General Andrew Jackson, the city's most prominent citizen who would soon become the nation's most prominent Indian hater, and soon enough after that its tenth president.[1]

The cause of Benton's famous fight with Jackson was both obscure and stupid—a series of slights passed between the aggrieved parties like a bad debt. The first act culminated with a duel between Benton's brother, Jesse, and a military subordinate and friend of Jackson's named William Carroll. Jackson was Carroll's second, which meant it fell to him to arrange the dueling conditions on behalf of the challenged party. Jackson secured an agreement to duel with pistols under

mortally dangerous conditions: the men would stand back to back only
ten feet apart, then turn and fire simultaneously. When Jesse Benton
shot first and missed, he sensibly and even instinctively—that is to say
dishonorably—turned his back and tried to curl himself into a smaller
target for Carroll, who cold-bloodedly—that is to say honorably—shot
him in the seat of his pants.[2]

The short distance later seemed to Thomas Hart Benton to have
unjustly favored Carroll, a notoriously bad shot. In the weeks that followed, Benton shared his unfavorable evaluation of Jackson, Carroll,
and the circumstances of the duel far and wide. Jackson sent Benton
a note requesting an explanation. Benton replied that he believed that
Jackson had failed to forestall a potentially fatal encounter between
overheated young men, and that he would not be cowed into keeping
the general's name out of his mouth. Jackson responded that he would
"horsewhip" Benton the next time he saw him in the street, and on
September 4, 1813, he attempted to do just that when he, along with
two friends, encountered the Benton brothers in the Talbot Hotel in
Nashville. As Jackson advanced, whip in hand, Benton reached for the
pistol in his belt. But Jackson was faster, and he began, gun drawn,
to back Benton down the hall of the hotel. Coming in from behind
Jackson, Jesse Benton shot the general in the back, shattering his left
shoulder, just as Jackson let loose an errant shot at Thomas Hart Benton. Jackson's friends then set upon Benton with knives, stabbing him
in five places before he was saved by tumbling down the back stairs of
the hotel. As Jackson's friends carried the grievously wounded general
away to safety, Benton staggered, bloodied, into the street and broke
Jackson's sword over his knee.[3]

Although he may not have realized it at that moment, Benton
was done in Nashville. After brief and undistinguished service in the
War of 1812 under Jackson's command—the general kept Benton away
from most of the military action the younger man would have needed
in order to enhance his reputation—Thomas Hart Benton decided to
move to Missouri.

St. Louis in 1815 was an outpost at the beginning of a furious transformation: from the westernmost hub of the fur trade to the eastern hub of the nation's settler empire. Over the first decades of the nineteenth century, the fur trade produced income that was invested in the city fabric of St. Louis, and the city grew from a few square blocks on Pierre Laclède's landing, southward along the banks of the Mississippi toward Carondelet, westward to St. Charles, and northward to St. Ferdinand (today's Florissant). In 1820, the city was designated the western terminus of the National Road, which was to connect the Mississippi Valley to the Potomac River and the East Coast. The scattered log cabins of the fur trade world would soon give way to a grubby host of riverfront warehouses and small manufactories—brickyards, tanneries, and smelters. The Chouteaus' stone mansion, which had once stood apart from the city (close by today's Busch Stadium), was gradually surrounded by it. By 1840, the city's propertied leaders were surveying and selling off the commons that had once served to graze the city residents' stock—it had become too valuable to leave as open land. By that time, the mixed population of trappers and traders—French, Indian, Negro—had long since been transformed into a populace organized by the rigid forms of racial hierarchy and white supremacy that prevailed farther to the east and that the city of St. Louis would play a key role in transmitting to the West. In 1810, the population of the city was less than fifteen hundred; by 1840, it had grown more than twentyfold, to around thirty-five thousand, with westering white men like Benton making up the bulk of the increase.[4]

Benton found work in the law office of Charles Gratiot, a Chouteau in-law whose primary business was turning territory into property—the legal aspect of settler colonialism. As the Chouteaus and the rival Lucas family surveyed, staked, and claimed the area that would become downtown St. Louis (the area to the west of Third Street), Benton worked on what would become a career-making case: the registration under US law of Spanish land titles held by the city's Creole elite. (The Louisiana Territory had been under Spanish control from

1763 to 1803, when it was transferred back to France, only to be sold to the United States.) The Chouteau family alone had almost two hundred thousand acres of disputed property, bought up at bargain prices from risk-averse titleholders, and the Chouteaus stood to make a killing if they could establish clear title before the claims commission first established by Thomas Jefferson in 1805.[5]

Benton's work in Gratiot's office thus put him in touch with the first family of the city of St. Louis, whom he faithfully served up to his election to the US Senate in 1821, and indeed, ever after. His first speech in the Senate was delivered on behalf of the Creole speculators who had sent him there to do their bidding. And as the business interests of the city's leading families gradually turned from the fur trade to Indian removal—that is, from using Indian labor to control resource extraction to using the control of Indians to extract revenue from the government—Benton was there every step of the way. In 1822, he termed the government-controlled trading factories in Indian country a "pious monster" and sponsored a bill that abolished them, effectively taking Indian trade out of the hands of the US Indian Agency and placing it in the hands of the American Fur Company and a seemingly endless supply of settler competitors. In 1825, Benton shepherded an Osage removal treaty through the Senate that included the direct transfer of hundreds of thousands of acres to the Chouteau family in repayment for Osage debts supposedly incurred at the family's company stores; in 1851 he did the same in relation to a Sioux treaty that had been arranged by the American Fur Company agent J. A. Sanford. As the fur trade world gave way to settler colonialism and land speculation in the Midwest and the Great Plains, Benton helped his St. Louis patrons make the transition. "Senator Benton seems to have been as much an employee of Chouteau and Company as a representative of the people of Missouri," one historian has mordantly observed.[6]

And yet it is as a champion of the people rather than as a corporate tool that Benton was known in the nineteenth century. Certainly Benton owed part of his populist persona to his reputation as a duelist, which he built on shortly after moving to St. Louis by killing the fur trade scion Charles Lucas on Bloody Island. The cause was once again both trivial and stupid—an argument in court between two lawyers that involved an escalating exchange of uses of the word "puppy." His reputation as a duelist certainly helped his populist reputation, but Benton owed his status as the officially recognized voice of "the West" mainly to his vision of federal land, to the liberality he proposed in distributing lands taken from Native Americans to migratory white men like himself. Though it might seem ironic at first glance that a man who had gone to Washington as the Chouteaus' prize pig, trussed up for sale to the highest bidder, made his reputation in the Senate as a stubborn and tireless advocate of the common man, there is actually no irony in it at all. Thomas Hart Benton was the type of populist fixer beloved by plutocrats throughout American history. Turning the attention of ambitious but impoverished white men like himself away from the ruling class as they sought an explanation for why rich men had so much when they had so little, he pointed them instead to the West: toward Indian lands and Indian wars. For Benton, Indian lands and empire (rather than class politics or revolution) held the promise of white equality.[7]

Benton's signature issue was the Graduation Bill, which proposed the distribution of unsold federal lands at prices that declined twenty-five cents an acre every year until the entire public domain of the United States was privately owned. What could not be sold in the end should simply be given away. Thus would the West be whitened and cemented to the United States. "The tenant has, in fact, no country, no hearth, no domestic altar, no household god," Benton famously declared, transforming the class conflict between white renters and landlords into a call for westering imperialism. "The freeholder, on the contrary, is the natural supporter of a free government. . . . I say give, without price, to those who are not able to pay. . . . It brings a price above rubies—a race of virtuous and independent farmers, the true supporters of their country." Benton's scheme was, at once, a spatial fix for class conflict in the East, a conversion of expropriated Indian lands into a subsidy for whiteness, a privatization of the public domain, and an effort to expand the imperial domain of the United States. It identified the national interest with the endless serial reproduction of white family farms as far as the sovereign power of the United States could reach, which, by the final time Benton went through the annual ritual of calling for graduation in 1854, was all the way to the West Coast. Benton's graduation speeches were printed throughout the West, and his admiring supporters "had the terms of it by heart," in the words of another senator. "They called their counties after him; they called their towns after him; they gave his name to their children; and it had secured to him an influence which nothing else could have obtained for him."[8]

Though Benton was never successful in convincing his fellow senators to simply give away the public domain (that would have to wait for Abraham Lincoln), he did convince them to allow white settlers to pay bottom dollar. Following the provisions of the Indian Intercourse Act (1790), and according to the decision of the US Supreme Court in *Johnson v. M'Intosh* (1823), it was illegal for Indians to sell land directly to whites. Indian lands could only be transferred—by treaty or by sale—directly to the United States of America, whose General Land Office then surveyed and sold them at auction. All of the surveying, sale scheduling, and auctioning took time, however—time that restless and entitled white settlers resented and refused to endure. Long before the sales, white settlers from Georgia to Illinois simply moved onto Indian lands and started to farm them. In some cases, they literally drove people out of their own houses and moved in; on occasion they harvested fall crops that had been planted by Indian farmers that spring. Settler colonialism prevailed in the shadow of empire.

The problem was that the settlers were operating outside the effective administrative reach of the government upon which their claim to the land legally and practically—and militarily, in the final instance—depended. It was only the federal government that could legalize their land claims, but the government simply did not have time to survey all of the Indian lands it had taken. The solution was preemption. In

1830, along with his fellow Missouri senator David Barton, Benton sponsored a bill that gave white settlers who built a house and improved the land around it a preemptive claim on any 160-acre quarter-section eventually laid over their homestead by the General Land Office's surveyors. That claim allowed them to purchase the land at the federally stipulated minimum price of $1.25 an acre before it was put up for auction—indeed, it allowed them to delay the auction of the land for two years while they farmed it in order to raise the money they would need to purchase it.

Administratively speaking, the policy was a disaster. It took the surveyor's abstract grid on the maps in the Land Office and scrawled across them a chaotic social history of existing settlement, partial payment, and fraudulent claims of precedence. But politically speaking, it made Benton a hero not only in the West but among the emergent Jacksonian coalition of western farmers and eastern laborers. "The manufacturers want poor people to do the work for smaller wages; these poor people wish to go to the West and get land; to have their own fields, orchards, gardens, and meadows—their own cribs, barns, and dairies; and to start their children on a theatre where they can contend with equal chances with other people's children for the honors and dignities of the country," Benton intoned. Philosophically speaking, the policy of preemptive claims represented the elevation of settler colonialism to a principle of federal governance.[9]

Benton, promoter of preemption, thus made peace with the prime mover of Indian removal, Andrew Jackson, on the basis of their shared imperial ambitions for the nation's common whites. After an elaborate series of deferential gestures involving the scheduling of meetings, pleasant inquiries about the health of one another's wives, and an exchange of home visits, the old antagonists had established a working relationship during Jackson's years in the US Senate. With Jackson's election to the presidency in 1828 on a platform of "Indian removal today, Indian removal tomorrow, Indian removal forever," Benton became one of his ablest allies and staunchest defenders in the halls of Congress. In Jackson, Benton found an ally willing to further the course of empire by any means necessary—and then some.[10]

From the beginning of his political career, Benton's imperial ambition was scaled to the size of the globe. In 1819, while the United States was negotiating with Spain about the future of Florida, Benton was already writing an article in the *Missouri Enquirer* suggesting the further acquisition of Cuba, support for the independence of Mexico, and the development of trade routes to the Pacific and beyond.

> The disposition which "the children of Adam" have always shown to "follow the sun" has never discovered herself more strongly than at present. . . . In a few years the Rocky Mountains will be passed, and "the children of Adam" will have completed the circumambulation of the globe, by marching to the west they arrive at the Pacific Ocean, in sight of the eastern shore of Asia in which their first parents were originally planted. The Van of the Caucasians and the rear of the Mongolians must intermix. They must talk together, and trade together, and marry together.

This passage, in its unwavering focus on the age-old dream of Pacific empire, its grandiloquence, and its racial and sexual entitlement was emblematic of the man. The serial restatement, revision, and practical application of this set of ideas consumed Benton for the thirty years of his career in the Senate, and even afterward, until his death in 1858.[11]

Benton's unwavering focus on the West isolated him from the leading men of the Senate during much of his time in Washington. He was a vigorous opponent of the tariffs promoted by John Quincy Adams and Henry Clay, which would subsidize eastern manufacturers at the expense of western consumers and, more important to Benton, provide the federal government with a revenue stream other than from wholesale liquidation of the public domain: the Indian lands he wanted to make sure were sold off to the common (read: white) man. As the issue of slavery moved to the center of federal politics, Benton clashed repeatedly with both committed opponents of the institution, like Daniel Webster, and its most ardent proponents, like John C. Calhoun. Benton was a slaveholder, but for him the politics of slavery was simply a distraction from the business of developing the West; indeed, it was in empire that the conflict over slavery could be resolved, as expansion abroad would inevitably have "the effect at home of producing a more perfect fusion of the different elements composing our own National Union."[12]

Benton was not so much the architect of the US Pacific empire as he was its prophet. In 1822, Benton proposed the creation of a military line of control along the spine of the Rocky Mountains, a set of forts in lands that were then in Mexico, to ensure American domination of the Indian trade as well as the Pacific trade he expected to emerge in the wake of the fur trade. During his time in the Senate, Benton sponsored four western expeditions, each of which departed from St. Louis to survey a route through Alta California (that is, Mexico) to San Francisco, the presumptive wellspring of the western empire, and each of which was led by the senator's son-in-law John C. Frémont, "the Pathfinder." Frémont's expeditions of 1842 and 1843–1845 surveyed the Oregon Trail with the goal of providing a pathway for the wealth of Asia to make its way to the heart of the continent—St. Louis itself. In 1845–1846 and, finally, over the winter of 1853–1854 (by which time the United States had seized Alta California in the war with Mexico between 1846 and 1848), he traveled across the Rockies, seeking a gap that might allow the building of a transcontinental railroad along the thirty-eighth parallel, from St. Louis to San Francisco.[13]

It was in support of that railroad that Benton gave what is perhaps his best-remembered speech, at a railroad convention held in the Mercantile Library in downtown St. Louis in October 1849. The transcontinental railroad, Benton intoned, would be a "Western route to Asia."

And from empire in the Pacific and the exchange of goods, Benton imagined, would follow the progress of civilization:

> The furs of the north, the drugs and spices of the south, the teas, silks and crapes of China [silk fabrics, or "crêpe de chine"], the Cashmeres of Thibet, the diamonds of India and Borneo, the various products of the Japan Islands, Manchooria, Australasia, and Polynesia, the results of the whale fishery, the gold, silver, quicksilver, jewels, and precious stones of California. . . . Our surplus . . . products would find a new . . . market in return, while the Bible, the Printing Press, the Ballot Box, and the Steam Engine, would receive a welcome passage into vast and unregenerated fields, where their magic powers and blessed influences are greatly needed.

Benton outlined a history of the future, of the American Dream of a Pacific empire, that reverberated through the late nineteenth century and even beyond. Seen in this light, it is unsurprising that Benton's first and most admiring biographer was the man who is credited with bringing so many of the Missourian's imperial dreams into martial being: Theodore Roosevelt.[14]

But not even the Seer of St. Louis, the prophet of Pacific empire, could foretell the future with perfect accuracy. Benton topped off his speech to the railroad convention with a brighter vision of the future of St. Louis (well, of the whole world, really) than he would be able to provide in reality. "Three and a half centuries ago," he concluded, ending at what he thought of as the beginning of the history he was trying to make,

> the great Columbus . . . departed from Europe to arrive in the East by going to the West. It was a sublime conception. . . . It lies in the hands of a Republic to complete it. . . . Let us rise to the grandeur of the occasion. Let us complete the grand design of Columbus by putting Europe and Asia into communication . . . through the

heart of our country. . . . Let us beseech the National Legislature
to build the great road upon the great national line which unites
Europe and Asia—San Francisco at one end, St. Louis in the middle, New York at the other; and which shall be adorned with its
crowning honor—the colossal statue of the great Columbus.

Benton is today memorialized in St. Louis's Lafayette Park with a
statue carved by Harriet Hosmer in 1861 in the way he had imagined
Columbus: clad in the toga of a Roman senator over his suit and shod
in the heavy boots of a nineteenth-century explorer, gazing westward,
above the inscription THERE IS THE EAST. THERE IS INDIA—the most
famous line of the railroad convention speech.[15]

Of the actual Indians who lived along the route of Benton's railroad, or the Indians he commonly saw on the street in St. Louis and
considered during his years on the Senate committees on military and
Indian affairs, Benton said very little. Of the Shawnee, the Delaware,
and the Osage in Missouri, he wrote with none of his accustomed
grandiloquence, but rather with a succinct and implacable savagery
more often associated with Andrew Jackson: "Sooner or later they must
go." Where many whites, including imperialist whites, continued to
support the Jeffersonian notion of the Louisiana Purchase lands as a reserve for Indians forced off their lands on the east side of the continent,
Benton insisted there should be no political limit to white settlement.
There was simply no place for Indians in Benton's imagined global order of the imperium of the city of St. Louis.[16]

Benton's prophetic vision took the earthly shape of Indian wars. Indeed, the post–Revolutionary Army began as an Indian fighting
force (the Patriots of the first generation were suspicious of standing
armies in general, but devoted to Indian killing), with Benton's St.
Louis at the center of its strategic configuration. As early as 1804, General Nathaniel Wilkinson, in St. Louis to oversee the transfer of Upper

Louisiana to the United States, outlined a vision of western dominion predicated on the control of the trade systems of the Missouri and Mississippi Rivers once "we get possession of the interior of their country." From 1805 until 1826, the army maintained a garrison at Fort Belle Fontaine, north of the city, near the confluence of the two rivers. It was on the grounds of the fort where William Clark signed some of the dozens of land cessions he negotiated during his time as the superintendent of Indian affairs. In the aftermath of the War of 1812, Wilkinson's vision was taken up by then–secretary of war John C. Calhoun, who proposed the creation of a military line defending the northern boundary of the country from Great Britain, anchored to the United States through its connection to St. Louis. In 1826, the garrison at St. Louis was moved south of the city, to Carondelet, where the newly constructed Jefferson Barracks soon became the nerve center of the Army's Department of the West. This arrangement was given official sanction in a series of military reforms in the 1830s and 1840s in which varied deployments of frontline forces were tied by supply lines and a chain of command that traced back to St. Louis. "In no other way, can an extensive line of frontier, like that of the United States, be defended by a small army such as ours," wrote Secretary of War Joel Poinsett in 1843 of the idea of a far-flung arc of lightly defended forts reinforced by soldiers concentrated at a central hub—Jefferson Barracks.[17]

During the years leading up to the Civil War, about 80 percent of the army's active-duty soldiers were stationed west of the Mississippi (179 of the army's 197 companies in 1860, for instance) and depended upon Jefferson Barracks for their supplies, reinforcements, and marching orders. At this time, Indian wars and treaty costs (annuities, etc.) were by far the largest elements of the federal budget, and Jefferson Barracks was arguably the single most significant material manifestation of the United States of America other than the Capitol and the National Road. Between 1826 and 1865, every western Indian war fought by the United States was staged out of or supported from Jefferson Barracks in St. Louis: in addition to the Sauks and the Foxes, the Osages, the

Winnebagos, the Ho-Chunks, the Comanches, the Pawnees, and the Sioux were all involved in significant battles with the United States in these years. Troops from Jefferson Barracks also played a central role in the Second Seminole War (1835–1842) in Florida, the Cherokee removal in Georgia, and the run-up to the Mexican-American War on the southwestern border. During that same period of time, virtually every officer who rose to prominence during the Civil War spent time at Jefferson Barracks—Braxton Bragg, Jefferson Davis, John C. Frémont, Ulysses S. Grant, Joseph Hooker, James Longstreet, Robert E. Lee, George Pickett, Philip Sheridan, William Tecumseh Sherman, James Stoneman, and J.E.B. Stuart. Before these men were legends, they were Indian fighters.[18]

In the decades before the Civil War, Indian fighting was big business in the city of St. Louis. In addition to the subcontracting of Indian removal and annuity payments to the Chouteaus and others in the city, the footprint maintained by the army at Jefferson Barracks provided merchants, manufacturers, and farmers throughout the region with steady income. St. Louis grocers and Missouri farmers provided most of the food consumed by soldiers (and later their horses) at Jefferson Barracks and at many of the army's frontline bases. Indeed, the city provided much of the military hardware for most of the US Army: guns, ordnance, ammunition, uniforms, and eventually horses—all were provided to the government by merchants and manufacturers in the city of St. Louis.[19]

In other words, in addition to its overall strategic setting, the city of St. Louis had important connections to the developing defense industries of the first half of the nineteenth century. Jefferson Barracks sat midway between two of the richest lead belts in North America: one centered in Herculaneum and Potosi in southeastern Missouri (and controlled by the Chouteau family), and the other in Galena in the northwestern corner of Illinois. Lead was to the military-industrial complex of the nineteenth-century United States what rubber, then oil, then uranium, would be to the military-industrial complex of the twentieth century: an indispensable extractive resource. In 1824, when Congress doubled the tariff on lead, the industry exploded in the United States. The population of the lead district around Galena, where the federal government leased mining rights to settlers, increased twenty-fold in the immediate aftermath of the change; subsequently, in 1827, 580 US Army soldiers were deployed from Jefferson Barracks under the command of General Henry Atkinson to inflict "exemplary punishment" on Ho-Chunk farmers who had come into conflict with the white settlers. In the years following, lead smelting grew into the first heavy industry in the city of St. Louis. When the New York merchant Phillip Hone toured St. Louis as the guest of Thomas Hart Benton in 1847, it was "immense piles of lead" on the levee that struck him more than anything else. By the 1840s, St. Louis boasted the largest smelting plant in the nation—providing the raw material of empire.[20]

The most famous war staged out of St. Louis in the years before the Civil War (though far from the only one) was the conflict that came to be known as the Black Hawk War in the summer of 1832. At stake were issues that dated to 1804, when a delegation headed by the Sauk leaders Pashipaho and Quashquame had traveled to St. Louis to meet William Henry Harrison. At the time, the future president was the territorial governor of the Missouri Territory, and his nickname, Tippecanoe, referred to his own legendary status as an Indian killer. The Sauk went to St. Louis to negotiate the release of a Sauk farmer who had been accused of killing three white settlers.[21]

The Sauk delegation had no authority to cede land, but Harrison nevertheless began by asking for land in return for a presidential pardon for the Sauk man he had in custody (and a promise not to pursue three others similarly accused who were not). Harrison kept no records of the negotiations, but Quashquame remembered that the Indians were "drunk the greater part of the time they were in St. Louis." By the end of that time, according to Harrison, who had a signed treaty to

The Sauk and Fox leader Black Hawk led an effort to resist white settlers in Illinois in 1832. At the beginning of August, many of his followers were massacred by US soldiers operating out of Jefferson Barracks in St. Louis. This portrait was painted while Black Hawk was imprisoned in St. Louis following his surrender to Jefferson Davis, the future leader of the Confederacy. (Smithsonian American Art Museum)

prove it, in return for the release of one man, the Sauk had ceded most of what is today western Illinois, southwestern Wisconsin, and a small strip of eastern Missouri to the United States, including the sacred city of Saukenuk (known today as Rock Island, Illinois), the ancestral home of the Sauk.[22]

The 1804 treaty, which provided that the Sauks and Foxes would continue to inhabit their ancestral lands up to the moment when the United States surveyed and sold them, never enjoyed a high degree of credibility among the Sauks and Foxes whose removal it promised. They stayed on the land and continued to gather at Saukenuk. In 1828, the federal government began to survey the lands in expectation of their sale, and Thomas Forsyth, the US Indian agent in Saukenuk, acting under the authority of William Clark in St. Louis, informed Black

Hawk that the time had come—a quarter-century after the signing of the infamous treaty—for them to leave Saukenuk and move to the west side of the Mississippi.[23]

Much of what we know of the conflict that follows comes from the autobiographical *Life of Black Hawk*, which was dictated by the Indian leader to a translator (and recorded by an amanuensis) in 1833, after his capture and confinement at Jefferson Barracks. *Life of Black Hawk* is thus a slippery source. At best, it is a story told by a man who had little left to lose, but perhaps much to gain, by presenting himself in a way designed to placate his captors. Indeed, the book is dedicated to General Atkinson, the commander who oversaw both the war and its brutal denouement on the banks of the Mississippi. At worst, it is a mostly fabricated account composed out of the interaction of a loose translation and creative transcription. The enormous success (indeed, the bare existence) of *Life of Black Hawk*, however, suggests that, at the very least, the Sauk leader was canny enough to flatter his captors into allowing him to mount a publicity campaign for his people when he was, for all intents and purposes, a prisoner of war.

And yet the autobiography presents its central character as a bewildered naïf, more puzzled than outraged, at least in the first instance, by the ways of white settlers. On one occasion in the late 1820s, he remembered, "one of my camp cut a bee tree and carried the honey to his lodge. A party of white men soon followed him, and told him the bee tree was theirs, and that he had no right to cut it." However much Black Hawk (and his scribes) might have exaggerated his perplexity at the property rights claimed by the white settlers, he was conveying to his audience the basis of the conflict between Indians and settlers over the meaning (and control) of land. In the winter of 1828, *The Life* tells us, Black Hawk, who was away hunting, received word that white settlers had arrived in Saukenuk and were fencing the land and destroying Indian lodges. When he returned to his lodge in the village, he "saw a family occupying it." Again, even allowing for an increment of strategic literary effect, Black Hawk's narrative conveyed the essential character of settler imperialism: one group of people moving into the houses of another, taking over the land they had cleared and cultivated, calling their actions progress, justifying them by race, and enforcing them by violence.[24]

Every spring after 1828, Black Hawk returned to Saukenuk, each year with a larger group. They repaired their damaged lodges and planted corn at the margins of the land that had been claimed by the whites. But the whites were running fences across the fields, and the Indian women who tended the crops "had great difficulty in climbing their fences . . . and were ill-treated if they left a rail down." Often the whites plowed up the Indian corn. One hungry Indian woman was assaulted by a settler for eating a few ears of corn picked from the edge of "his" field; two others beat a young Indian to death for removing a rail from a fence that had been built directly across an Indian roadway. Black Hawk complained to Forsyth, and through Forsyth to William Clark, but heard back that Clark was receiving a constant stream of complaints about Indians from white settlers in Illinois. "THEY made themselves out the *injured* party, and *we* the *intruders!* . . . How smooth must be the language of the whites, when they can make right look like wrong, and wrong like right," Black Hawk remembered in a passage that stands as one of the earliest analyses of the quicksilver process by which white entitlement is synthesized into feelings of white vulnerability and then back again into a standing justification of imperial aggression and white supremacist violence.[25]

While away for the winter hunt in 1830, Black Hawk received word from Saukenuk that the city had been divided into lots and sold. One of the white traders with whom the Sauks had once done business had bought a home lot on the site of the tribal graveyard and was plowing up the bones of their ancestors. In contrast to the white settlers, who based their claim to the land on imaginary lines drawn on the surface, Black Hawk rooted his people's claim in the past and the earth. But the time for arguing had passed, and Black Hawk began to plan for war.[26]

Black Hawk had fought alongside the British during the War of 1812, and the Sauks and Foxes maintained trade ties to British traders in the Great Lakes region. He spent 1831 traveling around the Upper Midwest, consulting with other Indians and with British traders and agents. The following spring, Black Hawk had led his people, now known among the settlers as "the British Band," back from their winter hunt to the east side of the Mississippi. By the middle of the month, his army had grown to about 1,100, enough to attract the attention of General Henry Atkinson, who was stationed at Jefferson Barracks in St. Louis. When Atkinson received word that the Foxes had joined Black Hawk, he wrote to the governor of Illinois, James Reynolds. Informing him of the situation, Atkinson implied that Black Hawk was intending to attack white settlements, and he urged the governor to take whatever action he thought "proper."[27]

Atkinson's message to the governor signals the complex nature of the relationship between the US Army and the settler militias in the ethnic cleansing and annihilation of Indians in the 1830s. The official role of the army was to maintain peace while overseeing Indian removal. In practice, this often meant trying to avert conflicts between white settlers and Indians who—whatever their so-called representatives had agreed to, or been forced to agree to—were reluctant to leave their ancestral lands for ecologically and spiritually alien lands on the west side of the Mississippi. In times of war, however, the comparatively small regular army relied upon support from state militias. Which is to say that they mobilized the radicalized, leading-edge settler whites whose actions had occasioned the conflict in the first place.[28]

None of that is to suggest that the officers of the US Army resisted or even significantly mitigated the ethnic cleansing of the eastern United States. Removing Indians while writing anguished letters home (for example, William Tecumseh Sherman on the Cherokee) is still removing Indians. There is, however, an analytical distinction to be made between the sovereign imperialism represented by the US Army and by the settler colonialism of the white militias, between ethnic cleansing and annihilation. "The material was an energetic and efficient troop, possessing all the qualities except discipline, that were necessary in an army," wrote St. Louis–based General Edmund Gaines of the Illinois militia in 1831. "They also entertained rather an excess of *Indian ill-will*; so that it required much gentle persuasion to restrain them from killing indiscriminately all the Indians they met." It would not be long, however, before indiscriminate killing became the official policy of the US Army in Illinois and, not long after that, throughout the West. But, in Illinois in the summer of 1832, US Army officers were officially in command, but the actions and intentions of the white-settler militia determined the nature of the conflict—not least because, unlike the army, the settlers had horses and could operate well in advance of the trailing forces of the regular army.[29]

According to Black Hawk's subsequent account, it became clear to him in the spring of 1832 that the hopes he had entertained of alliances with other Illinois Indians had been misplaced. Without hope of support from the Winnebagos and Potowatomis, whom he had believed would join him, nor from the British, whom he had believed would supply him, Black Hawk "concluded to tell my people that if the White Beaver [Atkinson] came after us, we would go back—as it was useless to think of stopping or going on without provisions." He decided to make peace with the United States and move west. On May 14, 1832, Black Hawk sent three men under a white flag to assure Atkinson of his intention to return to the west bank of the Mississippi. When those men did not return in the expected time, he sent five others to see what had happened. Three men from the second party shortly returned at full gallop with the news that the two remaining members of the party had been killed, and that they were being pursued by "the whole army." Black Hawk's messengers had delivered his message not to Atkinson's men, but to Reynolds's—not to the regular army, but to the white-settler militia.[30]

Black Hawk later remembered that he had been preparing for a council with Atkinson when the men he had sent out under a white flag returned in full flight from the pursuing whites. He had only about forty men with him, but Black Hawk rallied them, saying, "Some of our people have been killed!—wantonly and cruelly murdered! We must revenge their death!" As the Indians advanced in alternating ranks, the white settlers began to turn and run. "Never was I so much surprised in my life as I was in this attack," Black Hawk later remembered. "An army of three or four hundred, after having learned that we were suing for peace . . . that I might return to the west side of the Mississippi, to come forward with a full determination to demolish the few braves I had with me, to *retreat*, when they had *ten* to *one*, was unaccountable to me." The militia's leader, Isaiah Stillman, was unable to rally his men, some of whom only resurfaced after two or three days in full flight. Twelve of them remained behind, dead on the field. Among those eventually detailed to bury them was a settler militiaman who would later become the nation's sixteenth president, Abraham Lincoln.[31]

For Black Hawk, whose force emerged intact from the battle, it was a Pyrrhic victory. After burying the two men Stillman's rangers had killed and taking up the arms, ammunition, and provisions Stillman's men had left behind, Black Hawk directed his band northeastward, toward Wisconsin. Everywhere the Indians went as they traveled, the white settlers of the Upper Midwest were hearing the news of Stillman's Run and catching fire with rumors of an army of two thousand savages.[32]

General Atkinson, leading the combined forces of US regular soldiers from St. Louis and Illinois volunteers, had his own problems. Settler volunteers like those under Stillman's command were, to the general's way of thinking, unreliable and prone to outbursts of indiscriminate violence followed by serial desertion. He considered them a force unsuited to what was increasingly looking like an extended effort to track Black Hawk across a landscape that was known to very few whites in 1832. Through the month of June, Atkinson pursued and engaged raiding parties but was unable to capture Black Hawk, or even divert his northward progress. By the end of June, Atkinson's struggles were national news. The general received word from President Andrew Jackson that he must bring the war to a "speedy and honorable termination" lest other Indians in other places come to see the army's difficulty in capturing Black Hawk as a sign of more general weakness. Secretary of War Lewis Cass warned Atkinson that "an example [must] now be made" of Black Hawk. "A War of *Extermination* should be waged against them," wrote William Clark, the superintendent of Indian affairs, from St. Louis. "The honor and respectability of the Government requires this: the peace and quiet of the frontier, the lives and safety of its inhabitants *demand* it." The war had evolved from a conflict over the removal of the Sauks and Foxes into a campaign of exemplary genocidal violence led by the US Army—imperial annihilation designed to communicate to both the Indians and the settler whites that the US Army had the fortitude and the wherewithal to pacify the frontier.[33]

In Washington, the War Department began to organize a thousand-soldier expeditionary force (one-sixth of the entire regular army) under the command of General Winfield Scott to be sent to Illinois. But by the beginning of July, Black Hawk's people had run out of food. "We were forced to dig *roots* and *bark trees* to satisfy hunger and keep us alive! Several of our old people became so reduced as actually to *die with hunger!*" Black Hawk later wrote of the last weeks of his march. He decided to try to work his way northwest, toward the Wisconsin River, in an effort to "remove my women and children across the Mississippi, that they might return to the Sac nation again." Atkinson, closing in on the British Band and aware of the possibility that Black Hawk would try to recross the Mississippi, was determined to prevent the Indians from doing so. As the army pursued the Indians, the trail began to yield evidence of desperation—such as kettles and mats thrown away to cut weight in an increasingly headlong flight.[34]

Slowed by hunger and exhaustion, Black Hawk's column made its way toward the river and what it thought was safety. "At length," Black Hawk remembered, "we arrived at the Mississippi, having lost some of our old men and little children, who perished on the way with hunger." The signs of starvation were everywhere along the trail that the soldiers and militia were following in pursuit of the retreating Indians: abandoned packs, butchered horses, and the emaciated bodies of the dead. Black Hawk reached the Mississippi near the mouth of the Bad Axe River on August 1, 1832. As the Indians prepared to cross, the steamboat *Warrior*, operating out of St. Louis, rounded a bend in the river. The *Warrior* had been chartered by the army to carry troops up from St. Louis. On board were fifteen regular army soldiers, six volunteers, and a six-pound cannon.[35]

Black Hawk knew the *Warrior*'s captain, who had traded along the Mississippi between St. Louis and Galena, Illinois, in the years before the war, and believed that he could convince him to let the women and children cross to the west bank of the Mississippi. He stood on the shore and waved a white flag. In response, the soldiers turned their cannon on the Indians and fired volley after volley of grapeshot. The slaughter went on for more than eight hours. "As many women as could, commenced swimming the Mississippi with their children on their backs," Black Hawk recounted. "A number were drowned, and some shot, before they could reach the opposite shore." On the other shore of the Mississippi, the Dakotas, Menominees, and Ho-Chunks—Indians who wanted the Sauks to stay in Illinois just as much as the white settlers wanted them to leave—were waiting. They killed many of those who managed to make the crossing and took many of the rest captive.[36]

The Black Hawk War ended there, near the mouth of the Bad Axe River, on the morning of August 2, 1832. "After the boat left us," Black Hawk later remembered, "I told my people to cross, if they could and they wished." Black Hawk gave himself up at the US Indian Agency at Prairie du Chien, Wisconsin, on August 27, 1832. Handed over from the Indian Agency to the army, he was placed by Colonel

Zachary Taylor under the control of Lieutenant Jefferson Davis, who took Black Hawk down to St. Louis: "On the way down, I surveyed the country that had cost us so much trouble, anxiety, and blood, and that now caused me to be a prisoner of war," Black Hawk remembered in defeat. "I reflected on the ingratitude of the whites, when I saw their fine houses, rich harvests, and everything desirable around them; and recollected that all this land had been ours."[37]

After eight months of confinement at Jefferson Barracks, where he was forced to wear a ball and chain, Black Hawk was furloughed on the orders of President Andrew Jackson and taken on a tour of the eastern cities of the United States, the tour that occasioned the publication of *Life of Black Hawk*. Jackson's intent was apparently to exhibit the defeated Black Hawk as a talisman of his own potency—"to be gazed at," as the painter George Catlin put it—while also overawing him through a full-spectrum sensory exposure to the sights and sounds of industrializing America. Along the way, especially in the East, Black Hawk was treated as a heroic curiosity, especially after the publication of his *Life*, and large crowds of whites gathered to gawk at and applaud the conquered Indian in their midst. When he was released by the government near the end of 1833, Black Hawk settled in southeastern Iowa, where he died in October 1838 and was buried near the banks of the Des Moines River.[38]

For a time, Black Hawk was the most famous Indian in the United States. After dining with William Clark on Beaver Pond in 1832, Washington Irving rode down to Jefferson Barracks to gawk at Black Hawk in his cell and wrote about the experience in his *Western Journals*. The western artist George Catlin also rode out to Jefferson Barracks, where he sketched the captured leader, sitting in his cell. Catlin's Black Hawk, painted in October 1832, sits stoically, in the artist's words, "dressed in a plain suit of buckskin, with strings of wampum in his ears and on his neck, and [holding] in his hand his medicine-bag, which was the skin of a black hawk, from which he had taken his name, and the tail of which made him a fan." His eyes seem fixed on a distant horizon, a view inaccessible to the viewer of the sketch. In reality, Black Hawk was looking out on the headquarters of the US Army Department of the West, the administrative center of the wars that the United States would wage against western Indians for most of the rest of the nineteenth century.[39]

The Black Hawk War was the final impetus for the transformation of the US Army into a force designed to fight Indians, a transformation that was centered in St. Louis. From the mid-1820s, commercial interests in Missouri, and especially in the city of St. Louis, had been insistently urging the militarization of the Santa Fe Trail, which connected St. Louis via St. Joseph, Missouri, to the Southwest and Mexico and was emerging as a principal source of wealth for city merchants. Indian attacks along the trail, editorialized the St. Louis–based *Missouri Republican* in 1825, were more than a threat to the lives and livelihoods of individual traders; they were "a *public wrong*, a *national insult*, and one which will bring down upon the heads of the guilty the strong arm of national power." Never mind that the attacks took place in territory that was either Mexico or Comancheria, but definitely not in the United States of America. The deployment of the US Army along the trail in the late 1820s, spearheaded by Thomas Hart Benton, among others, represented a novel assertion of extraterritorial, indeed imperial, authority in the Southwest. It also, at least at first, represented a colossal failure. The foot soldiers deployed by the United States along the trail were no match for mounted Indian raiders—indeed, that was part of the point of the trail: horses taken from Mexico by Comanche raiders were sold through Santa Fe to St. Louis.[40]

The ongoing difficulty of patrolling the Santa Fe Trail, combined with the de facto subordination of the regular army to the mounted militia in Illinois and the national puzzlement at the army's inability to capture the Sauk leader, prompted a midstream correction during the Black Hawk War—a transformation of doctrine in the War Department that would reverberate across the West for the next sixty years. In January 1830, the commanding general of the US Army reported to Congress that mounted troops were the only way that "the Indians can be properly punished, should they molest the inhabitants who are settled on the frontiers, or who may be engaged in the trade with Santa Fe." And in April, the army's quartermaster argued that mounted soldiers were the essential condition of continental empire: "The means of pursuing rapidly and punishing promptly those who aggress, whether on the ocean or on the land, are indispensable to a complete security; and if ships-of-war are required in one case, a mounted force is equally so in the other." The deployment of mounted soldiers was inextricable from the emerging doctrine of exemplary punishment.[41]

The First Battalion of the US Mounted Rangers was formed at Jefferson Barracks in June 1832. Major Henry Dodge, still chasing Black Hawk across Illinois at the time, was appointed battalion commander; Captain Nathan Boone, the son of Daniel Boone, headed one company; Captain Jefferson Davis, upon his return from Illinois, was appointed to head another. By the end of the year, the mounted unit had been expanded to a regiment, renamed the US Dragoons, and permanently headquartered at Jefferson Barracks. Five of the ten authorized companies were fully outfitted and mounted on colored horses—grays, chestnuts, buckskins—matched to their unit. Even when the Dragoons left St. Louis for forward operating bases elsewhere in the West, Jefferson Barracks remained their primary base for intake and resupply. Based at Jefferson Barracks from the time of their creation, the US Dragoons (renamed the First Cavalry in 1861) took part in virtually every significant military action for the rest of the nineteenth century: action against the Seminole, Cherokee, Iowa, Kansas, Mahas, Pawnee, Potawatomi, Osage, Sauk, and Sioux, as well as service in the Mexican-American War, the Civil War, and the Spanish-American War. For most of the nineteenth century, St. Louis was home to the frontline force of exemplary imperial punishment: annihilation.[42]

Among the Dragoons, one man stood out: William Harney, the "Prince of Dragoons," was athletic, imperious, vainglorious, and violent even by the expansive measure of the Age of Jackson. Born in Tennessee in 1800, Harney soon grew into the type of man whose character and practical morality were based solely on his greater size and strength relative to others. Harney was white supremacy and empire embodied. Commissioned as a second lieutenant in the US Army in 1818, he was first stationed in Natchitoches, then Baton Rouge; by 1823, he was stationed at Jefferson Barracks.[43]

Along with other soldiers from Jefferson Barracks, Harney fought the Arikaras in 1824 and the Winnebagos in 1827. By the time of the Black Hawk War, Harney was notorious in the army for his stubbornness and volatility. At Jefferson Barracks, he refused to drill his men because of the pain caused by his gonorrhea, and he feuded with his commanding officer, Stephen Kearney. He viciously beat a dog that lifted its leg in the direction of his garden and tied a trader who sold whiskey to his soldiers to a post and beat him. Harney became close friends with Jefferson Davis and, later, Abraham Lincoln. He marched with the army that pursued Black Hawk to the mouth of the Bad Axe River and participated in the slaughter there.[44]

On June 26, 1834, in St. Louis, Harney beat an enslaved woman named Hannah to death. He had misplaced his keys and blamed her for hiding them. When Hannah's body was discovered, there was a great deal of public outrage about the senselessness and wonton violence of the murder—enough to send Harney into hiding for a time. But by the time he returned to the city, his case had been assigned to a friendly judge, the aptly named Judge Lawless, who suggested that Harney was in danger of becoming the victim of the fury of an unreasoning mob and transferred the case to neighboring Franklin County—a markedly more proslavery jurisdiction. Harney was acquitted of Hannah's murder after a daylong trial in March 1835. A little over a year later, he was promoted to the rank of lieutenant colonel and given command of the Second US Dragoons. By 1837 he was in

Florida, fighting the Seminole. Perhaps it goes too far to see in his case an uncanny premonition of the unpunished murder of Michael Brown almost two centuries later.[45]

On the night of July 23, 1839, Harney was camped with a detachment of Dragoons along the Caloosahatchee River, east of present-day Fort Myers, when he was attacked by a larger group of Seminoles. Harney had spent the day hunting wild boar in the swamps, and his men had gone to bed without having been issued ammunition for their arms. When the attack came, they could do little but run. Harney himself fled in his socks and underwear, returning to camp only after daybreak to find that most of his twenty-two men had been killed, some of them mutilated. In September of that year, he wrote to his commanding officer, Zachary Taylor, who had just requisitioned a pack of Cuban bloodhounds to hunt the Seminole in the swamps. (Thomas Hart Benton was among the measure's few civilian supporters.) "There must be no more talking—they must be hunted down as so many wild beasts," Harney wrote. "Let everyone taken be hung up in the woods to inspire terror in the rest."[46]

It was not long before Harney made good on his genocidal vision. In December 1840, near where the Miami River drains from the Everglades, Harney dressed a small company of Dragoons as Indians (a tactic seen as dubious even according to the corrupted standards of the Second Seminole War) and went in search of the Seminole leader Chakaika. When they came across two Indian families crossing the water in their canoes, they chased them down and hung the men in front of their wives and children. The next day they surprised Chakaika at camp and killed and scalped him. That night Harney hung the dead man's body from a tree, along with two others, in plain sight of Chakaika's wife and children, who had been captured earlier in the day. The Second Seminole War ground on for five more years— seven years all told, longer than any American war before Vietnam. Eventually around four thousand Seminole were removed to Oklahoma, including many Black Seminole—fugitives from slavery and

their descendants, whose claims to being Indian would later be disputed by the "full-blooded" among the Seminole. After that December
1840 day in the Everglades, Harney's historical reputation was firmly
set. Henceforth, he was viewed as one of the army's most merciless and
effective Indian fighters. In St. Augustine that winter, the white citizens
saluted Harney with cannon fire, a marching band, and a gigantic illuminated sign that read LIEUT. COL. WM. S. HARNEY—EVERGLADES—
NO MORE TREATIES—REMEMBER THE CALOOSAHATCHEE!—WAR TO
THE ROPE.[47]

Over the following years, Harney cemented his historical reputation as both a bully and a sadist. He reprimanded his men by grabbing
their two ears and shaking their heads back and forth, and he punished soldiers who fought with one another by pitting them in punitive
fights against slaves at Jefferson Barracks. Eventually court-martialed
for abusing the men under his command, he was ordered suspended
from rank and command for four months, with a recommendation that
his suspension be itself suspended by his commanding officer. Harney
served in the Mexican-American War between 1846 and 1848 and
was delegated responsibility for hanging thirty of the legendary San
Patricios—Irish Americans who fought for the Republic of Mexico.
This he did by placing the men on the backs of wagons and forcing
them to watch the climactic battle of the war unfolding in the distance
with nooses hanging around their necks. At the culmination of the
battle, the wagons were driven forward; Harney left the bodies hanging from the gallows. "I was ordered to hang them, and have no orders
to unhang them," he said.[48]

In 1854, stationed once again at Jefferson Barracks, Harney was
selected by Secretary of War Jefferson Davis to lead a punitive expedition against the Sioux. The expedition was designed as a retaliation
for the so-called Grattan Massacre—the killing of twenty-six US
Army soldiers who had begun shooting during a fairly routine piece
of western diplomacy and ended up dead. Harney, commanding six
hundred soldiers, including the Second Dragoons, caught up with the

Brulé Sioux in September of the following year at Ash Hollow on the North Platte River in what is today western Nebraska. The leader of the Brulé, Little Thunder, rode out under a white flag to negotiate. Harney told the bewildered Little Thunder that he would not consider any terms, but that the "day of retribution" had come and the Indians "must fight."[49]

While Harney sent the infantry northward after the retreating Little Thunder, his Dragoons circled east to block the Indians' escape. As the Indians ran out through a narrow ravine, pursued by the infantry, the Dragoons fired down on them from above. By the time Harney's men stopped shooting, eighty-six Indians were dead. Men, women, and children lay amid the detritus of their headlong flight, the things they had tried to carry away—the women's moccasins, the children's toys. "The sight," remembered one of Harney's soldiers, "was heart-rending." In the aftermath of the massacre at Ash Hollow, General O. O. Howard termed Harney "the most renowned Indian fighter that we had." From Harney's perspective, the massacre was a perfect success; "the result was what I anticipated and hoped for," he crowed in its aftermath. From that time forward, Harney was known among the Sioux as "Woman Killer."[50]

It is for this man that Harney Avenue in St. Louis, running parallel to West Florissant, near the historical site of Fort Belle Fontaine and not far from the site of the Ferguson uprising in 2014, is named. In a way, it makes sense. For Harney is a perfect emblem of his age. He was not some frontier curiosity, a weird relic of another time, but a man who stood at the leading edge of the empire, pulling it into the future: lead, horses, and Indian fighting (the military-industrial complex of the nineteenth century); the militarization of the Santa Fe Trail and the Great Plains (the theaters of imperial battle for most of the remainder of the century); the annihilationist fury of Ash Hollow. If Thomas Hart Benton was the prophet of the westering imperium of the city of St. Louis, William Harney was its avenging angel: volatile, implacable, and unrepentant.

Genocide was the vanguard of the empire, and anti-Blackness followed immediately in its wake. In the South, and in the more familiar story, anti-Blackness took the form of slavery, and there was certainly slavery in St. Louis. But western anti-Blackness, the sort pioneered and promulgated in St. Louis, had as much to do with the model Indian removal and empire as it did with the exploitation of enslaved labor as it asserted its vision: there was no room at all for Black people—at least not free Black people—in the city of St. Louis.

3 | NO RIGHTS THE WHITE MAN
IS BOUND TO RESPECT

The n—r, like the Inj—n will be eliminated. It is the law
of races, of history.

—WALT WHITMAN to Horace Traubel, September 8, 1888

ON APRIL 28, 1836, FRANCIS MCINTOSH, A FREE BLACK STEW-
ard aboard the steamboat *Flora*, disembarked on the levee in St. Louis,
not far from the spot where Lewis and Clark had landed on their
return to St. Louis three decades earlier. Best as anyone could later
tell, as McIntosh crossed the levee and walked into town he was overtaken by a pair of sailors who were running from the police. Whether
he impeded the police, ignored their shouted commands, or simply
did not understand what was happening around him, Deputy Sheriff
George Hammond and Deputy Constable William Mull abandoned
their pursuit of the two sailors and instead took McIntosh into custody. Within an hour, McIntosh would be dead, the victim of what
was arguably the first lynching in the history of the United States. As
Abraham Lincoln later put it, "His story is very short, and is perhaps

the most highly tragic of anything of the length that has ever been witnessed in real life. A mulatto man, by the name of McIntosh, was seized in the street, dragged to the suburbs of the city, chained to a tree, and actually burned to death; and all within the single hour from the time he had been a free man, attending to his own business, and at peace with the world." McIntosh, who had begun the day as a free Black sailor, was, by nightfall, a grisly landmark in a campaign of ethnic cleansing that sought to remake St. Louis, Missouri, and the West as a "white man's country," linking together the imperial practices of Indian removal and war to the jurisprudential annihilation of the 1857 *Dred Scott* decision.[1]

Because there was no uniformed police force in the city in 1836, there was no way for McIntosh to easily distinguish Hammond and Mull from anyone else when they accosted him. As the policemen tackled him and attempted to drag him to jail, McIntosh drew a knife from his coat and cut Hammond's throat. He then turned to Mull and drove his knife upward into the constable's stomach. McIntosh began running down Fourth Street, toward Market. As he passed across the front of the courthouse square, Mull, in pursuit, called out for help before collapsing in the street. McIntosh made it as far as Walnut Street before he was surrounded by as many as fifty men, taken to jail, and locked in a cell.[2]

Outside the jail, a crowd began to gather. There were later reports that Hammond's widow and orphaned children were there, and that their keening grief enraged the crowd. A group of men soon forced their way into the jail, seized the key to McIntosh's cell from the overwhelmed sheriff, and pulled the Black man outside. The mob dragged him a couple of blocks up Chestnut Street, where they tied him to a tree. Members of the neighborhood fire company stacked wood around his feet. McIntosh was silent while they worked. Only as the flames rose around him did he begin to pray and then to scream. Some of those who watched in the crowd later remembered hearing him beg to be shot as he was consumed by the flames.[3]

Francis McIntosh was a free Black sailor who was lynched in St. Louis in April 1836. The violence was emblematic of the white fears of free Black people that prevailed in the city in the decades before the *Dred Scott* decision in 1857. (Library of Congress)

The lynching of Francis McIntosh transfixed the nation. Elijah Lovejoy, who would later become celebrated as the nation's first (white) antislavery martyr, detailed the murder and its aftermath in a series of articles published in his newspaper, the *St. Louis Observer*. By the end of May, the reaction to his reporting had forced Lovejoy to leave St. Louis for Alton, Illinois, across the Mississippi. In November of the following year, a St. Louis mob followed Lovejoy across the river to set fire to the Illinois warehouse where he kept his press. When Lovejoy tried to save the building from burning, someone shot him; as he lay dying, the mob carried his press down to the banks of the Mississippi, broke it into pieces, and threw it in. No one was ever convicted of his murder, which John Quincy Adams termed "a shock as of an earth-quake throughout the continent."[4]

Both murders caught the attention of twenty-eight-year-old Lincoln, a legislator in the Illinois House of Representatives known at that point mostly for his strong support of African colonization—the idea that free people of color in the United States should be sent "back" to Africa. In January 1838, Lincoln delivered a speech before the Young Men's Lyceum in Springfield on the theme of "The Perpetuation of Our Political Institutions," which has since become known as "the Lyceum Address." It remains one of the most pointed and eloquent defenses of the rule of law in the history of the United States. Lincoln's address began with the lynching of Francis McIntosh and ended with a reference to the murder of Lovejoy. Lincoln argued that the lynching of McIntosh augured "the increasing disregard for law which pervades our country, the growing disposition to substitute the wild and furious passions in lieu of the sober judgment of courts, and the worse-than-savage mobs for the executive ministers of justice."

Lincoln did not account the life of McIntosh to be a great loss in itself; he knew that McIntosh was a dead man the moment he cut Hammond's throat. For Lincoln, it was the way in which McIntosh had died that had implications beyond the bare fact of his death. "This mobocratic spirit," he wrote, would eventually drag down the innocent with the guilty; destroy "the walls erected for the defense of the persons and property of individuals"; and finally, and tragically, cause even the best among Americans to lose faith in their government. "Whenever the vicious portion of the population shall be permitted to gather in bands of hundreds and thousands, and burn churches, ravage and rob provision stores, throw printing presses into rivers, shoot editors, and hang and burn obnoxious persons at pleasure and with impunity, depend on it: this government cannot last."[5]

In the place of the law, Lincoln feared, had been thrust the body of Francis McIntosh: "his body, or the remains of it," left "at the place of execution" and the burned tree left standing on the corner of Seventh and Chestnut for years afterward, an attraction for whites traveling west and a grim warning for Black passersby. Lincoln, who believed in constitutional governance and rational debate, could not quite bring himself to say what everyone who saw the body of McIntosh must have known. The mob that had burned him to death was not simply a manifestation of some abstract and irrational extraconstitutional energy among the masses. It was an assertion of white rule over and against the rule of law: white power.[6]

That the argument over whites' ability to lynch with impunity had its origins in St. Louis should not be surprising. Nor should the fact that it began with the question of the spatial aspect of racial hierarchy— with the regulation of free Black mobility. For the imperial economy of the city of St. Louis depended upon motion—upon dynamic, uncontrollable connections with the rest of the nation. In the years between 1820 and 1860, the population of St. Louis increased sixteenfold, from 10,000 to 160,000. The first upriver steamboat arrived on the levee in St. Louis in 1819; by 1855, there were 3,450 annual arrivals—more even than in the city of New Orleans. In the same span of time, the value of real estate in the city increased tenfold. The growth of the city depended upon empire and trade: on the Missouri and the Mississippi, on trade with Indians and traffic in slaves; on steamboats that brought white migrants from Virginia and the Ohio Valley, furs from the Dakotas, and lead from Galena, and that delivered barrels of pork, bottles of wine, bushels of grain, and thousands and thousands of enslaved people to market in New Orleans. On the levee in St. Louis, the *Missouri Republican* enthused in 1855 that "the sugars of the South lay mingled with the cereals of the North, and the manufactures of civilization contrasted with the peltries of the Indian." Those same steamboats also carried—too often for the taste of many whites—free men and women of color upriver and downriver as they sought new homes, new jobs, and new chances. The body of Francis McIntosh was a lesson for those who needed guidance in the midst of this dynamic, changing world about its foundational principles: Black slavery and white supremacy.[7]

In St. Louis, that mute lesson was given voice by the judge who presided over the grand jury that investigated McIntosh's lynching—the self-same Judge Lawless who had helped William Harney evade justice after he murdered the enslaved woman Hannah in 1834. When it came time to instruct the members of the grand jury about their legal responsibilities, Judge Lawless provided them instead with an account of the metaphysics of white supremacy. A lynch mob was "a force unauthorized by law," and burning alive "a mode of death forbidden by the Constitution," he admitted. But in the action of the mob, Lawless discerned "a principle of even higher import to the community . . . a higher law." The mob had responded at once to the murder of Hammond, the piteous tears of his widow and orphans at the scene, and "similar atrocities committed in this and other states by INDIVIDUALS OF NEGRO BLOOD AGAINST THEIR WHITE BRETHREN." For Lawless, McIntosh himself had been the "incendiary," the product of the exposure of the "fiery, unreasoning mind" of a free Black man to the "doctrine of abolition." And on the other side of the torch that actually set McIntosh alight was a higher law, one beyond the Constitution or human reason itself, a "mysterious, metaphysical, and almost electric phrenzy." The mob was moved by a spirit greater than that of law or constitutional order: the spirit of white rage.[8]

The foreman of the grand jury to which Lawless addressed his argument, and which eventually decided to bring no charges in the murder of Francis McIntosh, was one of the city's leading citizens: the nephew and ward of William Clark, John O'Fallon. O'Fallon had begun his career in St. Louis working in the Indian Agency under Clark, and he had gone on to make a fortune in defense contracting— supplying the soldiers at Jefferson Barracks and farther west during the military buildup of the 1820s and 1830s. By the time of the Civil War, he would be the richest man in Missouri, and a principal patron of Washington University, which was founded in 1853. In 1838, O'Fallon was already a notable landowner and prominent civic leader, and his presence on the grand jury suggests that the decision not to take any action against the men who had dragged McIntosh out of jail and burned his body in the street reflected the views of the leading citizens of the city. This is not surprising, for the para-legal authority that Judge Lawless discerned in the action of the mob had its closest legal analogue in the debate that had framed the entry of the state of Missouri into the Union in the first place.

In December 1818, the territorial legislature of Missouri petitioned the US Congress for admission as the twenty-fourth state in the Union, a request that occasioned a landmark debate in the history of the United States. On February 13, 1819, New York representative James Tallmadge added a rider to the Missouri statehood bill that came to consume Congress for almost a year and shaped the legal history of slavery and constitutional history for the next forty-five years—up until the issues it raised were adjudicated in the form of 600,000 dead on the battlefields of the Civil War. Missouri, Tallmadge suggested, should be admitted to the Union only if it outlawed slavery. In the admission of Missouri, Jefferson wrote, the "knell of the Union" was sounded—a note that might be temporarily "hushed" by compromise, but could never be unstruck.[9]

Because of its obvious sectional aspect, the sharp words used in the debate have generally been read as premonitions of civil war. Representative Cobb's invocation of a sin "[which] all the waters of the oceans cannot wash out, which only blood can wash away," sounds like a presentiment to those who know that Lincoln would later state that the nation needed to balance "every drop of blood drawn with the lash" with the sea of blood shed in the Civil War. But the men who debated the Missouri Compromise knew only dimly that they were on their way to civil war, if they knew it at all. More familiar fears shadowed their steps.[10]

"This momentous question, like a firebell in the night, awakened and filled me with terror," wrote Thomas Jefferson of Missouri. The image Jefferson used—a firebell in the night—was a fearful one for a slaveholder, who knew arson to be among the most murderous of the "weapons of the weak." Early in Missouri debate, Edward Colston of Virginia interrupted a speech by Arthur Livermore to warn the representative from New Hampshire that his speech might incite slaves listening in the gallery to revolt; indeed, to suggest that such a speech might justly end in the speaker's hanging. Tallmadge responded with a speech that referred repeatedly to "seas of blood" and the possibility of civil war and asserted that slaveholders had "whet the dagger and place[d it] in the hands of a portion of your population stimulated to use it," and on and on. For these men, who did not know the end of the story, the Missouri question was, from the beginning, edged with white fear and the possibility of slave revolt—with race war. The Indian wars upon which the whole enterprise depended, one way or the other, were simply assumed: it went without saying.[11]

In 1820, the threat to the Union was allayed, or at least delayed, with the Missouri Compromise. Tallmadge's amendment failed; slavery would not be banned in Missouri. Instead, in exchange for Missouri's admission as a slave state, Maine was admitted as a free state, and a line was drawn at parallel 36°30' (the southern border of Missouri) across the Louisiana Territory—a compromise over slavery that both assumed and forecast a future of empire. Below the line, slavery would be allowed; above it, there would be only freedom, or at least the freedom imagined by white settlers and supremacists. Historians have generally followed Jefferson in treating the Missouri debates as a landmark episode in the history of sectionalism. What emerged, in Jefferson's words, was "a geographical line, coinciding with a marked principle, moral and political"—the history by which the states north of the boundary became the North, and those to the south became the South.

As well as a new sectional orthodoxy on the slavery question, the Missouri debates inaugurated a new phase in the history of proslavery thought in the United States. Up to the time of the Missouri controversy, most defenders of slavery had described the institution as a necessary evil, a regrettable, even unjust inheritance of the past that was nevertheless essential to continued economic development as well as to the safety of southern whites. Jefferson was typical. "We have the wolf by the ear, and we can neither hold him, nor safely let him go. Justice is in one scale, and self-preservation in the other," he wrote.[12]

For most of the first decades of the nineteenth century, these ostensibly reluctant defenders of slavery had relied upon the argument that the institution, left to its natural course, would die out on its own. Allowing slavery to spread into the Louisiana Purchase Territory, argued Kentucky senator (and Jefferson's future attorney general) John Breckinridge in supporting the same, would, counterintuitively, bring that slow, peaceful end to slavery closer; it would "disperse and weaken that [African] race and free the Southern states from a portion of its black population and its danger." But by 1819 it was clear that those taking this position had been grossly mistaken. Slavery was not disappearing. It was expanding. And to justify that further expansion, the defenders of slavery would need a new set of terms. They could not simply keep arguing that slavery was a necessary evil that was bound eventually to disappear. They needed an argument that, at once, explained slavery's growth in the United States and celebrated it as a positive good.[13]

For much of the Missouri debates, the proponents of slavery stumbled from one argument to another: from proclaiming that slavery was a necessary evil to suggesting that if slavery had been good enough for the founding fathers it was good enough for the nineteenth century, to declaring that slavery was God's Providence and nothing less. By the time debate ended and Missouri was admitted to the Union, the "positive good" defense of slavery had emerged on the national stage. The next forty years of proslavery intellectual history would be devoted to the elaboration of this idea; even today we live in its cold shadow. The basic premises of the "positive good" argument were outlined by soon-to-be senator Thomas Hart Benton at the time of the Missouri Compromise. Slavery was good for Black people, Benton insisted, because it channeled their feral energies into productive labor and introduced their heathen hearts to the gospel truths of Christianity. Slavery was good for white slaveholders, he further argued, because it allowed them to convert savage wilderness into staple crops that could be sold on the open market. Finally, slavery was good for non-slaveholding white people because it alleviated class differences among whites by providing the South with a racially distinct working class—Black slavery, he noted, was the foundation of white equality. Benton in later years would diverge from the most spirited of the proslavery evangelists; he would prove much more interested in making compromises in the name of empire than fighting for slavery. But in 1820, he was one of the first to enunciate the terms that soon became the settled doctrine of the slaveholding confession of faith: slavery was not a threat to democracy and progress in the United States, it was their guarantee. Residents of St. Louis celebrated the Missouri Compromise by creating a giant illuminated display of a happy slave, grateful for the opportunity to follow his owner to Missouri. And yet the power of this saving stereotype was never quite enough to convince slaveholders, or still less their non-slaveholding white neighbors, that they could sleep soundly at night without worrying about being awakened by the mad-panicked ringing of a firebell in the night.[14]

Once the forces of compromise and union in Washington, DC, had mustered bare majorities in both houses of Congress, Missouri's admission to the Union had been balanced with Maine's, and a line had been drawn westward to the Pacific and forward into perpetuity, Missouri was given permission to draft a state constitution. The constitutional convention, held in the Mansion House Hotel in St. Louis, lasted thirty-eight days and produced a document that threatened to unravel the delicately balanced congressional compromise that had been almost a year in the making. For in addition to sanctioning slavery, the Missouri Constitution of 1820 directed the legislature of the new state "to prevent free negroes and mulattoes from coming to and settling in this State, under any pretext whatsoever."[15]

The provision reflected the variety of white supremacy that defined the emergent non-slaveholding and working-class white population of the state of Missouri and the city of St. Louis. It was consonant with the politics of the American Colonization Society, which had emerged on the East Coast in 1817 to advocate and seek to effect the removal of free Black people to Africa. In Missouri, however, Black exclusion was particularly resonant with the state's ongoing Indian removal, with which it shared a kind of malignant affinity backed by the fear—and the fantasy—of race war. "The cry has been raised—'Missouri for white men!'" recalled the free Black barber and chronicler of Black life in St. Louis, Cyprian Clamorgan. Indian removal and Black exclusion were aspects of the same imperial and territorial project, and Missouri in 1820 was its leading edge—what the abolitionist William Lloyd Garrison would later call "whitemanism." It was no accident that in 1820 the western metropolis serving as the epicenter of Indian removal produced the nation's most controversially anti-Black state constitution. Nor was it surprising that one of the first actions taken under that constitution was the resounding electoral repudiation of territorial governor William Clark, who was seen as too friendly to Indians (for removing them too slowly) and too cozy with the new state's slaveholding elite, their

mixed-race families, and their free Black economic partners, employees, and political clients.[16]

St. Louis was a city populated and inhabited by men on the make,
most of whom did not own slaves. In spite of its status as the largest city
in a state whose admission to the Union would soon become so identified with proslavery politics, St. Louis was much less dependent upon
slavery than other notable slaveholding cities. In 1820, there were just
over 8,200 whites in St. Louis County, as compared to 1,810 enslaved
people and 225 free people of color. In 1860, the census taken in the
county recorded 182,597 whites, 3,825 slaves, and 2,134 free people of
color. No other southern city had such a small proportion of slaveholders
among its white population: in St. Louis only about 14 percent of white
households contained a slave, whereas in Charleston, South Carolina,
that figure was 75 percent. For the non-slaveholding and working-class
white men who predominated in the state, Indians were a barrier to
cheap land and enslaved people and free Black people were a barrier to
high wages. "The attitude of the West toward Negroes," wrote W.E.B.
Du Bois of the era of the Missouri Compromise, "became sterner than
that of the East. Here was the possibility of direct competition with
slaves and the absorption of western lands into the slave system . . . but,
beyond this, even free Negroes must be discouraged."[17]

Many of these tetchy white men were migrants from Virginia,
where representation in the state legislature, like representation in the
US Congress, had been apportioned on the basis of population rather
than suffrage—an effective political subsidy to slaveholders, who were
able to increase their political representation in proportion (three-fifths
proportion) to the number of people they owned, and a perfect example of the racial capitalist process by which derogation of Black people
is generalized into the disenfranchisement of impecunious whites. In
Missouri, things would be different. Along with the provision forbidding the in-migration of free people of color, the Constitution of 1820
contained a provision apportioning representation in the Missouri
House and State Senate according to a census of the state's "free white

male inhabitants." This provision reflected the interests and perspective of the migrants who had come to Missouri in the years after 1816, seeking land and economic advancement; these men had seen their hopes diminished—or dashed—by the depression in 1819. They were wounded white men whose interests had an unsteady relationship to those of slaveholders: they might hold out hope of one day becoming slaveholders themselves, but meanwhile the political preferment of slaveholders was an occasionally galling constraint on their own skin privilege. Missouri, under the Constitution of 1820, was ruled by and for white men, not simply slaveholders. "They had," W.E.B. Du Bois wrote of the hundreds of thousands of white Virginian (and Carolinian and Tennessean and Kentuckian) immigrants to Missouri and the Midwest, "a very vivid fear of the Negro as a competitor in labor, whether slave or free."[18]

This was the germinal ideology of the militant wing of the white republic, later known as the "free-soil" movement and then finally the mainstream of the Republican Party. The politics of the second-chance white migrants was violently anti-Indian, but also antislavery, or at least anti–slaveholding aristocracy. It was a white supremacist anti-slavery argument in defense of a white man's democracy. But that is getting ahead of the story.

In order for Missouri to be admitted to the Union, the constitution that had been approved by the St. Louis convention had to be sent to Washington and approved by the US Congress. In the textbook history of the Missouri Compromise, the story moves on at the end of the debate over the future of slavery in the West and the line at parallel 36°30' and on to the Compromise of 1850 and beyond. But in Missouri, that was just the beginning of the debate: at stake was the question of Black exclusion. Article IV, section 2, of the US Constitution provides that "the Citizens of each State shall be entitled to all Privileges and Immunities of Citizens in the several States." Termed the principle of "interstate comity," in practice this clause means (and in 1820 was taken to mean) that individual states were not allowed to discriminate against the citizens of other states. The Missouri Constitution of 1820's deliberate exclusion of the free Black citizens of other states declared that when it came to free people of color, the state of Missouri was a territory apart. It was whitemanism beyond even the wide latitude provided white men by the US Constitution—at least up until the time the US Constitution was reconfigured around the politics of Missouri in the *Dred Scott* decision.[19]

A long and unusually pointed debate in the US Congress—the second Missouri Compromise debate, now mostly forgotten—considered the fate of this apparently unconstitutional state constitution. In February 1821, the final admission of Missouri to the Union was approved by Congress provided that the state constitution's stipulated ban on free Black migrants "shall never be construed to authorize the passage of any law . . . by which any citizen, of either of the states of this Union, shall be excluded from the enjoyment of any of the privileges and immunities to which such citizen is entitled under the Constitution of the United States." What that actually meant was anyone's guess. The state of Missouri was admitted to the Union under the auspices of a willful misunderstanding of its explicitly white supremacist, Black removalist constitution.[20]

Under the Constitution of 1820, the state of Missouri insistently curtailed the rights of free people of color. According to the 1835 revision of the Statutes of Missouri, the school-aged children of free people of color were to be bound out by the courts for apprenticeship. A record of their names, their ages, and their appearance, though not of the names of their parents, was to be recorded by the county clerk, along with a register of the names of the whites to whom they had been bound out. According to the contemporary theory of the 1835 law, free Black people in Missouri were denizens, not citizens; much like Indians, they were subject to the law of the state but lacked the ability to invoke its provided protections. (Indeed, according to Article 2 of the 1948 UN Convention, these threatened forcible separations would have qualified as "genocide.") An 1843 revision to the state code pushed at the limits of the creative misunderstanding that underlay the second compromise by restricting the immigration of any free Black people unless they could demonstrate that they were citizens of another state—a near-impossibility for most, because states did not issue proof-of-citizenship documents. And in 1847, the state of Missouri explicitly violated the terms of article IV, section 2, by reviving the language of the Constitution of 1820 and making it state law that "no free negro or mulatto shall under any pretext, emigrate to this state from any other State or Territory." After 1847, it was the legal duty of every justice of the peace, county clerk, and judge in Missouri to violate the US Constitution in the name of whites-only state law. In 1854, the free Black minister Hiram Revels, who would eventually be elected to replace Jefferson Davis as US senator from Mississippi, was imprisoned in St. Louis for "preaching the gospel" to free Black people and teaching their children to read.[21]

Most of the free Black people whom white Missourians so feared were second-chance strivers like themselves, although they strove without the entitlement of white skin. They worked as firemen and cooks on the western waters, as artisan barbers in the city's hotels, and as steamboat stewards (like Francis McIntosh). As described by Cyprian Clamorgan, the self-defined social luminaries of free Black St. Louis were people like Albert White, "one of the most expert chin scrapers in the city," who kept a shop on the corner of Fourth and Pine, near the courthouse; Frank Roberson, "one of the talking barbers," who worked out of a shop in Barnum's Hotel; Henry Alexander Meliée, a seller of vegetables who was "much patronized by steamboatmen"; James Nash, the steward aboard the *D. Perry*, which ran packet service up and down the Missouri, the itinerary of empire; James Williams, "a good workman" with a weakness for driving his buggy too fast on the plank road north of town; Pelagie Rutgers, "a brown-skinned, straight-haired woman of about fifty years of age . . . fine looking and healthy, and . . . worth a half million dollars"; and Antoine Labadie, who began as a butcher and made a fortune shipping beef to the southern market. In the aftermath of the 1847 code, which made further free Black immigration to Missouri illegal, many of these resident free Black people—all of them hardworking, fortunate people—were able to continue living in St. Louis only after posting a $1,000 bond. They lived in a condition of temporary exemption: awaiting removal.[22]

Among these remarkable people was James Thomas, who had been born a slave in Tennessee in 1827, and whose life allows us to understand some of the possibilities as well as the limits of free Black life in St. Louis in the years before the 1857 *Dred Scott* decision. While still enslaved in Nashville, Thomas had trained as a barber, and by the late 1850s he had gained his freedom and was running his own shop. In 1857, following his trade, he arrived in St. Louis. By the time he sat down to write his autobiography, he had made a fortune in real estate (and been described in the *New York Times* as "the richest Negro in St. Louis") and then lost it again. But it is not so much the trajectory of Thomas's extraordinary life that is of interest here as his keen observations about the racial politics of St. Louis in the 1850s.[23]

For Thomas, as for many of the men in Clamorgan's list of "Colored Aristocracy," barbershops and steamboat parlors were his domain, and he described them in detail in the early chapters of his autobiography. These were spaces of comfort, service, and aspiration for the white traders and travelers of the Mississippi and Missouri Valleys, and Thomas was one of the Black men who cared for them, making them feel important and at ease, even as he lathered around their noses and their eyes and then drew a straight razor across their necks. It was his business to know white men, and he observed them keenly—the way they all kept their papers in their hats and wore their cravats wrapped twice around their necks, the way they caviled and complained if a barber forgot to wash his hands or had breath that "smelt of Onions or his hands smelt of a common cigar." He noticed that they "had to be shaved low on the neck" to stem the tide of "hair on the chest that didn't know where to stop," and that the hair of their eyebrows was so long that he wondered that his clients did not "wear a bandage to keep their Eyebrows up out of their eyes"; he saw the hair on the ends

of their noses. Even as he recoiled at the way they picked their noses
or dribbled tobacco juice on the ruffles of their shirts, Thomas treated
these men with elaborate courtesy and respect. "The barber was safe so
long as he showed a cheerful willingness to please," he wrote. Thomas's
proximity to whites made him acutely sensitive to the contradictions
of free Black life. He looked down on white men, with an acuity that
makes one cringe at a distance of more than a century and a half. But
he also knew whites well enough to fear them.[24]

In time, Thomas developed relationships of patronage and perhaps
even friendship with the white men who spent time in his chair. When
the perimeter of the freedom allotted him began to close in the 1850s,
Thomas and those like him kept their heads down, took note of what
they could overhear of the conversations of their clients, and "stayed
in near touch with their white friends to have a good word spoken
for them." These were the sorts of relationships that separated Thomas
from other Black people in St. Louis—from enslaved people certainly,
but also from many free people of color. And not coincidentally, these
were the type of relationships that could drive resentful whites to make
apoplectic speeches in the Missouri House, arguing that free Black
people should be barred from the state.[25]

Thomas's view of poor and working-class whites was framed by
his experience in barbering and the views of his wealthy white clients.
"Gentlemen would not have a white man around him as a waiter or
barber. They wanted nothing to do with a white man that could not
rise above that," he remembered of the period before the Civil War.
"If a white man came towards him to shave him, he would jump out of
the chair. . . . The true Southern gentleman had no use for poor white
people." Thomas obviously approved, and as he recalled, so did most of
"the blacks," who called the poorest whites "trash" and those with a little
more "strainers." He remembered that these whites responded to his own
success with threats ("if I could get a hold of that n—r, I would take him
down a peg or two") and reminders of their own sense of imperial entitlement: "You fellows must remember, this is a white man's country."[26]

Thomas, who it should be clear was a very close observer of what
W.E.B. Du Bois would later call "the Souls of White Folk," located the
source of white racial enmity in the labor market. He had seen the look
in the eye of a work-seeking white sent away with a patronizing pat on
the back and a "well, my man, I'll tell you I have the best mechanic in
the state. The boy that does my work cost me a big price. He knows
what I want and he does it." Pushed to the margin of the economy,
Thomas suggested, poor whites "attempted to bring themselves into
notice of the better class" by policing their Black neighbors, arrogating
to themselves the "duty to watch the Negroes as a measure of public
safety," shaking them down in the dark, waiting for someone to run
away, gaining the reward for pulling them in. For Thomas, the violence with which poor whites policed the boundaries of slavery could
be understood as their own misbegotten effort to gain the favor of their
social betters.[27]

The "Colored Aristocracy" of St. Louis was not composed of revolutionaries or, according to Clamorgan, even political visionaries.
James Thomas built his fortune by making house calls to shave white
clients (and then selling real estate). Antoine Labadie became rich selling preserved meat downriver to feed slaves. The stewards among them
ran steamboats that carried slaves to market. The draymen pulled the
spoils of empire across the levee and traded them for the plunder of
slavery. And so on. And yet their hard work, their wealth, their confidence, their style, their pretension, even their pettiness, enflamed the
resentment of the economically unsuccessful, the psychically wounded,
and the resentfully entitled among the city's working-class whites.[28]

In 1859, the Missouri State Legislature approved what Thomas
remembered as the "Free Negro Bill." The bill provided for the removal
of free people of color from the state. Those who remained in Missouri would be enslaved. The property owned by the removed and the
enslaved was to be expropriated and applied to the education of poor
whites. If the legislature could not elevate all of Missouri's white people by making them masters, it could at least ensure that all the state's

Black people would either be slaves or be gone. Though it was never signed into law by the governor, the 1859 bill stood as a warning of what whiteness could do.[29]

It was a reminder that James Thomas himself probably did not need. Standing in his shop, Thomas could look out the window onto Fourth Street. Almost every day in 1859, he remembered, he would see Dred Scott, walking along Fourth Street between the courthouse and the slave market. It was the 1857 *Dred Scott* case that had provided the constitutional background of the 1859 law. Indeed, the decision of the Supreme Court of the United States in that case had retroactively thrown the full authority of the Court behind the Missouri Constitution of 1820 and all the laws to police and exclude free Black people that had followed. And yet, for Thomas, there was still another dimension to the dark irony of watching Dred Scott pass in front of the slave pen. Thomas's own white father, the father who had once held him as a slave, was a Tennessee judge who had gone on to become an associate justice of the US Supreme Court, Justice John J. Catron. Catron had joined Chief Justice Roger Taney in the majority decision in the case of *Scott v. Sandford*, decided in 1857.[30]

The *Dred Scott* decision is the defining ruling in proslavery jurisprudence. That it should have come from St. Louis, a city where slavery played a marginal role in the economy, is only a seeming contradiction; the deeper truth is that slavery in St. Louis was especially precarious, and because it was especially precarious, it was especially violent. William Wells Brown, who worked as a steward on the Galena packet and for a slave trader in the Mississippi River trade, suggested in his memoir that "no part of our slaveholding country is more noted for the barbarity of its inhabitants than St. Louis." Brown went on to cite William Harney's murder of the enslaved woman Hannah as a prime example, and indeed much of the slaveholder violence in St. Louis was of that type: enraged owners in private domestic spaces losing their minds over trivial problems. The majority of enslaved people in St. Louis were domestic workers, and the majority of these were women. Elizabeth Keckley remembered working so hard at making dresses for the leading ladies of St. Louis that her health began to fail. Lucy Delaney remembered the white woman who owned her attacking her with shovel, tongs, and broomstick for failing to get the stains out of an old shawl. Enslaved people in St. Louis lived not only on the violent terrain of slaveholding but in the shadow of the slave market, one of the nation's largest. St. Louis traders, among them a Captain Walker—who, for a time, owned William Wells Brown—were especially active in the interstate trade: they would buy those judged by the slave owners of mid-Missouri's "Little Dixie" region to be personally resistant or economic surplus and sell them south to New Orleans.[31]

And yet it is no accident that St. Louis yielded several published memoirs of an institution that left almost no survivors—including three of the nation's very few narratives published by Black women in the nineteenth century. For the violence of slavery in St. Louis was an index of the institution's vulnerability, not its vitality. The proximity of the "free" state of Illinois, the river linkages to the Northwest, and the imperial deployment of slaveholding soldiers beyond the boundaries of the settled law of slavery—all of these created avenues of escape for enslaved people in St. Louis, as well as uncertainty among whites as they tried to figure out just who was who.

One way of understanding the white supremacist fundamentalism of the second Missouri Compromise and the mean-spirited laws leading up to the proposal of the free Negro law in 1859 lies in the smoldering resentments of second-chance whites, who felt marginalized by slaveholding whites, threatened by the accomplishments and wealth of the "Colored Aristocracy," and anxious about economic competition with slavery. Another lies in the daily uncertainties of slavery and race in St. Louis itself, where slavery was not so much a legal condition as a state of low-intensity open war. One could never be certain if things were actually as they seemed—and never more so than in 1841.

Not far from the slave market, next to the National Hotel, lived the man who, for a time before the *Dred Scott* case, was the most famous slave in St. Louis—Madison Henderson. Henderson had been born a slave in Virginia and was sold as a child to a slave trader who carried him to New Orleans. Little in his early life was remarkable: Henderson was one among hundreds of thousands of enslaved people who were sold from the Upper South to the Lower South, from declining tobacco plantations to booming cotton plantations, from the Atlantic imperial fringe of the eighteenth century to the harsh, Indian-removing, slave-labor-dependent "empire for liberty" (as Jefferson called it) of the nineteenth. Then, in 1841, along with three others, Henderson was convicted of murder in a trial that transfixed the city; he was subsequently hung near the courthouse, close by the spot where Francis McIntosh had been burned alive in 1836—the same courthouse where Dred Scott would file his first suit seeking freedom five years later.

Henderson's full "confession" was eventually published, along with those of his three accused accomplices, in a pamphlet that was printed and distributed throughout the city and up and down along the Mississippi in the aftermath of the trial. In the days after bodies were discovered inside a burned-down riverfront store, the four were tracked down outside the city, bound in chains, and interrogated aboard boats headed back toward St. Louis. It was under these circumstances that their stories began to be told. Uncannily, the white men who took down these confessions each claimed, one after the other in court, to have been absent—taking the air, having dinner, getting some sleep—when the black men had begun to talk. They had no knowledge, they professed, of why the prisoners had chosen to confess. One of the prisoners, a man named Amos Warrick, later said that he was told that if he did not confess, the "people at St. Louis would burn him." Another, James Seward, believed likewise: "Feeling sure that I would be burned or destroyed on reaching St. Louis, unless I made a confession, I did confess to them."[32]

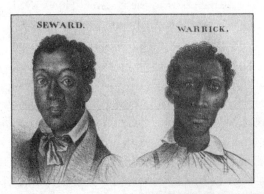

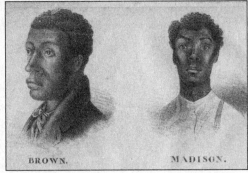

The "Madison Henderson Gang" represented many of the fears that whites in St. Louis had of both slavery and free people of color. The four men—one enslaved, three free—were executed in 1841. (Cornell University Law Library)

The fact that the stories in the pamphlet were almost certainly the result of torture reduces its value as a means of documenting with empirical certainty the lives of the four men whose testimony it contains. It seems likely that the recorded testimony reflected the prejudices, the fears, and the fantasies of the white interrogators as much as it did the stories of the four accused Black men. And it is precisely this that makes it valuable for understanding the prejudices, fears, and fantasies of the white population of Missouri in the 1840s: their sense of what it was possible for Black people to do in Missouri, and the ways in which it had become impossible for white people to control them. The pamphlet thus provides a road map—a sort of highwayman's map—to the fears that haunted white St. Louisans living on the imperial edge of the slaveholder's republic in the 1840s.

In the postmortem pamphlet, Henderson stood out: he was brilliant and ambitious and ruthless. Henderson served the slave trader who had enslaved him as a fixer. "If there was any Negroes whom we wished to purchase who were unwilling to be sold," he later remembered, "it was my duty to overcome their objections, and by false tales of what my master would do for them, or the purposes for which they were wanted, induce them to agree to be sold." One could write an entire book about the cross-cutting power relations that framed such an undertaking: the world-destroying power of those with the authority to buy and sell other people; the capillary resistance that might befuddle that power in any given instance; people moved where they were demanded, presented as they were desired, and sold for a profit. For now, however, it is enough to focus on one aspect of Henderson's story.[33]

As he later told it, Henderson's ostensible job as a fixer was a cover for his real work—stealing slaves. This man, who seemed in some ways to be a faithful adjutant of the slaveholding social order, a Black man who sent other Black people "down the river" for sale, was instead a secret agent. Slave-stealing was a shadowy form of hyperparasitism practiced at the edge of the interstate slave trade. One form was brutally straightforward, and common in the southern Illinois borderlands of slavery: small parties of kidnappers snuck across the river, snatched free Black people, and sold them down the river as slaves. As Henderson's interlocutors no doubt knew, there had been several high-profile cases of this type of body-snatching in the 1830s (and unbeknownst to them, there would be several more in the 1840s), as well as episodic shoot-outs between the snatchers and free people of color (and their defenders) in southern Illinois: slavery as a state of war. Henderson specialized in another form of slave-stealing: selling people to whom he had no legal title. Henderson and his white owner would quietly approach several slaves and offer them freedom in exchange for running away and participating in an extended con game. The slaves might then be sold several times over to different buyers from whom they would subsequently run away.[34]

After several years and a hundred such hustles, or so the confession went, the slave trader sold Henderson to a merchant in New Orleans. In New Orleans, Henderson met a free man of color, Charles Brown, who had spent much of his adult life spiriting enslaved people away from their owners, providing them with counterfeit papers provided by white abolitionists, and sending them upriver. Brown had arrived in New Orleans as a young man and taken a job as a pastry chef in one of the city's hotels. Shortly after settling in New Orleans, he traveled upriver to attend a meeting of the Anti-Slavery Society of Ohio, at which he pledged to return to New Orleans to work as an "agent" in aiding slaves to escape to Ohio. During the 1830s, Brown later estimated, he had helped as many as eighty people escape slavery in New Orleans, and another seventeen in Vicksburg.[35]

Remember that we do not actually know if any of what Brown and Henderson told their interrogators was true. What we do know is that it was credible to an audience of white interrogators and eventually jurors, who heard in these biographies two versions of the same terrifying story: a story about the vulnerability and violence of slavery in the borderland of St. Louis. To slaveholders, it mattered little if their slaves were stolen to be sold south or sent to Canada. In St. Louis, backed up to the border with Illinois and "freedom," maintaining slavery depended on force. Proslavery violence might be dispersed across the landscape of the Lower South, where an enslaved person would have to travel hundreds of miles in order to escape, but in St. Louis that violence was concentrated on the levee and across the river, in the Illinois borderlands. In St. Louis, the state of war latent in much of southern slavery was manifest as armed abolitionists and proslavery kidnappers fought a running series of battles that began on the riverfront and stretched across the prairies of southern Illinois.[36]

In New Orleans, Brown and Henderson began talking about how to "make a big raise, and quit the business" by escaping to Canada to begin new lives. Their pathway to wealth and freedom led through St. Louis, where they linked up with two free men of color, Amos

Warrick, an old friend of Henderson's, and James Seward, who had experience cheating at cards, working on steamships, and making a living on the periphery of the law. The four men began to talk about a job a few blocks away at Pettus's countinghouse, near the waterfront, where they had heard that the steamboat *Missouri* was due to deposit a load of upriver money.[37]

According to their later testimony, on the night of April 18, 1841, the four men gathered aboard the steamboat *Missouri*, pretending to inspect the boat's engines. They then walked together to the countinghouse at the bottom of Pine Street. Henderson, holding a bill in his hand, asked the clerk at the desk to look at it to determine whether it was a counterfeit. As the clerk bent to inspect the bill in the fading light, Henderson struck him on the head with an iron pry bar. Brown also hit the man several times and then handed the bar to Seward: "If you don't strike him, I'll strike you!" Seward struck the man on the floor twice, and then went outside and threw up.[38]

Inside the shop, Brown and Warrick wrapped the now-dead clerk in a blanket and dragged his body into the back bedroom. They found the keys to the cash drawer, which Henderson later specified contained $200 in Illinois and Miner's paper. But their real target, the safe, was unyielding.[39]

The men had been inside Pettus's for a couple of hours when they heard the other clerk who boarded there coming down the street, whistling. Brown hid next to the door. When the clerk entered, Brown hit him repeatedly on the head with the iron bar. When Brown was finished, Warrick pocketed the dead man's watch. Henderson and Warrick worked through the night on the safe. Finally, as the sun began to rise, Henderson gave up, declaring "that we might just as well try to break open the bank in the day time as to get into that vault." The men set the store on fire, locked the door behind them, and parted.[40]

Over the next few days, each of the men left St. Louis: Henderson headed toward New Orleans on a steamer, Warrick shipped for Galena, Seward traveled to Cairo on the *Atalanta*, hoping to catch another boat for New Orleans, and Brown headed for Cincinnati aboard the *Goddess of Liberty*. And, over the next few weeks, bounty hunters from St. Louis tracked them down, one by one, and brought them back to the city to stand trial.[41]

Recall once again that all of this is based on testimony that was elicited under duress and may have been freely rewritten, elaborated, and enhanced before being published in a pamphlet. All of this tells us as much about white fears about Black life on the Mississippi as it does about actual Black life on the Mississippi, maybe more. These are men you need to fear, the pamphlet told its readers: they move freely on the waterways and throughout the city; they have thought about murdering white men while walking along Church Street, Front Street, and Pine Street. They have been allowed to hold a razor to a white man's throat, openly and brazenly in the barbershop on the corner of Franklin and Tenth. They sow dissatisfaction among our contented slaves and steal them off—whether to slavery or freedom it hardly matters.

Above all, the trial, the pamphlet, and the accompanying panic betrayed profound anxiety about Black mobility on the rivers of the imperial West. No matter whether enslaved or free, these men moved easily along the Mississippi from New Orleans to St. Louis, and northward from there: to Alton, Galena, and even Prairie du Chien—the archipelago of American empire and white settlement. This episode also reveals a pervasive anxiety about the breakdown of the visual code of the slaveholding republic. Whites could no longer tell slave from free, most obviously, but they also had difficulty figuring out which Black people were connected to which white people. Indeed, we see in the forced confessions of the "Madison Henderson Gang" an insistent anxiety that these Black bandits were in league with powerful and unseen whites, from the men through whom they fenced their stolen goods to the slave traders with whom they collaborated to resell stolen slaves, to the abolitionists across the river. The fear was that these powerful players, with their Black minions, were pursuing schemes that targeted the ordinary, honest, God-fearing white people who were the bedrock of the slavery and white supremacy social order that was supposed to prevail even on the borders of the slaveholding republic, right up to the banks of the Mississippi.

Whether or not the men who served on the juries that convicted Henderson, Brown, Seward, and Warrick believed that every detail presented to them in court came from honest, forthright, and freely given confessions, they apparently shared this anxiety. Each of the four was convicted in the course of a daylong series of trials on July 9, 1841, and sentenced to hang. Uncannily, or perhaps emblematically, among the jurors who sent the four Black men to their untimely deaths was John F. A. Sanford, future owner of the man whom *Frank Leslie's Illustrated Magazine* would later term "the most famous coloured man in the world"—Dred Scott.[42]

In the years before Dred Scott sued John Sanford on the grounds that the time that he had spent in an area of the country where slavery was illegal made him free, similar cases were quite common in St. Louis—in the borderlands of slavery. The grounds upon which these freedom suits were filed were various. Some were filed by litigants who claimed that they were Native American; some claimed that they were born of free mothers; some claimed that their owners had agreed to allow them to buy their freedom, but had pocketed the purchase price and continued to claim their labor and their lives. The largest group, like the Scotts, claimed that they had traveled as slaves to regions of North America where slavery was forbidden by law and that they had, therefore, become free. The vast majority of this last group of cases involved people who claimed freedom by virtue of the time they had spent living where the Northwest Ordinance of 1787 had outlawed slavery: present-day Ohio, Indiana, Illinois, Wisconsin, Michigan, and a portion of Minnesota. These were people who had been enslaved along the northern frontier of the fur trade world and the empire that followed in its wake. Their cases represented a contradiction between the spatial character of the empire and the spatial limits of slavery—between the mobility necessary to the maintenance of military and commercial hegemony in the West and the locked-down control characteristic of the system of racial slavery.[43]

In the years before the US Supreme Court's 1857 decision in the *Dred Scott* case, the Missouri state courts usually decided cases like Scott's in accordance with the precedent set by a case known familiarly in the city as "Winny's case." Winny was born a slave in the Carolinas and taken by her owner to the Illinois Territory in 1793 to live on the east bank of the Mississippi, between Cahokia and Kaskaskia, across the river from St. Louis. At the end of the eighteenth century, Illinois was on the edge of the western empire of the United States, perhaps beyond the edge, and Winny's owner was an Indian-fighting settler as well as a slaveholder. He was also living in territory governed by the Northwest Ordinance.

When her owner moved to St. Louis in 1818, Winny sued him in the Missouri state court there, perhaps fearing that such a move presaged a drastic transformation in what it meant to be enslaved, from the comparative autonomy of the imperial frontier to the more rigidly prescribed social order of slaveholding Missouri. And she won: "We did not suppose that any person could mistake, the policy of Congress," the Missouri court wrote, declaring that a slaveholder "by such residence, declare[s] his slave to have become a free man."[44] Her case became the precedent of choice for the litigants in about three hundred similar cases filed in the Missouri state courts during the nineteenth century, the vast majority of them in St. Louis, and the vast majority of them successful.[45]

The case filed by Dred and Harriet Scott followed an imperial itinerary similar to that of Winny's case. Dred Scott was born in Southampton County, Virginia, in 1799, and moved with his owner's family, the Blows, to St. Louis, where he was sold in 1830 to John Emerson, a doctor attached to the US Army at Jefferson Barracks. Enslaved to a soldier, Scott followed the course of empire. He traveled upriver with Emerson in 1834, to Fort Armstrong in Rock Island, Illinois, and then in 1836 up north to Fort Snelling, on the west bank of the Mississippi, near present-day Minneapolis, on land that the Dakota called Bdote. There he met Harriet Robinson, who had been born around 1815 in Virginia. As a teenager, she had been given to Ensign Lawrence Taliaferro, who was stationed at the Indian Agency near Fort Snelling beginning in the 1820s. Taliaferro's business at the fort was to oversee relations between the nearby Dakota and Ojibwa and the American Fur Company (among whose principals was John Sanford).[46]

Dred Scott and Harriet Robinson were married at Fort Snelling in 1836. On the occasion of the marriage, Taliaferro transferred ownership of Harriet Robinson—now Harriet Scott—to Emerson. When Emerson traveled back down the river to St. Louis in the fall of 1837, the Scotts stayed behind at Fort Snelling. This was no small decision. Once the river froze, Emerson and the Scotts knew, it would be impossible for them to leave. They spent a long cold winter without any word from Emerson; as long as the river was frozen, so too was communication in either direction. When spring came, the ice in the river broke up, and the first steamboat of 1838 arrived at the fort, the Scotts received word that their owner had married in Louisiana and instructed them to travel there to meet him. Dred and Harriet Scott's first child, a little girl named Eliza, was born aboard the steamboat *Gypsy* as they traveled south. By 1840, both Emerson and the Scotts had returned to St. Louis, and in 1843, when John Emerson died, the Scotts became the property of his widow, Irene Sanford Emerson.

Somewhere along the line, the Scotts had decided to seek emancipation for themselves and their daughters, the second of whom, Lizzie, had been born in St. Louis in 1840. Dred Scott first tried to purchase freedom for himself and his family from Irene Emerson. When that failed, he filed suit in circuit court against her in 1846, alleging that the time he and Harriet had spent in Illinois and the Wisconsin Territory—time in the empire beyond the law of slavery—

had made them free. In 1850, in accordance with a quarter-century of precedents in the Missouri state courts, Scott won.

But in 1852, the Missouri Supreme Court overturned the lower court, invoking the Constitution of 1820's proscription of free Black immigrants and the interest of public safety in a state threatened by the "dark and fell spirit" of abolition. "Every State," the Supreme Court of Missouri declared, "has the right of determining how far, in a spirit of comity, it will respect the laws of other States." In 1853, the Scotts refiled the case in federal court in St. Louis. The defendant they named in this second suit was John Sanford.[47]

In the years since he had started out as a junior agent in the office of Superintendent William Clark, Sanford had worked his way up through the American Fur Company and been married for a time to Pierre Chouteau's daughter, Emilie. At the time Scott sued him, he was one of the founding directors of the Illinois Central Railroad (the line that would in the twentieth century carry Black migrants from the South to the city of St. Louis and on to Chicago). The judges of the federal district court in St. Louis ruled that the case was one properly settled in state court, thus deferring to the 1852 ruling that the Scotts remained slaves. Then the Scotts appealed to the US Supreme Court, where the case was heard in the December term of 1856. The decision of the court was announced on March 6, 1857.

For Chief Justice Roger Taney and the six other justices who concurred with his decision, the principal issue at stake was the question of whether Dred Scott had any right to sue in the first place. The chief justice's decision defined the right to seek redress in federal court as the sole prerogative of "citizens" of the United States, and like the debate over the Missouri Constitution of 1820, Taney's decision hinged on article IV, section 2, of the US Constitution: the question of the "privileges and immunities" of the citizens of the various states. For Taney, only the United States of America could make a "person" into a "citizen." Whatever the governments of any given state might choose to do with those residing within their borders, they could not make them "citizens," for they could not speak for the governments of other states in making such a determination. The Constitution would not allow any single state to "embrace the Negro African . . . raise him to the rank of a citizen, and immediately clothe him with all the privileges of a citizen in every other state."

And if only the federal government could make a person into a citizen, Taney was certain that the framers of the Constitution had never intended to do so in the case of Black people. Never, he argued, could the framers have imagined that the "class of persons . . . whose ancestors were Negroes of the African race, and imported into this country and sold and held as slaves," could "become entitled to all the rights and privileges and immunities" guaranteed the citizens of the United States. Would the founders have been so stupid as to give members of the "African race" exemption from the "special laws" that regulated their behavior? Would they have allowed them to travel from state to state "without pass or passport," and "go where they please at every hour of the day or night without molestation?" Would they have allowed Black people to "hold meetings upon political affairs and to keep and carry arms wherever they went?"

Of course not, he answered himself, for so doing would inevitably have "endanger[ed] the peace and safety of the State." The possibilities of Black citizenship, which Taney represented through a set of images of Black mobility, posed a threat to public safety. Taken together with his parting images of Black men holding mass meetings on public affairs and carrying guns, it seems very clear that Taney saw a pathway that led fairly directly from Black citizenship to race war—to the world of Black mobility and violence that the white citizens of St. Louis had seen exposed in the press coverage and pamphlets that circulated in the wake of the trial of the Madison Henderson Gang. Slowed down, the logic went something like this: to recognize the rights of Black people to sue in the nation's courts would be to tacitly countenance their legal right to constitutional protection. That, in turn, would protect their movements from state to state under the principle of interstate comity.

Once allowed to move about freely, they might gather in assemblies and even arm themselves like a militia.

Sped up, Taney's logic went something like this: there were two possible outcomes stemming from the issues presented in this case—slavery or race war. Taney vastly preferred slavery; indeed, he thought it the natural condition of Black people. Surveying the legal history of the United States, Taney found countless instances in which whites had held African Americans to be "of an inferior order and altogether unfit to associate with the white race, either in social or political relations." And for him, the frequency of the racist claim was proof enough it was right: among other things, the *Dred Scott* case was a landmark in the white supremacist use of white supremacist legal precedent in establishing white supremacist constitutionalism. From there, it was but a short leap to Taney's infamous conclusion that African Americans were "so far inferior that they had no rights which the white man was bound to respect."[48]

For Taney, "the Negro" stood exposed—naked—before "the dominant race . . . and had no rights or privileges but such as those who held the power and the government might choose to grant." The Negro existed by the pleasure of white people, by their grace. For the Black barber James Thomas—whose white father, the white man he might in another world have thought to be the person most likely to speak up for him in a moment of extreme danger, had concurred in Taney's decision—this was the lynching of McIntosh made sovereign law. "That 'the Negro has no rights that a white man is bound to respect' is shown by the mob going after the blacks and endeavoring to 'wipe them out,'" he wrote.[49]

The *Dred Scott* decision reflected the politics of race and slavery in the city from which it emerged. The case has been justly treated as a landmark in the history of slavery in the United States, but it turns out to have as much to do with freedom as with slavery: specifically with defining the condition of free people of color in the United States, and indeed, with extraterritorializing or even exterminating free people of color. It took the proslavery stance of the South and recalibrated it to the whites-only removalism of the West—the state of Missouri and the city of St. Louis from whence the case emerged. And it looked westward, toward empire: it was predicated upon the notion, too obvious to even need to be spelled out, of Indian removal and genocide, upon the idea of the "white man's country."

There was no room for Black citizenship in the empire of white fear, a place where a sitting judge might argue that a free Black man who had been burned to death by a mob was an "incendiary"; where 1,700 beleaguered free Black people living amid 150,000 whites might occasion a removalist race panic; where the effort of a middle-aged man, his middle-aged wife, and their two small children to gain their freedom in the courts of the slaveholding state of Missouri according to three decades of settled precedent was evidence of the "dark and fell spirit" of abolition; where poor whites were so arrested by the image of free Black competition that they could only dimly understand that they too toiled and suffered in the service of wealthy whites.

In the following decades, however, the struggling second-chance whites of St. Louis would be offered an unprecedented, even revolutionary alternative: to ally themselves with the slaves and overthrow their masters—to choose hope over fear, and solidarity over skin privilege. That the idea came slowly to most, and never stuck with many, should not blind us to the extraordinary challenge it represented. But neither should we lose sight of the fact that even the most radical imaginings of freedom in the history of St. Louis were hedged in by the limits of empire.

4 | EMPIRE AND THE LIMITS OF REVOLUTION

Labor cannot emancipate itself in the white skin where
in the Black it is branded.

—KARL MARX, *Capital*

IN MISSOURI IN THE YEARS LEADING UP TO THE CIVIL WAR,
the studied silence that had come to characterize the Bentonite approach to the question of slavery in the early 1850s—the doomed effort
to insulate the promotion of the western empire from the question of
whether or not white settlers would be able to own slaves—had given
way to a more pointed argument over the proper relation of race, property, and empire. On the one hand were proslavery politicians, most of
them Democrats, like Claiborne Jackson, the slaveholding governor of
Missouri at the time of secession, and Sterling Price, the commander
of the Missouri state guard who eventually oversaw the Confederate
war effort in the state. Support for slavery was particularly strong in
central Missouri's hemp-producing Little Dixie region, the slaveholding counties along the state's western boundary with Kansas, and
among the St. Louis elite. For these Democrats, the questions of white

supremacy, slavery, and expansion were aligned according to the logic of the *Dred Scott* decision: Black slavery and white ascendency without territorial limit.[1]

On the other hand, the election of 1856, in which John C. Frémont had been the presidential nominee of the new Republican Party, represented the national emergence of a powerful reworking of the question of the relationship of slavery to white equality, as prefigured in the removalist politics of the city of St. Louis and the state of Missouri between the second Missouri Compromise of 1821 and the attacks on free Black citizenship that had followed in its wake. These "free-soilers," arguing that slavery raised one class of white men (slaveholders) above others (workers and farmers, the "producers"), fought to keep the institution out of the West, often with the codicil familiar to readers of the Missouri Constitution or the "Free Negro Bill" of 1859—that the West should be a "white man's country." As far as the West was concerned, however, and as far as Indians were considered, both the expansionist proslavery position of the Democratic Party and the settler whitemanism of the free-soil movement were simple variants on the imperialist theme that stretched back to Jefferson Barracks, Benton, the Black Hawk War, and beyond.

Captain John C. Frémont—"the Pathfinder," the son-in-law of Thomas Hart Benton, and the founding figurehead of the Republican Party—was an imperialist and, by any modern standard, a war criminal. In April 1846, operating about nine hundred miles west of where he was supposed to be surveying a pass across the Rockies in Colorado, Frémont came upon about a thousand Indians—probably Wintus—gathered on the banks of the Sacramento River to catch salmon as they swam upstream. Though the reason for their assembly in the Sacramento Valley was obvious and easily explained, the Indians were rumored among nearby settlers to be planning an attack on a white settlement about ninety miles northwest of present-day Sacramento. For Frémont, that rumor of war was enough, and he ordered a preemptive attack on the large encampment. "The settlers charged into the village taking the warriors by surprise and then commenced a scene of slaughter which is unequalled in the West. The bucks, squaws, and paposes were shot dead like sheep and those men never stopped as long as they could find one alive," remembered one observer. As the Indians fled on foot, Frémont led a mounted party that literally "cut a path through the fleeing crowd." It was, as Frémont said of the Indians in another massacre in which he participated, "a story for them to hand down while there are any" left to tell it. It was, as the leading historian of the genocide in California has put it, "pedagogic slaughter"—killing in excess of any strategic justification, intended to demoralize the population into submission. Before he was through in California, Frémont would find himself at the head of a settler army and declare himself the leader of the short-lived (and arguably treasonous for a US military officer operating outside the chain of command) Bear Flag Republic.[2]

For Frémont and the Republican Party, empire (and thus Indian-killing) was the key to white freedom. In their imperial ambition, the Free Soil Republicans were the intellectual heirs of Benton, committed to the expropriation of Indian lands and their distribution to white settlers and to a transcontinental railroad. But where Benton had tried to defer the question of slavery, Free Soil Republicans sought to agitate it. The free-soil synthesis that formed the ideological infrastructure of the Republican Party that cohered around Frémont in 1856 suggested that white labor could thrive, and white men advance, only in the absence of slavery. For them, the future of Missouri as a "white man's country"—as an empire—depended on the territorial limitation of slavery or even its abolition. The politics of the party was rooted in the material experience of the ambitious westering whites who had followed their hopes to Missouri in the decades after the War of 1812—Bentonite whites turned Free Soil Republicans. In the November 1860 presidential election, St. Louis voted two-to-one for the Free Soil Republican Abraham Lincoln over the proslavery Democrat Stephen A. Douglas.[3]

In the aftermath of Lincoln's election, as the southern states began to secede from the Union and the United States prepared for war, St. Louis became a divided city. Sometime around Christmas Day in 1860, armed antislavery paramilitaries began training in the parks and parading in the streets of St. Louis. On New Year's Day, armed men attended a court-ordered slave sale on the steps of the courthouse where the *Dred Scott* case had been heard a decade earlier and held the bidding on the first lot of people sent to auction to $8—their presence an implicit threat to anyone who dared bid more than the value of the clothes in which the slaves had been dressed for sale. (The moment was later commemorated in a famous painting by Thomas Satterwhite Noble misleadingly entitled *The Last Sale of Slaves in St. Louis.* The crowd returned to the courthouse on another day, and the enslaved people were sold; indeed, enslaved people in St. Louis continued to be sold southward by profit-taking owners well into the early years of the Civil War.) By the end of February, two months before the shelling of Fort Sumter, the streets of St. Louis were controlled by armed antislavery "wide-awakes" (thus known for the style of hat they wore) numbering about 1,400 men, divided into sixteen companies, many of them armed with Sharps rifles, the most deadly infantry weapons available on the planet in 1861.[4]

Proslavery Democrats in the city soon organized their own paramilitary units, the most notable called the "Minute Men" and led by Basil Duke, a St. Louis lawyer who would go on to fame as a Confederate general and chronicler of the Confederate war effort. The families of the old-money fur-trading and slaveholding elites, as well as working-class white Democrats and Irish immigrants (as much as 16 percent of the city's population by 1860), looked to the state government and Democratic governor Claiborne Jackson for direction. At the behest of proslavery Democrats, Jackson placed the city's police department under state control (where it remained until very recently). He then appointed a police board composed of four men whom the antislavery St. Louis minister Galusha Anderson later termed "three of the most outspoken virulent secessionists in the city," led by Basil Duke. The police and the proslavery militias began to drill in the city's parks and to march in its streets. The city, in the words of Anderson, was coming to resemble an "armed camp."[5]

With the shelling of Fort Sumter on April 12, 1861, and the beginning of the war, all of the factors that had contributed to St. Louis's position as the capital city of the nation's western empire were transformed into strategic resources in the emergent struggle between North and South: control of the nation's western waters and its best overland connections to the Pacific, the lead mines in Potosi and Galena, and the largest military base in the West. Years after the war, Ulysses S. Grant reflected on the strategic significance of the Union defense of St. Louis in 1861: "If St. Louis had been captured by the rebels it would have made a vast difference. . . . It would have been a terrible task to recapture St. Louis, one of the most difficult that could have been given to any military man. Instead of a campaign before Vicksburg, it would have been a campaign before St. Louis."[6]

In the earliest days of the war, all of that strategic significance centered on the question of who would control the US arsenal located just south of the city's downtown. In the weeks after the shelling of Fort Sumter, pro-Confederate state militias all over the South had been seizing federal arsenals, and the arsenal at St. Louis was by far the largest prize. As the arms depot of the nation's western empire, St. Louis had the second-largest arsenal in the United States: 60,000 long arms, 1.5 million cartridges, 90,000 pounds of gunpowder, and 40 cannons. And in command was the man whose bloody record on the plains followed his murder of an enslaved woman named Hannah: General William S. Harney, the commander of the US Army Department of the West, the man the Sioux called "Woman Killer."[7]

But as Lincoln's national call for volunteers was ignored by Missouri's proslavery governor and armed paramilitaries paraded in the city's streets, Harney, known throughout his career for taking precipitate, even rash, action, moved with a deliberation that suggested an unspoken sympathy for secession to his critics. When he received orders from Washington to reinforce the arsenal, he moved three hundred men from Jefferson Barracks, but left the high ground above the riverbank depot undefended. When the Republican congressman (and Lincoln confidant) Francis Preston Blair Jr. tried to have the Home Guard, the antislavery paramilitaries, mustered into the US Army to defend the city, Harney refused to swear them into federal service or to provide them with arms. When General Nathaniel Lyon, who had direct command over the arsenal, suggested that some of the weapons stored there be transferred to Illinois volunteers who had been pledged to the United States by their governor, Harney asked to have his subordinate transferred. "He is a Southern man," the well-connected Blair wrote to his friends in Washington; he noted in that letter that Harney was a chronically indebted slaveholder whose wife's family owned a number of slaves he might one day hope to inherit. Not long after Blair sent his letter, General Harney was ordered to Washington to deliver a full report on the situation in St. Louis. Acting in his stead, General Lyon occupied the hills that overlooked the arsenal and mustered the antislavery Home Guard into the service of the United States.[8]

While Harney dithered, proslavery St. Louisans fell in behind Missouri's Democratic governor, Claiborne Jackson. Acting under the authority of the state of Missouri, General Daniel Frost called up about seven hundred volunteers and began to drill them at the edge of the city, at a place called Lindell's Grove, near the site of present-day St. Louis University. They drilled beneath the flag of Missouri, called themselves the militia, and claimed to be acting as neutral peacekeepers in the divided city. But events left little room for doubt about their true purposes. The site soon became known as Camp Jackson, after the proslavery governor, and through Governor Jackson, Frost was in touch with Confederate commander Jefferson Davis, who arranged for artillery seized by the Confederacy from the US armory at Baton Rouge to be sent upriver to St. Louis, packaged and labeled as marble in order to escape attention. On the evening of May 9, 1861, local legend has it, General Lyon confirmed for himself what everyone already suspected. Disguising himself in women's clothes, Lyon rode through Camp Jackson in a carriage owned by Blair's widowed mother, a blind woman known for touring the city with her coachman. Whether the heavily bearded general actually rode around Camp Jackson disguised as a blind woman or instead observed the camp from the vantage point of a nearby ditch, as one of his German-speaking officers remembered, he saw enough to convince himself once and for all that General Frost was planning an attack on the arsenal. The state militia had taken down the street signs around their camp and replaced them with signs honoring the leaders of the Confederacy. Beneath those signs, boldly displayed, were the field pieces stolen from the armory in Baton Rouge.[9]

And so, around midday on May 10, 1861, General Lyon stole a march on Camp Jackson. Under his command were some eight thousand men—a small army composed of the army's US Volunteers and locally organized Home Guards. As they spread out and marched in parallel columns down four different streets leading to Camp Jackson, many of the volunteers and all of the Home Guards received their orders in German.[10]

Throughout the 1850s, many in St. Louis used the word "white" in a way that would have been familiar to Thomas Hart Benton—as shorthand for a certain kind of person: a yeoman-farming or wage-working, vote-casting person. "Free soil, free labor, free men" went the slogan of the Republican Party to which, in Missouri at least, these men increasingly belonged. Their city had changed, however, in the decades since Thomas Hart Benton first championed Missouri to poor whites from Virginia, Tennessee, and Kentucky as the "best poor man's country," as the place where they might get out from under the bloated aristocracy of slavery and inherited privilege, escape competition with slaves and even free people of color, and get what was by right their own. These men, we will see, were well represented in the US Volunteers.

But by 1860, one-third of the city's population had been born in the German-speaking territories of Europe, and some of them had brought with them very different notions about property and democracy than those held by men like Benton and his Republican successors (not to mention those men's more conservative antagonists assembled at Camp Jackson).[11]

The German-speaking population of the city dated to the 1830s, but the largest part of St. Louis's German-speaking population had arrived in the city after the European revolutions of 1848. In that year, across large portions of continental Europe—France, Sicily, the German Confederation, and throughout the sprawling territories of the Habsburg Empire, from Milan and Prague to Budapest and Vienna— an anti-absolutist alliance of peasants, artisans and journeymen, students, and liberal professionals succeeded for a time in taking control of the cities and forcing the monarchs and their armies into retreat. The demands of the revolutionary alliance spanned the spectrum from the introduction of constitutional monarchy and the "rule of law" to the redistribution of land and, in the most radical cases, the abolition of private property. In time, however, the monarchists regained their footing, and taking advantage of the fear of too-radical change among the moderates who had opposed them, used their overwhelming military force to crush the revolt. Many of the defeated revolutionaries, including the most radical among them, were forced into exile and fled to Switzerland, London, the Ottoman Empire, and the United States, especially St. Louis.[12]

In St. Louis, as elsewhere in the United States, German-speaking immigrants were met with nativism and violence. Many native-born St. Louis whites resented the Germans, who they thought would take away their jobs and diminish their political power, and the politics of the city in the 1850s was shaped around sharp divides between nativists and immigrants, cutting across both the Republican and Democratic Parties. Jealous of their office and political emoluments, both old-line Whigs and working-class white Democrats resented

German (and elsewhere, Irish) voters, and officeholders. The Order of the Star Spangled Banner, a nativist political party, emerged nationally in 1856 and captured the state governments in Pennsylvania and Massachusetts, although only after they rebranded themselves as the Know-Nothing Party. (The name referred, not to their being ignorant xenophobes, although one could surely make a case for that, but to the response they were bound to make to any questions about the semi-secretive workings of their party: "I know nothing.") In the 1855 municipal election in St. Louis, Know-Nothingism divided the Bentonite Democratic Party and took control of the city. "Crass nativism and intolerant temperance oppressed the entire population with an iron hand," wrote the newspaper editor, theater owner, and brewer Henry Boernstein (for whom nativist attacks on German beer halls and breweries were particularly galling). "The people were held in virtual slavery through restrictions on their freedom" enforced by the native-born police force.[13]

In the German neighborhoods of South St. Louis, men organized themselves into hunting clubs, which served the dual function of recreation and armed self-defense. The iconography of anti-German nativism focused mostly on beer and potatoes, but beneath the tired jokes was a deeper disquiet: many of the German immigrants to St. Louis were experienced political organizers, and some of them were quite radical. There were German slaveholders in St. Louis as well as Germans who cared very little one way or the other about the issue, but it was Germans who in 1861 would form the backbone of the Union Army in St. Louis. These were men who had fought against monarchical rule and hereditary privilege in Europe only to come to the United States and find a variant form of aristocracy in the entrenched power of slaveholders. For some of them, free-soil politics made the same sort of sense that it did to the non-slaveholding settler whites who were the bedrock of the Republican Party. And for an influential few, the struggle against slavery offered an opportunity to continue a struggle not simply against inherited privilege, but against property itself.

The commanders of the regiments that marched on Camp Jackson provide an emblematic roll call of the politics of Unionist St. Louis: there was a regiment of US Volunteers under the command of the Bentonite Republican Francis Preston Blair Jr., known in St. Louis as Frank; a regiment of German-speaking Home Guards under the command of Nikolas Schüttner, a German brickmaker from South St. Louis; another regiment under the command of the German immigrant theater impresario and newspaper editor Henry Boernstein; and yet another under the command of Franz Sigel, a veteran of the revolution in southwest Germany and a military theorist who would soon become the most famous German in the Union Army. Held in reserve were still more Germans, under the command of the Republican political leader B. Gratz Brown. They were united by their opposition to slavery, although there were deep differences among them about the question of "freedom"—about what, concretely speaking, the overthrow of slavery would mean for Black people, for Indians, for settler whites, and for property in general. In the end, it would be the politics of the neo-Bentonite Republicans—imperialists whose greatest hope for African Americans was that they would get out of the way—and the liberal (not radical) Germans that would point the nation's course. But that, again, is getting ahead of the story.

Saturnine and handsome as he led his troops up Laclede Street toward Camp Jackson, Frank Blair was the namesake and third son of one of the most powerful Democratic politicians of the Jacksonian era, and he had become a Free Soil Republican by the time of the Civil War. It was the younger Blair, as much as anyone other than Frémont, who transformed the Bentonite vision of settler colonialism and Pacific empire of the 1840s into the free-soil imperialism of the 1850s. His most famous speech, "The Destiny of the Races of This Continent," delivered in Boston in 1859, began where Benton left off: with a vision of American commercial empire that linked the Atlantic to the Pacific by way of a "great national highway between the oceans"—the imperium of St. Louis. Blair found in Indian removal an example for the process by which African Americans might be removed from the central commercial corridor at the heart of his vision of national and imperial greatness. "The races of this continent" could flourish only if separated from one another, each allotted to the climate that suited them best, their "true zone" of hemispheric habitation: Black people in "the tropics," white "redeemers" in the "temperate central latitudes," and "wild beasts and the wild tribes of men who pursue them" pressed out to the margins of white settlement and finally southward into Mexico.[14]

For Blair, the alternative to emancipation, colonization, and expulsion ("the gradual transfer of four million of our freedmen to the vacant regions of Central and South America") was what would today be called "white genocide." Black slaves would out-reproduce working-class whites until "the wages of free labor would be so reduced as to destroy its existence." "All who labor" might soon be reduced to "the condition of Slavery." Neither Black nor working-class whites, he warned in a pointed invocation of the language of the *Dred Scott* decision, "will have rights which those holding power in the state are bound to respect."[15]

Blair's free-soil synthesis of the history of Native American genocide and white supremacy stopped short of calling for an end to slavery; his family's roots were in the Democratic Party, after all, and he was himself a slave owner in 1860. But in 1857, Blair's cousin and sometime political rival, the St. Louis newspaper editor and state representative B. Gratz Brown, had done just that, outlining a free-soil position that was equal parts antislavery and white supremacy. For Brown, who rose in a debate in the Missouri House to speak in favor of the gradual emancipation of Missouri slaves, the question of "humanity"—indeed, the question of "the emancipation of the black race"—was of no independent concern. He spoke instead of "The Emancipation of the White Race." As he explained, "I seek to emancipate the white man from the yoke of competition with the Negro."[16]

Brown is often remembered as a radical, and that is certainly how his proslavery colleagues in the Missouri House viewed him; they received his speech with a slack-jawed horror that gradually thickened into dyspeptic nausea. His political vision, however, was framed by the historical limits of his experience in St. Louis—that is, by the logic of ethnic cleansing that framed the Missouri State Constitution, Indian removal, the free Negro laws, and the *Dred Scott* decision. And above all, his vision was shaped by the politics of empire, commerce, and the railroad. If Brown's opposition to slavery turned out on further inspection to be an aspect of his devotion to white men, that devotion itself turned out to be an aspect of his commitment to a Bentonite vison of western empire, and especially to the railroad.

In the decade before the Civil War, the state of Missouri spent more money on railroads than any other state in the Union. Construction had begun on the Pacific Railroad line, originating in St. Louis, in 1851. Though construction was slow, by 1855 the line had reached Jefferson City, the state capital, about 120 miles west of St. Louis. On November 1, 1855, many of the city's leading citizens, including the mayor and several prominent railroad investors, set out on an inaugural trip on the Pacific line to Jefferson City. In the early afternoon, about 90 miles out, they reached the Gasconade River, where a temporary trestle had hurriedly been built to support an unfinished bridge so that it could accommodate the vanity train ride. Overnight rains had turned the banks of the river to mud and loosened the moorings of the temporary bridge, and as the train headed out over the river the trestle began to lean, and then it collapsed. Forty-three people died in the river, many of them crushed beneath the weight of the locomotive, which fell backward on top of the first coach, in which many of the dignitaries rode.[17]

By the time of the Gasconade disaster, the politics of railroads and the politics of slavery in Missouri had become as twisted together as the rails over the Gasconade, and with much the same result. The Kansas-Nebraska Act (introduced by Senator Stephen A. Douglas of Illinois in an effort to provide the federal jurisdiction necessary to expropriate Indian land and protect railroad property) had established "popular sovereignty" (that is, a territory-wide referendum) as the mechanism for deciding the future of slavery in the West. The new standard, an explicit repudiation of the Missouri Compromise, had set off a contest over migration to Kansas between easterners on either side of the slavery question. The competing migrations soon developed into a shooting war in "Bleeding Kansas," which was a direct precursor of the Civil War and the occasion for the emergence of "Osawatomie" John Brown and "Bloody Bill" Anderson, for the Lawrence Massacre, and for the caning by Congressman Preston Brooks of Senator Charles Sumner on the floor of the US Senate.

A direct rail line from St. Louis was understood by those on both sides of the conflict in Kansas as a potentially decisive strategic advantage for the free-soil side of the struggle, and so railroad bills were repeatedly obstructed and slow-walked by proslavery representatives in the Missouri legislature. Among those most concerned with capitalist development and imperial expansion, the functionally proslavery imperialism of Thomas Hart Benton, who had hoped to endlessly defer conflict over slavery until the railroad reached the Pacific, gave way to the antislavery imperialism of the free-soil movement and the Republican Party. This slow-rolling transformation in Missouri politics was dramatically accelerated by Gratz Brown when he rose in the state legislature in February 1857 to denounce proslavery Missourians for standing in the way of the city's western empire and effectively delivering commercial control of the Missouri Valley—the wellspring of the city's wealth and its history—to Chicago. If forced to choose between slavery and empire, Brown declared, Missouri should choose empire and set about making plans to emancipate its slaves.[18]

For Brown, the combination of empire, emancipation, and annihilation held the key to freedom—for white people. "Paper edicts and proposed statutes will be of little force or effect until population—and free white population at that—shall insist upon its rights of labor and supply that great substratum upon which society rests for support." It was white people themselves, through the act of being white and moving

to Missouri, who would abolish slavery: "The African race and its con-
comitant slavery, will go down and vanish in these United States as the
Indian race has gone down and vanished beneath the tread and march
of the Anglo-Saxon and nothing else under God's blue heaven will ever
supplant it in the State of Missouri." As to what would happen to the
slaves whom nature had condemned to recede before the Anglo-Saxon
advance, Brown was fairly vague—he assumed that their owners would
be compensated for recognizing the racial writing on the wall and acced-
ing to the "deportation" of their human property.[19]

At the head of a column that marched along Olive Street was the
beady-eyed, nervous, and observant Henry Boernstein, another veteran
of the European revolutions of 1848, this time from Austria. Boernstein
was the editor and publisher of the *Anzeiger des Westens*, a German-
language paper printed in St. Louis. After growing up in Austrian Gali-
cia, he had made his way to Paris with a company of traveling actors. In
Paris, he settled in among that city's radical émigrés and fell under the
influence of the brilliant and charismatic Karl Marx. In 1844, he took
over a theretofore moderate weekly newspaper and transformed it into
a vehicle for the city's emerging radical leftists: Marx, Heinrich Heine,
and Karl Ludwig Bernays. The paper was suppressed by the French
government in 1845, and Boernstein emigrated to the United States,
first to Illinois and then to St. Louis. In St. Louis, Boernstein became
a fervid supporter of Thomas Hart Benton, whose efforts to distribute
the public domain to working-class migrants had become a model for
one stream of radical thought in Germany during the 1840s.

Boernstein, that is to say, fell victim to a problem that has bedev-
iled the American left down to the present day: a failure to reconstruct
a vision of democracy rooted in European social theory around the
specific history of the United States. In Europe, the land that radicals like Boernstein imagined redistributing belonged to aristocrats; in
the United States the land belonged to Indians. European radicalism
translated to the American context could become a vexed whites-only
liberal imperialism, a tendency that Boernstein seems to have exempli-

fied in the years leading up to the Civil War. In those years, Boernstein became a political supporter and ally of Frank Blair and Gratz Brown, serving for the latter as a liaison to the city's German neighborhoods. In Missouri, Boernstein's revolutionary liberalism was translated into a variant strain of the aspirational whiteness of so many of the migrants who had followed Benton west—the settler vanguard of the white man's country who had turned to free-soil politics as a way to preserve the West for themselves. As much as to end slavery, Boernstein went to war in defense of the rights of white men to hold property in the imperial West.

A block to the south, Franz Sigel marched along Pine. By the time Sigel had arrived in St. Louis in 1857, he was already a renowned revolutionary. Of medium height, slim and severe, with hollow cheeks and deep-set dark eyes, he looked like Johnny Depp dressed up to play Dracula. When the revolution broke out in Baden in March 1848, he had been one of the few men among the revolutionaries with any military experience, and in 1849 he became the war minister of Baden's provisional revolutionary government. With the defeat of the revolution, he fled to Switzerland, where he contributed to a study of the revolution (*Geschichte der Süddeutschen Mai-Revolution*) that was intended to provide a manual of practical instruction for imagined future revolutionaries.

This handbook for aspirant revolutionaries combined a reading of the German military theorist Carl von Clausewitz with the political economy of the *Communist Manifesto*. Clausewitz had argued that "general insurrection" was a "natural, inevitable consequence" of modern warfare, and that the revolt of people against their leaders was of decisive importance in the conflict between states. Sigel and his co-agitators combined Clausewitz's argument with their own experience in 1848 and their communism to conclude that a "total levy"— the militarization of the common man—was both good strategy (Clausewitz) and good politics (Marx). "Red republicans, the socialist democrats, have as their political principle the solidarity of all peoples;

they know that, in the freedom struggle of any one land, the fight is for freedom of all humanity," they wrote. "This governing principle secures from neighboring lands not just sympathy, but concrete assistance." Their views tracked Sigel's own, which Andrew Zimmerman, the most careful scholar of his political thought, has termed both "revolutionary" and "anti-capitalist." "Strictly speaking, there is no such thing as property," Sigel wrote after arriving in New York in 1852, before going on to declare, "We, the socialists, are the Muslims of the modern World. In one hand, the Quran—*our* Quran—in the other the saber—need commands it."[20]

Sigel's political writings are aphoristic, abstract, written in an archaic alphabet, and almost illegible. They are punctuated by harsh declarations ("war is the teacher of politics") and portentous dialectics ("the revolution must unite beast and spirit; it must humanize society"). And they outline a vision of the world in which revolution, class conflict, and the uprising of slaves against their masters were distinct aspects of a single struggle toward human emancipation: "The socialist and communist has to want Revolution even in its mildest form, just like the worker has to want the worst work. But both must, through superior effort and superior talent, gain dominion [*Herrschaft*] over the masters. The slave must make himself master [*zum Herren machen*]."[21]

He sought, he wrote, to develop a "system of war" that would join the talents of "soldiers" to the aspirations of "communists" in launching an anticapitalist "crusade" from their redoubt in the United States. When the war began with the shelling of Fort Sumter on April 12, 1861, Franz Sigel had already been organizing working-class German radicals into paramilitary self-defense battalions for over a year. And when the first significant military action following the shelling of Fort Sumter (and the first significant Union military victory) occurred in St. Louis on May 10, 1861, Sigel was in the midst of the fight. Almost immediately, he became a hero to German Americans, and going to "fight mit Sigel" became a tagline for the 200,000 German-born soldiers who eventually fought in the Civil War.[22]

That's the long version of the story. The short version is this: Sigel, one of the most celebrated figures in the history of Civil War St. Louis and the Civil War, a man whose service is today memorialized in a striking twenty-foot statue in St. Louis's Forest Park, was a stone-cold communist.

And then there was Nikolas Schüttner, who marched along Market, a block south of Sigel, at the head of a regiment of erstwhile paramilitaries who had been mustered into the service of the United States. Huge and heavily bearded, the brickmaker Schüttner was the longtime leader of the Schwarze Jager, or Black Hunters, a rifle club based in the German neighborhoods of South St. Louis that had been marching in the streets of St. Louis since the beginning of the year. The members were mostly veterans of the European wars of 1848 and 1849, "strong, bearded, full-grown men" who owned their own weapons and marched with a menace that caused what one onlooker termed "holy fear" among the proslavery Minute Men with whom they contended for control of the streets. With Schüttner, too, were three armed companies of Turners, members of the Turnverein, or Turner's League, whose sports club (the Turnhalle) was one of the poles of German social life in St. Louis. Almost two hundred of them had been training for armed combat since the beginning of the year and carried arms that had been bought by the Turnverein after an appeal to its members.[23]

The German-speaking soldiers who marched with Schüttner and the others held a variety of views about slavery and race. Along with radicals like Sigel, who saw the struggle against slavery as part of a larger revolutionary struggle against property, there were many who took a different view of the relation between slavery, freedom, property, and empire. Like aspirant white settlers, many previously agnostic Germans felt threatened by the Kansas-Nebraska Act and the possibility of the westward extension of slavery. Slavery in Kansas would mean lower wages in St. Louis (as wealthy slaveholders bought up all the land that provided wage workers with an alternative to poorly paying jobs, or so the argument went). More than that, it was not even clear whether Germans would be allowed to vote in the elections that would decide the future of slavery in the West. The debates over the Kansas-Nebraska Act had featured a long sidebar about whether or not non-naturalized German immigrants would be allowed to vote in Kansas at all. Among the German readers of Boernstein's *Anzeiger des Westens*, it was an article of faith that slaveholders viewed German workers as men in need of masters, indeed, as "white n—s." Like Blair or Brown, many Germans supported the territorial limitation of slavery or even gradual and compensated emancipation out of concern for their own interests rather than out of any concern for the slaves—they were anti-slaveholder and anti-Black as much as they were antislavery.[24]

At the head of the forces marching on Camp Jackson was Nathaniel Lyon, a Connecticut-born graduate of West Point and recent veteran of the terroristic paramilitary border war in Kansas. Like William Harney, the man whom he was replacing as interim commander of the US Army Department of the West, Lyon had been an officer in the First US Dragoons. Eleven years earlier and two thousand miles to the west, near Clear Lake in California, Nathaniel Lyon had led a company of Dragoons on an expedition against the Pomo. His orders were "to chastise the Pomo." Many of the Pomo had reportedly been held on the west side of the lake by a couple of self-styled grandees in a sort of settler-gothic slavery—raping the women at will and driving the men to death mining for silver. In the spring, the Pomo on the west side of the lake rose up and killed the whites; some then went to an island at the north end of the lake, where hundreds of Pomo had gathered to participate in an annual gathering. Representing the US Army, Lyon marched on the Pomo gathered on what came to be called "Bloody Island" and killed as many as two hundred of them. "Little or no resistance was encountered, and the work or butchery was of short duration," reported the *Daily Alta California*, "nor sex, nor age was spared, it was the order of *extermination* fearfully obeyed." Lyon and his men then moved west, toward the Russian River, where, according to a Pomo survivor, they killed seventy-five more, "mostly women and children," whom they chased through the thick brush surrounding the Pomo camp and killed with their bayonets, hatchets, and knives. The massacre at Bloody Island, argues the leading history of the genocide in California, was one of the largest in the history of North America, and it marked the moment when the full force of the US Army was brought into alignment with the murderous white settler government of Gold Rush–era California.[25]

Just as the political philosophy of the more conservative of the Republicans drew on images of Native American dispossession and disappearance to frame their predictions about the western apotheosis of the white man, the military careers of the radical Republicans emerged out of the crucible of empire and Indian killing. And just as their radical German supporters and allies brought with them to Missouri a vision of war-making that was inseparable from their vision of social transformation—a revolutionary vision—men like Lyon brought the experience they had gained in California to the war they fought in Missouri—uncompromising, brutal, civilizational, total war.[26]

B y the time the federal forces reached Camp Jackson, a large crowd of onlookers had gathered, waiting to see what would happen. Among the crowd of observers at Lindell's Grove that day were two men whose names would become bywords for pedagogic, punitive, total war over the course of the Civil War: Ulysses S. Grant and William Tecumseh Sherman. Grant's first posting after he graduated from West Point in 1843 was to Jefferson Barracks, and it was in St. Louis that he met his wife, Julia Dent, the daughter of a slaveholding farmer. Posted to California in the years after the Mexican-American War, he was rumored to have begun drinking regularly, and to excess. He resigned from the Army in 1854 and returned to farm his wife's property (and oversee her family's slaves) in St. Louis County, south of the city. Grant was an indifferent farmer, and in 1860 he quit altogether and moved with his family to Galena, where his father had offered him a job and a regular income in his tannery. (His wife's property would later be incorporated into the estate of the beer-brewing Busch family, Grant's Farm.) When Lincoln sent out the call for soldiers after the attack on Fort Sumter, Grant raised a company of men and was commissioned as a captain in the Illinois Volunteers. In May 1861, Grant was stationed at Belleville, Illinois, across the river from St. Louis, and he had come to the city out of professional curiosity, which quickly hardened into the murderous fury for which he was later known: "After all, we are not so intolerant in St. Louis as we might be," he wrote from the tense city. "I have not seen a single rebel hung yet, nor heard of one; there are plenty of them who ought to be, however." Early in the afternoon of May 10, Grant reached Lindell's Grove just as Lyon's column approached and, to quote legend once again, wished the general good luck moments before Lyon laid siege to Camp Jackson.[27]

Also at Camp Jackson that day was William Tecumseh Sherman. After graduating from West Point, Sherman had fought in the Second Seminole War and in the Southeast, where he participated in the removal of the Cherokee. He spent the years of the Mexican-American War on an exploratory expedition to Brazil (along with Henry Halleck, who would command the Department of the West from St. Louis in the latter years of the Civil War), and like Lyon and Grant, he was stationed in California during the years of the genocide. In 1853, Sherman resigned from the army to become the principal of the San Francisco branch of the St. Louis–based bank Lucas, Turner, and Company (the Lucas in question being a descendant of the fur-trading and land-speculating St. Louis Lucases). Several ventures later, Sherman was in St. Louis, where, in 1861, he began a job as the president of the St. Louis Railroad Company, a streetcar company connecting the city's expanding western suburbs to the downtown. On the afternoon of Friday, May 10, Sherman was at Lindell's Grove with his young son, waiting, along with the rest of the crowd, to see what would happen. Sherman, perhaps the most infamous of all Civil War generals, began

the day as a retired military man who had turned to business. By nightfall he had witnessed one of the earliest skirmishes of the Civil War. By
the following Tuesday, Sherman, who had been skeptical about Lincoln's call for volunteers a month earlier, had been commissioned as
a colonel in the Union Army and given command of the Thirteenth
Infantry, which was being organized at Jefferson Barracks.[28]

At 3:15 in the afternoon, as his forces deployed around Camp
Jackson, Lyon gave General Frost a half-hour to surrender. Frost, who
was outnumbered by ten to one, had little choice but to comply with
a demand that he nevertheless insisted was "illegal and unconstitutional." Sigel's regiment disarmed the rebels and took control of the
weapons that had been shipped upriver from Baton Rouge. Frost's
captured men were divided into two columns, one superintended by
troops under the command of Frank Blair, the other by troops under
the command of Henry Boernstein. Around six o'clock, as the federal
band struck up "The Star-Spangled Banner" and the troops started
marching their prisoners to the arsenal, some in the crowd began to
jeer at the German soldiers—"Hurrah for Jeff Davis" and "Damn the
Dutch"—and to throw stones at them as they passed. No one knows
who fired the first shot, or indeed whether it was fired by a soldier in
the ranks or an armed onlooker, but there was an exchange of gunfire
from both sides. Many in the crowd panicked and crushed one another in what Sherman later termed a "stampede." There with his son,
Sherman crouched behind an embankment during the gunfire and
then "jerked" his son by the arm into a gully in the surrounding grove
of trees when the soldiers paused to reload. By the time the soldiers
stopped firing, twenty-eight of the onlookers were dead.[29]

For several days, the city of St. Louis teetered on the brink of
an all-out war. As the soldiers returned to the arsenal with their secessionist prisoners, they were surrounded by a crowd that threatened
to "lynch" the prisoners of war. Armed mobs roamed the streets. Saloons and restaurants boarded up their windows, and citizens barred
their doors. The US Volunteers, the German Home Guard, and the

St. Louis Police all deployed in the street to show force and claim turf in the time-honored name of "keeping the peace." On the night of the eleventh, as Home Guard troops paraded through the downtown, an ambush by a group of armed men hiding amid the columns of a Presbyterian church on the corner of Walnut and Fifth Streets left six dead. Rumors spread through the German neighborhoods on the Southside (known to this day as "Germantown") that "the American-born citizens to the North were coming down to loot and burn their dwellings and kill them."[30] Boernstein recalled crowds gathering in front of the Planter's House Hotel and the courthouse shouting at the troops as they passed—"damned Dutch" and " Hessian hirelings"—and threatening to "exterminate" the Germans. Both the *Demokrat* and the *Anzeiger des Westens* were targeted and put under armed guard.[31]

Still, it was clear who had won the battle, and slaveholders and southern sympathizers, including some of the wealthiest families in the city, began to make plans to leave. "Sunday morning presented the spectacle of the general flight of the 'upper ten,' the rich proud slaveholders who had looked down on the Germans only twenty-four hours before with such contempt," remembered Boernstein. "Coaches from every livery stable, furniture wagons, drays, and every sort of vehicle was requisitioned. The best furniture, trunks and chests with clothing and linen, women and children, and anything that was not nailed down were loaded up" and hauled down to the levee, awaiting shipment out of town.[32]

General Harney returned to St. Louis on May 12 and deployed regular army troops to keep the peace in St. Louis. A wary quiet settled over the city. For a brief moment, even the skeptical Francis Blair thought that Harney had returned from Washington a changed man: the general was unequivocal in terming the action taken by Frost at Camp Jackson "unconstitutional" and illegal, and he ordered his troops to search the city's Confederate-aligned police stations, where they discovered several of the cannons that had been shipped from Baton Rouge. But by the end of the month, Blair had tired of Harney's insistence on treating the statements of Claiborne Jackson, the state's pro-slavery governor, and Sterling Price, the commander of its proslavery militia, as if they were reliable. Again and again they assured Harney that they were neutral actors committed to "keeping the peace" in Missouri, and again and again their best efforts fell short of actually ending the attacks of proslavery "bushwhackers" on their antislavery, unionist, or even agnostic neighbors. By the end of the month, Blair had presented Harney with a letter from Abraham Lincoln that reassigned the general to Washington, effective immediately, and elevated Nathaniel Lyon to commander until a permanent commander could be found for the Department of the West. Blair had been carrying the letter in his pocket for weeks, a trump card he could no longer hold in reserve.[33]

Once Lincoln's order was revealed, Lyon acted quickly. Even before Harney's removal, Lyon had overseen the fortification of the city, setting up checkpoints at the rail stations and river landings and ordering that every conveyance be stopped and searched on its way into the city. He had likewise ordered the military occupation of Potosi, downriver from St. Louis in Washington County, where federal troops had taken control of over sixty thousand pounds of lead. Now fully in command, he met with Jackson and Price at the Planter's House Hotel in St. Louis. After several hours of fruitless discussion, Lyon abruptly ended the meeting: "Rather than concede to the State of Missouri for one single instant the right to dictate to my Government in any manner, however unimportant, I would see you . . . and every man, woman, and child in the state dead and buried." And then, in case they had missed the point: "This means war." Lyon provided his visitors with safe conduct through his lines and began to plan his attack on the state capital. As they traveled back to Jefferson City, Jackson and Price ordered that the railway bridges over the Gasconade and Osage Rivers be burned behind them.[34]

Lyon's march across Missouri has been largely forgotten by a Civil War historiography focused on the eastern theater and the Battle of Manassas, which was fought on July 21, 1861. Lyon's battles in

Missouri, however, were the only Union military victories in 1861; more than that, the actions taken by his army presaged the course of the war. For as Lyon's army worked its way across Missouri, the conduct of some of its officers and many of its soldiers began to diverge from the orders they were receiving from Washington. Many of the soldiers in Lyon's army adopted a genuinely "revolutionary" strategy: to fight a war against slaveholders, they had to declare war upon slavery. Or, as an editorial in St. Louis's *Westliche Post* put it as Lyon marched across Missouri, "The more one encourages slaves to escape from the South, the more one weakens the rebellion and the sooner one defeats it." Emancipation, in this view, was not simply a goal of the war, and still less a possible outcome to be repeatedly disavowed in favor of an exclusive focus on the question of "union." Revolutionary alliance with runaway slaves was a strategic imperative. It would take Abraham Lincoln and his eastern generals another year to absorb the lessons of Lyon's campaign. By then, Lyon would be dead, the first Union field-grade officer to die in battle in the Civil War.[35]

Lyon first marched on Jefferson City, the state capital. Finding that Jackson and Price had left the city and traveled west on the Missouri River, Lyon left Boernstein in control of the capital and continued westward. Boernstein found the city a ruin—most city officers had fled with the governor. "Everything would have to be recreated, if the usual course of bourgeois life was not to be interrupted," he later wrote. Boernstein, the onetime radical turned ally of Benton and Blair, stuck close to the orthodox distinction between a war to preserve the union and a war to abolish slavery in a handbill he had printed and distributed throughout the city. "Your personal security will be Guaranteed. Your property will be respected; your slave property will not be touched by any part of my command, nor shall any slave be allowed to come to my lines without written permission from his master . . . at the same time I shall not tolerate the slightest attempt to destroy the union and its government." Boernstein had hoped to pacify the population of the city by guaranteeing their property and promising not to interfere with their slaves, but he soon found that these assurances did him little good. The residents of the city tore up his proclamation and used it to litter the streets. Those who had slaves ran them off to counties out of the reach of the Union Army. Boernstein, feeling isolated and undermanned, finally resorted to simply jailing five of those whom he took to be his most fervent antagonists for crimes no greater than flying the Confederate flag. Under the pressure of events, Boernstein's liberalism quickly collapsed into its opposite.[36]

Along Lyon's westward march, the army made another kind of history—no less violent, to be sure, than its military actions, but a history in which the violent exercise of authority was fitfully but significantly aligned with the cause of human emancipation rather than simply with that of national preservation. As Lyon's army marched west it relied on runaways for information about their owners, the landscape, and the whereabouts of pro-Confederate troops in the field. At Boonville, German Home Guards who had joined the federal forces armed three fugitives and fought beside them in the trenches. After their defeat near Springfield and Lyon's death, the federal force, now under the command of Franz Sigel, retreated to Rolla, where their encampment became a magnet for escaping slaves from south-central Missouri. Many of those who made it to the encampment at Rolla were given uniforms and put to work in support of the army. In Rolla, at least, emancipation was less a disputed aspiration of the war effort than a means of its practical prosecution.[37]

Fall turned to winter, and escaped slaves—self-emancipated African Americans—continued to make their way to the Union camp at Rolla, part of an uprising across the South that W.E.B. Du Bois termed "the General Strike"—the mass withdrawal of the laboring class of the South. The emerging policy of the government in Washington was to treat them as "contraband"—the property of disloyal owners that might be confiscated like any other property. But they did not act like property: these Black Americans told their stories, denounced their erstwhile owners as traitors, and offered their labor and even their lives.

They put on the uniforms and took up the arms provided them by the army. In the camp in Rolla, Sigel finally met the flesh-and-blood front-line soldiers of the revolutionary war against property he had imagined in his notebooks.[38]

The politics of the camp in Rolla—the combination of the political radicalism of Sigel and the revolutionary action of the African Americans who joined his army—came for a brief moment to define the approach of the entire US Army Department of the West, still headquartered in St. Louis but now under the leadership of John C. Frémont. In St. Louis, Frémont surrounded himself with European revolutionaries. He moved through the city with an armed guard of 150 mounted men, headed by the Hungarian Charles Zagonyi (Károly Zágonyi); they wore uniforms a shade darker than Union Army blue, with distinctive plumed hats, and carried German-made pistols. Another Hungarian, Alexander Asboth (Asbóth Sándor), was Frémont's chief of staff until he was sent to Rolla to replace Sigel; there he continued to embrace fugitives from slavery with the same revolutionary pragmatism demonstrated by his predecessor. For many Germans in St. Louis, Frémont represented not simply a military commander whom they could respect and trust, but one whose appointment reflected their own devotion to the cause. "Will not everyone reach for his sword with courage and enthusiasm when he knows a Frémont is within our walls?" asked the *Anzeiger* in August 1861.[39]

Perhaps the most interesting member of Frémont's staff in St. Louis was Joseph Weydemeyer, whose arrival in the United States in 1851 has plausibly been called "the beginning of the history of American Marxism." Weydemeyer, whose politics had led him to resign his position as an artillery officer in the Prussian Army in 1842, had been a collaborator and close friend of both Marx and Engels since the mid-1840s, and he had spent the years immediately after the 1848 revolution underground in Europe, editing a series of radical newspapers in which he published their (illegal) writings, including Marx's *The German Ideology* and Engels's *The Condition of the Working Class in*

Joseph Weydemeyer was the most prominent communist in the United States at the time of the Civil War. Friend and frequent correspondent of Karl Marx and Friedrich Engels, he was a colonel in the US Army and oversaw the wartime fortification of the city of St. Louis. (Library of Congress)

England. As the authorities closed in, Weydemeyer fled to New York, arriving in November 1851. In New York, he founded *Die Revolution*, the original publisher of Marx's *Eighteenth Brumaire*, which was not published in Europe until 1869. During the 1850s, Weydemeyer moved between Milwaukee, Chicago, and New York, contributing to and editing a succession of radical German-language newspapers and acting as a de facto literary agent for Marx and Engels, whose writings he helped to place in papers throughout the United States (and whose frequent and affectionate correspondence provides the best means of tracking Weydemeyer's movements during these years—Weydemeyer was Zeppo, the least remembered of the Marx Brothers, to Marx and Engels's Groucho and Harpo). Much of his time was spent organizing for the Proletarian League, the first Marxist organization in the United States, and the Communist Club, which was committed to "the abolition of private ownership of the means of production" and "the equality of all human beings, irrespective of color or sex." In an 1860 letter to the German socialist Ferdinand Lassalle, Marx referred to Weydemeyer as "one of our best people" in the United States.[40]

Among the communists, Weydemeyer stood out for his insistence that the condition of the white working class could not be addressed separately from the question of slavery. Weydemeyer's materialist Marxism convinced him that the abolition of private property and the "dictatorship of the proletariat" (the idea itself is a theoretical innovation in the history of Marxism for which Weydemeyer is sometimes credited) could not occur until capitalist industrial development had reached its apogee. For him, slavery was an economic drag on that development, and it was only with the abolition of slavery that all labor might be truly free. At the time of the Kansas-Nebraska Act, he urged his followers not to adopt the narrow position of the white supremacist free-soilers, but rather to "protest most emphatically against both Black and white slavery." Where Bentonite liberals like Boernstein favored distributing the public domain to working people on the basis of individually held parcels of private property, Weydemeyer advocated state ownership and "large-scale agriculture" under the direction of "workers' associations." Whatever its virtues, it should be noted that this too was a solution that subordinated any consideration of Native American sovereignty, humanity, and ultimately survival to the "march of progress." With the outbreak of the war, Weydemeyer enlisted and requested a posting to Missouri, which he considered the strategic key to a Union victory. In St. Louis, he joined Frémont's staff and was assigned the task of coordinating the deployment of artillery and the construction of forts in defense of the city of St. Louis.[41]

On August 28, Frémont called Sigel to St. Louis for a meeting with the rest of his general staff, including Weydemeyer. Two days later, Frémont followed Lincoln's lead in Maryland by placing Missouri under martial law. But he also went beyond the action the president had taken in Maryland by declaring that any civilian found to have taken up arms against the United States would be tried by a military court and executed if convicted. And then he did something revolutionary. On August 30, General Frémont issued an order emancipating the slaves of disloyal owners in Missouri, adopting the views of the communists Sigel and Weydemeyer, legalizing the situation on the ground in Rolla, and putting the force of the US Army behind the revolutionary actions of escaping slaves.

The response in the German papers in St. Louis was immediate and enthusiastic. The *Anzeiger des Westens* noted that Frémont's action drastically exceeded his legal authority, but praised it nevertheless: "This goes quite a bit further than the confiscation law of Congress—it is a measure of war and extreme necessity. In other words it is a dictatorial act, an act à la Jackson." It soon became clear that Lincoln (and his local proxy, Blair) had been blindsided by Frémont's order and would not allow it to stand. But the *Anzeiger* stuck by Frémont, unfavorably contrasting the actions of Lincoln's chief of staff, the Democrat George C. McClellan, "who orders escaped slaves held and returned to their masters," to their hero Frémont, "who issues manumission out of hand to slaves." In conclusion, the editorial implied—threatened, really—that Germans in St. Louis would stop supporting the Union war effort if Frémont was removed from his command. When Blair used the pages of the *Missouri Republican* to make the administration's case, criticizing Frémont and his emancipation order for alienating the conditional unionists who were the focus of Lincoln's effort to hold the border states in the Union, Frémont closed down the paper and threw Blair, who was a US congressman and general in the US Army as well as a friend of the president, into jail.[42]

Lincoln's response was immediate. Writing to Frémont, he noted that the military trial and execution of Confederate prisoners of war would surely be met with immediate retaliation against Union prisoners of war. He then noted that Frémont's emancipation provision "will alarm our Southern Union friends" and asked Frémont to modify his order to match the Confiscation Act, which treated self-emancipated people as "contraband of war"—as confiscated property temporarily held (a position that the *Westliche Post* had termed the "nonsensical contraband-fiction" two months before). When Frémont refused, insisting that if Lincoln wanted to countermand the emancipation order, he should do so publicly, Lincoln immediately obliged.[43]

By the beginning of November 1861, Frémont had been relieved of his command—an act that was accompanied by a genuine fear that German troops in St. Louis would mutiny when they heard the news. He was called to Washington to stand trial for the misappropriation of military funds, a charge of which he was eventually acquitted. The general was given another command (in the Shenandoah Valley, where he spent the rest of war being outmaneuvered by Stonewall Jackson). But he remained guilty of fighting the wrong war in Lincoln's eyes (and in the eyes of historians who have, by and large, adopted the president's pragmatic moderation as their own moral center and treated Frémont's emancipation as an outlying footnote to the real story)—of fighting against slavery and property when he should simply have been fighting for the United States of America and for union. Jessie Benton, Frémont's wife, remembered that when she met Lincoln shortly after the president had rescinded her husband's emancipation order, the "Great Emancipator" was livid about the matter and declared to her: "It was a war for a great national idea. . . . *General Frémont should never have dragged the Negro into it.*"[44]

In St. Louis, however, Frémont remained a hero to many and was presented with a ceremonial sword upon his return to the city after being relieved of his command. In December 1861, the *Anzeiger* invoked the general's name and the example of his forces in the field in demanding that Lincoln reverse course and emancipate the slaves: "When we use the word *emancipation* we are not thinking of something that would have to wait until the conclusion of the peace but rather of emancipation on the basis of martial law, as Frémont tried to do." At least 15,000 Missouri slaves had "run away to freedom," the paper estimated, predicting that, no matter how the Lincoln administration worked to preserve it, slavery in Missouri could not last another year.

Indeed, as well as the example of Frémont, the *Anzeiger* invoked the example of Sigel and Rolla: "Wherever we occupy them [slaveholders] an active war party in our favor must be created. . . . But since only the slaves are available to do the work, then it is necessary to train a proper number of them in weapons."[45]

The man Lincoln appointed to replace Frémont, a lawyer, translator, and author of a book on strategy entitled *Elements of Military Art and Science*, was as deliberate as Frémont was rash, as studious as Frémont was vainglorious. He was also a man who adjudged Franz Sigel to be "unworthy of the rank he now holds." Like Frémont and Lyon, General Henry Halleck had served in California. He had, indeed, been called upon to try to establish military order in the state in the aftermath of Lyon's well-publicized atrocities against the Pomo. In November 1847, Halleck placed the state of California under martial law and instituted a statewide pass system to lock down the new territory's Indian population. The system required California Indians either to be employed by non-Indians or to be defined as "thieves and marauders"—designations that rendered them vulnerable to (officially sanctioned) massacre. "Any Indian found beyond the limits of the town or rancho in which he may be employed," it read in part, "without such certificate or pass, will be liable to arrest as a horse thief." Drawing upon the disciplinary repertoire of the slaveholding South, the order effectively legalized the enslavement of California Indians.[46]

In St. Louis, Halleck struggled to reassert the officially authorized and legalistic account of the war as a struggle for the Union rather than against slavery and property: "Military officers cannot decide about the rights of property," he declared. As for the small-scale revolution that was occurring in Rolla, Halleck instructed officers there to stop admitting self-emancipated Black people into their lines.

For the moment, Lincoln remained more interested in shoring up his standing with border-state Unionists than he was in emancipating the slaves. But the enslaved continued to escape and to present themselves as human dilemmas to the officers in Rolla: What about this family who will otherwise starve? What about this woman who has been cooking for the troops and doing their laundry? What about this man with a disloyal master? What about this woman who gave us information about the movements of the proslavery guerrillas? What about men who were willing to take up arms and risk their lives alongside white soldiers in the brutal guerrilla war unfolding along the border with Kansas? As the *Anzeiger* editorialized in December 1861, Halleck's orders notwithstanding, slavery in Missouri was "disintegrating" under the pressure of strategic alliance between radical soldiers and rebellious slaves.[47]

Even after the Emancipation Proclamation in 1863, the *Anzeiger* editorialized that Lincoln and his supporters had "gone as far toward the abolition of slavery as ink, pens, and paper would let them," but that it would take men like Frémont and Sigel to really do something about it. In the summer of 1863, radical Germans in St. Louis used the anniversary of the march on Camp Jackson to demand the removal of General Halleck, whom they thought insufficiently committed to emancipation. Frémont and Sigel, however, were fulsomely praised by speaker after speaker that day. In 1864, the St. Louis Germans were among the principal supporters of Frémont's brief presidential candidacy as the nominee of the Radical Democracy Party on a platform committed to emancipation, equal rights for African Americans, and the confiscation of Confederate property, and Frémont was also supported by the abolitionists Frederick Douglass, Wendell Phillips, and Elizabeth Cady Stanton.[48]

And yet, in the coming years, it was the ghost of Thomas Hart Benton that would haunt the city of St. Louis. The national government emerged from the war pledged to the white settlers and railroads at the heart of the Bentonite vision, and it began a decades-long campaign of military pacification, ethnic cleansing, and, finally, annihilation in the West. The apotheosis of the Bentonite vision for the city represented a triumph for Frank Blair, Gratz Brown, and Henry

Boernstein over Franz Sigel, John Frémont, and Joseph Weydemeyer, as well as over Basil Duke, Claiborne Jackson, and Sterling Price. But on the streets of St. Louis, as both Black and white migrants crowded into the city, the question of freedom remained an open and contested one. And indeed, at the end of the period of Reconstruction, radicals in St. Louis would once again provide the nation with an example of Midwest-style communist revolution.

5 | BLACK RECONSTRUCTION AND THE COUNTERREVOLUTION OF PROPERTY

> God wept; but that mattered little in an unbelieving age; what mattered most was that the world wept and still is weeping and blind with tears and blood. For there began to arise in America in 1876 a new capitalism and a new enslavement of labor . . . united in exploitation of white, yellow, brown, and Black labor, in lesser lands and "breeds without the law."
>
> —W.E.B. DU BOIS, *Black Reconstruction in America*

SOMETIMES WHEN PEOPLE WHO LIVE IN ST. LOUIS TODAY TRY to explain the racial inequality they see in the city around them, they rely on the fact that "there was no Reconstruction in Missouri." Unlike the slaveholding states of the Deep South, Missouri was not placed under federal military occupation after the war; nor was the state, which had never officially seceded from the Union, required, like the slaveholding states farther to the south, required to ratify the Reconstruction Amendments to the Constitution in order to reenter the Union. And yet, in many ways, it was the state of Missouri in general and the city of St. Louis that epitomized both the most radical version of "abolition democracy" in the aftermath of the war (especially the General Strike of 1877) and the pitiless and cynical triumph of capitalism and imperialism—the counterrevolution of property—in the growth of the "liberal" wing of the Republican Party out of the state's Bentonite legacy.[1]

Although many secessionists had left the city in the days immediately following the surrender of Camp Jackson, and more continued to leave throughout the war, St. Louis was a fiercely divided city for the duration of the war. The city and county had been placed under martial law by Frémont on August 14, 1861 (the order was extended to the rest of the state at the end of the month) and were governed throughout the war from the office of the army provost marshal. Residents of the city were required to be off the streets by 9:00 p.m., and those who crossed into or out of the city or the county were required to carry a written pass that could only be obtained after they swore an oath of allegiance to the United States. Newspapers critical or even insufficiently supportive of the United States of America, the Union Army, or its various offices in St. Louis could be suppressed (as, indeed, was the *St. Louis Republican*). And individuals who spoke intemperately in public—yelling "Hurrah for Jeff. Davis" at a passing column of Union troops, for example—could be imprisoned (as was Frank Blair). Under General Halleck, martial law in St. Louis only intensified. All state and local governmental officials, attorneys, jurors, university officials, and voters were required to swear the oath of allegiance—a requirement that was eventually included in the wartime Missouri State Constitution. Exhibiting the Confederate flag in the city of St. Louis was punishable by imprisonment. And as elsewhere in the United States, the property of traitors was subject to confiscation.[2]

Although Maryland was the first state that Lincoln placed under martial law (and the state that produced the emblematic struggle over the right of habeas corpus during wartime, *Ex parte Merryman*), it was Missouri where the suspension of civil law had the deepest effect upon the population and everyday life. Almost half of all trials of civilians by military commission during the Civil War occurred in Missouri—close to five thousand in all, and one for every three hundred males in the state. In St. Louis, the provost marshal struggled to find enough space in the city to house all the prisoners. The McDowell Medical College on Gratiot Street was turned into a prison that held as many as two thousand inmates. Prisoners from St. Louis were sent across the river to Alton, Illinois, where as many as five thousand were eventually incarcerated in a facility with 256 cells. Most famously, prisoners were held in the Myrtle Street Prison, the converted slave pen of the St. Louis trader Bernard Lynch. Outside, Union soldiers sang "John Brown's Body" as they marched by in the street.[3]

Meanwhile, as Grant moved down the Mississippi in the campaign that culminated in the Union victory at Vicksburg in July 1863, St. Louis once again became a city of refugees. The antislavery minister Galusha Anderson recorded the stories of some of the self-emancipated people who made their way to St. Louis. "The contrabands usually trudged into the city in groups, bearing in their hands or on their shoulders budgets, filled with old clothing or useless traps, their heads covered with dilapidated hats or caps, or, in the case of the women, wrapped about with red bandanas. Their garments were coarse, often tattered, and usually quite insufficient to shield them against the cold of winter." Some, he remembered, came barefoot, their feet frostbitten and bleeding from the frozen road, their shoes in some cases having been seized by bands of white irregulars they met on the road; others had had their shoes confiscated for the night by owners who thought it would keep them from leaving. "St. Louis was for them," Anderson wrote, "a city of refuge." Between 1860 and 1870, the Black population of the city of St. Louis increased by 600 percent. Although African Americans made up a higher proportion of the population of many cities in the United States by 1880, only Philadelphia and Baltimore had larger Black populations when measured in absolute terms.[4]

The congregation of freed people in St. Louis was a revolutionary challenge to the notion of it as the imperial capital of the "white man's country" of the West. From the time of the War of 1812, the bedrock racial policy that governed the city of St. Louis had been whites-only settlerism. The broad consensus shared by both Free Soil Republicans and the proslavery Democrats who supported the *Dred Scott* decision was that there was no place in St. Louis (nor really in the United States of America) for free Black people. And yet, during the war, they came to the city by the thousands. They set up mutual aid societies and schools, they organized in neighborhood watches for self-defense, and they raised money to feed and clothe their neighbors. They went to the office of the provost marshal and swore out complaints when their white employers refused them wages, or beat them, or tried to rape them or their children. Black workers, mostly women, insisted that the conditions under which they worked were a matter of federal concern and demanded an end to white impunity, to the world in which the "Negro has no rights which the white man was bound to respect." Sometimes the soldiers intervened, many other times they did not, but gradually the freed people made a larger point: you white men must respect the fact that we have rights. The nature and limits of Black freedom remained uncertain and fiercely contested—indeed, they still are today—but the days of *Scott v. Sandford* were gone, for the moment at least.[5]

The strategic and symbolic center of Black freedom in Civil War St. Louis was Benton Barracks, in North St. Louis, on the site of present-day Fairground Park. Benton Barracks was established by John C. Frémont in 1861 and overseen by William Tecumseh Sherman (in his first command as a general officer) and Benjamin Bonneville over the course of the war. Originally intended as an intake and training base for the US Army Department of the West, Benton Barracks gradually grew into a combination military base and hospital, prisoner-of-war camp, and refugee camp. By the end of the war, the military barracks alone could house thirty thousand soldiers, somewhere between one-fifth and one-sixth of the resident population of the city, and the site was jointly administered by the army; the federal Bureau of Refugees,

Freedmen, and Abandoned Lands; and the Western Sanitary Commission (founded in St. Louis in 1861 to aid in the support of escaping slaves). The first regiments of US Colored Troops—the Sixty-Second, Sixty-Fifth, and Sixty-Seventh US Infantry—were formed at Benton Barracks in May 1863, months before the formation of Black regiments elsewhere. By the end of the war, over eight thousand Black men from Missouri, a full 40 percent of the Black men of military age in the state, had enlisted in the US Army and gone into battle singing "Give Us a Flag":

> *Oh, Frémont he told them when the war it first begun,*
> *How to save the Union and the way it should be done.*
> *But Kentucky swore so hard and Old Abe he had his fears,*
> *Till ev'ry hope was lost but the colored volunteers.*

By the time the Missouri State Constitution of 1865 made their legal emancipation official and irrevocable, most of those who had been enslaved in St. Louis had long since claimed freedom for themselves.[6]

Black volunteers—formerly enslaved—from all over the western theater went to Benton Barracks for training. There they were provided (by the Western Sanitary Commission, overseen by William Greenleaf Eliot) with copies of *Sargent's Standards Primer* and taught to read. Black women, meanwhile, were trained as nurses and eventually oversaw a military hospital for Black soldiers set up on the grounds in 1864. Black soldiers, together with paroled Confederate prisoners of war, guarded the camp and the largest military hospital in the West, built to accommodate 2,500 patients at a time. By the end of the war, Benton Barracks furnished the city of St. Louis, as well as the nation as a whole, with an example of Black capacity-building, self-care, and self-determination. Some of the most prominent Black political figures of the postwar period spent time there. Hiram Revels, who recruited an entire regiment of Black soldiers in St. Louis during the war, was the first African American elected to the US Senate (from Mississippi)

This African American soldier was one of the thousands who enlisted and served at Benton Barracks (on the site of today's Fairground Park) during the Civil War. After the war, Black soldiers from St. Louis were deployed to protect white settlers in the West. (International Institute of Social History, Amsterdam)

during Reconstruction, and Blanche K. Bruce, elected to the Senate (also from Mississippi) shortly after Revels, also spent time at Benton Barracks during the war. Although it would be a mistake to overstate the democratic significance of what was, after all, an armed camp that was segregated and rampantly overcrowded, subject to periodic epidemics, and ruled in the final instance by open force, it is nevertheless the case that the soldiers and scholars, the nurses and teachers, the refugees and the ruined, mendicant beggars, represented a collective challenge to the half-century-long hegemony of the "white man's country."[7]

Public conveyances, especially streetcars, were other defining sites of Black struggle in St. Louis. During the war, Black passengers were banned from the inside of the cars, allowed only to ride exposed on open balconies at the front of the cars. "I have seen neatly dressed colored females on cold days stand on the front platform with tender infants in their arms," wrote one sympathetic observer. For the Black citizens of St. Louis, who rode outside in the rain and freezing winter, this was an issue as important as any other, although it was generally treated as a distraction by the "radical" Republicans, who thought Black activists should focus on the struggle for suffrage (and become loyal supporters of the Republican Party). Beginning in 1865, Black passengers began to push their way inside, and in 1868 they won a judgment in circuit court allowing them to ride inside the covered cars.[8]

In response, the *Anzeiger*, which quickly abandoned its radicalism in the years after the war, joined the Democratic (that is, white supremacist) *St. Louis Republican* in editorializing against the integration of hotels, ballrooms, and so on, in the city. In essence their argument was that public accommodations were private property and that property should be exempted from the struggle for social equality: "according to the terms of the federal Constitution today every proprietor of an omnibus, hotel, concert hall or ball room is permitted to decide himself who he will admit and who not." The party of property had survived the war and emancipation; it was only a matter of time before it regained its footing.[9]

Black activists were able to gain a slightly larger degree of white support in their struggle for public education. Black educators in St. Louis had been running underground schools for decades, and in defiance of an 1847 state law that forbade teaching Black people to read. During the war, Black veterans and local Black activists had built "freedom schools" where children and adults alike could learn to read and reckon. Under the state constitution of 1865, the Missouri General Assembly was empowered to establish public schools "for the children of African descent." The privileges of white supremacy and property were entwined in the bilious response of the *St. Louis Republican* to the supporters of (segregated) public schools for Black children: "If they like to associate with the n—rdom, as would seem to be the case, let them go to [the Black schools], but not at the expense of white men." The fact that Black St. Louisans had long been paying taxes to support schools they were not allowed to attend did not receive a hearing in the pages of the *Republican*.[10]

In 1866, the St. Louis School District opened three public schools for Black children, including Toussaint L'Ouverture Elementary School, the alma mater of both US poet laureate Maya Angelou and St. Louis activist Percy Green. In 1875, the city's Sumner High School became the first public high school for Black students west of the Mississippi River. And the Black veterans of the fight for public schools—men like James Milton Turner, who had served General Lyon as a personal attendant and would go on to be appointed ambassador to Liberia, and future senator Blanche K. Bruce, who had been a schoolteacher and steamboat porter along the Mississippi—led the way in founding, at a meeting held in St. Louis in October 1865, the Missouri Equal Rights League, which became the principal Black organization fighting for suffrage in Missouri. "Had it not been for the Negro schools and colleges," W.E.B. Du Bois later wrote, "the Negro would to all intents and purposes, have been driven back to slavery."[11]

Along with the Black refugees to the city during the war came tens of thousands of whites. Galusha Anderson remembered them as coming in even greater numbers than the Black migrants, and as equal in their poverty. "They entered St. Louis in rags, often hatless and shoeless, sallow, lean, half-starved, and unkempt. Very many of them were women and children, in pitiable plight, half-naked, shivering, penniless, dispirited," he wrote. Anderson found them, on the whole, unwilling to work and unfathomably hostile to making common cause with their Black neighbors, who were mostly refugees themselves. "They regarded manual labor as a disgrace. They had been taught in the school of slavery that honest toil was servile and ignoble," he wrote. He went on to tell the story of visiting a white family at a federal refugee center that had been set up at the Virginia Hotel. Even though their squalid room offered a sharp contrast to the clean and "homelike" room of the Black man who lived next door, they expressed their dismay that the superintendent would put them in a room on an integrated hallway.[12]

Anderson held out little hope for poor white people whose imagination was bounded by the political horizon of the white republic. His disappointment suggests that he had imagined that over the course of the war white St. Louisans would gain some empathy for their Black neighbors. Their resentful statement of their own embattled entitlement—the idea that only "the dutch and the darkeys" were free in St. Louis—had embedded within it a recognition of the ways in which their own social and political condition had come to resemble that of erstwhile slaves. They had become subject to the same 9:00 p.m. curfew and pass laws that had defined the lives of slaves and free Black people in St. Louis since the 1830s and 1840s; they had been placed under surveillance and subjected to the rumors spread about them by their neighbors; and they had been deprived of their property, governed by force, and imprisoned in Bernard Lynch's downtown slave pen. The question, in Anderson's mind, was whether they would declare that their poverty and poor treatment were unjust because they were white, or because it was unjust for anyone to be treated that way.

Among those who did make a direct connection between the plight of the city's poor whites and their Black neighbors was Joseph Weydemeyer, who had finished out the war as the military governor of the eastern district of Missouri, which stretched westward from St. Louis to the German settlement in Hermann. In a series of editorials published over the summer of 1866, first in German in the *Westliche Post* and then in English for the *St. Louis Daily Press*, Weydemeyer outlined a case for the limitation of the working day to eight hours as the defining struggle for the interracial (and national and eventually global) working class. "The eight-hour movement," Weydemeyer wrote, "slings a common bond around all workingmen, awakens in them a common interest, pulls down the barriers too often raised between different trades, declares war against all party prejudices of birth and color, and thereby clears the ground for the formation of a real workingman's party, in whose hands soon will be held the future of the country."[13]

For Weydemeyer, the eight-hour movement was only a first step, a way for workers to overcome the historical, racial, and economic divisions that had undermined their solidarity: after emancipation, all workers were paid by the hour, and so it was in a struggle over the length of the working day that they might discover their commonality. When the *Anzeiger* mocked the "radical Germans" who would "give [the Negroes] voluntarily their most beautiful plantations; they would divide their belongings with them; they would give them all the political rights which they themselves exercise . . . every Teuton would instruct a Negro in German philosophy," and seek them as marriage matches for their sons and daughters, they were thinking of Weydemeyer. Still, the communist colonel was popular enough among St. Louisans that he was elected St. Louis County auditor in 1866. But before the "radical auditor" could fulfill his promise to collect back taxes from war profiteers and reform the city's property-friendly tax laws, he died in a late-summer outbreak of cholera.[14]

The struggle for Black suffrage marked an inflection point in the historical transition back from the revolutionary possibilities of wartime toward the whites-only pro-property liberalism that determined the political vision of Boernstein, Brown, and Benton. At the state constitutional convention in 1865, there was a good deal of support for Black suffrage expressed by radicals, and especially by Germans from the city of St. Louis and by the vice president of the constitutional convention, Charles Drake, who exerted so much influence over the proceeding that the result came to be known as "the Drake Constitution." And yet, from the beginning, there was an audible backbeat of white fear: If Missouri allowed Black men to vote, wouldn't the state become a magnet for cheap labor in the shape of emancipated slaves? Why should Black men be allowed to vote immediately when immigrants were required to wait a year before naturalization? Why should Black men be allowed to vote when white women were not? And finally, most pertinently and destructively, why should Black men vote when former Confederates could not?

Even among the radicals, there was little hope of getting the state of Missouri to produce a constitution that would allow African Americans to vote. In 1865, the voters of the state approved a new constitution that limited suffrage to "every white male citizen of the United States" and "every white male person of foreign birth who may have declared his intention to become a citizen." The constitution extended the privileges of whiteness to immigrants, while denying citizenship to freed people—it extended the mantle of whiteness to the Germans, chiseling off the liberals who were willing to abandon common cause with former slaves from the radicals. African Americans in Missouri—or, more properly, African American men in Missouri—would not gain the right to vote until the passage of the Fifteenth Amendment in 1870.[15]

Having failed in their effort to broaden their political base, the "radicals" had instead focused on narrowing the political base of their opponents (read: former Confederates). The result was the so-called Iron-Clad Oath, or Test Oath, the various provisions of which accounted for thirteen of the constitution's twenty-six articles concerning suffrage, including a page-long itemization of eighty-one ways in which a prospective voter might have demonstrated "sympathy" for the Confederacy. Those who wished to vote or hold office in Missouri were required under the constitution to swear that they had "always been truly and loyally on the side of the United States against all enemies thereof." Under the Missouri Constitution of 1865, the politics of the state came to be preoccupied with questions about white life, white politics, white rights, and white reconciliation in a way that foreshadowed the course of Reconstruction nationally. Indeed, St. Louis, the politics of Missouri, and the struggle over the Test Oath produced the political leadership that pointed the Republican Party and the nation toward the end of Reconstruction and the demise of the federal effort to guarantee the constitutional rights of the freed people.[16]

The position of the "liberal" opponents of the Test Oath was undergirded by a sometimes-spoken-sometimes-left-unspoken white supremacy. Even many of those who had opposed slavery before the war agreed in its aftermath that it was wrong to deny *white* men the right to vote. When B. Gratz Brown, now a US senator from Missouri, said in 1866, "Universal suffrage will triumph in the end," he was defending the rights of ex-Confederates in Missouri to vote, not ex-slaves. Brown was joined in the struggle for the rights of whites by Carl Schurz, who soon became the most famous German inhabitant of St. Louis, succeeding Sigel as surely as Marx argued that comedy succeeded tragedy in the *Eighteenth Brumaire*. Tall, thin, bearded, and bookish, Schurz had been a Prussian student radical who took up arms in 1848. With the collapse of the revolution, he went into exile in Switzerland in 1849. The following year, he returned to Prussia, where he collaborated with a sympathetic guard to rescue his onetime professor and radical mentor, Gottfried Kinkel, from the notorious Spandau Prison—an act that gained Schurz international acclaim among radicals. By 1851, he was in London, where he met the exiled revolutionaries Louis Kossuth (Kossuth Lajos), Giuseppe Mazzini, and Karl Marx. He moved to the United States in 1852. By the time of the Civil War, Schurz had become a well-known Republican orator, a fierce opponent of slavery, and an enthusiastic supporter of "free labor." In the American context, however, Schurz was no revolutionary. He was an unapologetic skeptic about the abilities and capacities of the Black people about whom he so regularly spoke. After the war, he settled in St. Louis, where he was hired by Joseph Pulitzer to edit the German-language *Westliche Post*.[17]

With the collapse of the Confederacy and the end of slavery, radicals like Drake, who had supported emancipation beginning in 1861 and presided over the Confederate-disenfranchising constitutional convention of 1865, and liberals like Schurz could no longer find common ground. The politics of the national Republican Party increasingly divided those for whom the struggle for "freedom" was predicated on the promotion and protection of African American voting rights (not to mention the more thoroughgoing human emancipation imagined by Sigel or Weydemeyer) from those for whom "freedom" meant the freedom to own property and to go on doing whatever they were doing without having to bother about other people's rights. The latter sort came to be called "liberals," and Carl Schurz became a leading figure in the liberal wing of the Republican Party, first in Missouri and, soon after, nationally. For Schurz, association with radicals—and thus with Black people—drew unnecessary attention to the history of German radicalism and divided them from the mainstream of the Republican Party. Asked again in 1868 to support Black voting rights, Germans joined the rest of the city in voting two-to-one for white supremacy. The Republican Party was leaving African Americans behind, and the St. Louis Germans were becoming white.[18]

In the meantime, the Bentonite center of gravity in Missouri politics reconstructed itself around the question of the voting rights of former Confederates. Schurz and the railroad Republican Gratz Brown were joined in the struggle against the Test Oath by Frank Blair, whose 1888 statue in Forest Park remembers him not only as "the Indomitable free-soil leader of the west," but also as "the magnanimous statesman, who, as soon as the war was over, breasted the torrent of proscription, to restore to citizenship the disfranchised Southern people." After the war, Blair returned to the Democratic Party as a candidate for the vice presidency in 1868. Even in the context of the Reconstruction era, Blair stood out for his willingness to suggest that Black suffrage would naturally and inevitably lead Black men to, as he put it, "subject white women to their unbridled lust." Postwar party politics in Missouri, like prewar party politics, was thus framed almost entirely within the logic of the "white man's country."[19]

In the aftermath of the passage of the Fifteenth Amendment in 1870, Brown and Schurz convened a convention of self-styled liberal Republicans in St. Louis. The initial impetus of the meeting was to work toward the final repeal of the civic disabilities of post-Confederate whites that had been written into law in the 1865 state constitution, now made even more galling to the liberals by the Fifteenth Amendment's guarantee of Black male suffrage. But the result of the meeting was the emergence of a new movement within the Republican Party, known at first as "the Missouri Plan" but soon known as Liberal Republicanism. By 1872, Schurz and Brown had become rivals, but Liberal Republicanism had grown from a splinter tendency in Missouri politics into a national movement—and a significant challenge to both the re-election of President Ulysses S. Grant and the continued reconstruction of the South.

Liberal Republicanism was a white nationalist movement. Emblematized by the famous words of their 1872 presidential candidate, Horace Greeley—"root, hog, or die," an animalizing and degrading translation of the commonplace directive to fend for one's self—the Liberal approach to the freedmen was to abandon them. The question of Black freedom was to be left to the states as the federal government turned to promoting the economic development of the West and getting out of the way of capital—in other words, as it turned once again to empire. It was a political vision not so different from that of Thomas Hart Benton. Genocide was a predictable result.

The disputed presidential election of 1876 resulted in the extra-constitutional appointment (by a bipartisan backroom bargain) of the Liberal Republican Rutherford B. Hayes to the presidency. In exchange for the elevation of Hayes, the Liberal Republicans agreed to end the federal military occupation of the South, leaving the region's Black citizens to fend for themselves against the voter-suppressing, night-riding, sharecropping, convict-leasing, and lynching of the period that historians still, outrageously, generally refer to as "Redemption." The end of Reconstruction was a negotiated settlement between the Republicans and the Democrats that was also, in effect, a bargain between capitalism and white supremacy. In return for southern Democratic support for the railroad and tariff, the Republicans would abandon their commitment to Reconstruction and the federal protection of Black freedom. It was an agreement that reflected the final triumph of the Missouri (or Liberal) tendency in the Republican Party—a victory effectively announced to the nation days later when Hayes appointed Carl Schurz to be his secretary of the interior.[20]

For Du Bois, Reconstruction had represented a potentially revolutionary alliance of poor whites and newly emancipated African Americans—an alliance of precisely the sort forecast in the camp at Rolla and celebrated by Weydemeyer in the pages of the *Westliche Poste*. Correspondingly, the end of Reconstruction represented not simply the unleashing of white supremacy on the South, although that was surely part of it, but also the alliance of white supremacy with property, for as both the most radical and most conservative among nineteenth-century observers noted, the right to hold human property might have been the first to be challenged, but there was no necessary reason that it should be the last. It was, then, no accident that the counterrevolution of property had its earliest political precursors in the politics of Missouri, where the most radical wartime critique of both slavery and the rights of property more generally had taken root. Nor perhaps was it an accident that it resulted in the meteoric rise of Carl Schurz, a German liberal from Missouri. Nor, indeed, was it an accident that Schurz became the secretary of the interior—the man with the final say about the disposition of federal lands and policy toward western Indians, the Bentonite legacy of the "white man's country."

In St. Louis, the intellectual and political heirs of Sigel and Weydemeyer mounted a final battle. The St. Louis General Strike of 1877 provided the nation with the era's most compelling example of interracial radicalism—a final flash-lit image of the fading promise of abolition democracy. In July of that year, railway workers on the Baltimore and Ohio went on strike in Martinsburg, West Virginia, protesting long-standing grievances about dangerous working conditions, wage cuts, speedups, and union-busting blacklisting. The strike spread along the rail lines: to Louisville, Pittsburgh, Cincinnati, and Chicago; to Kansas City, Omaha, and as far west as San Francisco. In several cities, including Pittsburgh and Chicago, there were violent clashes between police and state militia forces called up to clear the tracks and strikers intent on shutting them down. And in several others, the radical Workingmen's Party, a largely immigrant group composed of socialists and Marxists, took center stage—nowhere more so than in St. Louis.[21]

On the afternoon of July 22, railroad workers gathered in the rail yards in East St. Louis for a rally in support of the strike. Their speeches decried the way "capitalists" treated "the workingman" and compared the condition of railroad workers to that of serfs and slaves. "Brother slaves!" one speaker addressed the crowd, "Yes, brother slaves. We are also serfs if we continue to work on the present reduction of wages on which we can barely live." It was not long before the radicals of the Workingmen's Party marched in, to raucous cheers. Five hundred strong, divided into German, Bohemian, French, and English sections, singing "La Marseillaise" and waving the red flag of revolution, they urged the railway workers to shut down the lines and take to the streets. One by one, the rail workers' unions voted to go out, and the strike was scheduled to begin at midnight on July 23.[22]

On the night of the twenty-third, the Workingmen's Party staged a massive rally at Lucas Market in downtown St. Louis. Speakers urged the strikers to be ready to fight when the military intervened on the side of the railways. "We have now a worse time than the slaves had in the 1850s," one of the speakers told the crowd. "If it must be by arms, let it be by arms." The assembly elected a committee to visit the mayor of St. Louis and apprise him of their determination to support the striking railway workers. Among the five elected was a Black man who was remembered by onlookers only as "Wilson." The Workingmen's Party, which had theretofore resisted any call to try to organize Black workers, was being led by the exigency of the moment and the logic of its own rhetoric toward a revolutionary alliance with the Black workers of St. Louis. Representatives of the party began to go door to door in the city, urging workers to strike in support of the railway workers; in shop after shop, they did.[23]

The next day, July 24, three hundred soldiers from the Twenty-Third Infantry and two Gatling guns arrived in St. Louis. They were commanded by Jefferson C. Davis (no relation), who had just finished a tour fighting the punitive, genocidal Modoc War in California. His presence in St. Louis exemplified the generalization of imperial violence in the service of capitalism and racial order that has repeatedly occurred in American history: machine-gunning the Modoc Indians in California made it that much easier to imagine doing the same in St. Louis. Davis was notorious in the army for having murdered a superior officer during the Civil War (General Halleck, by that time in charge of all of Lincoln's armies, had deemed a trial inexpedient due to a shortage of competent officers) and for having abandoned a large number of escaping slaves to a murderous Confederate cavalry charge, for which he had been briefly suspended from command.[24]

On the night of July 24, an estimated ten thousand workers rallied at Lucas Market. They cheered speakers who urged them toward an armed conflict with the federal force and stoked their willingness to "die in the struggle." "Negroes, too?" someone shouted from the crowd, and the crowd shouted "Yes!" A Black stevedore was called onto the stage, and he spoke to the crowd about the specific condition of Black workers on the levee—starvation wages in the summer and unemployment in the winter, when the river trade slowed. He then challenged the crowd: "Will you stand for us regardless of color?" "We will! We will!" they shouted back. The leaders of the Workingmen's Party then organized the crowd into patrol companies to prepare for street battles against the police and the military and to "protect property." At the end of the night, the crowd voted to declare a general strike, demanding the enforcement of an eight-hour day in all branches of industry and an end to child labor. Proclamations, printed in English and German, were posted throughout the city. Eleven years after his death, the emancipatory vision of Joseph Weydemeyer rose again in St. Louis.[25]

On July 25, 1877, the St. Louis General Strike took hold of the city. Historians have termed it the first general strike in the history of the United States, and it was clear to contemporary observers that something extraordinary was happening in St. Louis that summer. "It is wrong to call this a strike; it is a labor revolution," wrote the *Missouri Republican* disapprovingly. Workers of "all colors" marched through the city carrying the tools of their trade and waving the red flags of the railway signalmen. As they marched through the streets, workers inside businesses came out to join them; they left in their wake a pathway of closed shops—foundries, flour mills, smelters, bakeries. By the end of the day, sixty factories had been shut down and the crowd was in control of the city, and nowhere more so than on the railway, where the strike had begun: the strikers had reopened the lines and begun collecting fares. Soon a flour mill was opened in order to provide bread for the strikers and the city, and businesses across the city began to reopen under the control of armed strikers and in compliance with the demand of the strikers for an eight-hour day. For a time, the city of St. Louis was governed by a workers' collective of the sort imagined by Joseph Weydemeyer. "The cool audacity and impudent effrontery of the communists have nowhere shown so conspicuously as in St. Louis," wrote the *Chicago Tribune* of the inauguration of what was soon referred to in newspapers across the nation as the "St. Louis Commune."[26]

To onlookers, especially unsympathetic onlookers, the most remarkable aspect of the strike was its interracial solidarity, coolly described by a reporter from the *New York Sun* as "a novel feature of the times." In St. Louis, however, the response in the mainstream media was more heated, incendiary even. "There was something blood-curdling in the manner in which they shouldered their clubs and started up the levee whooping," wrote the *Missouri Republican* of the Black strikers; the "insidious influence of the International" had delivered the city into the hands of "notorious Negroes." In an interview given shortly after the strike, one of the leaders of the German section of the Workingmen's Party told a sympathetic reporter that the strike organizers were surprised by the role that Black workers had played in the strike and had tried "to dissuade any white men from going out with the n—s." That is to say, the whites-only leadership had lost control of the strike—and of the possibilities of interracial working-class solidarity being made plain in the streets.[27]

To regain control, the leadership ordered the suspension of mass outdoor meetings—and thus surrendered control of the streets to the police. As the strike leadership met behind closed doors on the morning of July 27, a crowd of workers—white and Black—gathered outside, demanding that the committee distribute arms to the strikers, including "a company of colored men." Eventually, a group of workers broke into the room where the leaders were meeting but were turned away by the strike leaders, who said they had no weapons to provide to the crowd and admitted that they intended to surrender if the police stormed the building. That afternoon, the St. Louis Police, supported by a deputized citizens' militia and armed with shotguns contributed by the St. Louis Gun Club and rifles from the federal arsenal in Rock Island, Illinois, arrested the leaders of the General Strike without a shot being fired. Two days later, US Army troops secured control of the rail yard in East St. Louis. Directing the deployment of federal forces in support of capital from Washington was the US secretary of the interior, Carl Schurz.[28]

The Civil War in St. Louis ended with the overthrow of the Commune. The city's leading men celebrated with a midnight parade the following year. Clad in a white hood and robes, the "Veiled Prophet" first patrolled the streets of St. Louis on the night of October 5, 1878, a revolver in one hand, a rifle in the other, a bowie knife looped through his belt. The parade was organized in a series of invitation-only meetings by elite St. Louisans in the aftermath of the General Strike. The Veiled Prophet that inaugural year, and the only one whose name has been officially acknowledged in the ongoing 140-odd-year history of the parade, was the city police commissioner, John G. Priest, who had continued to drill his deputized reserves—the reserve army of capital, as many as five hundred men—in the streets and parks of the city. Next to Priest on the Veiled Prophet's float, reported the *Missouri Republican*, stood a "villainous looking executioner and a blood curdling butcher's block."[29]

An 1870s image of the Veiled Prophet from the Veiled Prophet parade, which was inaugurated in 1878 by city leaders anxious to reassert control over the streets of the city in the aftermath of the 1877 General Strike. The parade continues to the present day. (*Missouri Republican*, October 6, 1878, Missouri Historical Society)

It is as an aspect of the eventual success of the counterrevolution of property, rather than as simply "the politics of Reconstruction," that we should understand one of the most notorious episodes in the municipal history of St. Louis—the so-called Great Divorce of 1876. In 1869, to punish and discipline "radical" Republicans in St. Louis (those who were supportive of the public education of Black children and insufficiently eager to reenfranchise former Confederates), the state government of Missouri had transferred the power to assess, tax, and audit property within the city to County Court, a body that had until very recently boasted Joseph Weydemeyer as its auditor. By 1870, a secessionist movement had emerged within the city, with large taxpayers and business owners at its center decrying the high cost of "double government" and the effective subsidy provided by wealthy city dwellers to their rural neighbors in the county. In 1875, a freeholders board composed mostly of candidates endorsed by the Merchants Exchange and the Taxpayers League (to wit: property) was chosen in a special election and set about separating the city from the county ("home rule") and designing new systems of government for each. The boundary of the city was stretched west to encompass the western edge of Forest Park. It is this line, an artifact of the Reconstruction-ending reconciliation of Liberal Republicans and propertied Democrats in their shared support of economic development and antipathy for taxes, that defined the hard boundary between city and county that hobbles the city's development to this day.[30]

In the West, the counterrevolution of property took the shape of empire and Indian killing. Abraham Lincoln emerged from the Civil War as the "Great Emancipator," but his political roots had more to do with the Black Hawk War than they did with the Black freedom struggle, and his political base lay in the free-soil wing of the Republican Party: antislavery, white supremacist, imperialist, and removalist. In St. Louis, the politics of the Republican Party was complicated by the leading role played by German liberals (like Boernstein), and even by German radicals (like Sigel and Weydemeyer). And yet, at the heart of all of these factions of the Republican Party were presumptions of empire: the idea that land in the West was there to be used as the standing reserve of white freedom, settler, liberal, or radical. All of the elements of the party of Lincoln in the West were imperialist, and all grounded their politics and their hopes on Indian land.

During the war, the president balanced his steps toward emancipation with a set of massive effective handouts to the free-soil wing of his party—that is, to whiteness and empire. Up to and even after the Emancipation Proclamation, Lincoln remained a committed colonizationist. In his annual message to Congress in December 1862—a month before the Emancipation Proclamation—the president assured the nation (or at least the West): "I cannot make it better known than it already is, that I strongly favor colonization," arguing that "by colonizing the Black laborer out of the country . . . by precisely so much you increase the demand for and wages of white labor." Through the later

years of the war, Lincoln sought land in Panama and the Caribbean for
Black resettlement, and, as late as April 1865, days before he died, he
wrote of Black Union Army veterans: "I believe it would be better to
export them all to some fertile country with a good climate, which they
could have to themselves."[31]

As much as he remained committed to ethnic cleansing, Lincoln
remained a supporter of empire—the other aspect of the Benton-Blair
tendency in the politics of westering white supremacy. In July 1862, as
Congress passed a renewed Confiscation Act, which allowed for emancipation of enslaved people whose owners had been convicted of treason, the president signed the Morrill Act, which provided large land
grants to the states that had remained in the Union in order to support
the foundation of institutions of higher learning. Lest the meaning of
"land grant" be misunderstood, it should be emphasized that these were
grants of large sections of land (over seventeen million acres all told)
that were to be sold to raise money to pay for the fabrication of entire
institutions of higher education—facilities, faculties, future endow-
ments—rather than the bare perimeters of land on which the buildings
were later built. Indeed, some of the grants were quite distant from the
campuses they eventually subsidized—the founding of Cornell University in New York State, to give only a single example, was partially
funded by the sale of timberland in Wisconsin. The Pacific Railroad
Act was signed into law the same month. It provided railroad rights-
of-way and large adjacent grants of land to corporations seeking to
build railways in the West. But the bulk of the subsidy came in the
form of land that was far from any railway, almost 200 million acres
of far-flung land that could be sold to finance the building of the railroad along the narrow path of its right-of-way. The Homestead Act,
signed into law in May 1862, arguably the culmination of Benton's
vision, provided white settlers free access to 160-acre tracts if they
settled west of the Mississippi; as many as 1.5 million of them did in
the years after the war, spread across 300 million acres of the West,
or about a half-million square miles. Although it is conventional to

understand the Civil War as a civil war—as a domestic conflict between the North and the South—from the vantage point of St. Louis
(and, indeed, Washington), the war also had much to do with empire
and the West.[32]

Taken together, the expropriating, land-distributing laws of 1862
and 1863 were the bill of rights for settler whites and corporate colonists
in the nation's postwar western empire—a neo-Bentonite program of
western imperial development. They aligned the United States with
pro-property liberals and settler whites in the West over and against
the communists' critique of property. And they were guaranteed by
the power of the US military. In August 1862, Dakotas in present-day
Minnesota rose against white homesteaders, killing as many as eight
hundred in a thirty-seven-day war. Two thousand Indians were eventually rounded up and imprisoned at Fort Snelling (where Dred and
Harriet Scott had met thirty years before), and 392 were tried for murder by the soldiers who had just defeated them in the field. In the mass
trial, 323 were convicted and 303 sentenced to death. On the day after
Christmas in 1862, a week before he signed the Emancipation Proclamation, Abraham Lincoln ordered the simultaneous execution by
hanging of thirty-eight Dakota men, in an exemplary act of retribution
that remains the largest mass execution in the history of the United
States (as well as a marked contrast from the emergent laws of war that
governed the treatment of Confederate prisoners of war).[33]

Through the remaining year of the Civil War and the first years
of Reconstruction—the years in which the United States defeated
the Confederacy and ratified the Thirteenth and Fourteenth Amendments—the US Army pursued a slow-rolling genocidal campaign on
the plains. Emancipation in the East was shadowed at every step by
imperialism in the West, as if the laws of the settler republic, or at least
the racial prerogatives of the "white man's country," required that every step toward Black freedom be compensated with a step toward Indian annihilation. Then, in September 1863, US Army soldiers under
the command of General Henry Sibley attacked a Dakota and Lakota

summer camp, killing more than four hundred, mostly women and children. According to the Standing Rock historian LaDonna Brave-bull Allard, in the chaos of the initial attack women in the camp tied their babies to the backs of their dogs and drove them out of the camp in a desperate effort to save them. As the dogs drifted back into the smoldering camp, the soldiers killed the babies one by one. In November 1864, Colorado volunteers under the command of US Army Colonel John Chivington massacred more than two hundred Cheyennes and Arapahos at Sand Creek, in the Colorado Territory; they celebrated their victory in a grisly festival of desecration and sexual mutilation of the dead.[34]

In 1868, to make way for the railroad, the army sent a treaty delegation to sue for peace with the Cheyenne, Arapaho, and Dakota. The US commissioners included William Tecumseh Sherman, who would shortly succeed Ulysses S. Grant as the commanding general of the US Army, and the "Woman Killer," William Harney. The resulting Treaty of Fort Laramie prescribed the boundaries of the Great Sioux Nation over almost 70 million acres of present-day South Dakota and Wyoming, including 32 million acres of "permanent reservation," and it committed the Sioux, in return, to allow for the construction of the transcontinental railroad. The treaty, which required the approval of "three-quarters of adult male Indians" for amendment, remains the legal ground of Sioux claims against the United States: its terms have never been amended by the seven nations of the Sioux, although they have been sequestered in ever smaller portions of their domain in the 150 years since its signing.[35]

The US Army and the railroad men worked together to build the western empire. The railroad made it easier for the army to move soldiers and supplies from place to place, and the army provided security for railroad crews as they built their way across the Indian nations of the West. In 1867, Grant, as commanding general of the army, had declared that the completion of a transcontinental railroad would "go far toward a permanent settlement of our Indian difficulties." To that

Along with General William Tecumseh Sherman, who moved the War Department to St. Louis in the 1870s, General William Harney represented the United States at the signing of the Treaty of Fort Laramie in 1868. Harney, who murdered an enslaved woman in St. Louis in 1834, was known among the Sioux as "Woman Killer." He is second from the left among the white men seated in chairs, Sherman is third. (National Archives and Records Administration)

end, an 1871 federal law unilaterally declared that the United States would make no further Indian treaties; over the following years, the army herded those Indians it could onto reservations and pursued the rest across the plains. Sherman, Grant's successor, moved the headquarters of the army to St. Louis in 1874, hoping that he could more vigorously (read: murderously) prosecute the Indian wars away from his erstwhile civilian overseers in Washington. "We are not going to let a few thieving, ragged Indians stop the progress [of the railroads]," he declared in a letter to Grant. Under Sherman, the railroadization and racialization of the West went hand in hand. Indians found outside the boundaries of their reservations were to be "regarded as hostile and treated accordingly." As Sherman wrote in 1873, "we must act with vindictive earnestness against the Sioux, even to their extermination, men, women, and children." The term "settler colonialism" seems scarcely adequate to describe the close coordination of the railroad and the army—of investment and imperialism—in the West.[36]

Many of the US Army troops pulled out of the South at the end of Reconstruction were immediately redeployed to an arc of forts moving westward like a shock wave from St. Louis. Though US Army operations and bases moved farther west in the years after the Civil War, the city remained the site of the War Department, under General Sherman, and it continued to be the headquarters of the army's Department of the West as well as its Quartermaster Corps. Jefferson Barracks would be the intake and training base for all US Army cavalry units for the duration of the nineteenth century. Confederate as well as Union Army veterans served at Jefferson Barracks and in the western army of the 1870s, just as Confederate as well as Union Army veterans worked on the railroad and provided security along its leading edge. In these years, the reunification of the United States was accomplished not through the pacification of southern whites and the revolutionary elimination of white supremacy, but in continental conquest in the service of capitalist expansion. The counterrevolution of property and what the historian David Blight has termed the "romance of re-union" followed the parallel tracks along the lines of the Union Pacific, Central Pacific, and Southern Pacific Railroads.[37]

As well as former Confederates, Black soldiers fought Indians in the West. The famous Black soldiers of the Ninth and Tenth Cavalries, colloquially known as the "Buffalo Soldiers," were inducted into the army and trained at Jefferson Barracks. Even with the tactical advantages afforded by the railroad, the US Army would have been unable to wage war on the plains without horses, and the Ninth and Tenth made up about 10 percent of the army's mounted units, a percentage comparable to that of Black soldiers in the infantry. Often romanticized by historians, Black soldiers in the West slept in segregated quarters (as they had in training at Jefferson Barracks) and were provided with separate chaplains so that the segregation could be maintained through the Sabbath. Their own white officers and white soldiers in other units abused them and taunted them, and there were occasional fights between Black and white soldiers, for which the Black soldiers were almost uniformly held responsible. Their story is often told as an emblematically American fable: men so devoted to freedom that they were willing to suffer injustice in order to exemplify a better pathway to their white antagonists. And perhaps that is true. But so is this: the pathway to freedom in the late nineteenth-century United States was through Indian killing. It is, as the historian Quintard Taylor has written, "a painful paradox" that Black soldiers in the West risked their lives in defense of the imperial promise of the "white man's country." The legend of the "Buffalo Soldiers" became an alibi for empire, cloaking annihilationist wars in the trappings of freedom.[38]

It was Carl Schurz, the German radical turned Missouri liberal and Bentonite imperialist, who outlined the most coherent alternative to Indian-killing-as-the-course-of-imperial-progress in the 1870s and 1880s. As head of the US Interior Department, Schurz had nominal jurisdiction over Indian affairs, and beginning in 1877 he sought to transform that administrative responsibility into actual control. Schurz's main antagonists in the effort were Generals Sherman and Philip Sheridan, who tried in 1878 to have Indian affairs moved out of the Interior Department and into the War Department. In contrast to Sheridan's notorious statement that "the only good Indian is a dead Indian," Schurz advocated a policy that was later summarized by Richard Henry Pratt, a onetime lieutenant in the Tenth Cavalry and founder of the Carlisle Indian School in Pennsylvania, as "kill the Indian, save the man"— pacification through the separation of Indian children from their families and their reeducation in eastern boarding schools. In other words, cultural genocide. Upon the founding of Carlisle in 1879, Pratt stated that the Indian school model had no greater advocate than Schurz.[39]

Within a few years, three-quarters of Native children were being taught in boarding schools run by the Bureau of Indian Affairs (within the Interior Department), one-third of these in off-reservation schools like Carlisle. For Pratt and Schurz, education and privatization of tribal lands were pathways by which Indians might move from being the "occupants of the soil" to actually being able to have land "they could call their own." In Schurz's vision, citizenship and private property were mutually defining: only by learning how to cultivate the land as owners could Indians become citizens; only by learning to be citizens could they become worthy of the land upon which they had always lived, but never truly possessed according to Schurz.[40]

It was under Schurz that the push for the privatization of Indian lands culminated in the Dawes Severalty Act of 1887. The Dawes Act dissolved the common holding of American Indians and pulverized their nations into 160-acre plots, assigned one at a time and on the basis of individually held parcels of private property to every Indian head of household. Because the reservation lands and other common lands, as restricted as they were, had once included land for hunting and seasonal migration, there was a great deal of unassigned land left over after severalty—as much as three-quarters of what had been Indian territory in the years leading up to 1887. The Dawes Act deemed this unassigned Indian land "surplus" and provided for its distribution to white homesteaders, who once again began to embark from St. Louis by the tens of thousands.[41]

For a moment following the Civil War, it seemed as if St. Louis, the city of both Sherman and Schurz, would become the first city of the American empire, advancing "steadily and surely to her predestined station of first inland city on the globe," in the words of the journalist Horace Greeley. Boosters in the city led a brief campaign to have the nation's capital moved west to the banks of the Mississippi, going so far as to propose the brick-by-brick dismantling of the Capitol and the White House and their reassembly on the grounds of Jefferson Barracks. The idea's principal local booster was newspaperman Logan

Uriah Reavis, who argued that "the ruling power of a country should be located in the midst of its material power." Walt Whitman and William Tecumseh Sherman supported the plan, as did *DeBow's Review*, the principal journal of the commercial South, and an 1869 convention held at the Merchants Exchange in St. Louis at which the governors of twenty-one states expressed their support for the proposal.[42]

In the end, the Capitol remained intact and in Washington, but the fact that the proposal was taken seriously provides a reminder of the status of St. Louis, the West, and the empire in the minds of white Americans in the years after the Civil War. As one of those who lingered on the idea long enough to take it seriously reasoned, "St. Louis is the center of the Mississippi Valley—that this Valley is the center of the United States—and the United States the center of the whole world." According to the logic of the imperial reason, there was a case to be made for St. Louis, one that was only bolstered in the eyes of the western visionaries by the fact that the 1870 census revealed that the city had passed Baltimore, Boston, New Orleans, and Cincinnati to become the fourth-largest in the United States—behind only New York, Brooklyn (which did not merge into New York City until 1898), and Philadelphia and, most importantly, still ahead of Chicago.[43]

But if the Mississippi River was the historic reason for the city's imperial rise, it was also the limit. On May 10, 1869, standing on the traditional lands of the Western Shoshone at what is now called Promontory, Utah, Leland Stanford had driven a golden spike into the ground, securing the link between the Union Pacific and Central Pacific Railroads, and between the East, the Midwest, and the Pacific. At the other end of the line, however, was not Benton's St. Louis but the mushroom metropolis on the banks of Lake Michigan—Chicago, which, by way of Rock Island, had a bridge. Indeed, by 1868 there were three bridges across the Mississippi that connected the East to the West via Chicago. St. Louis had none.[44]

There were both simple and complex reasons for the difference. The simple reason was that Missouri was across the river from Illinois.

Any bridge that crossed the Mississippi at St. Louis would have to be built in coordination with a state government that had little to gain by promoting competition with the city of Chicago. The complicated reason had to do with the fact that the American empire in the West was not simply built out of iron, steel, and lead, blood, sweat, and tears; it was also built out of paper. It was an empire of capital as well as arms. And it turned out that there was almost as much money to be made in not building railroads as there was in building them.

The efforts to build or block the bridge pitted St. Louis railroad interests in combination with downstate Illinois commercial interests, who wanted a bridge across the Mississippi at St. Louis, against Chicago railroad interests and St. Louis ferry interests who did not. In the years before the war, Chicago-based investors had managed to acquire the sole rights to build a bridge across the river in St. Louis, which they held, doing nothing, as they unfolded link after link of railway lines connecting the Windy City to the West.

Excavation for the bridge piers finally began at the foot of Washington Avenue in November 1869. The principal investor in the project was the New York magnate and banker J. P. Morgan, and the principal engineer for the project was the visionary James B. Eads, who had started out as a salvage man working (literally) on the bottom of the Mississippi River. For the bridge across the Mississippi, Eads used a method never before employed in the United States—pumping compressed air into underwater caissons, effectively creating a giant submarine, inside of which the piers of the bridge could be built up toward the surface. The method was ingenious but, in an era before the connection between rapid decompression and the formation of nitrogen bubbles in the bloodstream was widely understood, deadly: of the nearly 600 men who worked in the caissons, 119 became severely ill and 14 died, each death evidence of the bridge builders' daily decision that construction must continue no matter the human cost. The bridge, which, at its opening, boasted the longest rigid span in the world (its 520-foot central arch), was completed in July 1874 and named for James Eads.[45]

When the Eads Bridge was completed in 1874, it tied St. Louis into the emerging network of transcontinental railroads. By the 1890s, twenty-two railways converged in the city, more than in any other city in the United States. (Calvin Milton Woodward/ Library of Congress)

By the 1890s, twenty-two railways had converged at St. Louis, more than at any other point in the United States (although rail traffic through Chicago was greater), and the city had completed the massive, Romanesque Union Station, billed as "the largest, grandest, and most completely equipped railroad station in the world," in 1894. But the railroads were impressive not only as material objects but as opportunities for the wealthy and the canny to extract wealth from empire. In 1878, the Washington Avenue Bridge Company was forcibly dissolved by J. P. Morgan, acting on behalf of those who held the first and second mortgages on the bonds that had been sold to finance the bridge's construction. Acting through a partner, Morgan promptly repurchased the company at auction and thus ended up with the bridge while bilking the lesser-status bondholders out of their share. By the 1890s, the financier Jay Gould controlled enough of the traffic across the bridge that he could also control economic development in the city of St. Louis by setting the rate for transporting a ton of coal across the river. At the going rate of twenty cents per ton, it was worthwhile for industrialists to build their steel mills and packing plants in East St. Louis, which experienced terrific growth under the dominion of what those on the west side of the river came to call "the bridge arbitrary." While the railroads brought business to St. Louis, they also shaped the city's economic geography in their own image and their own interest.[46]

Still, there was plenty of money to be made in the imperium of St. Louis. In 1870, the Missouri-Kansas-Texas Railroad (the MKT, or the Katy), having reached the border of Indian Territory in Oklahoma, acquired the right to land grants to build through to Texas and Mexico. In the following decades, both the city's railway network and its financial interests unfolded toward the Southwest and Latin America—the quarter-section of the continent between the city's long-standing trade routes along the Santa Fe Trail and up and down the Mississippi and out into the Gulf. Tracing out the pathway of the MKT on the map in 1873, the *Missouri Republican* enthused that "all of Mexico would become part of the commercial empire of St. Louis," momentarily diverting Benton's dream of a pathway to the Pacific toward the commercial (and military) conquest of the Southwest. It was the MKT line and land grants, among other factors, that provoked the Red River War of 1874 and the final military defeat and forced sequestration of the Comanche, Kiowa, Southern Cheyenne, and Arapaho.[47]

In the last decades of the nineteenth century, St. Louis again became a hub for the processing and resale of resources extracted from the West. On the Southern Plains, as cattle replaced bison—which were overhunted in the early 1870s and wantonly slaughtered by soldiers in the later years of the decade—the packing plants in East St.

Louis came to occupy a position second only to those in Chicago in the burgeoning "Republic of Red Meat." In these years, the city of St. Louis itself became the third-largest miller in the nation—shipping flour to Mexico and on to Central and South America via its southwestern rail link—and the third-largest market for pressed cotton in the United States. As well as agricultural processing, trans-shipment, and export, the city developed a large manufacturing sector in the years after the Civil War, second only to Chicago's in the West in terms of capital investment. Flour mills and cotton presses, breweries and cigar factories, shoe and shirt manufacturers; rolling mills, iron foundries, and eventually steel mills; streetcar, carriage, and railcar factories; stoveworks and sofas—all manner of goods were made in St. Louis and destined for sale in the emerging markets of Texas and the Southwest, the Pacific, and especially, Latin America.[48]

In 1875, the St. Louis pharmaceutical exporter John Cahill founded a new commercial magazine focused on the export trade that he believed would save the city from "commercial stagnation." Called *El Comercio del Valle*, it was printed largely in Spanish, with some English, and featured an engraving of the Eads Bridge on the masthead. By the 1880s, *El Comercio del Valle* had twenty-four thousand subscribers in the city, throughout the Midwest, and in Latin America— Mexico, Costa Rica, Honduras, Nicaragua, Cuba, Brazil, Chile, and Venezuela. The magazine soon came to serve as a sort of official organ of the Mexican & Spanish-American Commercial Exchange, which was housed in a large three-story building in the heart of the city's downtown, on the corner of Eighth and Olive Streets. Though the articles in *El Comercio del Valle* were generally printed in Spanish and English, the advertisements were only in Spanish, and they provided a view of the city's manufacturing and export sector comprehensive enough that it could have served as a ready alternative to the city directory: the William Lemp and Anheuser-Busch breweries; Shapleigh and Simmons Hardware; Meyer Brothers Drugs and Mallinckrodt Chemical; the St. Louis Car Company and the MKT; the Hamilton-Brown

Shoe Company; Shapleigh rifles and revolvers, and ammunition from the Western Cartridge Company; and on and on.[49]

The election of Porfirio Díaz as president of the Republic of Mexico in 1877 provided the capitalists of the Mexican & Spanish-American Commercial Exchange with a terrific opportunity. Díaz almost immediately appointed Cahill, a US citizen, as Mexican consul in St. Louis, a position from which Cahill and *El Comercio del Valle* could assist in Díaz's effort to draw foreign capital to Mexico by putting the country's assets up for sale. In these years, the MKT linked directly into the trunk line of the Mexican National Railway.[50]

Over the last twenty years of the nineteenth century and into the first decade of the twentieth, St. Louis capitalists bought mines, railroads, factories, and farms all over Mexico. In 1883, Díaz visited the city and gave a speech in which he promised that the city of St. Louis had a "deep and permanent interest" in the future of Mexico. By that time, the St. Louis oilman Henry Clay Pierce had become the chairman of the Mexican Central Railway, the Mexican Pacific Railway, the Mexican-American Steamship Company, the Mexican National Construction Company, the Mexican Fuel Company, the Tampico Harbor Company, and the Mexican Bank of Commerce and Industry. He had built and owned oil refineries in Mexico City, Monterrey, Vera Cruz, and Tampico, and since 1886 he had held an exclusive license to sell Mexican Fuel Company petroleum in Mexico. So great were St. Louis's interests in Mexico that the revolution that finally overthrew Díaz in 1911 was portrayed in some quarters as a simple proxy struggle between St. Louis capitalists and interests based in Great Britain: "A fight which will have on one side the interested of the oil department of Weetman Pearson of Great Britain, and on the other side the Waters-Pierce Oil Company of St. Louis is promised Mexico in the near future," predicted the *Mexican Herald* in January 1908.[51]

The merchants and manufacturers of St. Louis had been enthusiastic supporters of the 1898 Spanish-American War, which they viewed as an opportunity to expand both their commercial reach and their way out of the depression that had begun in 1893. St. Louis had long-standing connections to Cuba, having served as a refinery for Cuban sugar brought up the Mississippi River since the 1840s, and the city had shipped flour, shoes, and machinery for sugar mills to the island since the 1880s. In the years after the war, St. Louis had become the second-largest producer of shoes in the nation (behind Boston), and the St. Louis–based *Shoe and Leather Gazette* editorialized strongly in support of Cuban independence through much of the 1890s. But it was not just Cuba that these inland imperialists imagined as a part of the commercial dominion of St. Louis: "The Stars and Stripes should henceforth float forever from the Philippines," declared an editorial in the *St. Louis Star* in 1898. Benton's dream of Pacific empire found second life in the counter-revolution of property.[52]

The merchants and manufacturers of St. Louis and East St. Louis made good money off the Spanish-American War (as they did from Great Britain's Boer War between 1899 and 1902 in South Africa). Horses, mules, saddles, and shoes were hallmark products of the city of St. Louis, and in the last years of the nineteenth century they were shipped all over the world in the service of empire. Business only improved in the wake of the 1898 war. The St. Louis Car Company was soon shipping streetcars, freight cars, and locomotives to Manila, Honolulu, San Juan, Havana, Mexico City, Santiago, Buenos Aires, Lisbon, Rio de Janeiro, London, Berlin, Bordeaux, Cape Town, and Odessa. Shoes from St. Louis were shipped all over the world in the years following the war, $2 million worth in 1906 alone. "American shoes are certainly following the flag," enthused the *Shoe and Leather Gazette*, emphasizing the connection between war, empire, and the sale of shoes. In these years, St. Louis companies like Mallinckrodt Chemical and Anheuser-Busch became global brands, building on existing connections throughout the Americas but also expanding to Asia and even Australia; Anheuser-Busch reported a 50 percent rise in its global sales over one year in 1899. It was perhaps no coincidence that Thomas Hart Benton's vision of the commercial imperium of the

city of St. Louis found its fullest historical expression partly under
the military leadership of Lieutenant Colonel Theodore Roosevelt,
who would publish a fawning biography of Benton in the year following the war.[53]

Of the neo-Bentonites, only Carl Schurz expressed any doubts
about the conquest of Cuba and the Philippines (as well as Hawai'i in
1893), but his worries were strictly racial in character. Hearkening back
to the imperial white supremacy of the free-soil movement, Schurz
simply did not think that the United States should risk bringing any
more dark-skinned people—"tropical peoples and more or less barba-
rous Asiatics"—under the jurisdiction of the United States, no matter how far-flung their precincts. Schurz supported war in Cuba and
the Philippines, but only to provide their markets access to American
goods, not to provide their people access to American citizenship (or
even quasi-citizenship). Although he would probably have favored the
term "Anglo-Saxon racial purity," Schurz was outlining the premises of
what would later be known as "the imperialism of free trade": the process by which the US government and American corporations sought
to exert indirect rule across the globe in the interest of capital.[54]

According to the standard measures, these were good years for the
city of St. Louis. The population, which had been 350,000 in 1880,
rose to 450,000 in 1890, then to almost 600,000 in 1900. Beginning in
the 1870s, the capitalists of the counterrevolution were building man-
sions on Vandeventer Place, an almost mile-long gated street that had
its own private security force and whose residents included Henry Clay
Pierce and Edward Mallinckrodt. In the 1880s, they began to move to
Compton Hill, just east of Grand Avenue, where the Busch family had
a mansion, and then to Westmoreland and Portland Place in the Central West End, where there were other members of the Busch family,
as well as railroad magnates, bank directors, import-export merchants,
and large manufacturers. By 1900, the city's power brokers had come to
be known collectively as "the Big Cinch." These heirs of the old families and sons of the new ones lived within a few blocks of one another

and the corner of Lindell and Kingshighway (and Vandeventer Place), and their names—Carr, Glasgow, Maffit, O'Fallon, Lucas—still adorn the street signs and city limits that define space in the St. Louis metropolitan area. The de facto leader of the group was David Francis, the erstwhile bridge entrepreneur who would forever be remembered in St. Louis for presiding over the World's Fair in 1904. They had retaken the city from the mob in 1877, and for the next three decades they did more or less what they wanted with it. Du Bois termed them and those like them across the country "the dictatorship of property."[55]

On May 8, 1900, 3,325 streetcar workers seeking recognition of their union, the reinstatement of fired organizers, and a ten-hour workday went on strike in St. Louis. The strike was a direct challenge to the local rule of the city's imperial merchants, manufacturers, and bankers, though not to the city's racial order; by 1900, all of the streetcar workers were white, and thus their strike might be seen as a demand for inclusion in the spoils of white supremacy and empire as much as a genuine challenge to their accumulation. "Sons of ditch-diggers aspired to be spawn of bastard kings and thieving aristocrats rather than the rough-handed children of dirt and toil," Du Bois wrote of the white working class in the era after the suppression of the General Strike.[56]

The St. Louis Streetcar Company, which had recently consolidated control over all the lines in the city, brought in strikebreakers from Cleveland in order to keep the trains running, and it successfully petitioned a federal judge to allow the formation of a property-protecting posse comitatus, drawn from among the self-declared "better elements in the city." The workers and their families organized alternative public transportation on horse-drawn freight wagons, threw dead frogs and bricks at the windows of passing trains, and built fires on the tracks. There were even reports of dynamite being found concealed beneath cabbage leaves on the rails heading out to the comfortable suburbs of the Central West End.[57]

On June 10, a parade of striking streetcar workers marched across the Eads Bridge and up Washington Avenue on their way home from a picnic in East St. Louis, where they had joined with striking workers from that city. They were carrying flags and marching to the beat of a drum as they passed the downtown "barracks" that housed the "posse" the sheriff had raised to ride the streetcars during the strike. There was a shot, fired by whom no one ever really established, although the sheriff later said that one of his men had dropped his gun on the ground while chasing a striker who had thrown a brick. Then there were many more shots from pistols and riot guns as the posse shot down the marchers "like dogs," in the words of the president of the Streetcar Workers' Union.[58]

Three of the marchers died at the scene, and one other made it, fatally wounded, to City Hospital. Eight others were seriously wounded but survived. Although the posse later alleged that a series of unlikely coincidences had preserved the police from injury at the hands of marauding workers—workers aiming at policemen being jostled as they shot, the guns of workers in the act of shooting policemen jamming, a gun barrel protruding from a knothole in a fence behind which an old man who had nothing to do with the strike was shot dead by the police mysteriously disappearing—and although the police later exhibited cards embossed with the words "Union or Nothing. Liberty or Death," which they said many of the marchers had been carrying hidden in their hats, there was no evidence that any of the marchers had been armed, or that they had intended to fight with the police or the posse.[59]

Twenty of the striking marchers were arrested and held for trial in the aftermath of the violence, and the following day the city's mayor issued a proclamation barring the city's citizens from "gathering in numbers on the streets or in public places" and declaring that "jeering or abusive language" would not be tolerated within the limits of the city of St. Louis—effectively outlawing the ongoing strike for the duration of the three-day order. The governor, having spoken to the mayor by telephone, made a statement that he was entirely satisfied that the posse had acted properly. Meanwhile, twenty-three of the city's lawyers formed a new posse, arming themselves and patrolling the streets to make sure that armed men stayed off the streets, as the mayor had ordered. Indeed, the sheriff announced, application to join the posse had skyrocketed after the massacre, and he soon expected to have as many as 2,500 deputies patrolling the streets and riding the streetcars along their reopened routes. The following day, sixty Civil War veterans were deputized and, dressed in the outfits worn by Teddy Roosevelt's "Rough Riders," turned out for duty. Before long, workers began to be brought before the Police Court and charged with the offense of "jeering" at passing train cars and policemen. The habits of imperial rule died hard.[60]

By September, the strike had been broken and the streetcar workers were forced to apply for those of their old jobs that were still available alongside the men who had been hired to replace them. But in a way, they had made their point: the imperial spoils of the counterrevolution were creating a class of men in St. Louis who were answerable to no one but themselves, a "local nobility," in the words of W. M. Reedy, the iconoclastic journalist and author of a history of the 1877 General Strike, "that controlled everything worth owning" and "bought aldermen like cattle." It was in this context of class conflict turbocharged by the accumulation of the spoils of empire that St. Louis entered the twentieth century.[61]

6 | THE BABYLON OF THE NEW WORLD

By the rivers of Babylon, there we sat down, yea, we wept, when
we remembered Zion.

We hanged our harps upon the willows in the midst thereof.

For there they that carried us away captive required of us a song;
and they that wasted us required of us mirth, saying, Sing us one
of the songs of Zion.

How shall we sing the Lord's song in a strange land?

—Psalm 137:1–4

THE 1904 WORLD'S FAIR IN ST. LOUIS IS REMEMBERED BY SOME
as the high-water mark of the city's history—the moment when all the
world was assembled in tribute to the city's greatness, the moment at
the crest of the rise, before the beginning of the long decline. But for the
railroad barons and industrial princes of the Big Cinch, the fair was intended to mark not an end, but a beginning—the self-conscious passage
from one period of imperial history into another. Termed the Louisiana Purchase Centennial Exposition, the 1904 World's Fair celebrated
the "civilization" of the continent. And on that legacy of conquest,
it founded a vision for the coming century—modern, technological,

commercial, imperial, American. "The Babylon of the New World," the civic booster and impresario of the move-the-capital-to-Missouri movement Logan Uriah Reavis termed St. Louis at the turn of the century. Reavis meant it as a compliment, emphasizing the idea of an imperial capital to which all of the known world paid tribute, a center of learning and culture. And indeed, in its ambition, scope, and arrogance, the fair was a Babylonian gathering-in of all the peoples, things, and knowledge of the known world, a vast imperial harvest. But the comparison was double-edged, at least for anyone who had read the Old Testament. For St. Louis at the turn of the century was more like the Babylon remembered by the Israelites: presenting itself to the world in the splendor of its boundless ambition, but rotten at the core.[1]

If St. Louis was Babylon, the city where the assembled wonders of civilization could never quite conceal the imperial corruption, then Theodore Dreiser was its chronicler—or at least its gossip columnist. The journalist and novelist, author of *Sister Carrie* and *An American Tragedy*, began his career as a newspaperman in St. Louis, and the city figured prominently in his autobiography, *Newspaper Days*. Dreiser is often credited as one of the progenitors of American naturalism, the effort to set aside conventional morality in favor of the unstinting representation of the base motivations and animal urges that explain human behavior and the Darwinian underpinnings of modern social existence. St. Louis was Dreiser's laboratory for the exploration of human urges and desires, his test kitchen. He devoured St. Louis, moving freely between the enclaves of imperial whiteness and the leftover spaces inhabited by the driven-out and the left-behind, those fighting for survival on the underside of the history of American freedom. His chronicle of Gilded Age St. Louis provides an itinerary of the pleasures of impunity and empire, of the places a man like Dreiser could go and the things he could do—the things that money would buy and whiteness would allow—as well as a sense of the disquiet and moral decay at the heart of the city that W. C. Handy called "the Capital of the Sporting World." St. Louis was the players' playground, a place where the right kind of man with the right kind of money could get anything he wanted.[2]

Dreiser, writing for the *Globe-Democrat* and then the *Republic*, spent a lot of time in the taverns and alleys of the city's downtown, where the poor built a vernacular metropolis interleaved with the busy streets of the rising city. These were people who had come to St. Louis in the years after the Civil War and the failure of Reconstruction, seeking safety and a better life and looking for work in the breweries and foundries and brickworks of the city: African Americans from the South, leaving behind the lynching, white-capping, and sharecropping of the period historians often refer to as "the Nadir" of Black life in the United States; Russian Jews fleeing pogroms; poor whites from rural Missouri. Between 1880 and 1890, the population of the city grew by almost 30 percent, to 450,000; by 1900, it was closer to 600,000. The rail networks and rivers that accounted for the city's continued imperial rise also facilitated a second-order accumulation of racial, political, and economic refugees.

Dreiser was both attracted and repulsed by the raw, open lives of the city's poor: by the chop suey houses that were "hangouts for crooks and thieves and disreputable tenderloin characters generally"; by "those horrible grisly waterfront saloons and lowest tenderloin dives and brothels"; by "the patois of thieves and pimps and lechers and drug fiends"; by the "Jews" and the "Blacks" and the "rundown Americans," by which he meant poor whites, who lived in wooden shanties built up in the alleys where even the police were afraid to go alone; by "the ragpickers, chicken dealers, and feather sorters . . . the tang of the life here, rich, complicated, and mystic."[3]

In the summer of 1893, in the first months of the depression that would later serve as the frame for *Sister Carrie*, Dreiser received a tip that took him to "an old half-decayed brick barn" in an alley behind North Levee Street. An old man had been caught paying a girl of eight or nine a couple of pennies and a piece of candy to give him what Dreiser winkingly referred to as a "French Massage." The police had rescued the man from an angry mob and taken him to the station on North Seventh Street, but by the time Dreiser arrived the man had been released. Indeed, there was no record of his having been arrested at all. When Dreiser finally managed to wring the man's name out of a police captain he knew, he was told that the man, named Nelson, had been let go without charges. "He's an old man with a big wholesale business in 2nd Street, never arrested before, and he has a wife and grown sons and daughters," the policeman explained. So great was what he had to lose that it could not be taken from him, not for the sake of a crime against a poor little refugee girl in any event. Not in St. Louis.

Dreiser took the streetcar out to the West End, where he found Nelson sitting on the steps of his large brick house. The wholesaler sprang up, hurried to meet Dreiser at the gate, and offered him a bribe to kill the story. In his own telling, Dreiser was neither surprised by what the man had done nor terribly upset by it. Dreiser "could not," he wrote, "help sympathizing" with him. "Sex vagaries, as I was beginning to see were not as uncommon as the majority supposed . . . was not the child, with its instinct to accept almost as much to blame as the man?" He was only surprised that the man had offered him just $10 to kill a story he thought was probably worth a thousand. Not until he tried to submit the article he wrote on the streetcar going back downtown did he realize that the wealthy man was playing a deeper game than he had anticipated. "You can't make much out of a case of that kind," the editor at the *Republic* told Dreiser. "The public wouldn't stand for it. You can't tell what really happened. And if you attack the police for concealing it, then they'll be down on us." The crimes of men like Nelson were recorded in white ink.[4]

Dreiser's trip out to the West End was not his only experience, or even his primary one, with the passageway between St. Louis as represented in the stately brick facades and St. Louis as lived in the back alleys and bordellos. Indeed, Dreiser was at that very moment on a journey of discovery, celebration, and full-scale philosophical elaboration of his own "idiosyncrasies." Through his work at the paper, he had learned to see what others referred to as the "vice" district as something else, as what a later generation of scholars might call an "interzone" where white men went to seek forbidden pleasures—"a banker, who had an amazing studio in the red-light district"; "a clairvoyant" who lived near the banker; "a lawyer and a railroad man, both *bon vivants* in the local sense, and both having rooms away from their wives . . . and presumably a wider knowledge of the world than the rest of the city provided them." Before long, Dreiser himself decided to join them and took a room on Morgan Avenue downtown.[5]

Like the vice sojourners whom he emulated, Dreiser was a sybarite—a seeker of sensations beyond the ordinary or allowed. Dreiser's autobiography is 673 pages long, and perhaps fully one-third of those pages are devoted to a minute accounting of his sexual fantasies, frustrations, flirtations, and episodic fulfillment. Although these passages are wildly more interesting than his detailed accounts of the haberdashery and grooming habits of the various men he met in the newspaper business, they are so alarmingly specific as to be what young people today call "cringey." Neither Dreiser's self-abuse nor his self-satisfaction, both of which his autobiography documents in detail, require description. All that is relevant is his fear that youthful masturbation might have made him impotent and his constant anxiety that he had not pleased the women he slept with—an anxiety about women's sexual self-possession that turns out to have been less a personal peculiarity of Dreiser's than an index of a deeper societal reckoning.[6]

During the same years that Dreiser was living on Morgan Avenue, the novelist Kate Chopin was living and writing in another part of St. Louis, the city of her birth. Though Chopin's fiction is largely set in Louisiana, where she lived during the 1870s, she had returned to St. Louis in 1882 and lived there until her death in 1904. Chopin's most famous novel, *The Awakening*, written in St. Louis during these years and published in 1899, tells the story of Edna Pontellier, a society woman, wife, and mother who has an affair with the younger Robert Lebrun. It is the story of life lived along the shoreline of white female sexual longing and fulfillment, a world whose existence Dreiser could intuit, but only imagine through the parallax of his own anxiety. Dreiser's anxiety—or at least the anxiety that white women might have unfulfilled sexual desires and that those desires might lead them into the arms of darker men like the suggestively named Lebrun—was perhaps shared by some of the leading men of St. Louis, who saw to it that *The Awakening* was removed from the shelves at the Mercantile Library and that Chopin would no longer be received in polite society.[7]

Closer to Dreiser's beat at the newspaper, his new apartment, and his understanding of sexuality and desire is the autobiography of Nell Kimball, which provides a catalog of the tricks used by sex workers to please men like Dreiser; indeed, so luridly detailed is that catalog that some have speculated that it was written by a man. However one reads it, one thing is clear: at the center of paid sex was the performance of female pleasure. "We became very good actresses in faking through the sexual pleasure game to a full blown orgasm, thrashing about and crying out love talk and rolling our heads. Most of the time feeling nothing, and thinking all the while maybe the codfish cakes were too salty at lunch, or wondering if tassled high-buttoned shoes were proper for Sunday walking in the park?" That was supposed to be funny, but the insight at its core, about the alienation of spirit from the business of sex in the downtown brothels, was treated with more gravity elsewhere in Kimball's memoir in the observation that the knives in the downstairs kitchen were locked up at night to make sure that the girls did not cut or kill themselves.[8]

The fact that one could pay for a performance provided men like Dreiser with a shortcut around the question of female desire—a contractually agreed fiction that was enough to get successfully to the end of the script. But the existence of that shortcut was also an insistent reminder of something that men could never really know. For Dreiser, the uncertainty—the epistemology of desire amid the social architecture of deception—left him wondering many years later whether he had been up to the job in long-ago sexual encounters. It could be said that the knowledge of female pleasure—that women might or might not enjoy sex—was something from which Theodore Dreiser never recovered.

Whether dogged by fears of sexual inadequacy or perhaps simply seeking something new, Dreiser moved to the apartment on Morgan Avenue late in the summer of 1893. His room overlooked a glass-roofed music hall, "whence nightly and frequently in the afternoons, especially on Sundays, issued all sort of garish music hall clatter . . . until far into the night." He thought he was close to getting what he was seeking one night in his room when he kissed two women in turn. The three of them were fantasizing out loud about dressing the women as men and sneaking into the club downstairs—a place forbidden to white women. Just the proximity of that club electrified the atmosphere in Dreiser's room up above.⁹

Not long after Dreiser moved to Morgan Avenue, a Black man named John Buckner was lynched in Valley Park, west of St. Louis. Buckner was accused of raping a white farmer's daughter, and on January 16, 1894, he was kidnapped by a mob from police custody and hung from a railroad bridge over the Meramec River. Dreiser covered the lynching for the *Republic* and arrived in Valley Park in time to witness both the kidnapping and the hanging. He took notes while lurking in the mob and filed his story that night. "Buckner's crime had been an awful one . . . and proved that this character was that of a brute," he wrote. "Swinging so in the cool morning breeze, with the river's bright waters rippling merrily over innumerable pebbles below, the administrators of such summary justice were fully assured that at least he would not further disturb the peace of their pleasant homes."¹⁰

Writing two decades later, Dreiser described the lynching in one of the most disorienting and revealing passages in his extraordinary confession. "A Negro in an outlying county assaulted a girl," he wrote, "and I arrived in time to see him lynched. But walking in the woods afterward, away from the swinging body, I thought of her." Then, directly following the mention of the lynching of John Buckner, he continued: "If I had been alive before, now I was much more so, within my own blood and nerves. I fairly tingled all over with longing and aspiration. . . . Love—all its possibilities—paraded before my eyes a gorgeous fantastic and sensual procession. Love! Love! The beauty of a woman's body." Something about the lynching of Buckner aroused Dreiser and transformed his anxieties into optimism, his fears of sexual inadequacy into a sensation of erotic potency. His arousal seems to have captured something about the energy of the mob, the sexual energy that these white men felt as they murdered a Black man whose projected animal appetites they openly condemned and secretly desired.[11]

Elsewhere in his autobiography, Dreiser remembered experiencing a similar thrill on the back of a different kind of sexual violence. A friend of his named Peter McCord, who served him as a sort of Virgil of the vice world, shared with him one night the wonders of his particular fetish in "a shabby, poorly-lighted, low-ceiled" brothel where he watched a group of "absolutely black or brown girls with their white teeth and shiny eyes" dance naked while his friend played the flute. They danced, he wrote, "in some weird savage way that took me instantly to the central wilds of Africa . . . so strange they were." As he wrote about it years later, Dreiser remembered sitting there for two or three hours. At first, he felt low, almost criminal. But then he began to "enjoy it intensely." He soon began to elaborate that pleasure into a philosophy, for his enjoyment felt "anything but evil" to him. There, in the brothel, watching naked Black women paid to play out an exoticist's fantasy, Dreiser located the germ of a new morality. "Our theology is too narrow . . . something we haven't the brains as yet to comprehend." There, in the brothel, Dreiser began his quest to imagine a moral order beyond good and evil, beyond the piebald morality of a world "dull enough to make a sacrament of marriage." A new kind of "freedom."[12]

Though Dreiser was not a great philosopher, he was a fearless ethnographer, at least of himself and his kind—the white "sports" of the city of St. Louis. What the progenitor of American "naturalism" took to be an extraordinarily complicated and unorthodox moral position—one that could lead him to understand and sympathize with a wealthy old man who traveled downtown to get sexual service from a little girl—was, in reality, a simple restatement of the practical morality of his time and the society in which he lived: the circular expression of inadequacy, entitlement, privilege, and violence we might call imperial whiteness. The license of empire.

Dreiser did not have the wit to recognize it, but there *was* a moral and philosophical revolution taking place in St. Louis, though it did not have to do with his fantasies of the effect on his sex life of a world where marriage was laid aside in favor of "polygamy and polyandry." Indeed, it was happening in the very neighborhood where he lived, in the dance hall downstairs and in the music that drifted up through his window. The music Dreiser heard, unrecognizable to him but somehow still alluring and stimulating in its exotic proximity, was ragtime—the soundtrack of the emergence of modern African American urban culture.[13]

O n Christmas Day of 1895, just a few blocks from where Dreiser had rented his small flat at the center of empire, Stagolee shot Billy Lyons in a conflict over a Stetson hat. In toasts, in tales, and finally in the famous folk song, the story of Stagolee spread throughout the Mississippi Valley and along the rail lines around the turn of the century. Ma Rainey (backed by Louis Armstrong) would sing about Stagolee, as would Duke Ellington, Cab Calloway, Woody Guthrie, Bob Dylan, and the Grateful Dead. Stagolee is the subject of the song, but he is not its hero. In the classic version, recorded by Mississippi John Hurt in 1928, Stagolee is "cruel," a "bad man": "Do I care about your two babes / Or your loving wife? You done took my Stetson hat / I'm bound to take your life." The song neither questions the wisdom of shooting a man over a hat nor celebrates the vengeance of a man so proud that he would shoot someone for touching his Stetson. It simply recites the elements of the legend: the Stetson, the .44, the wife and children, and the gallows. Stagolee was an African American legend, not a role model. He was the original gangster.[14]

When he shot Billy Lyons, Stagolee was in Bill Curtis's saloon on the corner of Eleventh and Morgan in St. Louis. His government name was Lee Shelton, and he had come to St. Louis on the MKT rail line from Texas, where he was born in 1865. He was known as "Stack Lee" or "Stacker Lee" after a steamboat on the Lee Steamboat Line, which ran between Memphis and St. Louis. The ships of the Lee Steamboat Line were favored by Black passengers and also, it was rumored, by pimps and prostitutes. And indeed, Lee himself was a pimp—or as they said on the street in St. Louis, a "mack," after the French *Maquereau*. When Shelton walked in, wearing a long cape over a bright blue suit, a pleated shirt, yellow calfskin gloves, and narrow-toed patent leather shoes, with a ring on his finger, a stickpin in his lapel, and a high-crowned, soft-brimmed white Stetson hat, Lyons was standing at the bar. Shelton called out, boldly, "Who's treating?" Lyons was a substantial man himself, brother-in-law to a saloon-keeper, a Black ward boss and a tough guy. He knew Shelton, however, and bought him a drink, and the two men sat at the bar and laughed and talked.

Soon the conversation turned into an argument, and Shelton took Lyons's bowler hat and crushed in its crown. Lyons grabbed Shelton's hat, demanding that Shelton pay him "six bits" for his own crushed bowler. Shelton drew the famous Smith and Wesson .44 and told Billy Lyons he would kill him if Lyons did not give him back his Stetson. Lyons pulled out a knife and walked toward Shelton. "You cock-eyed son of a bitch, I'm going to *make* you kill me," witnesses remembered him saying. Billy Lyons's death certificate records that Shelton shot him in the "abdomen." The dying man staggered toward the bar, still holding the Stetson, until Shelton snatched it from his hands and walked out of the bar. "N—r, I told you to give me my hat."[15]

The neighborhood where Lee Shelton shot Billy Lyons, the neighborhood where Dreiser sojourned and fantasized about the things he could do if only he had the courage and the chance, was known as

"Deep Morgan," for the east-west street along which the barrooms and bordellos—many of them Black-owned—were arrayed. Although Lee Shelton's house on Twelfth Street still stands, most of the structures in the architectural record of these times have been torn down and covered over. Today there is a bank on the corner of Eleventh and (what was) Morgan, just up the street from the America's Center Convention Complex and the Dome at America's Center, the onetime home of the St. Louis Rams football team. Morgan Street is today known as Delmar—a street name that has become a byword for segregation in the city of St. Louis. Ask anyone from the city and they will tell you: south of Delmar is white, north of Delmar is Black.

But in the 1890s, Deep Morgan was something different. Along with Chestnut Valley, the east-west corridor a few blocks to the south, Deep Morgan was the domain of pimps and prostitutes, like Lee Shelton and his best girl Lillie, but also of Black saloon-keepers and ward bosses, like Bill Curtis and Billy Lyons's powerful brother-in-law Henry Bridgewater, who was one of the richest Black men in St. Louis and owned a saloon nearby, on the corner of Eleventh and Lucas. Henry Bridgewater's, Bill Curtis's Bar, the Silver Dollar, Tom Turpin's Rosebud Bar, Madam Babe's Castle Club, Jim Ray's Falstaff Club, William Walker's Alcove Café—these are just a few of the best remembered of the Black-owned clubs of the 1890s. The Black population of St. Louis had increased by 600 percent during the 1860s, and their numbers continued to grow as refugees came north to escape the sharecropping and night-riding white supremacy of the 1880s and 1890s South.[16]

The Black clubs in Deep Morgan and along the Chestnut Valley were sites of economic power and political organization. Men like Tom Turpin and Henry Bridgewater were property owners and emergent political bosses—participants, like their white counterparts, in the pay-to-play political world of police protection and ward-heeling machine politics. Several of the clubs served as meeting places for Black men's social organizations, like the Four Hundred Club; others hosted ward meetings for the Republican Party and, after 1896, even meetings of Black Democrats. Some Black leaders in St. Louis, most notably James Milton Turner, became disillusioned with the city's Republican machine; indeed, the leading historian of Deep Morgan attributes the quarrel between Shelton and Lyons to the fact that Shelton had become so frustrated with the Republicans' inattention to the Black voters who had traditionally supported them that he had become a Democrat.[17]

Another St. Louis murder ballad of the 1890s (the genre can fairly be said to have originated in the city), "Frankie and Johnny," tells the story of Johnny getting caught dancing with the wrong woman by his "sweetheart" Frankie, who had walked down to the corner to buy a bucket of beer. "Frankie and Johnny," a love story, begins, "Frankie and Johnny were lovers / Oh Lordy, how they could love." And it is a story of the anger of a woman who cared for her man: "Frankie and Johnny went walking / Johnny had a brand new suit / Frankie paid a hundred dollars / Just to make her man look cute." And of unfaithfulness: "Johnny, man, a lovin' up, That high-brow Nellie Bly" on Clark Avenue, a couple of blocks over from Chestnut. "Frankie and Johnny" tells a story about Black love in St. Louis—a certain kind of story, to be sure, about the hurting kind of love, for it ends with Frankie shooting Johnny dead with his own .44. But the ballad is a story about Black love nonetheless: about the fierce attachments between people whom the minstrel shows and "darky songs" of the day portrayed as feckless followers of fleeting pleasure. And finally, it is yet another story about a Black woman's sexual self-possession: about Frankie keeping Johnny in clothes because they were in love and he made her happy; about Frankie refusing to allow Johnny to be in the arms of Nellie Bly, because "he was her man"; about Frankie shooting Johnny, "roota-toot-toot," as he tried to run away, because "he done her wrong." It is a story about the density and complexity (and fragility) of life in Deep Morgan and along the Chestnut Valley, neighborhoods for which St. Louis was famous in the 1890s, and about the lives of those who lived there and are all but forgotten today.

St. Louis was known in the 1890s as a "sporting city"—indeed, as *the* sporting city. For a brief period after the Civil War, St. Louis had been the only city in the United States where prostitution was legal. Under the city's "Social Evil" laws, passed between 1870 and 1874, sex workers were licensed by the board of health and brothel-keepers paid fees that were put toward the care of "abandoned women" in the city's Institution for the Houseless and Homeless and the treatment of the carriers of sexually transmitted disease at City Hospital. An 1871 police census found that there were over 1,200 prostitutes in the city, working out of about 150 houses. By 1894, prostitution had been outlawed for two decades, but little had changed. In that year, the city declared the entire area bounded by Market, Washington, Jefferson, and Twelfth Street—a seventy-two-square-block area—to be overrun with houses of "ill-repute." Whatever was on the books in St. Louis in 1894, however, in Chestnut Valley and Deep Morgan—the "sporting" part of St. Louis—the law was something different. Patrolmen demanded and were provided with meals, liquor, cigars, and sex in exchange for looking the other way during periodic vice reform panics and providing protection from violent johns. "The police, the law courts, and the whorehouse with solid protection worked together," concluded the autobiography of the sex worker Nell Kimball.[18]

Along with the sex trade, St. Louis was famous for gambling— poker, faro, and the numbers (also known as "the state lottery" and "the policy"). Here, too, the police took a cut, and they were frequently involved in scandals. For instance, an 1868 investigation cleared officers on the beat (not for the last time) of allegations of being drunk on duty and, in one case, riding a horse into a saloon while in uniform; sexually abusing women in their custody under the pretense of "searching" their persons; dining in the brothel of the notorious Madame Callahan; turning a blind eye to gambling and the rampant violation of the "blue laws," which legislated the closing of barrooms, music halls, and theaters on Sundays; and standing idly by when a bull and a bear were pitted in a fight against one another for public entertainment. In the same vein, it became apparent in 1878 that the gambling interest in the city was making decisions about hiring, firing, and promotion within the police department, and in 1883 an internal investigation revealed that several members of the Police Commission had been forced to submit undated letters of resignation upon their appointment to the commission to ensure their compliance while they served. Later in 1883, the records of an investigation into police corruption that had begun earlier in the year disappeared from inside the Four Courts building downtown. St. Louis was a gangster city with a gangster police department, much of which operated as the uniformed wing of the Babylonian capitalists of the Big Cinch and the various smaller cinches that ran the demimonde in Deep Morgan and elsewhere.[19]

In 1882, the *St. Louis Post-Dispatch* ran an extraordinary series of articles entitled "Where's the Policy?" that simply listed the addresses of all the gambling houses in the city; shortly thereafter, in another series, it published the addresses of all the brothels that were hiding in plain sight, cloaked only by the impunity of police protection. In the early 1890s, Theodore Dreiser remembered, women were openly arrayed in the windows and on the porches of the "bagnio district, stretching from 12th and Chestnut to 22nd or 23rd . . . and girls walked the streets for hire [on] Olive Street between 6th and 12th." For those on the outside of the game, St. Louis could be a tough place to survive. Dreiser remembered watching a "large powerful Irish policeman" on a sidewalk dragging an old woman, in the gutter, down the street by her hair, the other passers-by either "thinking nothing of it" or being "too cowardly" to intervene—a judgment that applied, unsurprisingly, to Dreiser himself. "You goddamned bitch . . . goddamned drunken fucking old whore," the cop screamed as he beat her with his nightstick. Among the police, this was known as "curbstone justice." The bluesman W. C. Handy, who spent a formative year in St. Louis, remembered the city for "the brutality of the police," who would use yard-long nightsticks to drive vagrants off empty lots at night. For the poor and the vulnerable, the message was clear: either join the hustle and get some protection, or get out of town.[20]

Along with "Stagolee" and "Frankie and Johnny," Deep Morgan was memorialized in the song "Duncan and Brady"—or, as Handy remembered it, "Brady, He's Dead and Gone," another of the classic murder ballads of the 1890s and a classic anthem of the fight against police brutality. The song tells the story of the shooting of patrolman James Brady in Starkes's Tavern on Eleventh Street in the fall of 1890. The government record of the case portrays Brady's death as the result of an ambush: drawn into the tavern to stop a fight, he was shot in the head by an out-of-control Black man, William Henry Harrison Duncan. The song remembers Brady differently, describing him as "King Brady," a crooked cop who had "been on the job too long"; as a "big fat man," with "a mean look in his eye," who would "shoot somebody just to see him die"; and as a cop who tried to break up the wrong card game, a gangster cop temporarily (and fatally) out of his depth:

> Well, Duncan, Duncan was tending the bar
> Along comes Brady with his shiny star
> Brady says, Duncan, you are under arrest
> And Duncan shot a hole right in Brady's chest
> Yes, he been on the job too long
>
> Brady, Brady, Brady, well you know you done wrong
> Breaking in here when my game's going on
> Breaking down the windows, knocking down the door
> And now you're lying dead on the barroom floor
> Yes, you been on the job too long

If you listen, you can almost hear how the vernacular wisdom of that refrain sounded on the street in Deep Morgan: "You been on the job too long."[21]

The barrooms and bordellos in Deep Morgan and along the Chestnut Valley all employed piano players, virtually all of them Black men, to entertain their guests, and out of the crucible of imperial license, sexual longing, and artistic genius in the brothels of St. Louis came one of the definitive art forms of the twentieth century—ragtime. Johns looking for sex in St. Louis first entered a parlor where they were served drinks and met the girls. The girls themselves got a fifth of the price of the drinks the men bought downstairs, as well as a third of what they paid to go upstairs. So the music had to be right: cheery and sexy and suggestive. In the United States after the Civil War, that meant that it had to be Black. Through the 1870s and 1880s, the music played in the houses was the minstrel music of Stephen Crawford, and a generation of Black pianists began their careers playing "darky song," which served as the background music for the for-a-fee sexual license of men like Dreiser. Scott Joplin, generally recognized as the greatest of the ragtime composers and the founder of the form (or at least the first to successfully sell it in standard notation), was one of them.[22]

Joplin, like Lee Shelton, had come to Missouri from Texas on the MKT. He began his musical career as a member of the Texarkana Minstrels, a quartet that performed at reunions of Confederate veterans. By 1890, he had made his way to Sedalia, a railroad boomtown in central Missouri, where the new "piano-thumping" music was starting to be played in the brothels and Black clubs along the main drag. Joplin often sat in at the Maple Leaf Club, where he began to bend the phrases through which minstrelsy had represented the arrival of a Black character onstage into a new sort of music. The music Joplin played was insistently syncopated: it separated the beat played in the bass clef from that played in the treble, creating novel depth and counterpoint within each piece. Where the bass maintained the continuous 4/4 (or, less frequently, 3/4) tempo of the popular music of the era, the treble sped and slowed polyrhythmically and discontinuously. Although there was syncopated music before ragtime (musicologists often point to several bars of Beethoven's Piano Sonata, Op. 111), it

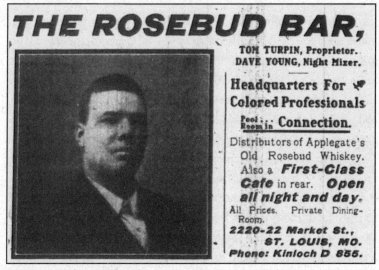

In the 1890s, the city of St. Louis was known as a "sporting city"—an "anything goes" city of players, pimps, and prostitutes. The city's nightlife supported a number of Black-owned bars and a rich musical scene out of which ragtime music emerged. (State Historical Society of Missouri)

was from Joplin and the pianists he met, played with, learned from, and influenced in St. Louis that the characteristic ragtime rhythm of modern jazz and the blues emerged.[23]

In the 1890s, Joplin took the MKT back and forth from Sedalia to St. Louis, where he played in the clubs in Chestnut Valley and along Market Street. The piano player Charles Thompson recalled that Joplin and his fellow player and composer Louis Chauvin "had a string of followers as they strutted about the district," remembering that "when Joplin returned for a visit there would be just like a parade down Market St." They played at the Silver Dollar Saloon, where Tom Turpin, a man so large he could not sit down at the piano, and the composer of the genre-defining "Harlem Rag" in 1892, presided behind the bar.[24]

W. C. Handy remembered that Black quartets from all over the nation, his among them, gathered in St. Louis in 1892. Many of them, including Handy, had first traveled to Chicago, intending to be there for

the World's Fair. On arriving, they found that the fair had been post-
poned for a year, and so, rather than staying in Chicago, they moved on
to St. Louis, whose sporting reputation promised more opportunities
for musicians. By the mid-1890s, the city was crowded with musicians.
In fact, by the time Joplin started traveling to St. Louis, he sometimes
had a hard time finding a piano to play. So deep was the talent in the
barrooms and theaters along Chestnut Valley that one of the nation's
most renowned musical innovators, however talented as a composer,
found that he did not have the technical ability to hold his place on
the stage. It was in St. Louis that Handy—who was sleeping rough in
a vacant lot at the corner of Twelfth and Morgan, a block up the street
from where Billy Lyons would shortly meet his untimely end—first
heard the music that he said inspired the rhythms of the blues.[25]

Ragtime, which took its name from the ragpickers at the edge of
the city's economy, sounds bright and colorful on the topside and is
usually propelled by a rolling, oblong stride in the bass. Sometimes,
as in Joplin's most famous pieces, "The Maple Leaf Rag" (1899) and
"The Entertainer" (1902), the bass seems to lead into and support the
treble. In others, like "A Real Slow Drag" from Joplin's 1911 opera
Treemonisha, the bass and treble almost seem to work at cross-purposes
as the bright melody is insistently pulled back by the heavy, repetitive
bass line. Common to all the songs is a play of surface and depth, of
lines diverging from one another and then coming back together, of
the insistent tinkling melody pushing out to the front and then being
called to account by the implacable rolling bass—the way Lillie Shelton and Lee Shelton might have looked as they walked down the street
together, or the way Frankie and Johnny loved and the undertow in
her love that would never let him go. Joplin wrote the soundtrack for
desire and dread, for the inflated festivity of the night before and the
pounding payback of the morning after, for pleasure rung out of pain,
for the hard work that subtended the easy life. For the rumble and the
bell of the streetcar that carried the wealthy white men of the West
End downtown to Chestnut Valley and Deep Morgan.[26]

Beginning in 1889, the first electric streetcar in St. Louis ran along Lindell Boulevard, from the middle of downtown out to Forest Park, where the rich people lived. It was a sensation at the time and even found its way into the song "Duncan and Brady." Middle-class whites began to move out to the West End and use the cars to commute into the city to work; it was in these years that "inner-ring" suburbs such as Webster Groves, Maplewood, and Shrewsbury were incorporated. Suburbanization transformed the geography of domestic service and white supremacy (not to mention sexuality) in the city. To this day, St. Louis is a city of alleyways—small service roads bisecting residential blocks along the backsides of the lots. In the years after the Civil War, as the population of the city expanded, people crowded into these alleys and built small shanties that housed the cooks and cleaners and child-minders who staffed the pleasant outward-facing, street-numbered houses that they entered only through the back door. It was in these alleys that Theodore Dreiser sought out the thick, teeming life of *lumpen* and working-class St. Louis. But as wealthy and even middle-class whites moved out to the suburbs, from which they took the streetcar into work, their domestic servants—largely though not exclusively African American women—began to take the streetcars out from the city to work in the suburbs. Increasingly, the ad hoc pattern of squatter settlement in the alleyways was regularized into a new pattern: real estate "development" in pursuit of rent from working-class tenants.

As wealthy whites moved to the suburbs, the houses and apartments they left behind were transformed into income streams for landlords. In the real estate markets, sellers and landlords extracted income from segregation: surcharges imposed for both the whiteness of the suburbs and the increasingly bounded space of racial reservation in the older parts of the city. Streetcars, suburbs, and segregation reformatted the space of racial capitalism in St. Louis in a pattern that would be eventually formalized in the city's 1916 segregation ordinance, which forbade Black St. Louisans from establishing a residence on any block that was at least "seventy-five percent white."[27]

And where there was money to be made in St. Louis, there was corruption. In an urban replay of the imperial corruption of racial capitalism and the railroad, St. Louis at the turn of the century was the most outrageously and notoriously corrupt city in the nation—the city of "the boodle," a single word denoting both the practice and the take. In 1902, muckraking journalist Lincoln Steffens wrote an essay on St. Louis for *McClure's* that became the introduction of his landmark account of urban political (and police) corruption in the United States, *The Shame of the Cities* (1904). A year later, amazed at how brazenly the city's elite kept up the vote-buying and boodling even after a bright light had been shined into their backrooms, he wrote a follow-up essay about the city, "The Shamelessness of St. Louis."[28]

St. Louis, according to Steffens, announced itself to the world as "the worst-governed city in America," a city where the leading men were single-mindedly engaged in a ravenous competition to "devour their own city." Even as the central core of the city presented a portrait of urban decline—taps oozing muddy water ("too thick to drink, too thin to plow," Mark Twain famously dubbed the water in the city); "poorly paved, refuse-burdened streets"; and "dusty or mud-covered alleys" in back of crowded "fire-trap" tenements—the city's businessmen and politicians were busy selling off its future. And the corruption followed from the vice. The city government was so full of saloon-keepers, Steffens remarked, that an old joke had it that city hall could be emptied by hiring "a boy to rush into a session and call out, 'Mister, your saloon is on fire!'"[29]

According to Steffens, everything in St. Louis politics—every franchise approval, every property easement, every vote in favor, every vote against—had a price. "There was a price for a grain elevator, a price for a short switch; side tracks were charged for by the linear foot, but at rates which varied according to the nature of the ground taken; a street improvement cost so much. . . . As there was a scale for favorable legislation, so there was one for defeating bills." And the biggest hustle of them all: the fraudulent sale of the suburban railway to its only competitor, the St. Louis Transit Company—a sale that promised its principals millions in return for what turned out to be the $144,000 it took to buy the St. Louis city council.[30]

The occasion for Steffens's piece was a years-long investigation of municipal corruption led by a maverick district attorney named Joseph Folk. Over the course of several years, Folk investigated a rolling set of conspiracies between local businessmen, bankers, and political leaders to buy and fix virtually every matter that came before the St. Louis city council. By the end of Folk's time in office, a cross-section of the city's elite had either gone to jail or fled to Mexico, and he had been propelled to national prominence as "Holy Joe," the governor of Missouri, and the paladin of the "Missouri Idea," which became the inspiration for much of the Progressive emphasis on "good government" over the first decade of the century.[31]

The occasion for Folk's crusade was, as Steffens noted at the beginning of his first essay in *McClure's*, the city's bid to host the 1904 World's Fair—the grand scheme of the city's elite to turn the nation's sporting city into the global archetype of modern civilization. By 1890, St. Louis had slipped a place in the rankings behind Chicago, but was still the fifth-largest city in the United States. The city had the largest train station, brewery, chemical plants, brickworks, and electric plant on the continent. After mounting an unsuccessful bid to host the Columbia Exposition, which had gone off in Chicago in 1893, St. Louis succeeded in securing the 1904 fair, which was promoted as a celebration of the one hundredth anniversary of the Louisiana Purchase and organized by a board of local luminaries and philanthropists—eleven of the twelve were members of the Veiled Prophet organization—and headed by David Francis, the grand oracle of the Big Cinch, the boss of bosses. Seldom in the history of the world had there been (and rarely has there been since) such a gathering of professional racists, keepers of human zoos, and Western civilizational luminaries as there was in Forest Park and on the campus of nearby Washington University during the summer and fall of 1904.[32]

The conventional estimate is that 20 million people attended the fair, which began when Theodore Roosevelt pushed a gold button in the White House and instantaneously illuminated the fairgrounds eight hundred miles away in Forest Park. Because tickets to the fair were sold in books and visitors often went more than once (sixteen-year-old St. Louisan T. S. Eliot, for instance, used all but one of the fifty tickets in his own book, which is preserved today at the Missouri Historical Society), that number surely overstates the attendance figure. Nevertheless, the figure of 20 million entrances (as opposed to entrants) gives some idea of the terrific scale of the seven-month-long fair—it works out to just under 100,000 entrants a day in a city of around 600,000 inhabitants. On the weekends, a train a minute left Union Station for the fairgrounds.[33]

During the fair, something like 20,000 people lived and worked in 1,500 buildings scattered across the 1,300 acres of Forest Park. The same 264-foot, 4,200-ton, 2,000-horsepower Ferris wheel that had dominated the skyline of the Chicago fair now seemed small in St. Louis, where the fair was more than twice as big. The Ferris wheel had been transported at a cost of several hundred thousand dollars and the lives of nine men who died during its reassembly. The Liberty Bell, never loaned for exhibition before or since, was escorted from the rail depot to the grounds by a parade of 75,000 schoolchildren. One exhibit boasted dozens of babies living in incubators, who were rotated out into cribs as they became healthy enough to survive without intensive support. A 900-foot indoor whirlpool pumped 49,000 gallons of water (drawn from the Mississippi) per minute. A nine-acre reconstruction of the Tyrolean Alps, sponsored by the beer baron Adolphus Busch, hosted performances of the famous Oberammergau Passion Play, a reproduction of Mozart's Salzburg birthplace, and a café that seated 2,500 at a time. An eleven-acre reconstruction of Jerusalem and the Holy Land included reproductions of the stable where Jesus was born, the Garden of Gethsemane where he was betrayed by Judas, and the Temple of the Mount, where Mohammed ascended to Paradise. Visitors could see Ulysses S. Grant's St. Louis County log cabin and the train car that carried the assassinated Abraham Lincoln from Washington, DC, to his burial place in Springfield, Illinois. They could admire Jim Key, the educated horse who could spell, sort mail, make change, and remove a silver dollar from a glass jar without spilling (or drinking) a drop of the liquid inside. They could tour a transplanted California ostrich farm. They could dine on hot dogs, hamburgers, cotton candy, peanut butter, ice cream cones, and Dr. Pepper, all of which are credibly said to have been invented (or at least introduced as mass-market staples) on the grounds of the 1904 fair. As a sort of sideshow, St. Louis also hosted the Olympic Games, which were held on the adjacent grounds of Washington University during the summer of 1904. At the center of the grounds stood the Column of Progress, a ten-story classical set piece festooned with eagles and topped with a figure of Progress standing astride a giant garlanded globe.[34]

Combined with the fair and organized in coordination with Washington University was a series of academic events aimed at presenting, in the words of the German psychologist Hugo Münsterburg in his opening address to the International Congress of Arts and Sciences, a "Weltanschauung" for the new century: "a unified view of the whole of reality." Münsterburg's collaborator in industrial psychology, Frederick Winslow Taylor, who would publish *The Principles of Scientific Management* in 1911, was also at the fair, as were the pioneering German sociologist Ferdinand Tönnies, with whom originated the theoretical distinction between society (*gemeinschaft*) and community (*gesellschaft*); the historian Frederick Jackson Turner, whose "frontier thesis" shapes the study of the United States down to the present day; and the German economist and activist Werner Sombart, who would publish "Why No Socialism in the United States?" in 1905. Also in attendance were Woodrow Wilson, the Johns Hopkins historian who would soon become president of the United States; the historian Henry

Adams, the author of a nine-volume history of the early republic and, later, of one of the most famous memoirs in American letters; the philosopher, mathematician, and historian Josiah Royce; and G. Stanley Hall, the eugenicist first president of the American Psychological Association and promoter of the notion that the races of man followed a course of development analogous to those of individual human beings—from infancy and childhood to adulthood and senescence. Max Weber, who published *The Protestant Ethic and the Spirit of Capitalism* in 1905, made his first public appearance at the St. Louis World's Fair, following a five-year nervous breakdown. Mark Twain and Henry James sat down for dinner together at the fair, although both seemed depressed to observers and their much-anticipated conversation has gone unremembered. The teenage T. S. Eliot, we have seen, toured the grounds repeatedly, as did Thomas Wolfe, who remembered the fair in his lugubrious masterpiece *Look Homeward, Angel*; Frank Lloyd Wright, who first encountered Japanese architecture at the fair; and Kate Chopin, who collapsed and died after a humid 90 degree day at the fair in August 1904. On the closing day of the Congress, the mathematician Henri Poincaré delivered a critique of Newtonian mechanics that provided the intellectual foundation for Einstein's 1905 papers outlining the equivalence of mass and energy and the special theory of relativity. Nearby, in the Hall of Technology, a cube of Ernest Rutherford's radium glowed uncannily through the summer and into the fall. During the summer of 1904, St. Louis was not simply the hub of the nation's western empire—it was the center of the world.[35]

And yet it was the city's own imperial history and aspirations that framed the fair. The discipline that presided over the fair was neither psychology nor sociology, nor even physics, but anthropology. Prospero more than Prometheus was the spirit that prefigured the World's Fair in Forest Park. Like the rest of the exhibits on the grounds—like the baby incubators on the midway ("the Pike"), the miniature railways, the motorized airships, the X-ray machine, and the world's first air conditioner and player piano and cordless phone and wall plug and fax machine and answering machine—the world's intellectuals were self-consciously positioned by organizers to make a point about history and civilization. "Over and above all the fair is the record of the social conditions of mankind," wrote Frederick Skiff, the director of exhibits, "registering not only the culture of the world at this time, but indicating the particular plans along with which different races and different people may safely proceed, or, in fact have begun to advance towards a still higher development." The purpose of the fair, in the words of David Francis, the chief executive of the Louisiana Purchase Exposition Corporation, was to demonstrate to visitors that human history had reached its "apotheosis" in Forest Park. Were all the works of prior civilization to be blotted out, he concluded, the records of the fair would provide the "necessary standards" for its rebuilding.[36]

In Forest Park in the summer of 1904, the directors of the exposition's Anthropology Department, including the founder of American cultural anthropology, Franz Boas, presided over the assembly of the largest human zoo in world history. An estimated ten thousand people were conscripted to play a role in the account of progress by the Anthropology Department. Brought to St. Louis for the fair, they lived for its duration on the grounds and were exhibited in ersatz reconstructions of their "native habitats" for curious visitors to Forest Park. Among them were Ainu people from Japan, "Patagonians" from the Andes, and members of fifty-one of the First Nations of North America—including Chief Joseph of the massacred Nez Perce, the Comanche soldier Quanah Parker, and the Apache leader Geronimo. Geronimo was assigned to pose for nickel-apiece souvenir photographs with white visitors and play the part of the Sioux leader Sitting Bull in daily reenactments of the Battle of the Little Bighorn.[37]

Elsewhere on the grounds lived Ota Benga, who had been sold along with seven other people to the American Samuel Verner, who had traveled to King Leopold's Congo Free State under the auspices of the fair's Anthropology Department to purchase Mbuti "pygmies" with the sole purpose of exhibiting them at the fair. Benga, who was about twenty at the time of his sale, had had his teeth filed into sharp points as a child, and was exhibited at the fair as a "cannibal." Benga and the other enslaved Africans sometimes danced and performed before as many as twenty thousand people at a time. For a time after the fair, under the auspices of the white supremacist racial theorist Madison Grant, Benga was kept in a cage at the Bronx Zoo. After his release, Benga worked in a tobacco factory in Virginia, where he began to wear Western clothes and had his teeth capped. In March 1916, in Lynchburg, Virginia, Ota Benga built a large fire, danced, and then shot himself through the heart.[38]

These terrible, soul-warping images were designed to be that way: the fair intentionally produced instrumental images of Geronimo, Ota Benga, and other people of color that would be suitable for deployment in a larger argument about white supremacy and the pathway to racial progress. "There is no document of civilization that is not at the same time a document of barbarism," wrote Walter Benjamin in what might be seen as an evaluation of the savagery with which the organizers of the fair assembled living human beings in a zoo as a testimony to their own advanced position in the "march of human progress." The historical record of the fair tells us much more about people like David Francis and Franz Boas than it does about people like Geronimo and Ota Benga.[39]

The forty-seven-acre "Philippine Reservation" in the southwest corner of the fairgrounds was the 1904 fair's ideological core as well as its most popular attraction—ninety-nine out of a hundred visitors to the fair visited the reservation, estimated Francis. Although the US war against the Philippines had officially ended in 1902, American troops were still fighting insurgents on several of the islands of the Philippine archipelago. The Philippine exhibit in St. Louis was, at once, a celebration of conquest, an operation in an ongoing counterinsurgency campaign, and an argument about why the first two were necessary actions taken in the support of racial civilization and social progress. The War Department, with the support of William Howard Taft, the US military governor of the Philippines, coordinated the collection and transport of the one thousand eventual inhabitants of the Philippine Reservation, as well as of the battalion of Philippine Scouts—four hundred US-aligned Filipino soldiers, who served under white officers. The fair, Taft argued, would exert "a very great influence on completing the pacification of the Philippines" by creating a cadre of Filipinos who would be informed about the wonders of modern civilization and overawed by its inexorability. The Philippine Reservation was, one could argue, a civilizationist psyop—an act of psychological warfare.[40]

Visitors to the Philippine Reservation entered through a "Walled City" meant to recall the fortification of the conquered city of Manila. Arrayed around the grounds were villages populated by various officially designated ethnic "types," who were themselves categorized according to their supposed level of civilization: the "intelligent" Visayans; the "fiercely" Islamic Moros; the "savage" Bagóbo; the "monkey-like" Negritos, one of whom came to be known as "Missing Link"; and the "picturesque" Igorots. Camped around the edges of the Reservation, beyond the ersatz ethnic enclaves, were the Scouts, who were charged with keeping order inside the Reservation and exemplifying the final stages of the civilizing process.[41]

Like the Philippine Reservation, the human exhibits at the Louisiana Purchase Exposition were arranged spatially in a way that was meant to tell a story about racial progress. The idea was as destructively simple as it was sadly familiar: all of human history marked linear progress from less to more civilization, and the middling races—the Igorots, if not the Negritos—could be molded to become productive members of civilized society. In other words, they could be turned into workers. "There *is* a course of progress running from lower to higher humanity, and all the physical and human types of Man mark stages in that course," wrote William McGee, the leader of the fair's Anthropology Department and the man termed the "overlord of the savage world" by the *St. Louis Post-Dispatch*.[42]

That the Philippine Reservation was called a "reservation" in the first place reflected an important fact about the racial imagination of the fair organizers. In their view, the specific imperial history of the American West—the history that began with the Lewis and Clark expedition—provided the model for the future of the American empire and the world more generally. The legacy of conquest was celebrated throughout the park, in both the massive statuary of noble savagery—Cyrus Dallin's *Sioux Chief* being exemplary in this regard—and the daily restaging of the Battle of the Little Bighorn. But the overriding message of the fair was about consigning the "savage" past to the future progress of "civilization." The "method" of the Anthropology Department, according to McGee, was "to use living peoples in their accustomed avocations as our great object lesson . . . to represent human progress from the dark prime to the highest enlightenment." In McGee's vision, the Louisiana Purchase had begun the "purposeful . . . promotion" of Indians into American citizens. Slowing that down and spinning out the implications, we can see that McGee was proposing the "civilization" of Native Americans—the process of conquest, annihilation, subordination, sequestration, and reeducation that had begun with the Louisiana Purchase (this was the Louisiana Purchase Exposition, after all)—as the model for global racial governance.[43]

And at the center of this vision of global, imperial human progress was the Indian school model of Schurz and Pratt—"America's best effort to elevate the lower races . . . savages made, by American methods, into civilized workers." The Louisiana Purchase Exposition stood at the juncture between Indian wars and overseas imperial ambition, translating the supposed successful culmination of the former into an open-ended justification of the latter. The idea behind the fair was that civilization—racial progress—could take the place of violence as the principal tool of empire, or as one US general put it about the war in the Philippines, "The keynote of the insurrection"—the lesson to be learned—"is not tyranny, for we are not tyrants. It is race." In the eyes of the organizers in the Anthropology Department, as in the words of General Douglas MacArthur (the military governor of the Philippines and father of the more famous General MacArthur who would lead

American soldiers in the Pacific Theater of the Second World War), the fair was to be, like the Philippines itself, a "tuitionary annex" of the United States—a school for civilization.[44]

There was no room at the fair for a story about African American racial progress. The imperial notion of racial malleability and improvement was twinned with a Negrophobic belief in the implacable inferiority of African Americans. The very same Black soldiers who had served as imperial adjutants in the Indian wars, the Spanish-American War, and the Philippine-American War—which were endlessly replayed as the historical backstory of the 1904 fair—were not allowed on the grounds in uniform. All of the fairground restaurants were segregated. Plans for a building celebrating the advances and achievements of African Americans were broached, but never materialized. The plan for a single "Negro Day" at the fair was eventually canceled, and a speaking invitation to the ex-slave, educator, and up-by-your-bootstraps conservative Booker T. Washington was withdrawn. The only representation of African Americans on the fairgrounds was at "the Old Plantation," where Black actors tended a garden, staged a fake religious revival, sang minstrel songs, and cakewalked in an endless loop of white racial nostalgia. And though Scott Joplin composed "The Cascades" as a comment on the famous waterfall at the center of the fairground, ragtime music was banished from the grounds. Not only was ragtime a genuinely avant-garde challenge to the beaux arts classicism that provided the backbone of the fair's aesthetic vision, but its syncopated, polyrhythmic tempo implicitly challenged the linear developmental time of the fair's presentation of human "progress."[45]

The fair provided many opportunities for visitors to insert themselves into its overarching account of racial time. They could, in time-honored fashion, gawk and chuckle at the way other people in the world lived; they could even riot when those other people refused to perform for them, as happened when the crowds threw rocks at the small houses in which Ota Benga and his fellows took shelter when the weather got cold. While marveling at the technological wonders that attested to the ingenuity of their moment in time, they could cast a nostalgic backward glance at the simpler lives led by the human creatures on exhibit. They could draw sharp distinctions between the savage and the civilized based on how they washed and dressed themselves and on what they put into their bodies—the rumor that some of the denizens of the Philippine Reservation ate dogs provided one of the most durable memories of the fair in St. Louis. To this day one of the neighborhoods near the long-gone exposition grounds is called "Dogtown," because it is supposedly where the Filipinos got their dogs. White visitors to the fair had their heads measured ("cephalization") and their manual dexterity and sensory perception tested ("sensitization"), the emergent racial theory's key determinants of civilizational progress.[46]

In a city where one-fifth of the population was foreign-born and twice that many again had parents who were, the fair offered a powerful argument about the solvent character of imperial whiteness. It offered a dirty bargain to the working whites in a city with an enduring strain of labor radicalism: over two hundred stoppages and strikes had disrupted the preparations for the fair, and a property-protecting posse of hired guns in the service of capital had opened fire on a workingmen's parade only four years earlier. Come spend a day enjoying yourselves, the fair beckoned; lay down your placards and your pistols, and take up your rightful place in the front rank of the civilization and the "march of progress." The exhibits at the fair were explicitly designed, in the words of David Francis, to teach the "working citizenry" of the United States (another of the fair's boosters less delicately termed its intended audience the "unlearned" and "unlettered") "about the proper classification, correlation, and harmonization of capital and labor"—about capitalism as a form of racial progress. The fair exhibits were designed to domesticate the restive immigrant workers of St. Louis by turning them into white people.[47]

The Igorot village held a peculiar fascination for white fairgoers. From the moment the Igorot arrived in St. Louis, their near-nudity was a topic of debate. Local moralists feared the effect of so many naked and dark bodies on white women who visited the fair. Government officials, including Taft, worried that the nudity on the Reservation might undermine the case they were trying to make about the success of the civilizing mission of the United States in the Philippines. The leaders of the Anthropology Department, including Boas, argued that the ethnographic value of the exhibit would be destroyed if its inmates were dressed up like bankers or butlers or, as one of them put it in a letter to Taft, "plantation n—s." The question of the properly exotic and yet minimally erotic way to clothe the inhabitants of the federally sponsored human zoo was eventually decided by the president of the United States, Theodore Roosevelt, who reasoned that the stringed codpieces worn by the men in the villages could be draped with loincloths that covered their buttocks and bulges without essentially compromising the realism of the exhibit or its ability to convey the intended message about both the savage simplicity of the Igorot and their ultimate (under the proper imperial tutelage) human improvability.[48]

A photograph taken by Jessie Tarbox Beals, preserved today in the Missouri Historical Society, a short walk away from the place where it was taken, suggests some of the source of the anxiety. Entitled "Mrs. Wilkins, Teaching an Igorrote-Boy the Cake Walk," the image portrays a white woman and an Igorot boy. Dressed in a long white dress, she is lifting the hem with her left hand while reaching out to the boy with her right. He wears a loincloth, a necklace, and a top hat and holds a long thin stick like a baton in his right hand; his left hand, grasped by the woman at the wrist, is arrested, dead-center in the photo, offered, intercepted, and only half-accepted. They stand nearly side by side, the woman just a tiny bit behind and seeming to be stepping in time to the call of an unheard tune. They are laughing. The photograph portrays a moment of human contact, even intimacy, between two people from different worlds—or, as the fair would have it, different times.[49]

Like most any photograph, the image elides the circumstances of its own production, most notably the imperial violence that was the essential condition of its existence. It reframes the historical violence

The St. Louis World's Fair of 1904 sought to link the city's prominence in the history of continental imperialism to future leadership in the imperial management of the globe. The fair featured the largest human zoo in the history of the world and was characterized by an undercurrent of doubt about white women's sexual desire and self-possession. (Missouri Historical Society)

that brought the boy to St. Louis and confined him to the grounds of the fair as a lighthearted moment shared by people from two different places in time. And with the Cake Walk, a minstrel show staple, patterning their common steps, this momentary connection between white and brown is also framed in the dominant idiom of US anti-Blackness. And yet, all that said, the two figures are laughing as they stand there together. And that could be threatening.[50]

"Meet Me in St. Louis," the unofficial theme song of the 1904 fair and one of its most widely remembered artifacts, tells the story of a white woman named Flossie, who cleaned out her closet and abandoned her man to go to the fair. "Meet me in St. Louis, Louis," reads the note that she left him, which provides the song's chorus, "Meet me at the fair . . . We will dance the Hoochee-Koochee" / I will be your "tootsie-wootsie / If you will meet me in St. Louis, Louis / Meet me at the fair." The promised "Hoochee-Koochee" was a reference to the national sensation caused by the dancer Fahreda Mazar Spyropoulos, who, under the name Fatima, danced at the Columbian Exposition in 1893 so suggestively that she was banned from the St. Louis World's Fair. The "hoochie-coochie" was a racially tinted sexual promise. The song goes on to suggest just how far Flossie might go once she makes it to St. Louis:

> *There came to the gay tenderloin,*
> *a Jay who had money to burn,*
> *The poor simple soul*
> *showed a girlie his roll,*
> *and she said, "for some wine dear, I yearn."*
> *A bottle and bird right away,*
> *she touched him then said, "I can't stay."*
> *He sighed, "Tell me, sweet,*
> *where can you and I meet?"*
> *and the orchestra started to play*

The theme song of the 1904 fair was a song about a white woman gone sporting in St. Louis: about the allure of interracial desire and the dark pleasures of the tenderloin that might draw in a young white woman beguiled by the bright fair lights. And about a white man who lost control of his girl.

On July 3, 1904, the *St. Louis Post-Dispatch* framed the interracial imperial fascination that haunted both "Meet Me in St. Louis" and the photograph of "Mrs. Wilkins" as a threat to racial purity. "Filipinos Become a Fad with Foolish Young Girls," read the headline. Later in the week, a group of visiting schoolteachers invited some of the Philippine Scouts to escort them around the grounds. As they walked the grounds, whites in the crowd began to yell at the Scouts, calling them "n—s." The Jefferson Guards—the all-white private police who patrolled the fairgrounds, many of them veterans of the Philippine-American War—gathered and threatened to arrest the Scouts and any of the teachers who continued to stand there with them. Some uniformed US Marines, visitors to the fair, joined the Jefferson Guards in harassing the Philippine Scouts, and a riot ensued. Subsequent reports suggested that as many as two hundred Scouts had faced off with as many whites on the Pike, near the entrance to "Mysterious Asia." Even after the Scouts made their way back to the Philippine Reservation, the paramilitary park police pursued them, firing guns in the air and threatening to burn the Reservation: "Come on boys, let's clean the[m] off the earth!" Two weeks later, six white women and an untold number of Scouts were arrested on the Reservation following another riot at the Café Luzon.[51]

The Louisiana Purchase Exposition was an effort to codify the history that had begun with Lewis and Clark—the history of nineteenth-century St. Louis and the imperial project it sponsored—into a set of lessons that would guide the United States in the twentieth century. It was, in the words of one of its boosters, a "University of the Future." In that way, if in few others, the fair resonated with the work of W.E.B. Du Bois (officially suppressed on the fairgrounds), who had written in *The Souls of Black Folk* (1903) that "the problem of the twentieth century is the problem of the color-line—the relation of the darker to the lighter races of men in Asia and Africa, in America and the islands of the sea." It was against the backdrop of the St. Louis World's Fair that President Theodore Roosevelt, the former Rough Rider and the biographer of Benton, announced his corollary to the Monroe Doctrine while touring the grounds in November. Henceforth, the United States would reserve the right to intervene in the internal affairs of nations anywhere in the Western Hemisphere. The United States, he explained metaphorically, would be the hemisphere's "policeman." The racial and sexual order that prevailed in the city of St. Louis and on the Pike at the World's Fair was to be generalized as a principle of international order. Perhaps with the proper guidance, and under the proper constraints, the subjects of the racial and sexual order—women, workers, the darker races of the world—could learn to like it.

The World's Fair of 1904 was a sanitized and idealized projection of the self-regarding fantasy life of the city's ruling class and their intellectual and cultural collaborators from all over the world. It tried to channel all of the violence, steamy desire, and brittle masculine anxiety that characterized both the history of the city and its daily life into a set of pat lessons about white supremacy and racial progress. The fair was designed, at bottom, to pacify the city's white workers and ensure their proper alignment with the course of freedom-through-capitalism and imperial progress. It was designed, that is, to direct the attention of white workingmen to all of those who were below them on the ladder of civilization and away from those who presided over them from within glassed-in offices above the factory floors where they worked to earn the cost of a day's entrance to the fair. The proof of civilization that sustained the fair and made it materially possible was wrung out of their aching bodies in those factories—not only the machines and products exhibited on the midway but also the economic surplus necessary to the creation of something as grand and frivolous as a disposable material parable about the entirety of human history built out over hundreds of acres of forestland. The mixture of white entitlement and labor discipline, however, was an unstable compound, volatile and likely to explode.

7 | THE SHAPE OF FEAR

Are we not coming more and more, day by day, to making
the statement "I am white," the one fundamental tenet of our
practical morality?

    —W.E.B. Du Bois, "The Souls of White Folk"

On the Fourth of July in 1917, the sociologist, journalist, and activist Ida B. Wells disembarked in East St. Louis. The conductor and the Pullman porters on the train had advised her to stay on board. Fearful for their own safety, Black porters had been locking themselves into unoccupied berths on the sleeping cars as their trains approached the city. Over the past two days, more than a thousand white inhabitants of East St. Louis and several surrounding towns had turned on their Black neighbors, beating them, shooting them down, hanging them from lampposts, and burning their bodies in the street. Once again, the history of St. Louis forecast that of the nation. The 1917 East St. Louis Massacre was the first of several such enormities—most notably in Chicago and Washington, DC, in 1919 and Tulsa in 1921—and the deadliest.[1]

The official death count of thirty-nine seemed low at the time, and it has been questioned by historians ever since. In the immediate aftermath of the massacre, it was generally believed that hundreds had died, their bodies burned and thrown into the creeks surrounding the city. Over three hundred buildings had been burned down, many with their inhabitants inside. As many as five thousand of the twelve thousand or so African American inhabitants of the city had fled across the bridge to St. Louis during the violence, most of them never to return. In East St. Louis in the summer of 1917, the racism that had for so long served capital as a way of both separating and disciplining white workers—with the promise of a share in the spoils, the hollowed collegiality of shared skin, and the episodic threat of banishment and replacement with Black workers—slipped out of their control and ignited the city in a murderous, removalist frenzy of whiteness.[2]

The indomitable Wells walked from the Relay Depot across Cahokia Creek, where the bodies of the dead had been thrown during the massacre, and through the streets of East St. Louis alone, noting the absence of Black people, the burned-out buildings, and the soldiers in the streets. Along the way, she met a soldier, "a mere boy with a gun," who had been deployed by the Illinois National Guard to suppress the violence. "The Negroes won't let the whites alone," he told her. "They killed seven yesterday and three already this morning." If his account of the violence seems incongruous in light of what had actually happened—what anyone standing on the street where he stood could have immediately seen had happened—it was an accurate reflection of the approach to the violence taken by the Illinois National Guard. Rather than trying to end the violence, many had joined in the slaughter for several hours before finally taking control of the city. The first Black people Wells encountered were inside the city hall, where hundreds had taken refuge two days before and where the National Guard had established a command post. Several women were preparing to return to their homes under military escort, and Wells went along with them, riding in the back of a truck that the Red Cross had "commandeered" from the nearby Swift Packing Plant.[3]

Around her lay the smoldering ruins of a city built not just in the shadow but in the image of capital. From the moment of its founding in 1861 by a referendum of railway workers paid a dollar apiece for their votes, the city of East St. Louis was a municipal shell for un-bridled capitalist extraction and unchecked governmental corruption. Municipal government in East St. Louis was a convenient fiction. Where political theory would lead an earnest reader to believe that governments emerged from the shared interests of individuals who banded together to ensure their common welfare, East St. Louis took almost the opposite tack. Another city might try to diminish pollution and public nuisance by passing laws regulating which businesses might locate in which areas, as the city of St. Louis did in 1914, but East St. Louis existed to provide a haven from such regulations. Where another city might levy taxes on business in order to provide services for inhabitants—schools and parks and libraries—the low taxes collected in East St. Louis were generally kept by the tax collector. The city was sustained as a company bookkeeper's fantasy overhung with a sulfu-rous cloud.[4]

The city emerging in what had once been called the American Bottom was admirably situated for industry: at a bottleneck in the flow of agricultural goods from the west to the emerging industrial cities in the east, and near coalfields in southern Illinois that could provide the fuel for heavy industry athwart the Mississippi. The peculiar situation of East St. Louis ensured that it would thrive in the rail era. The Mis-sissippi River formed both a geographic and legal boundary, a point where, even after the opening of the Eads Bridge, rail lines on each side of the river had to converge to cross. That bottleneck provided an opportunity for extraction, and the robber barons of the "bridge arbitrary" responded to the opportunity by manipulating rates in ways that favored those who built their factories and produced their goods on the east side of the river. East St. Louis, Illinois, developed as a railway-rate-subsidized and lightly regulated alternative to St. Louis, Missouri—like Bayonne or Camden in New Jersey, or even Ciudad Juárez in Mexico. By the time of the First World War, twenty-six rail lines converged at East St. Louis, and the city had become a regional center of noxious industry and dangerous work. In East St. Louis, the city native and jazz innovator Miles Davis later wrote, "the smell of manure and cow shit mingled with [the] smell of death."[5]

Indeed, in what became the common pattern, large national corporations simply founded their own municipalities on the margins of East St. Louis, where even the comparatively low taxes (and the occasional cost of buying a local election) could be reduced to something close to zero: Alorton (Illinois) for the Aluminum Ore Company (today's Alcoa); Monsanto Town (now Sauget, Illinois) for Monsanto Chemicals; Wood River (Illinois) for Standard Oil and Roxana (Illinois) for Shell; and National City (Illinois), which was built out of the architectural remains of the 1904 World's Fair, for the National Stock Yards. By the time of the First World War, virtually all of the first families of American capitalism had an arterial tube sucking wealth out of the polluted bottomlands of East St. Louis: J. P. Morgan had the Eads Bridge; Jay Gould had the railroads; Andrew W. Mellon had Aluminum Ore; John D. Rockefeller had Standard Oil; Philip Danforth Armour and Gustavus Swift had their eponymous packing-houses. "East St. Louis," wrote W.E.B. Du Bois in the aftermath of the atrocity of 1917, "was a paradise for high and frequent dividends and the piling up of wealth to be spent in St. Louis and Chicago and New York." The congressional investigation into the violence in 1917 concluded that the corporations with plants in and around East St. Louis cared nothing for the civic life of the cities they founded and oversaw; rather, their sole concern was to "get the men into the plant to work, get the work, and then [do it] all again." It did not take a radical to recognize that East St. Louis was a capitalist wild zone where unbridled exploitation was twinned with formalized impunity.[6]

The city government of East St. Louis during the industrial era served mostly as a vehicle for funneling money into the pockets of the city governors, who made certain to stay out of the way of their corporate overlords. The 1917 investigation uncovered rampant corruption in the city government; indeed, terming it "corruption" seems to understate the issue, imagining as it does that the city government had any other purpose than lining the pockets of the local overseers of the out-of-town industrialists' interests. The city collector, allowed by law to retain 2 percent of city revenue up to a cap of $1,500, was instead keeping 2 percent of *all collections* and thus multiplying his stipend by something close to a hundredfold. In response to a 1913 investigative report in the *St. Louis Post-Dispatch* that the mayor, city attorney, and several aldermen were taking bribes from railroad companies, the city council simply recommended that the relevant city records be immediately destroyed. When a reformist mayor, who had run on the slogan "Make East St. Louis a little more like home, and a little less like Hell," expressed a willingness to release the records to the grand jury, those records mysteriously disappeared from the city vault, never to be seen again. At a similar juncture in an 1884 investigation of municipal corruption, parties unknown had simply burned down city hall.[7]

Locke Tarlton was the Democratic Party boss of surrounding St. Clair County in the years before the massacre, and he provides a convenient emblem of the cavernous greed and boundless cynicism of the political class in East St. Louis and St. Clair County, Illinois, more generally. Tarlton had become wealthy by using information he gained from serving on the county levee board to speculate in land—in one documented case, he made a 400 percent profit off of a swampy river bottom that he held for less than three weeks. In the years before the massacre, he controlled local politics by attempting to mobilize Black voters and then turning right around and creating panic among East St. Louis whites that their city was being "colonized" by Black immigrants. By 1920, according to one standard measure, East St. Louis had the second-poorest city government in the nation, and much of the revenue that actually made it past all of the outstretched hands and into the coffers of city hall was quickly paid out in the form of essential city services like fire and police donated by the city of East St. Louis to the surrounding tax-haven municipalities.[8]

For the out-of-town industrialists, however, the only parts of the local government that really mattered were the assessors and the boards of adjustment, and they got what they paid for: National City's gargantuan packing plants were assessed at cents on the dollar, as were the plants of Aluminum Ore, American Steel, and all the rest. The total assessed value of property in East St. Louis—a city in which *all* of the aluminum ore in the United States was processed, and which vied with Kansas City and Omaha for the distinction of being the nation's second-largest abattoir—was $13 million, a figure that might have been more accurately applied to just one of the larger plants. The novelist Sherwood Anderson wrote of East St. Louis that "nobody's home," and he termed it "the most perfect example, at least in America, of what happens under absentee ownership."[9]

In a pattern that would once again become notorious a century later, much of the revenue of the city government derived from fees and fines—as much as 50 percent from the licensing of saloons, and an additional increment from unlicensed saloons that were allowed to stay open but paid annual fines for their ongoing violation of the license law. Because there were no blue laws in East St. Louis, the city had long served as a Sunday getaway for the St. Louis sporting set. And by every contemporary account, East St. Louis was a "sporting" town: the saloons, storefront casinos, and brothels that surrounded city hall were the bedrock of the local economy. Their names suggest the tone of the city's civic life, among them: the Bucket of Blood, the Yellow Dog, the Monkey Cage, Aunt Kate's Honkytonk ("Something Doing Every Hour"), and Uncle John's Pleasure Palace ("Come In and Be Suited").[10]

Much of this activity was nominally illegal, but what passed for a city government was controlled by the vice lords' landlords, who were controlled in turn by the summer residents of Newport and Watch

Hill—all of whom were happy to allow the city to sink ever further into iniquity and corruption as the bottom line stayed dry. The saloons provided what policemen the city could afford to employ with free food as they walked their beats. The brothels, too, reached a set of accommodations with the local government: in the pre–World War I years, a joke made the rounds about a local judge who had received a new desk in return for going lightly on a prostitute in his court, the joke being that he walked around town saying he wished he had held out for an automobile. East St. Louis in 1917 was a rotten, dirty town; "there was no veil of hypocrisy here," wrote Du Bois, "but a wickedness frank, ungilded, and open." And into this cauldron of meat and steel, along with the greed and the sinfulness, along with the exploitation and the misery and the violence, "some unjust God leaned, laughing, over the ramparts of the heavens and dropped a Black man into the midst."[11]

From its beginnings as a railroad town in the 1860s, East St. Louis had a small, if slowly increasing, Black population. Numbering around one hundred, just 2 percent of the population, in 1870, it grew to about seven hundred (5 percent of the population) by 1890 and to almost six thousand (10 percent of the population) by 1910. Like the wartime migrants who followed them, the Black inhabitants of prewar East St. Louis were mostly migrants from the South who had come north on the Illinois Central seeking relief from the demeaning social rituals, economic exploitation, and relentless racial violence of the Jim Crow South. These were pioneers in the first wave of what came to be called "the Great Migration," and among the first of the million and a half migrants to the North between the beginning of the First World War and the end of World War II, who were themselves at the leading edge of a history that would see almost seven million Black people move from the rural South to the cities of the North and West by the 1970s. In 1910, almost 90 percent of the nation's Black population lived in the South; by 1970, the figure had fallen to 50 percent.[12]

Most immediately, they sought work, but East St. Louis was a hard landing place. "We give the white preference when hiring our labor—always have," the manager of the Armour processing plant testified in 1917. Before the war, Black workers were generally held "in reserve" by the city's leading employers—employed casually or seasonally, if at all. And even as Black workers increasingly found work in the plants during the war, they were almost always employed in unskilled positions: collecting manure in the stinking fertilizer division of the meatpacking plants; driving bolts into the brains of terrified animals on the killing floors; going unpaid during the "broken time" spent herding new animals into the factory; tending the molten metal and carrying the castings and hot slag in among the furnaces in the metal plants, where the temperatures reached 120 degrees.[13]

The racial order of production was mirrored in the racial order of organized labor in East St. Louis. In spite of the official colorblindness of the American Federation of Labor, Black workers were not welcome in the AFL locals in East St. Louis, which were generally limited, in any case, to skilled workers. In spite of the efforts of unskilled Black workers to band together in several of the plants, Black workers in East St. Louis were generally non-union. The white supremacist hiring practices at the factory gate, the racial organization of production inside the plants, and the whites-only unions combined to send an unmistakable message about the "wages of whiteness," the skin privilege and ready sense of social entitlement, to anyone seeking a job in East St. Louis: that, in the words of the white workingmen of East St. Louis, jobs "belonged to the white man"; "it don't require as much for a Negro to exist as it does for a white man"; and a white man needed to provide his family with "an American standard of living" and "raise his kids right and decent."[14]

The racial order of production was exemplary of the racial capitalism of the industrial era, which relied on a dual labor market and a segregated shop floor, Black workers being held in reserve as a counterweight to white organized labor, and white laborers besotted with skin privilege playing along. But threaded through this characteristically northern, industrial strain of white supremacy was an older tradition, one reminiscent of the 1850s and even earlier, of the Indian wars and colonization and the free Negro laws and Dred Scott, of removal and annihilation—the idea that East St. Louis was "a white man's town." In spite of the fact that virtually everything about the actual city—the violence, the corruption, the inequality, the pollution—represented a repudiation of the promise of shared spoils and imperial inclusion epitomized by the 1904 World's Fair, the white workers of East St. Louis kept on somehow believing that the city belonged to them rather than their corporate overlords. They believed it with such force and passion, such a sense of beleaguered entitlement, that when the time came, they would prove more than willing to kill for it.[15]

The First World War intensified the conflict between capital and labor in East St. Louis. Among the city's industries were several that were essential to the Allied war effort: most of the shell casings used by the Allied forces in the war were produced at the Western Cartridge (today's Olin) plant in East St. Louis; all of the aluminum produced in the United States (upon which all of the aircraft produced in the United States depended) was produced at Aluminum Ore; and an appreciable portion of the canned meats that were exported to the allies were likewise produced in Armour's and Swift's plants in East St. Louis. During the war, the plants ran around the clock, adding shifts and increasing the pace of work, doubling or tripling their production, and their owners made money hand over fist. Monsanto, which began World War I as a producer of the compounded precursors for high explosives, increased its profits a hundredfold before the war ended.[16]

War work meant jobs, and African Americans from the South began to move to East St. Louis in increasing numbers in the early years of the war. Because the number of migrants to the city became a central point of contention in the immediate aftermath of the violence in 1917, and because both the migration and the expulsion of many of those who lived and worked in wartime East St. Louis occurred in between the census years of 1910 and 1920, historians have found it difficult to settle on an exact number of migrants to East St. Louis during this period. The best estimates put the number at somewhere between two thousand and five thousand—a consequential, but not overwhelming, number of migrants to a city with a population of over sixty thousand, but more than enough to make many of their white neighbors paranoid about their ability to maintain their admittedly limited privilege.[17]

In a "white man's town," every Black face looked out of place. They were not, of course, out of place there: East St. Louis had a Black community of long standing, and even the recent migrants had a right to go to any town they pleased, seeking work or a better life or whatever caught their fancy. As one of the migrants explained in the aftermath of the massacre, he had just "taken a notion" to move to East St. Louis, but that should have been enough to justify his presence in the city. Nevertheless, the idea of the white man's town was so totalizing, so absolute, that it swept all nuance and all notion of right up in a fury of purification—one did not even have to believe in it to start to see the world anew, to become accustomed to a notion of race and space that was, at the root, removalist, even genocidal. Stories emerged to explain the presence of Black people in a "white" town, based on the harebrained magical thinking that has so often been the hallmark of white supremacy in the United States. These stories would have been laughable but for their murderous results: that persons unknown had hired entire trains to carry Black workers north; that two thousand African Americans a week were arriving in the city; that there were plans afoot to use the votes of migrants to "colonize" East St. Louis. Political bosses were rumored to be standing outside polling stations passing out $5 bills to Black voters. Soon Mayor Fred Mollman—who had courted Black voters with promises of municipal jobs, schools, and parks in 1915, only to turn right around and denounce them as fraudulent interlopers in 1916—was providing the newspaper with frequent, shifting updates of how many "Negroes" he thought were arriving from the South—two thousand a week, six thousand a month, five thousand in eight months, three to six thousand total. The Central Trades and Labor Union, the East St. Louis local organization of the American Federation of Labor, hired observers to sit at the train station and count the number of Black passengers arriving on northbound trains. "N—r after n—r came in—kept coming in. I have stood on the depot and seen them coming in, 200 at a time, barefooted . . . carrying some kind of bundle with some of their few n—r belongings that they owned. . . . They was thick here just like bees . . . six or seven or eight in a house . . . every evening if you was downtown you could see ten or fifteen of them coming along with their suitcases from the Relay depot, and they continued to arrive all the time," unrepentantly insisted a white labor leader in the aftermath of the massacre.[18]

Labor leaders began to float the idea of purging the voting rolls to make certain that their (completely sold-out and corrupt) city government was not "colonized" by Black voters. The outcry—repeated in several other midwestern cities that experienced "colonization" panics in 1916 and amplified by race-baiting newspapers, for which racial drama meant dollars—was loud enough to reach Washington, DC. President Woodrow Wilson responded by endorsing the connection between Black migration and voter fraud and ordering the US Justice Department to open a criminal investigation of Negro "colonization" and voter fraud in East St. Louis, Chicago, and several smaller Illinois cities. By the summer of 1917, the impulse toward ethnic cleansing that lies latent at the heart of our democracy—the weaponization by whites of the "we" in "we the people" over the course of American history along a spectrum running from gerrymandering and voter suppression to white-capping, cross-burning, and driving out—had been fanned into a full-on racial panic.[19]

The routines of city life became increasingly menacing to triggered whites. Black people walking down the street "*almost* shove all the white folks off the [side]walk," according to the *St. Louis Globe-Democrat*. Black people were taking over the streetcars, sitting in the breezy seats by the window or "jump[ing] in to get a seat beside a white woman," according to local Democratic Party boss Thomas Canavan. "You wouldn't think you were in the home town" anymore, testified one aggrieved white when asked to explain the violence of the summer of 1917. The oscillation of entitlement and fragility so characteristic of white supremacy reverberated through unsubstantiated stories about Black criminals. "Negroes" had murdered a white man "every other night or so" for six months running, wrote one newspaper man; white women were afraid to go out in the streets at night, reported another. According to a report commissioned by white labor leaders, Black bandits were responsible for eight hundred holdups, twenty-seven murders, and seven rapes between the fall of 1916 and the summer of 1917. "There was just a reign of terror in the city of East St. Louis for eleven or twelve months. Our women couldn't go out on the streets, sisters, sweethearts, mothers or children wouldn't be seen on the streets after dark at nighttime, after it became dark. The women refused to go out on the streets. They wouldn't go," insisted AFL organizer Harry Kerr.[20]

As they had been at the time of the *Dred Scott* decision, African American citizens of the United States were characterized in industrial East St. Louis not simply as inferior but as *outsiders*—as people who needed not so much to be kept down as to be kept out. The interest of politicians in exploiting Black residents' votes and capitalists in extracting their labor was met by an insistent extraterritorializing response from labor leaders and those who spoke in the name of the white working class: these Black people were out of place and they needed to be driven out. Or exterminated. Thus began the dialectic of segregation and removal that would define twentieth-century Black life in the United States—a shifting set of alliances between industrialists, real estate rentiers, and white labor to control the Black population and settlement, to take advantage of their Black neighbors when they could, and to drive them out when they could not.

In a 1926 essay entitled "The Shape of Fear," Du Bois explained the economic roots of these fantasies of persecution and their savage telos.

Before the wide eyes of the mob is ever the Shape of Fear. Back of
the writhing, yelling, cruel-eyed demons who break, destroy, maim
and lynch, and burn at the stake, is a knot, large or small, of normal
human beings, and these human beings at heart are desperately
afraid of something. Of what? Of many things, but usually of losing their jobs, being declassed or degraded, or actually disgraced;
of losing their hopes, their savings, their plans for their children;
of the actual pangs of hunger, of dirt, of crime. And of all this,
the most ubiquitous in modern industrial society is that fear of
unemployment.

The increasingly national and bureaucratic organization of the labor
movement had created a class of labor bureaucrat instigators: people
with both the interest and the capacity to get half the working class to
turn on the other half. And once they began to fan the flames, there
was ample frustrated entitlement and bottled-up rage to burn down
the entire city. There was no necessary reason to see Black people as a
threat to white aspirations (indeed, they might have been seen as allies
against the bosses)—no reason at all except for American history and
the toxic legacy of the "white man's country."[21]

The war could have changed all that, at least in East St. Louis.
High employment, with the plants producing products essential to the
Allied war effort running around the clock, gave labor leverage. The
white working people of East St. Louis saw the opportunity to renego-
tiate virtually every aspect of the terms of their employment—as long
as they could credibly threaten to shut down production by going on
strike. It was at this critical conjuncture that the fear and resentment
of Black workers—workers conventionally excluded from the plants
who could now be mobilized by capital—began to reach the temperature necessary for ignition. Although there were unquestionably Black
workers hired in East St. Louis during the war, there were never as
many as the unions claimed (or the managers threatened); indeed,
scarcely enough Black workers were hired to fill the jobs of immigrant

workers who had returned to Europe to fight in the war. But the *fear* of being replaced by Black workers had no necessary relationship to what was actually happening in the plants. In a full-employment (for whites) economy, the fear of replacement by Black workers became a tool for both capitalists and labor leaders trying to discipline working-class whites (who might otherwise make demands they had been unable to achieve in slack times, when there were more unemployed workers available to replace them). The managers threatened to replace them with Black workers if they did not behave, and the organizers of the American Federation of Labor (the umbrella organization to which most of the East St. Louis locals were pledged) used the threat of those same Black workers to motivate and discipline the rank and file.[22]

As the war continued, and as the unions continued to try to use the strategic position of East St. Louis industry to force their employers to address long-standing grievances, the specter of Black replacement workers came increasingly to dominate organized labor's efforts to explain what was wrong in East St. Louis. Rather than organizing the migrants feared by white workers, or, still less, staying focused on the already exploitative terms of workers' employment—for instance, packing plant workers were required to clock out before they cleaned up their stations and their tools at the end of their shifts—labor leaders focused on the threat of Black migrants. No less a figure than AFL president Samuel Gompers sent a letter to union locals warning of the "importation" of Black workers and urging them to "find out what they were being used for." Contemplating the similar racial stipulation of the labor movement at the moment of Reconstruction, W.E.B. Du Bois mordantly observed that "the laborers did not recognize that the exclusion of four million workers from the labor program was a fatal omission."[23]

Wild rumors circulated throughout the city in 1916: that the mayor had traveled to the South to recruit Black workers for the city's plants, that the Chamber of Commerce had taken out advertisements in southern papers recruiting Black migrants, that the industrialists had arranged for "fifteen hundred Negroes to be shipped to East St.

Louis" to break strikes. For the industrialists, who were accustomed to using race to segment their workforces and manage their employees, the terms of engagement were familiar: when they were forced by strikes to make concessions, they responded by firing union organizers and workers and replacing them with African Americans. Thus could white workers—blinded by their own whiteness to the larger dynamics of the racial organization of labor in the plants and to the self-defeating racism of their own union locals—enter 1917 believing, in the words of one, that their employers were "encouraging the Blacks by discriminating against the whites." "It was here that they entered the Shadow of Hell," Du Bois later wrote of the white working class, "where suddenly from a fight for wage and protection against industrial oppression, East St. Louis became the center of the oldest and nastiest form of human oppression—race hatred."[24]

It could have been another strike, another plant, or even another city. Instead, it was at Aluminum Ore in East St. Louis in July 1917 that the white supremacist spoils of racial capitalism—the satisfaction of the segregated saloon; the catharsis of *The Birth of a Nation*, which had shown in the city that spring to large audiences eager to see hometown superstar Lillian Gish on screen; the lived entitlement of the segregated streets and schools and parks—gave way to the rage that burned at the heart of whiteness. After a threatened union walkout in the winter of 1916, management at Aluminum Ore, following what had become the industrial protocol in East St. Louis, dismissed over two hundred unionized whites and replaced them with African Americans. True to form, union leaders responded not by redoubling their efforts to organize Black workers, but by ending an ongoing effort to organize Black workers in the plant, asserting that they were "taking work that belonged to the white man."[25]

In April 1917, as many as two thousand of the workers at Aluminum Ore went out on strike. They were soon joined by workers in other plants throughout the city. Then management began to grind them down. The United States had just entered the war, and the strategic importance of Aluminum Ore, upon which the strikers had rested their hopes for a quick resolution, was quickly mobilized by management to call the workers' patriotism into question. The manager of the plant was quoted in the local papers as saying that the strike was "pro-German in origin" and "using Kaiser money . . . in order to cripple or shut down" the strategically essential plant. If the threat was for any reason hard to interpret in a city where a large portion of the white working class had grown up in German-speaking households, it was made plain when the Illinois National Guard formed a fixed-bayonet picket around the plant in response to "reports of pro-German utterances."[26]

Among the replacement workers brought into the plant every morning under federal protection were a number of African Americans. The tacit prewar bargain between capital and labor in East St. Louis had been based upon a shared understanding of the importance of whiteness: plant managers freely admitted that they discriminated in favor of white workers, jobs were allocated by race in the production process, and trade union organization reflected the racist order of the shop floor and framed its demand in the language of racial entitlement. Outside the gates of Aluminum Ore in the summer of 1917, things looked different: it was the striking white workers who were being labeled as outsiders and Black workers who had taken up protected positions inside the plant.

With both the material and ideological aspects of their privileged position threatened, the white workers of East St. Louis began to lash out and to reassert their sole title to every job on the line—indeed, to the city itself. "The common talk around the town," remembered the manager of the Armour packing plant, was that the strikers were going to "drive the n—s out." Over the course of the summer, young men—both Black and white—began to carry guns whenever they went out in East St. Louis. In the city's African American neighborhood, in the shadow of Aluminum Ore, where the plant lights burned around the clock, a company of Black men began to drill under the supervision of a veteran of the imperial war of 1898. In case of an attack, they planned to muster in response to the pealing bell of a church at the corner of Sixteenth and Tudor.[27]

At a meeting on May 28, the Central Trades and Labor Union demanded a meeting with Mayor Mollman and the city council. "Negro and cheap foreign labor is being imported by the Aluminum Ore Company to tear down the standard of living of our citizens. . . . Come and hear the truth that the press will not publish," read a broadside published in advance of the meeting. The ensuing meeting began with a long discussion of the use of Black workers as strikebreakers, followed by the testimony of a number of white women that they had been robbed, grabbed, hit, and/or knocked down by recently arrived Black migrants; the meeting ended with the union leaders calling upon the mayor to end Black migration to East St. Louis. Mollman responded that he had written to southern governors asking them to keep Black people from boarding northbound trains, and he promised that the city council would consider taking additional measures, but the crowd remained restive. A local lawyer shouted out that there would be no way for the next Black family to settle in East St. Louis "if the house burns down" around them. Whites at the meeting began to shout that "East St. Louis must remain a white man's town."[28]

As the overheated whites began to leave the hall, rumors began to circulate among them: that a Black burglar had shot a white man; that a Black man had insulted a white woman; that two white girls had been shot; that a white woman had been shot. The crowd became a mob. As many as three thousand whites took to the streets, dragging Black men off of streetcars and beating those whom they found on the street. They looted a restaurant downtown, a barbershop, and several saloons. The East St. Louis police, all but a handful of whom were white, stood around and watched the violence before finally mounting an effort to disarm the city's *Black* inhabitants. The mayor's request that the National Guard units outside of the Aluminum Ore Plant be moved downtown was ignored by their commander, making clear that the soldiers were there to protect the plant, not the people who worked in it. By the early hours of the morning of May 29, the fury of the crowd had burned itself out, and the marauding whites returned to their homes. "Tomorrow night we'll be ready for them," one was overheard saying. "We are not armed now, but tomorrow we'll all have guns. We'll burn the Negroes out and run them out of town." While no one had died on the night of the twenty-eighth, the mob left a trail of Black men bloodied in the downtown streets. That night, hundreds of African Americans left the city, walking across the bridge to St. Louis, Missouri. At the request of Mayor Mollman, six companies of Guardsmen were deployed to East St. Louis overnight. Over the course of the day of May 29, they stood down mobs of brick-throwing whites, and a tense ceasefire settled over the city.[29]

Even before the violence was concluded, events in the city were being reframed according to the storyboard presented by the unions at the city hall meeting: embattled whites attacked by armed "Negroes." By the middle of the day on the twenty-eighth, Mayor Mollman had requested that the St. Louis Police Department prevent African Americans from coming across the river to purchase guns in Missouri. The East St. Louis police set up roadblocks on the bridges, stopped Black motorists, and searched their cars. Over the next several days, the Illinois National Guard searched the houses of Black residents of the city, and what the *East St. Louis Daily Journal* reported as "scores" of armed "Negroes" were pulled in by the police. Beneath the hypertrophic panic about armed African Americans lay a simple but nevertheless significant fact: confronted by armed whites trying to burn their houses down, some Black people shot back. Rumors began to spread among whites that their Black neighbors were planning to rise up and drive *them* from the town, the most common rumor specifying July 4 as the intended date.[30]

Through most of June, many of the union workers at Aluminum Ore stayed out on strike, but the plant stayed open around the clock. Replacement workers made their way through the gates under the protection of soldiers with bayonets fixed to the ends of their rifles as workers on the picket lines—baited, enraged, and increasingly desperate—shouted at them. For all intents and purposes, the strike at Aluminum Ore collapsed on June 21; a few strikers kept up the picket outside the plant over the following week, but most of the plant's striking workforce returned to the line. That week management at the plant culled the union leaders from the workforce and replaced them, one by one, with Black workers. It is hard not to wonder what the bosses thought would happen next; when later asked, the manager at Aluminum Ore said simply, "My principal business was running the Aluminum Company. That is what I make my bread and butter at."[31]

On the night of July 1, a carload of white terrorists whom history has somehow remembered as "joyriders" (such is the enduring power of whiteness to euphemize violence) drove a Ford Model T through the Black neighborhood on the Southside, shooting into houses. Someone rang the church bell to signal the attack that Black residents had been training to defend against. Officers from the East St. Louis Police Department were called on duty—not to rush to the aid of those being terrorized by nighttime drive-by shootings, but rather to determine if the pealing bell was the signal for the rumored Black uprising. Driving in an unmarked Ford Model T, several police officers headed toward the church, accompanied by a reporter from the *St. Louis Republic*, who rode outside the car, on the sideboard. Rounding the corner of Tenth and Bond, they encountered, according to the reporter, "more than 200 rioting Negroes," who began shooting at the car. The officers in the front seat of the car were hit. By the morning, both had died. Their bullet-riddled and blood-stained car was parked in the street in front of the police station—there for the white working people of East St. Louis to see as they made their way to their shifts in the plants.[32]

The violence began downtown around ten on the morning of July 2, when Black workers who had worked overnight at the plants began

to make their way home. "I saw a Negro coming north on Collinsville, and about the same time a large number of men, perhaps thirty
or forty went south on Collinsville Avenue . . . when they met this
Negro down there, somebody kicked him off the sidewalk, and he was
knocked down, and two or three of the men in the crowd stepped out
and kicked him in the face a few times, and some man walked up and
shot him—stood over him and shot him three or five times," remembered Paul Anderson, a reporter for the *Post-Dispatch*. Black men were
pulled off streetcars and beaten in the streets. The crowd downtown
soon numbered over a thousand: white workingmen, still identifiable
in the blue coveralls they wore to work, joined by the tough-guy denizens of the downtown saloons and any number of what appear in the
photos to be ordinary white men wearing jackets and ties, smile and
laugh as they stand behind a small fire built in the middle of the street
on which is burning the body of one of their Black neighbors. The violence was obscene, spectacular, wanton, and joyous: white men, egged
on by the crowd, taking turns throwing paving stones at a Black man
sitting stunned in the middle of the street, the contents of the lunch
pail he had packed that morning spilled out on the pavement beside
him; two men who had been shot dead with their hands raised above
their head, lying that way on the ground, arms outstretched; the crowd
shouting out support as a rope was thrown over a lamppost to hoist the
body of a man killed by the mob, laughing as the rope broke and the
body fell to the ground with a sickening thud, calling out for more, like
they were at a boat race or playing tug-of-war: "pull for East St. Louis";
white women shooting at the feet of a Black woman whose blouse they
had torn from her shoulders, forcing her to run terrified back and forth
between them until she collapsed in the middle of the road; a Black
woman trying to shield the baby she was carrying from a mob of whites
wielding broomsticks and a two-by-four, the woman staggering and
falling, and then stumbling on up the street.[33]

Several groups of armed Black men fought back, holding a line at
Thirteenth Street as the mob tried to press down Bond into the heart

of their neighborhood, fighting house to house downtown around the corner of Sixth and Broadway and, again, around Eleventh and Broadway. The most careful historian of Black self-defense in East St. Louis credits the organized defense of the Black neighborhood on the Southside with saving many lives over the course of the night of July 2. "The Negroes fought. They grappled with the mobs like beasts at bay. They drove them back from the thickest cluster of their homes and piled the white dead on the street," wrote W.E.B. Du Bois.[34]

The East St. Louis police either stood by and watched or took part in the violence. By the afternoon, several companies of the Illinois National Guard requested by the mayor had reached the city; they set up a checkpoint on the bridge into the city from predominantly Black Brooklyn, Illinois, where they searched Black workers coming off their shifts in the plant, confiscating any weapons, and then they too joined in the murder. An exchange between Charles Roger, the president of the J. C. Grant Chemical Company, and a congressional investigator in the fall of 1917 sums up the role of the soldiers in East St. Louis on the night of July 2:

Q: Were there any soldiers around?

A: One.

Q: What was he doing?

A: He was shooting n—rs.

Q: What?

A: Shooting n—rs.

Q: The soldier?

A: Sure.

With no effective protection from the police or the military, the plants locked their Black workers inside to protect them. The fortified walls of the plants marked the line between (and the contradiction between)

The East St. Louis Massacre was the first of several concerted efforts to drive Black people out of midwestern cities in the years around the First World War; other notable examples occurred in Chicago in 1919 and Tulsa in 1921. Thousands of African Americans fled across the river to St. Louis during the violence on July 2, 1917, never to return. (*St. Louis Globe-Democrat*)

the white supremacy of exploitation favored by the bosses, who used racism to pit workers against one another, and that of elimination latent within the false promise of the "white man's country" since the time of Thomas Hart Benton.[35]

As the sun declined in the sky, the Black residents of East St. Louis fled the downtown. Under the cover of darkness now, the mob splintered into marauding bands and headed toward the Southside and the other islands of Black settlement in the city. The violence downtown was bravely chronicled by Carlos Hurd, a reporter for the *Post-Dispatch*, and his published accounts of the violence have provided the template for subsequent historians. But even counting the number of buildings burned, or how many Black families made their way through the dark and across the Free Bridge to St. Louis, or how many days the thunderhead smoke plume overhung the city as the fires set that night smoldered out, fails to fully measure the savagery of that night. It is another type of violence that haunts the edges of accounts such as Hurd's. For many of the Black residents of East St. Louis, and particularly for Black women, it was the overnight violence that formed the basis of their recollection of the events of July 2. This violence was overlooked in Hurd's printed accounts but was central to the account of Ida B. Wells and that of W.E.B. Du Bois and Martha Gruening, who traveled to East St. Louis from New York to investigate on behalf of the NAACP.[36]

Wells heard a different story about the violence from the women she met at city hall on the morning of the fourth, and from others with whom she traveled back and forth across the river in the following days as they returned to their homes to see what could be salvaged from the remains and then made their way to a shelter in St. Louis to stay for the night. Emma Ballard had been in East St. Louis for seven years in the summer of 1917; she lived with her husband of twenty-four years and her four children in a "nicely furnished six-room house" with a piano. At around midnight on July 2, she heard a crowd of white men going up and down the street outside, calling "Come out, n—s!" She had her children gather their feather beds and pillows and dress in their best clothes, and they fled across the alley behind her house to the basement of a white neighbor, where they stayed until the morning. The mob outside was working its way along the blocks, one group setting fire to the houses from alleys behind while another waited in front to shoot at the Black families as they fled their burning houses.[37]

Some of those who escaped their burning houses hid in the high grass of abandoned lots overnight or in warehouses near the train tracks, while others tried to make it across the pedestrian bridge to St. Louis; a group of whites had taken up positions on the east side to shoot them as they crossed west. Some tried to take refuge with white neighbors, some of whom they had known for years. Clarissa Lockhart ran from her burning house carrying only a dog and a pistol to a nearby saloon, where the saloon-keeper and his wife took her in for the night, hiding her behind a piano in the barroom. After they went to bed, the barkeeper and another man tried to rape her, but she "drew her pistol and drove them off." She stayed there all day on the third, and then left for St. Louis on July 4. Under the cover of darkness, Lulu Suggs took her children to beg the white lady next door to let them hide under her house, but the woman said she had chickens in her side yard that she thought they would steal. She sent her mortally terrified neighbors back into the street, their lives apparently of less value to her than the comfort of a minstrel show jape about chicken-stealing Negroes. Mrs. Douglas Howard watched from her window as a child whom she had hired to go to the butcher was set upon by the mob. He had been riding a bicycle, and the mob knocked him off it and threw it over a fence. He ran into the house of some white people who lived on the street, but the mob threatened to burn the house down if they did not send the child out. "The tenants picked him up and threw him out in the street to the mob [w]here he was kicked and stamped on and beaten until they knocked out his teeth from his head and killed him."[38]

When they came upon empty houses, members of the mob took what they wanted and destroyed the rest. "When these cottages were found to be empty," Wells later wrote, "the mob went into them, threw the mattresses, quilts, blankets and wearing apparel that was not new, on the floor and then cut, tore and trampled these things under foot and set fire to them. Pictures, bric-a-brac, everything that they could destroy, they did." One Black woman returning later to see what she could salvage "found a few of her records, but her Victrola and most of the records had been taken away." Riding in a Red Cross truck with Wells on the fourth of July was Mrs. Lulu Thomas, who had been in East St. Louis for six years, and whose husband worked on the Illinois-Central. She returned to her home to find her mattresses smoldering in the middle of the street, "her pictures and bed clothes, wearing clothes, and furniture all broken and thrown about," and her white neighbor wearing her best dress.[39]

The oral histories recorded by Wells (as well as those of Du Bois and Gruening) go on for page after unrelenting page. In them the representative victims of the mob are women and children, and they have names and stories—a young girl whose photo has been reproduced in several of the standard histories of East St. Louis above a caption noting simply that she lost her arm to a gunshot wound is identified as Mineola McGee, who was shot by soldiers as she ran back into her house after trying to escape; an old woman with thickly scarred arms, unidentified beneath her photo in most published accounts, is identified by Du Bois and Gruening as seventy-one-year-old Narcis Gurley, who had lived in East St. Louis for thirty years, and who was trapped with her elderly sister inside their burning house with the mob waiting outside to shoot them when they ran. "When the house began falling in, we ran out, terribly burned, and one white man said, 'Let those old women alone,'" and so she lived.[40]

Historians have generally followed the usage established by the US Congress, which labeled the violence in East St. Louis a "riot" in the hearings it conducted later that summer. But "massacre," the term used by Du Bois and Gruening and Wells and drawn from the history of Indian killing and imperial violence, makes more sense. Consciously or not, the murderous white men of East St. Louis employed the tactics of their military forebears in the West—of Nathaniel Lyon on Bloody Island and, even more pointedly, William Harney at Ash Hollow in the Nebraska Territory. They burned their victims out and shot them as they ran. They drove them out of their houses and off their land. When these white men encountered resistance, they moved on in search of softer targets. This was an attack not just on Black voters or Black workers or Black migrants or Black "gun-toters": it was an attack on Black families, on women and children, on the fabric of Black domestic life, on Black houses and bedsteads and photographs and pianos and phonographs and bric-a-brac, on Black wealth as much as Black labor. It was an attack on the possibility that Black people might have a future in East St. Louis, might have families and leave a legacy for another generation.

The journalists who traveled to the city following the massacre searched for a way to describe the mood on the streets in the stories they would publish on the morning of July 4. Hundreds of buildings were still smoldering, and the streets were strewn with paving stones that the mob had used to stone fleeing neighbors. Cahokia Creek was clogged with half-submerged bodies, the unenumerated dead. Those who had been hanged from the lampposts downtown had been cut down, but the bodies of some of those who had been shot down as they fled the mob, their hands up above their heads in death, were still in the street. A Guardsman stood guard near the charred remains of a man who had burned to death. No one was really certain how many had died in the burned-out neighborhoods. There were some soldiers on patrol in the streets, and white people began to come out of their houses in the morning and walk around and look at the damage. The plants were closed. It felt "like Mardi Gras," the correspondent from the *St. Louis Globe-Democrat* finally concluded. A "roman holiday," the pan-Africanist organizer Marcus Garvey termed it. The white people out in the streets seemed relaxed, unburdened, happy. Meanwhile, a constant stream of their Black neighbors were making their way across the bridge to St. Louis, on foot, dragging carts, or riding in wagons and trucks, carrying everything they could, bound for the shelters on the other side of the river, where they would stay and try to find family members from whom they had been separated by the mayhem, as well as a place to start over.[41]

Justice in the aftermath of the massacre was neither swift nor certain. Guard units from across the state of Illinois had been deployed on the streets of East St. Louis throughout the night of July 2 and finally, under the threat of court-martial, had begun to restore order. As they spent the third escorting Black refugees to the base of the pedestrian bridge, an observer might have been forgiven for thinking it was a state-sponsored removal. The St. Clair County prosecutor's initial presentation to the grand jury was framed by the dry exasperation that pusillanimous men use to show they are in on the joke.

His investigators had not found a single person, he told the court, who would admit to having recognized any of the participants in the massacre. Under pressure from the industrialists, who could scarcely conceal their fear that Black workers might stop coming to their plants from the South, the governor of Illinois appointed a special prosecutor. Eighty-two whites and twenty-three African Americans were originally indicted; in the end, nine whites and twelve African Americans served significant time in the Illinois State Penitentiary. Most of the whites were eventually charged with simple misdemeanors and simply fined; fourteen served short stretches in the county jail. Seven of the implicated policemen were allowed to draw lots to determine which three of them would take a misdemeanor charge and pay a fine. All in all, it was the kind of "justice" that reflected the vision of the young soldier Wells had encountered on the street when she first arrived in town, the one who told her that the "Blacks" were armed and killing innocent whites: righteous, vengeful, fearful, implacable, murderous, unrepentant whiteness.[42]

Thanks mostly to the efforts of Illinois congressman William Rodenberg, the child of German immigrants who had been educated in St. Louis, and Missouri congressman Leonidas Dyer, who had represented the Twelfth District, including much of Black St. Louis, for almost twenty years and who would soon lead a long and bitter failed struggle to pass a federal anti-lynching bill, a congressional investigation chipped away a good deal of the surface of the "bad people on both sides" whitewash offered up in much of the press coverage of the massacre and the criminal trials. In keeping with the concerns of an era when progressive ("Progressive") politicians focused on poor municipal governance and corporate excess, the congressional investigation emphasized the corruption of the East St. Louis city government and the avarice of the absentee industrialists in explaining the root causes of the violence. The wide-ranging and substantive congressional investigation has provided the primary basis for many subsequent accounts, including mine here. But it stopped short of contemplating the nature of the violence to which it continually referred. Both the perpetrators and the victims of the massacre go largely undiscussed—the perpetrators because their actions were assumed, according to the stimulus-response economism of Progressive social theory, to be predictable results of municipal vice and corporate greed, and the victims because, with a few notable exceptions, the committee did not ask them to tell their stories.[43]

Writing in *The Crisis* in March 1918, W.E.B. Du Bois argued against the implication of the congressional report and a good deal of allied commentary that "the laborers of East St. Louis are innocent victims of the aggregation of capital." Du Bois noted that he had repeatedly "inveighed against color discrimination by employers and the rich and well-to-do," while knowing, as did every one of his "Negro readers," that the union label on the cover "was an advertisement that No Negro's hand is engaged in the printing of this magazine." There was nothing indirect about Du Bois's account of the origins of the violence: Black workers were not organized and included in collective bargaining, but instead, "by the deliberate advice and conspiracy of the labor leaders in East St. Louis, race prejudice was invoked as a weapon to secure labor shortage and monopoly." Further: "Labor Unions in East St. Louis and neighboring towns sent 5000 men and women into the town and . . . they caught the crowd of Black workingmen between their places of employment and their homes and beat shot and burned them to death." And further still: "We know perfectly well that what happened in East St. Louis may happen in a dozen other cities." East St. Louis was a harbinger of the Red Summer of 1919 and the coming identification of calls for civil rights as a stalking horse for bolshevism—of the blurring together of industrial, political, and racial contagions.[44]

Traced from East St. Louis, the problem of the white supremacy of the white working class runs like a red thread through some of Du Bois's most important subsequent writing, which, to this day, is some of the most searching and insightful writing about the history and practice of racial capitalism we have. In his 1926 collection *Darkwater*, Du Bois published a pair of interlocked essays on racial capitalism and whiteness. The first, "The Souls of White Folk," treats racial capitalism in light of the history of imperialism and the catastrophe of the First World War. The second, "Of Work and Wealth," treats the history of the massacre in East St. Louis.

"Of them I am singularly clairvoyant," Du Bois wrote of the subjects of "The Souls of White Folk." "I see these souls undressed and from the back and side. I see the workings of their entrails. I know their thought and they know that I know. . . . And yet they preach and strut and shout and threaten, crouching as they clutch at rags of facts and fancies to hide their nakedness, they go twisting, flying by my tired eyes and I see them ever stripped—ugly, human." That's only the first paragraph. The body of the essay focuses on "the discovery of personal whiteness" in the nineteenth and twentieth centuries—the idea that certain people are white and that their whiteness entitles them to the "ownership of the earth," and the idea, drawn from the *Dred Scott* decision and the history of St. Louis, "that a White Man is always right and a Black Man has no rights which a white man is bound to respect." For Du Bois, "the Negro"—essentialized, stigmatized, instrumentalized—arose in response to the predicament of whiteness. "It is plain to modern white civilization that the subjection of the white working classes cannot much longer be maintained," he wrote, "but there is a loophole. There is a chance for exploitation on an immense scale for inordinate profit, not simply to the very rich, but to the middle class and to the laborers. This chance lies in the exploitation of darker peoples. . . . In these dark lands 'industrial development' may repeat in exaggerated form every horror of the industrial history of Europe, from slavery and rape to disease and maiming, with only one test of success—dividends!"[45]

"There are no races," Du Bois wrote, as he turned his attention to East St. Louis, "in the sense of great, separate, pure breeds of men, differing in attainment, development, and capacity." Rather, he continued, there were great groups with common histories, common cultures, and, yes, common ancestry. But more and more, these groups were organized by their place in the imperial order: the whites who claimed ownership, the middle classes who did their bidding, and the darker peoples of the world, who worked at the bottom. Capitalism and Negrofication were mutually—dialectically—constitutive of the modern world. And for Du Bois, just as the First World War represented a crisis within the imperial history of racial capitalism—"the jealous and avaricious struggle for the largest share in exploiting darker races"—the massacre in East St. Louis represented a crisis within the emergent mode of industrial organization. "Westward, dear God, the fire of Thy Mad World crimsons our Heaven," he wrote of the war in Europe. "Our answering Hell rolls eastward from St. Louis."[46]

Both "The Souls of White Folk" and "Of Work and Wealth" are full of metaphors of whiteness as a form of ownership. Whiteness is "the ownership of the earth" and "title to the universe," it is a "bequest" and a form of "wealth." In treating whiteness as a form of property, Du Bois was able to understand how it was that people who were in no danger of starving themselves could lash out with such violence at those who actually were. "What they feared," he wrote, "was not deprivation of the things they were used to and the shadow of poverty, but rather the definite death of their rising dreams." For them, whiteness was a form of capital, and with capital came the promise of endless augmentation. For Du Bois, there was no sense in a critique of capitalism and class (or even what the pundits have come to call "economic anxiety" in our own feelings-first age) that was not also a critique of imperialism and white supremacy. In contrast to Du Bois's more familiar formulation, "the wages of whiteness," these essays put forward a notion of racial privilege that is built up over time and that emphasizes the historical and structural dimensions as well as the psychic and performative ones, what Du Bois terms "personal whiteness."[47]

Du Bois's essay on the East St. Louis massacre, "Of Work and Wealth," like the accompanying essay "The Souls of White Folk," is a brilliant exposition of a crisis of racial capitalism: of the ways in which white solidarity and entitlement (the broadly classless "imperial owner-ship" promised at the 1904 World's Fair) were threatened by the insis-tent demands of Black freedom (or, failing that, simply Black jobs). Like his essay on the First World War, it concludes with a pointed threat. Either the imperialists and the industrialists and their racially obsessed adjutants could reorganize the extraction, production, and distribu-tion of the bounty of the earth in a manner more just, or they could face the uprising of those whose entitlement had been stolen by them. "This is not the end of world war—it is but the beginning," he wrote of East St. Louis. On July 28, 1917, as many as fifteen thousand African Americans marched silently down Fifth Avenue in New York to protest the violence in East St. Louis, in a protest organized by the NAACP. Among those at the head of the column was W.E.B. Du Bois.[48]

And yet these dark and lyrical essays seem somehow to miss the point. The essays as a whole are like the sentences I have quoted from them, but more so: oracular, symbolic, portentous, written from on high: "the black man . . . born in a house of fear . . . slipping stealthily northward to escape hunger and insult, the hand of oppression, and the shadow death." Du Bois seems to search in them (and in the po-etry and allegory interleaved with the essays throughout *Darkwater*) for the words to convey the fury of the mob and the terror of its victims. Perhaps Du Bois had little choice but to try to sound the depth of the catastrophe by stretching language and image to its limit. "Ev-erywhere are brick kennels—tall, black, and red chimneys, tongues of flame. The ground is littered with cars and iron, tracks and trucks, boxes and crates, metals and coal and rubber. Nature-defying cranes, grim elevators rise above pile on pile of black and grimy lumber. And ever below is the water—wide and silent, gray-brown, and yellow . . . here then was staged every element for human tragedy, every element of the modern economic paradox."[49]

And yet, compare that to the plainspoken account of Ida B. Wells with which we began.

I accosted the lone individual in soldier's uniform at the depot, a mere boy with a gun, and asked him if the governor was in town. When he said no, he had gone to Washington the night before, I asked how the situation was and he said, "bad." I asked what was the trouble and he said, "The Negroes won't let the whites alone. They killed seven yesterday and three already this morning." It was only 7 o'clock in the morning and I decided he was lying, so said nothing more on that score.

Or to this, also from Ida B. Wells:

Mrs. Flake is a widow with three children, 11, 8 and 6 years old. She is a laundress who came to East St. Louis four year ago from Jackson, Tenn. She took care of her little family by taking in washing, and she worked from Monday morning until Saturday night at the ironing board. She too had three rooms full of nice furniture. Both of the two front rooms having nice rugs on the floor, a brass bedstead and other furniture to correspond. She had about a hundred dollars-worth of furniture ruined, fifty dollars-worth of clothing and about fifty dollars more of bedding, mattresses, etc. The mob had taken a phonograph for which she had paid $15.00 and twenty-five records for which she had paid 75 cents and $1.00 each. She got away with her children before the mob reached her house and she too came back that morning to get some clothes for herself and children. The mob hadn't left much, but out of the debris, she was able to pack one trunk with some clothing and quilts for herself and children. It was in this house that I picked up one child's new shoe and although we looked the house over, we couldn't find the other. In its spasm of wanton destruction, the mob had doubtless carried it away. Mrs. Flake also had life insurance policies for herself and children, but she couldn't find any of the books. She too had already found a flat in St. Louis and was only too anxious to get away from the town where such awful things were transpiring, and where not even widows and children were safe from the fury of the mob bent on killing everything with black skins.

In the end, violence like that in East St. Louis in 1917, like that of US history, exceeds analysis, even the analysis of as brilliant a thinker and prodigiously talented a writer as Du Bois. The violence and the loss reside instead in Wells's straightforward recounting of the scene she found in the city: A mere boy with a gun. A lie. A desecrated home. A child's new shoe. The world left behind by those who had come north in search of a better life as they pushed on into the terrifying unknown of the night, crossing the bridge to St. Louis.[50]

8 | NOT POOR, JUST BROKE

You may write me down in history
With your bitter, twisted lies,
You may trod me in the very dirt
But still, like dust, I'll rise.

—MAYA ANGELOU, "Still I Rise"

THE FIRST PANEL OF THE AFRICAN AMERICAN PAINTER JACOB
Lawrence's masterpiece visual history of the Great Migration depicts Black southerners lining up to buy northbound train tickets
in a crowded station. Along with ticket windows for New York and
Chicago, Lawrence included St. Louis as the third emblematic Black
metropolis of the migration. Tens of thousands of African Americans
migrated to the city, joining the refugees from East St. Louis, in the
years between the world wars. They came in search of sanctuary from
the white supremacist violence of the Deep South, of honest wages
instead of sharecropping contracts and company stores, of the chance
to vote, and of the hope of something closer to freedom. Hope was
enough to carry them north on a train traveling up the line to Union
Station. But, after that, they had to fight for everything—not just for

their dreams, but for their basic right, as citizens of the United States, as working people, as human beings, to the bare subsistence required to keep them alive, to living where they wanted, and to their children having safe places to play, to learn, and perhaps even to flourish. In the years between the world wars, the proportion of African Americans in the city's population almost doubled (to over 13 percent, about 100,000 people) as migrants from the South added their energy, creativity, and courage to the city's existing tradition of Black resistance and radical struggle and pointed the way forward to a brighter, more equitable future for all residents of St. Louis. Many were lost along the way, but their struggle persists down to the present day.[1]

On February 29, 1916, the city of St. Louis became the first in the nation to pass a residential segregation ordinance by popular referendum, part of a wider panic about Black refugees from the South in the first decades of the century. The ordinance was sponsored by a long list of real estate commercial interests and white neighborhood associations that came together as the Universal Welfare Association. It stipulated that no "Negroes" should move into neighborhoods where either 100 percent of the houses were owned by whites or 75 percent of the residents were white. The ordinance also banned whites from moving to neighborhoods in which the opposite set of circumstances prevailed. The ordinance's defenders claimed that its intent was not prejudicial, but rather mutually beneficial. "Our ordinance protects both the Negro and white man where he lives now," said the Universal Welfare Association in an early instance of the employment of false equivalence in the service of white supremacy. For, as everyone knew, the white supremacist and racial capitalist origins of the proposal were its chief selling point. "There has been for years a constantly increasing protest against the encroachments of Negroes moving into white neighborhoods, especially new, bright, and attractive neighborhoods built up by the home owners and paid for out of the hard earning of our representative thrifty, frugal, and home-loving people," the realtors began, before coming to the point. White St. Louis was under siege:

"There have been over 1,000 actual cases of Negro invasion," mostly to the detriment of "widows and dependents." Although it was opposed by the newspapers in the city—white and Black—the segregation ordinance was passed by an overwhelming majority of the voters (African American voting rights prevailed in St. Louis, but Black residents in the city were wildly outnumbered in the early years of the century) and became law in the spring of 1916.[2]

The US Supreme Court's 1916 decision in *Buchanan v. Warley*, a case that held that a Louisville ordinance very similar to the one in St. Louis violated the "equal protection" clause of the Fourteenth Amendment to the Constitution, put an end to the segregation ordinance, but not to its replication in various forms that persist down to the present day. Among white homeowners, there was (and is) an apparently unshakable belief in direct connections between the race of the inhabitants of a neighborhood and the value of the homes in that neighborhood—a belief powerful enough to transform itself into a social fact. By midcentury, realtors, city planners, and white homeowners would find ways of making the case for segregation in language that was almost completely devoid of overt allusion to the racial character of the wealth that was being protected. In the meantime, however, the neighborhood associations, which had been so active in supporting the segregation ordinance, turned to what became the dominant tool for realizing the extra increment of value to which they believed their whiteness entitled them: the restrictive covenant. Indeed, given the degree to which St. Louis was still a city of immigrants and the children of immigrants, the covenants might be seen as a way of whitening the city, of urging immigrant Germans, Scandinavians, Russian and Polish Jews, and others to declare for whiteness. In the period between the segregation ordinance and the US Supreme Court's 1948 decision in *Shelley v. Kraemer*, which held that racially restrictive covenants were not legally enforceable, Black St. Louis was surrounded and closed out by almost four hundred specifically covenanted white neighborhoods.[3]

The frontier of racial residence ran along Grand Avenue and produced value for the whites who owned the majority of the property on both sides. On the west side of the line, white homeowners and rentiers received a subsidy in the form of a guarantee that no prospective buyer or renter need ever worry about having a Black neighbor, with a corresponding boost to the value of their property. To keep up the covenants, the realtors turned to maudlin stories of widowed old ladies who needed to be protected, lest they be unable to rent their rooms to whites who would not live next door to African Americans (these old ladies apparently preferred foreclosure to Black tenants of their own), and maiden aunts who would be divested of half the value of the house they had saved their entire lives to buy if a Black family moved in next door. But the message on the flip side of these fears was also quite clear: whiten your block and your house might double in value.[4]

On the east side of the line, segregation produced housing scarcity, making Black migrants easy money for white landlords. And as the population of Black St. Louis grew through two phases of Black migration from the South in the years between 1910 and 1950, its geographic outline (tall tales of "Negro invasion" notwithstanding) remained roughly the same. Rather than expanding, the social and familial life of Black St. Louis was compressed into an area whose population density varied between 200 and 400 percent of that prevailing in much of white St. Louis. Apartments were subdivided into the kitchenettes that became characteristic of how urban African Americans lived: the familiar four-family St. Louis brick apartment building was cut up on the inside to accommodate twelve or even sixteen families in two-room apartments, with one room for cooking and eating and one for sleeping, and with no running water, indoor toilets, or reliable heat. The comedian Dick Gregory later recounted a childhood story of slamming the door on a white lady bearing a Thanksgiving-gift turkey, not because he hated turkey or Thanksgiving or even well-meaning white ladies, but because his family's apartment did not have an oven in which the bird could be cooked.[5]

All that segregation and compression was money in the bank for the white landlords who owned the buildings. The artificially created housing shortage enabled landlords to charge higher rents—contemporary estimates of the "Black tax" in rental property suggest that landlords charged as much as three times the rent for comparable apartments in Black neighborhoods as they did in white neighborhoods. And because their renters had few alternatives, landlords were able to save money by skimping on maintenance. The result was overcrowded, rat-infested, firetrap apartment buildings—the very sorts of buildings and conditions that the propertied would later turn around and use to justify tearing down the neighborhoods and removing their inhabitants (while blaming them for the poor conditions) when they thought they could make more money as real estate "developers" than as slumlords.[6]

The basic condition of Black St. Louis in the 1930s (as in the decades before and the decades after) was poverty, segregation, and exploitation. And yet, as Gregory remembered in a chapter of his autobiography entitled "Not Poor, Just Broke," these embattled neighborhoods were sites of human flourishing as well as suffering, spaces of joy as well as rage, and places where radical ideas and unaccustomed alliances took root in the 1930s, a decade in which St. Louis came as close as any other city in the nation to fulfilling the promise of the 1877 General Strike. It would take an enormous, sustained, and ongoing effort—a second counterrevolution of property, as destructive in its own way as the violence in East St. Louis—to destroy that radical possibility.

"It's a sad and beautiful feeling to walk home slow on Christmas Eve after you've been out hustling all day," Gregory's book begins. Then he takes readers on a soft-focused tour of the hard-life side of the Ville—the emblematic Black neighborhood on the city's Northside—in the late 1930s: ending a day's work shining shoes in the white taverns to buy a few presents (and steal a few more than that) in the five-and-dime; stopping by his best friend's house to drop off a ballpoint pen and look at the decorations on the tree; and waving to the neighbors and Mr. Ben, the Jewish corner grocer, whose credit would backstop the family through especially lean times, and even waving to Grimes, "the mean cop" standing out on the corner. "And then you hit North Taylor, your street . . . and for the first time the cracked orange door says 'come on in, little man, you're home now' . . . and you hug your Momma, her face hot from the stove."[7]

Gregory's autobiography is often excerpted to serve as an example of classism, colorism, and cruelty in the lives of poor Black children in the United States. Among the most common, most exalted, words in the book is "clean." Child of the Depression and a segregated cold-water tenement on the Northside, Gregory longed to be clean. Years later, he remembered the "clean little girl" who would wave at him when he finished his paper route in the morning, and his fantasy that one day his father would return home, "big and clean." He remembered the "goodness" and "cleanness" of his first love—he washed his socks and his shirts before school in hopes of impressing her—and he joined the school track team just so he could take a shower at school. He also remembered hunger and cold: breaking the window of Mr. Ben's store to steal food; eating paste at the back of the class just to taste salt on his tongue; doing his homework with a flashlight under the covers in a freezing bedroom, only to wake up and find that one of his younger brothers had peed in the bed and his work was too sodden and smudged—too shameful—to turn in at school. Better to fail.[8]

Even so, Gregory describes a neighborhood that was rich in decency and generous in support, a place where Black people, in the words of the historian Earl Lewis, "turned segregation into congregation." There was the family of a friend who fed him for a week, until the day he made the mistake of taking their generosity for granted by casually asking what time dinner would be served; the grocer who made sure Gregory's family had food even when they had no credit left and gave them all the perishables in the store before he closed up for the high holy days; his friend Boo, who played hockey with him in the street, with broom handles and bottle caps, and went with him in the summer to Forest Park to watch the outdoor performances (and gape at the rich white people); the counselors at Camp Rivercliff, the first Black people he remembered meeting who were high school graduates; the teacher at Cote Brilliant Grammar School who appointed him to be a crossing guard; the coach at Sumner High School who invited him to join the team after seeing him lurking outside the fence; and the high school kids who cheered him as he ran the mile and won the state championship, high-stepping down the backstretch of the last lap, wearing his signature argyle socks and bandana and saluting the flag. All these people were there in the Ville, along with the hunger and the cold.[9]

And above all, there was his mother, Lucille Gregory, who worked all day every day to keep him in food and clothes, bought him the wallet he wanted, called home every day from the white people's house to tell him how to cook dinner, and taught him that they were "not poor, just broke." Who got the landlord to let them move their furniture back in from the "streetcar zone" at the edge of the street and the electric man to turn the lights back on for Christmas, and who got the haughty light-skinned doctor to give them medicine. Who was the worst cook in the world ("whoever heard of burning Kool Aid?" was a Gregory standard in later years) yet stood by him and fed him and fought for him and loved him through all the years he told her not to come to his track meets and band performances because he was "ashamed when I saw her come in wearing that shabby old coat, her swollen ankles running over the edges of those dyed shoes that the rich white folks gave her, a little too much lipstick." Who sat on the bed with his head on her lap the night before he was to give a speech to his graduating class at Sumner, when he did not know what he would say. Who sat there and listened to him read the speech a sympathetic teacher had passed to him on his way into the auditorium, with tears in her eyes. "And she was moving her lips and I knew just what she looked like when she was alone and saying 'Thank God, oh, Thank God,'" Gregory remembered.[10]

Black St. Louis in the years of the Great Migration was home to some of the greatest artists, athletes, and entertainers of the twentieth century; they were the children of migrants who had left behind the sharecropping fields of Louisiana, Mississippi, and Arkansas for hardscrabble but hopeful lives working in brick kilns, packinghouses, flour mills, and domestic service in St. Louis. Maya Angelou spent some of her childhood on the Southside, where she lived in a kitchenette much like Gregory's on the Northside and attended Toussaint L'Ouverture Elementary School. Sent north from Arkansas by her grandmother to live with her mother, Angelou famously described St. Louis upon her arrival as "a new kind of hot, and a new kind of dirty," a city "with all the finesse of a Gold-Rush town." It was on the Southside that the eight- or nine-year-old Angelou was raped by her mother's boyfriend, an incident at the center of *I Know Why the Caged Bird Sings*. And it was on the Southside that her St. Louis cousins dispensed the rough, community-based justice that many remember as characteristic of Black St. Louis at the time: they beat the rapist to death on the eve of the one-year prison term he'd been given by the state of Missouri.[11]

The neighborhoods remembered by Gregory and Angelou were also home to Josephine Baker, who lived in Mill Creek Valley and started out singing and dancing while her friends made music with clotheslines strung between barrels and combs covered with paper. Later, she sang on the street in front of the Booker T. Washington Theater in Chestnut Valley, until they invited her inside to join the chorus line when she was thirteen years old. The city was also home to Chuck Berry, a graduate of Sumner High School and the Poro Cosmetology College; to Ike and Tina Turner, who got their start in St. Louis clubs a generation later, at the same time that Miles Davis was starting out across the Mississippi in East St. Louis; to Robert McFerrin, who graduated from Sumner High School and would become the first African American man ever to sing at the Metropolitan Opera; and a few years later, to the poet Quincy Troupe, who started out at Vashon on the Southside before graduating from Beaumont High School, next to Fairground Park. In the same way, the baseball Hall of Famer James "Cool Papa" Bell, who moved to St. Louis from Mississippi in the 1920s, was followed by Elston Howard, the first Black ever to play for the New York Yankees, after starring at Vashon High School. Similarly, Henry Armstrong, a Mississippi migrant and Vashon graduate who was the first boxer ever to hold three world championship titles at the same time, was succeeded by Archie Moore, the light heavyweight champion and another Mississippi migrant, and then by Sonny Liston, the heavyweight champion of the world, who lived as a teenager in Compton Hill. And Redd Foxx and Robert Guillaume, who would later represent the two caricatured poles of the class hierarchies of the Ville—the one as the uncouth junkman Fred Sanford (*Sanford and Son*), the other as a fastidious African American butler-turned-lieutenant governor (*Benson*)—grew up just a few years and a few blocks apart on the Northside.[12]

It was in these years, too, that St. Louis led the way in the national struggle for civil rights. In 1936, Lloyd Gaines sued the University of Missouri for denying his application to law school because he was Black, a case that was tried as *Gaines v. Canada* (Sy Canada being the name of the registrar at the university's law school). Gaines, who had been born in Mississippi in 1912 and migrated with his mother to St. Louis as a child, was the valedictorian at Vashon. He graduated from Lincoln University in Jefferson City, the state of Missouri's Black university, founded as a freedom school by Black soldiers at Benton Barracks. The case was tried in Columbia, the site of the all-white University of Missouri, and when the verdict went against him, Gaines appealed to the Missouri Supreme Court. Again, Gaines was unsuccessful, the court ruling that the state of Missouri's practice of providing tuition for Black students to attend out-of-state professional schools was sufficient to meet the "separate but equal" standard upheld by the US Supreme Court in *Plessey v. Ferguson* (1896). Gaines appealed to the Supreme Court, where his case was heard in November 1938.[13]

In its decision, the Court ruled for Gaines, holding that the state of Missouri was legally bound to provide Black citizens with an education that was functionally as well as formally equivalent to the education provided to white students, and it remanded the case to the Missouri Supreme Court. As a stopgap, the state set up a separate law school for Black students, Lincoln Law School, on the erstwhile premises of the Poro Cosmetology College on the city's Northside. While awaiting the state rehearing of the case, Lloyd Gaines, after stepping out on the night of March 19, 1939, to "buy stamps," disappeared under suspicious circumstances. He was never seen again. But the standard articulated by the court in *Gaines v. Canada* (1938)—that the formal "equality" represented by supplying the tuition dollars necessary to send well-educated African Americans out of the state for further education was not actually equitable—would finally be fulfilled with the ruling in *Brown v. Board of Education* fifteen years later.[14]

It was no accident that *Gaines v. Canada* originated in St. Louis, the city in Jim Crow's borderlands where the train cars were switched from segregated to integrated on the way north and from integrated to segregated on the way south. "A northern city with a southern exposure," Margaret Bush Wilson, the African American activist (and graduate of Sumner High School), termed it. Black St. Louisans had the right to vote and strong ward-based political machines (Maya Angelou's grandmother was a ward boss on the Southside, and powerful enough that white policemen stopped by the house to pay tribute), but segregated public accommodations—lunch counters, theaters, playgrounds, and schools. St. Louis was thus situated to produce tension over civil rights, being home to a Black middle class—educated at the city's nationally famous Black high schools and beyond—that was accomplished, ambitious, and frustrated enough to produce and support litigants like Lloyd Gaines at the upper end of the struggle for social inclusion.[15]

The condition of the city's Black neighborhoods was the primary focus of the interracial and middle-class St. Louis Urban League during the 1930s and 1940s. Every year, the league's annual report began with a summary of its fight against restrictive covenants and the effect of segregation and crowding on Black St. Louis. "At the end of 1944, there was hardly to be found a single vacant house or flat anywhere available to a Negro family. Neighborhood covenants among whites practically encircle the entire Negro areas and have the effect of ghetto walls," opened the organization's report for that year. The Urban League framed its argument to the white leaders of the city in the language of humanitarian relief organizations, focusing on the deplorable conditions of human life east of Grand: "the greatest proportion of obsolete houses in the city, infested with termites, crime, delinquency, and tuberculosis." In the real estate market, however, where the league's hopes for integration were opposed by the realtors and the rentier slumlords and hundreds upon hundreds of racially restrictive covenants, its organizational emphasis on fostering "substantial gains in friendliness to the Negroes among an ever-widening-circle of white people" was a nonstarter. Just as maintaining a dual labor market that pitted white and Black workers against one another was the principle of industrial labor management, housing segregation was an elementary aspect of real estate: the racial border at Grand was a frontier of racial capitalist accumulation. It was unlikely to give way to increased interracial benevolence alone.[16]

In 1945, J. D. Shelley, who had migrated to the city from Mississippi in 1930, purchased a house at 4600 Labadie that lay in a racially covenanted neighborhood well to the west of Grand. Labadie Avenue was named for a wealthy Black grocer from the nineteenth century; nevertheless, one of Shelley's white neighbors filed suit to void the purchase, based on a restrictive covenant signed when the house had last been sold in 1911. In 1948, the case came before the US Supreme Court, where it was heard by a panel of six justices, the other three having recused themselves because they lived in covenanted neighborhoods around Washington, DC. While holding that there was nothing inherently illegal about private agreements limiting the terms of association or membership—in the local private school or country club, for example—the Court ruled that racially discriminatory agreements were *not legally enforceable.* The members of a private club could do whatever they wanted, but they could not rely on the police power of the state to protect their right to do so. Having felled one of the principal legal supports of residential segregation, the Shelleys were able to remain in the house on Labadie. But covenants like the one they faced down in court in the 1940s remain in many city deeds today; though legally unenforceable, they nevertheless continue to threaten, humiliate, and intimidate Black home-buyers at their long-anticipated closings.[17]

As well as access to better and cheaper housing, the Urban League and the NAACP sought legal access to the city's whites-only playgrounds and swimming pools; Dick Gregory's nostalgic memories of playing hockey in the street were shaped by the fact that Black children were not allowed to play anywhere other than the street. In 1946, the Ku Klux Klan burned a ten-foot cross in the middle of the Buder Playground in St. Louis County after Black children began to play in the park. After decades of complaints by Black citizens and their elected representatives, the St. Louis Parks Department finally relented and opened the outdoor pool at Fairground Park to Black patrons. It had been the largest open-air swimming pool in the world since 1915. On June 21, 1949, the city of St. Louis announced that Fairground Park would be open that summer as an integrated pool.

Having heard on the radio that the pool would be open, dozens of Black children joined hundreds of whites in the line at the gate awaiting the opening. They were admitted, but as they played in the pool, a white mob gathered outside. By the time the afternoon session ended at three o'clock, there were hundreds of angry white men, women, and children waiting at the gate. The pool attendants shut the Black children in the locker room and, after searching their lockers for weapons, called for the police to escort them out of the park. Officers from the St. Louis Police Department arrived and did just that, but no more: they escorted the Black children through the howling mob—some of the angry whites were throwing bricks and rocks—to Natural Bridge

Road at the edge of the park and then told them, in effect, "Run, you're on your own." Robert Gammon, one of the Black children who swam in the pool that day, later remembered running as fast as he could toward St. Louis Avenue at the heart of the Ville and passing a white woman who broke stride while walking with a baby in a carriage to spit at him as he passed.[18]

Over the course of the afternoon and into the evening, as many as five thousand violent and enraged whites flooded into the neighborhood around the park, and roving bands armed with clubs and knives attacked any African Americans they found out on the street. "Want to know how to control these n—s?" *Time* magazine reported one of the marauding whites yelling at the crowd. "Smash their heads, the dirty, filthy fuckers." It took four hundred policemen twelve hours to restore order. By the time they did, fifteen Black St. Louisans had been seriously wounded, at least two of them stabbed. The following day the mayor closed the Fairgrounds Pool for the summer.[19]

The anaphylactic reaction to Black children wanting to swim in the summertime suggests that racial capitalism is something more than the mobilization of race prejudice to make money, as one might conclude after a study restricted to the labor market, or to the sporadic violence and protests that had attended the recent arrival of African Americans in the College Hill neighborhood north and east of the park. The violence in Fairground Park was well in excess of any economic calculation, no matter how cynical. It was a libidinal rage: psychic disgust externalized into the collective fury of race hatred. Racism and capitalism in the 1940s were inextricable. But racism and capitalism were not identical: one could not be reduced to the other. They were always in excess of one another—capitalism mobilizing and exploiting whites as well as African Americans, and white supremacy providing pleasure, even the filthy pleasures of racial disgust and collective violence, as well as profit. The Fairground Park pool was reopened in 1951 as an integrated facility under federal court order (a ruling that, along with *Gaines v. Canada*, was eventually used as a precedent in the

Brown decision), but it was boycotted by whites. In 1956, the parks department, apparently unable to imagine a pool that served only African Americans, closed down the Fairground Park pool and filled it with concrete, as if the once-hallowed facility—"the largest open-air swimming pool in the world"—were a landfill or a toxic waste site.[20]

I n St. Louis, as elsewhere, the legal struggle against Jim Crow tapped into a deeper and more radical history of grassroots organizing and direct action led by Black workers, especially Black women, and by communists. As in the nineteenth century, the working class in St. Louis was hit hard by economic depression. Industrial production in the city fell by almost 60 percent between 1929 and 1933, and unemployment increased from about 9 percent to 30 percent in the same period; 70 percent of Black adults were either unemployed or severely underemployed. During these years, a radical and powerful working-class movement emerged in Black St. Louis, threatening both the hegemony of the middle-class Black civil rights organizations, like the Urban League and the NAACP, and the racial and economic order of the city itself. For a time, working-class Black people in St. Louis, especially working-class Black women, managed to revive the revolutionary alliance of red and Black radicalism that had first been formed during Franz Sigel's 1861 march across Missouri and the St. Louis Commune in 1877.[21]

Following on from the history of the communists of the 1860s and the working-class German clubs of the Turnverein of the 1890s, St. Louis at the time of the First World War was a hub of anti-imperialist communism and anarchism. Both *The Communist* and *The Anarchist*, which circulated nationally, had been published in the city since the nineteenth century, and a noteworthy leftist literary circle gathered around William Marion Reedy, the editor of the literary journal *The Mirror* and the author of a history of the 1877 General Strike, and

Alice Martin and Harry Turner, editors of the political and cultural journal *Much Ado*. Martin and Turner were friends of the anarchist Emma Goldman, who stayed with Alice Martin when she was in St. Louis. The literary and bohemian scene in St. Louis shaded imperceptibly into radical politics. In addition to Goldman's frequent visits to the city, chronicled in *Living My Life*, the city was home to Kate Richards O'Hare, the Socialist Party candidate for governor of Missouri in 1916 and chair of the Socialist Party's Committee on War and Militarism. In 1917, O'Hare was convicted under the Espionage Act for speaking out against the draft and imprisoned at the Missouri State Penitentiary, where she served time with Goldman, who was imprisoned for the same offense in 1919.

Kate O'Hare's husband Frank was the founding editor of the *National Rip-saw* (later *Social Revolution*), published in St. Louis, which served as an intellectual clearinghouse for the Socialist Party in the United States. St. Louis was also home to Roger Baldwin, who began his career together with Emma Goldman in organizing resistance to the 1917 Selective Service Act during the First World War. Baldwin went on from the struggle against militarism and the draft to join the Industrial Workers of the World (IWW) and then became the founding director of the American Civil Liberties Union (ACLU). The city was also home to the Globetrotter Publishing House, which, in the years before the First World War, reliably turned out radical pamphlets on topics ranging from "Women under Capitalism," "Socialism for the Farmer," and "Socialism and Faith in Practice" to "Hands Up," "Sabotage," and "Militant Socialism."[22]

Reedy, Martin, and Turner were followed in the next generation by Jay and Fran Landesman, who founded the St. Louis–based literary journal *Neurotica* (later credited as inspiration for the Beat poets of the 1950s) and ran a nightclub called Little Bohemia on the riverfront, where avant-garde artists and radicals met, sat, smoked, and schemed in the 1930s. Svavo Radulovich partnered with the Landesmans in Little

Bohemia, and then later in Gaslight Square, as the scene moved farther uptown in the 1940s and after. "I found Bohemia on the Banks of the Mississippi," wrote Jack Conroy, himself a denizen of the riverfront dive bars, who is often credited as the progenitor of the "proletarian novel."[23]

It was out of this world that the most prominent St. Louis communist of the twentieth century, William Sentner, emerged. Sentner was born in 1907, the son of a Russian Jewish needleworker, and he grew up in and around the labor movement. He later joked that the first money he ever made was as a child paid to throw rocks at the windows of a factory where the workers were on strike. After two years at Washington University, where he studied architecture, Sentner dropped out to ride the rails, traveling west and eventually to Europe and the Middle East. Along the way he became a Marxist; when he returned to St. Louis, he joined Jack Conroy in the city's John Reed Club. Named for the American journalist, communist, and chronicler of the Bolshevik Revolution, the club was a cultural spin-off of the Communist Party's *New Masses* magazine and designed to channel the talent and energy of artists and writers toward revolution.

Sentner's organizing took him to the immigrant neighborhoods around Carr Square and the Wellston Loop, the bohemian dive bars along the riverfront, and then back again to party headquarters on North Garrison—"a long dingy room, bare save for a table and a scarred piano at the far end, a book case and a table piled high with pamphlets and magazines on one side," as Conroy described it in his novel *A World to Win*. During the Depression, Sentner organized—often through the Communist Party's Unemployed Council—among the unhoused and the hungry, who were living in Hoovervilles scattered throughout the city: on the riverfront, at several spots stretching from the area north of downtown to the base of the Free Bridge south of downtown, near Hyde Park on the Northside, and near the Busch Brewery on the Southside. Taken together, these shantytowns added up to what was arguably the largest encampment of the unhoused and the unemployed in the Depression-era United States. Residents lived in small houses built of driftwood and repurposed building materials. There were as many as 250 makeshift dwellings along the riverfront in the early thirties, and at least twice that many scattered elsewhere in the city. The communities were self-governing—contentiously so when it came to food distribution and the role of Christian aid organizations in a settlement's internal politics—and, by and large, self-policed.[24]

Sentner also organized in Black St. Louis, where, he later joked, he got stopped by the police every time he crossed Grand. The Black population of St. Louis had grown by over 50 percent, to around sixty-five thousand, in the years between 1910 and 1920—still less than 10 percent of the city's population, but the eighth-largest Black population of any city in the United States. Many of the Black migrants, most of them from Mississippi, settled in Mill Creek Valley, which stretched westward from Chestnut Valley along the corridor occupied today by Interstate 64. Another group, including many of those who had fled East St. Louis in 1917, settled west of the city, in Kinloch, which was the state of Missouri's first Black municipality. Much of the development around today's Lambert–St. Louis International Airport is built on the ruins of historic Kinloch. Middle-class African Americans, along with many of the working poor and the just plain poor, lived in the Ville, north of downtown, where many of the city's longest-standing Black institutions were located—the Poro Cosmetology College, with its historical ties to Madame C. J. Walker; Sumner High School, which had a national reputation for Black excellence in the 1930s; and Stowe Teachers College and Lincoln Law School, two segregated branches of the University of Missouri system.[25]

In November 1930, activists from eighteen states, including the organizer and theorist Harry Haywood, met at the United Brothers of Friendship Hall in Mill Creek Valley to found the League of Struggle for Negro Rights, a successor organization to the American Negro Labor Congress. They were women and men, Black and white, communists who sought to join the struggle for racial and economic justice in the United States to the global struggle against capitalism and colonialism.

The protest march signs they had printed for the occasion suggested the breadth of their vision: SUPPORT THE COLONIAL MASSES; EQUAL PAY FOR EQUAL WORK, REGARDLESS OF RACE OR NATIONALITY; DOWN WITH LYNCHING, DEMAND DEATH FOR LYNCHERS; CONFISCATION OF THE LAND FOR THE POOR BLACK NEGRO FARMERS IN THE FARMERS BELT; LONG LIVE NEGRO AND WHITE WORKERS. The league lasted through the early years of the Depression and was for a time led by the poet Langston Hughes. Even after its demise in 1934, the spirit that had brought the organizers together in St. Louis in the first place, the spirit of 1877, lived on in the city.[26]

On the morning of July 8, 1932, the disinherited of the city marched on city hall, demanding to be fed. More than a thousand were gathered in front of city hall, and many were African American, among them recent migrants from the South, veterans of the massacre in East St. Louis, and descendants of the revolutionary generation that had gathered at Benton Barracks during the Civil War. There were just as many whites—men, women, and children, communists, and unemployed workers. They carried signs with slogans like NO EVICTIONS OF UNEMPLOYED and WE WILL WORK BUT WE WON'T STARVE. A group of children carried a sign demanding FREE MILK FOR THE CHILDREN OF THE UNEMPLOYED. They had marched in groups from all over the city—from the Southside, the Northside, and the central corridor—singing "Solidarity" to the tune of "John Brown's Body." "The burden of the song," an observer relayed, "was that 'We're for inter-racial solidarity; we would rather fight than starve in slavery,'" with the refrain "Solidarity forever, our Union makes us strong."[27]

Twenty-five policemen barred the entrance to city hall, where the mayor was said to be meeting with business leaders to discuss the plight of the city's poor, and another twenty-five armed with "riot guns" and "tear gas bombs" stood ready in reserve at police headquarters, two blocks away. George Benz, an unemployed electrician and communist, stood on the steps of city hall and asked people in the crowd if they were willing to "fight" rather than "starve," in what the *Post-Dispatch* termed an "inflammatory" tone. "We will, we will!" they cried. A "young Negro, apparently well-known to his listeners," urged them on. "There is only one way left for the working class—that's the militant way. I am speaking for the Negro workers who know how to fight and will fight. We will not continue to starve peacefully."[28]

And they did not. Assembled under the auspices of the Unemployed Council of the Communist Party, a dozen of the demonstrators occupied the mayor's office on the morning of July 11, while a crowd of three thousand gathered outside. When word reached the crowd that the mayor had refused to meet with their delegates or address their demands, one of the CP organizers climbed the steps of the Market Street entrance and urged the crowd to enter city hall. They were led by Black women, about fifty of whom started up the stairs. As they pushed forward, the organizer called for the military veterans in the crowd to follow them in support, and over a hundred did so.[29]

As the crowd surged upward, one of the policemen stationed near the door threw a tear gas bomb into their midst. One of the demonstrators picked it up and threw it back, and the police themselves retreated into the rotunda of the building, blinded by the gas. Moments later, however, they regrouped and charged out of city hall, guns drawn, to disperse the crowd. More police arrived, some pushing their way out of city hall, some arriving in reserve from police headquarters. They began to drive the protesters back toward downtown, swinging billy clubs, throwing tear gas bombs, and shooting into the crowd.[30]

Within fifteen minutes, the crowd had been dispersed. Several policemen, the papers reported, were injured by bricks thrown from the retreating throng; one was treated for a sprained wrist sustained while swinging a club at a protester. Dozens of the demonstrators, many of them children, were trampled as the crowd retreated before the tear gas and charging policemen. Four men in the crowd, three white and one Black, lay bleeding in the street, shot by the police.[31]

In addition to the demonstrators inside City Hall, who were arrested, several dozen others were arrested in the immediate aftermath of what soon came to be known as the "July Riot."[32] A photograph of a court hearing on July 14 reveals that the "communists" accused of disturbing the peace were Black and white, men and women. On the same day the court issued warrants for eleven men and one woman, including all four of those who had been shot by the police, on the more serious charge of rioting, punishable by up to a year in the Workhouse (the name for the St. Louis City Prison down to this day) and a $1,000 fine. On the afternoon of the protest, the city's police commissioner, declaring himself in "sympathy" with the unemployed but intolerant of any further demonstrations, had instructed the force to break up any subsequent meetings of the Communist Party in St. Louis. In the following days, uniformed and armed policemen arrested suspected party members at a meeting of the Unemployed Council near Union Station and at party headquarters on North Garrison.[33]

The account of the violence that emerged on the left was of a peaceful march of the hungry and the unemployed that had been interrupted by a police riot. Speaking at a meeting of the Liberal Club, one of the organizers (who refused to give her name out of fear of police retaliation) described the demonstration in front of city hall as one in an ongoing series of "hunger marches" in the city. "People would just get up and state simply that they had nothing to eat," she recounted. "Women would get up and say, 'We can't go home because we have nothing to give our children and we just can't face them.'" If there were communists among them, that was nothing to be ashamed about, she argued: "Even a Communist can be hungry." If some among the crowd fought back when attacked by the police "with tear gas, clubbing, beating, trampling women and children," they could not really be blamed. "These people were not to be fooled with. They were hungry. They had nothing to eat and no money." Many of those who were arrested, the woman continued, had been beaten while in police custody. The police had instigated the violence by attacking a peaceful protest, beaten

The unemployed marches of the 1930s brought together Black and white working people, women and men. Out of them grew the strike at Funsten Nut, led by Black women. (*St. Louis Post-Dispatch*/Polaris)

prisoners in custody, and then turned around and charged the hungry and the innocent with "disturbing the peace."[34]

Whatever they thought of communists, Black people, or the unemployed, the members of the board of aldermen recognized that as long as people were hungry, further disturbances were likely. By the end of the week of the food riot, the board passed an emergency motion to appropriate $25,000 to set up food distribution centers throughout the city. In their assembly, the demonstrators at city hall had forced the government to account for them and their families. By the end of the summer, most of those charged in the aftermath of the violence were acquitted or sent home by hung juries.[35]

The following summer, a group of African American women employed as nutpickers went out on strike at R. E. Funsten Company, which had several processing facilities in St. Louis. The organizers included some of the veterans of the previous summer's action at city hall, including an African American woman identified in the relatively sparse archival record of the strike as "Mrs. Wallace," who had been among those arrested in the mayor's office. By the end of the summer, she and the others had led one of the largest strikes of Black women in the history of the United States.[36]

The vast majority of working-class Black women in St. Louis were employed in domestic service—cooking and cleaning in the homes of wealthy and middle-class whites who lived in the city's West End and emerging suburbs. These women, like Lucille Gregory, worked for wages barely sufficient to keep a roof over their own family's head, and often insufficient to keep their children fed. There were also many Black women who worked in food processing in St. Louis—and 2,500 of them worked at Funsten Nut, the largest single employer of Black women in the city.[37]

The production lines inside the sixteen Funsten plants scattered across the St. Louis metro area were segregated. Black women shelled the nuts, separating the meat from the hull, and a much smaller number of white women, many of them immigrants from Poland, sorted the nuts into halves and pieces. Because they were sorting nuts downstream on the line from the pickers, the white women in the plants were allowed to come into work fifteen minutes later than the Black women, and they were allowed to go home fifteen minutes earlier. The pickers worked twenty-five pounds at a time, and after each stage both hulls and meat were weighed to ensure that no nuts had been stolen. While the whites who worked in the plant were paid a weekly wage of around $3, the Black pickers were paid by the pound—three cents a pound for halves and two cents for pieces. Many complained that they were paid for totals smaller than what they had recorded during the day, but even under the best circumstances, it was very unusual for a picker at Funsten to make $2 in a week. They worked in poorly lit, unventilated basements where the air was so dusty that the workers at one plant kept the doors open through the winter. Their hands were cracked and cut by the work, and many developed chronic respiratory conditions similar to those suffered by men working in coal mines.[38]

On May 15, 1933, about five hundred Black women walked off their jobs at Funsten Nut, demanding that the company pay them a "living wage." The women had begun to organize in a series of secret meetings convened by the communist labor activist William Sentner and held over the course of the spring; first six, then twenty, and then fifty women were involved. On May 13, several women who had joined the Food Workers Industrial Union convened a meeting of seven hundred workers from various Funsten plants. They voted to go on strike if they did not receive an immediate raise. The first group to walk out on the fifteenth set out from the Delmar plant and marched to other plants located all over the city, urging the women inside to join them. Many did, although few of the white women on the production lines joined the Black women outside on the first day. One white worker, Nora Diamond, was quoted in the labor press as saying that she stayed on the job because the wages and working conditions of the Black workers "don't affect me . . . and because [the strike] was led by the wrong kind of people, Russians, foreigners," which was to say, communists. In spite of these time-honored, and self-defeating, prejudices against Black and red, many of the white women joined the picket lines on the second day of the strike, and the Funsten plants throughout the city were completely shut down.[39]

The scene outside the plants during the nine days of the strike was by turns (and depending on one's perspective) inspiring, chaotic, and violent. The women carried signs reading ANIMALS IN THE ZOO ARE FED WHILE WE STARVE, and FIGHT FOR THE FREEDOM OF LABOR—DEMAND UNEMPLOYMENT INSURANCE. Many carried their Bibles with them, and they periodically interrupted the picketing to stop and pray. Some of the striking women were joined on the picket lines by their husbands and children as they marched from plant to plant calling for the women inside to come out. The city police were soon deployed to the plants to escort strikebreakers through angry crowds of strikers.

Over the course of the strike, the police arrested at least ninety strikers (including Sentner) on charges of disturbing the peace. Some of the arrested strikers made their initial court appearances still bruised and bandaged from the curbside justice to which the arresting officers had subjected them.[40]

At the head of the crowd outside the closed plants was a Black woman named Carrie Smith, an eighteen-year veteran of Funsten, who had urged a strike vote at the meeting on May 13 with a Bible in one hand and a brick in the other; Smith was subsequently appointed chair of the strike committee. The strikers wanted to be paid, she said, "on the basis of ten cents a pound for half nuts and four cents a pound for pieces," or about $6 a week. "We believe we are entitled to live as well as other folks live, and should be entitled to a wage that will provide us with ample food and clothing," she told the mayor at a meeting called to mediate the strike. At the same meeting, Ardenta Bryant told the mayor that the money she earned at Funsten was not enough to feed her family and she was consequently forced to rely on public assistance to make ends meet, thus driving home the strikers' point that Funsten was taking a subsidy from the city: it was taxpayers who paid for the public assistance that as many as two-thirds of the nutpickers required to keep food on the table. Outside the meeting, 450 Black women protested, having marched from Communist Party headquarters on North Garrison.[41]

On the ninth day, Funsten folded. After a meeting with the mayor and company leaders Eugene and Fairfax Funsten on May 24, Carrie Smith emerged from city hall with an offer from the company to pay the pickers ninety cents per twenty-five-pound box, which represented a doubling of their wages and came close to the "ten and four" (ten cents for halves, four cents for pieces) they had struck to obtain. Along with the mayor, she drove to Communist Party headquarters, where seven hundred strikers had assembled, and presented them with the company's proposal for a vote. It was unanimously approved, and on May 25 the African American nutpickers and white sorters—many white

The Communist Party was active and influential in St. Louis in the 1930s, actively seeking Black members and supporting the struggle of Black workers. (State Historical Society of Missouri)

workers had joined the strike on the second day, and the settlement represented a substantial raise for them as well—returned, triumphant, to work at Funsten.[42]

Before the strike, the nutpickers had been ignored by mainstream civil rights organizations as well as the existing trade unions. After the strike, both the civil rights organizations and the labor movement sought to capitalize on their success. The Communist Party hoped that the Funsten strike would be a watershed moment in their effort to organize Black workers nationally. "You must follow these steps of these nutpickers," the Trade Union Unity League urged other St. Louis unionists in a pamphlet issued at the time of the strike. "You must organize yourselves and strike!" The leaders of the strike, including Carrie Smith, were held up to the nation in the party journals and at party meetings as examples for all workers. The nutpickers had provided a model "that can and should be followed in every section of the country against the slavery imposed on women," wrote a party journalist in *Working Women*. The nutpickers had "aroused the masses of St. Louis like no other strike in years," gaining the "full sympathy and solidarity of the St. Louis working class. . . . One would think that the Negro women had been for years trained in the working class movement." And indeed, in the aftermath of the strike, thousands of Black women, both in the nut plants and in other industries (especially meatpacking), joined the communist-aligned Food Workers Industrial Union.[43]

The conceit that the nutpickers had somehow managed to act and organize according to a party script they had never actually seen papered over a fundamental problem in the communists' approach to co-organizing with African Americans, and with African American women in particular. Both in St. Louis and elsewhere, party organizers were among the earliest and most stalwart supporters of Black workers. When Black women formed a picket line in front of Funsten, the communists walked with them; when they had to feed their families during the strike, the communists provided the food; when they went to jail for "disturbing the peace," the communists went too. But they did so according to an account of the strike understood as an action taken first by workers, second by women, and only incidentally by African Americans. Their theory made it hard for them to understand a struggle that was rooted in the material lives of working-class Black women in Mill Creek Valley and the Ville, in the specific forms of discrimination, exploitation, and violence faced by people who were, all at once, workers, women, and Black (not to mention wives, mothers, and Christians) rather than in the more general circumstances of "the working class." For the communists, the Bibles and prayers on the picket line were simple remnants of archaic ways of thinking, old superstitions and patterns of affiliation that would soon give way to the self-evident imperatives of working-class struggle.[44]

Years later, the Black communist Hershel Walker would remember the 1930s as a decade of terrific possibilities and lost opportunities for the Communist Party in St. Louis. Walker had been born in Arkansas in 1909, the son of a sharecropper. He migrated first to Memphis as a young man, and then to St. Louis in 1930, where he initially stayed with one of his brothers who had migrated several years earlier and lived on the Northside, near Carr Square. It was his brother who introduced him to the *Communist Manifesto*, the Unemployed Councils, and the party. Impressed that party headquarters on North Garrison was only a few blocks from where he lived, near the heart of Black St. Louis, and that the party membership (and leadership) was roughly equally divided between white and Black workers, Walker soon joined the Communist Youth League. He would later become the city's party chairman.[45]

Walker recalled the vibrancy and radicalism of politics in Black St. Louis in those years. In addition to the communists, there was the March on Washington Movement (Walker remembered it as "the Randolph Movement," in honor of one of the principal architects, A. Philip Randolph of the Brotherhood of Sleeping Car Porters), which was anticommunist but rigorously focused on economic justice. And there was what Walker called "the Japanese Movement," the Pacific Movement of the Eastern World, which promoted the idea that Japan would lead a worldwide uprising of the darker nations of the world against imperialism and white supremacy. Mostly forgotten today, the PMEW was centered in St. Louis, where it had thousands of adherents.[46]

In these years, the Black Marxists C.L.R. James and Claudia Jones visited Missouri—not because they thought working-class Black people in the Midwest needed their guidance, but because they wanted to find out what working-class Black people in the Midwest were doing and learn from them. Another regular visitor to the city was William H. Patterson, leader of the Communist Party's International Labor Defense section in the United States and future author of the charges contained in the book *We Charge Genocide*, which was presented to the United Nations in 1951 on behalf of Black Americans. In February 1942, Patterson gave a speech in the city entitled "Sikeston: Hitlerite

Crime against America," which condemned the lynching of the mill worker Cleo Wright and white mob violence in southeastern Missouri in January of that year. The historian Herbert Aptheker, the infamous communist intellectual and, later, the literary executor of W.E.B. Du Bois's estate, was also a frequent visitor to St. Louis during these years. Many years later, Hershel Walker cited the influence of Aptheker's work on his own thinking about the importance of the Black church, which he had underestimated during his days as an organizer.[47]

When he was later asked about the decline of interest of Black workers in the Communist Party, Walker recognized the effect of Cold War anticommunism, but emphasized the limitations of the party itself in its relation to the people in the Black neighborhoods of St. Louis in the 1930s and '40s. The party, he said, had been too focused on getting people to become communists and missed the opportunity to engage people who might have shared many of the party's positions but would never become communists—specifically church people like Carrie Smith. Walker was pressed by the interviewer: "You mean, you didn't bring them along?" No, he said, "We couldn't bring them along. We should have left them where they were." Not by ignoring them, he clarified, but by engaging them where they lived, in their neighborhoods, in the particularity of their own lives and beliefs.[48]

This is not to say that the strike had left the nutpickers' relationship to their churches and communities unchallenged. In spite of the entreaties of many of their parishioners, the ministers in the city's Black churches did not support the strike and focused instead on the foreignness of the communist organizers, many of whom were Jewish, and the hostility of the party to Christianity. Their resistance tested the allegiance of the strikers, who felt abandoned by Black ministers who refused to take up collections for their strike fund. "None came to our rescue but the Communist Party," Carrie Smith later wrote. Both the Urban League and the Universal Negro Improvement Association (the pan-Africanist Garveyites) sat the strike out—the UNIA because of the enduring sectarian polemic with the communists about whether African American workers were first and foremost workers or first and foremost African Americans, the Urban League because the middle-class nature of its prestrike version of racial uplift provided precious little in the way of resources for understanding a movement led by working-class women rather than educated ministers and wealthy professionals.

From the Urban League's perspective, the communists, far from addressing the population's true needs, had taken advantage of "hungry, destitute, and desperate people [who] would follow wherever there was a ray of hope for some kind of relief." "We felt the Negro was being used by something [he] was not a part of and which he was not in sympathy with," read one Urban League after-action account of the strike. The city's middle-class civil rights "leadership" was, by and large, unable to understand the capacity of the nutpickers to organize themselves and point the way forward for everyone else, just as it was apparently unable to find language to understand a struggle that was led by Black *women* rather than men. Even more revealing, perhaps, was the explanation offered by a longtime Urban League organizer: "The League did not take an active part in this Strike. . . . The Negro women working in these storefronts . . . many of them had open sores on their arms and their hands—no health requirements were enforced—and for that reason the League wasn't interested in furthering their cause." Perhaps the most charitable reading of that remark would be, for a time, the bourgeois integrationism and uplift ideology characteristic of the Urban League in the early 1930s made it difficult for some of its members to understand, make common cause with, or, still less, believe that they had something to learn from the Black women who went on strike at Funsten.[49]

But learn they did. The St. Louis Urban League had been founded in 1918 to "assist" southern migrants in their transition to life in the city. From that time on, the league's Women's Division served as a matchmaking agency for white women seeking domestic servants and Black women seeking jobs: league members evaluated the job-seekers' abilities, tried to place those whom they considered well mannered and tidy in jobs as cooks, maids, or laundresses in suitable white households, and steered job-seekers away from unsuitable jobs. In September 1933, however, the Women's Division began to follow a different pathway. Responding to the complaints of Black women—who accounted for about 40 percent of the domestic service employees in the city—the Women's Division held a mass meeting for the women to air their grievances. First among them was their exclusion from the protective provisions of the National Industrial Recovery Act, which excluded the vast majority of Black workers in the United States by offering no provision for domestic servants (or landless agricultural workers, many of whom also were Black).

But many of the thousand or so African American domestic workers who attended the meeting expressed more immediate concerns about the condition of their employment. They were forced to pay for uniforms and streetcar fare. They had to be available whenever their employers wanted them and to make ends meet whenever they did not—when their employers were away on vacation, for instance. At the end of the meeting, the women of the Urban League joined the domestic workers in agreeing to a set of industry standards: a maximum of forty-eight hours of work a week for live-out domestics and fifty-four hours for those who lived in; overtime pay by the hour; one week of paid vacation per year and one day off per week; private living space and bathroom for those who lived in; accident insurance; and transparent and binding agreements about who would cover work-related expenses. Although these standards were not binding on white employers, they represented a substantial evolution in the middle-class Urban League's attitude toward working-class Black women—from paternalistic "support" to something closer to actual solidarity.[50]

Black workers in St. Louis continued to strike through the years of the Depression and the Second World War. African American workers had long voted in St. Louis, and so the city's freedom movement, from the beginning (and to the end), emphasized economic equality in addition to issues of access to public accommodations, parks, and pools. The critique of economic injustice that historians identify as having come to characterize the mainstream of the civil rights movement only in 1968, with Martin Luther King Jr.'s support of the sanitation workers' strike in Memphis, had a much longer history in St. Louis. Organizing through the March on Washington Movement, the Communist Party, and the industrial unions of the CIO (the AFL locals remained segregated), Black workers in St. Louis sought both equal access to jobs and equal treatment on the production line once they got those jobs.[51]

In 1937, young women from the Black neighborhoods of St. Louis formed the Colored Clerks' Circle in order to pressure businesses that operated in Black neighborhoods to hire Black clerks. "Don't Buy Where You Can't Work," they urged Black consumers, coining a phrase that became a national standard. The Black women of the CCC demonstrated in front of Walgreen's, Gerken's Hats, the Matier Shoe Store, and the Nafziger Baking Company; at Kroger's for a month; and outside the National Clothing Store for twelve hours on a winter day when the temperature was three degrees. The result was 150 stores picketed and 200 jobs secured. The Urban League was grudgingly respectful of the young protesters who had secured these jobs for their community, but unwilling to acknowledge that the established civil rights organizations might have something to learn from the young people on the streets in front of the stores. "The one lamentable fact," St. Louis Urban League staffers wrote in the organization's national journal, "is that the mass-pressure method of securing jobs . . . does not seem to have evolved a well thought-out theory of action. Too many energetic Negro youths have gone to battle armed with no theory at all, but simply a rugged determination to get jobs." Their worry about the young people who were challenging the merchants and changing the city was a bourgeois mirror image of the communists' anxiety that Black women activists needed a proper theory.[52]

When workers at Emerson Electric, mostly white but including some Black porters and janitors, went on strike on March 9, 1937, Black workers elsewhere in St. Louis supported them. Workers at the downtown plant simply sat down on the job; by occupying the factory and shutting down the production line, they forestalled any possibility of bringing in replacement workers. The striking workers organized a three-shift security watch, played cards and checkers, staged shows, produced a daily newspaper, and held daily prayer services for the observant. They were visited by Norman Thomas, the Socialist Party candidate for president in 1936, who marched with protesters outside the plant carrying a sign reading CAN WE LIVE ON PROMISES?

William Sentner, now an organizer for the United Electrical, Radio, and Machine Workers (CIO), was one of the leaders of the strike. He led a march on city hall and a sit-in at the St. Louis Relief Administration office to demand that the city provide food for the striking workers and their families. When the mayor temporized, Sentner's small army of communists and trade unionists occupied city hall, just as they had done in 1932. And also as in 1932, the occupiers were both Black and white, women and men. Supported by a coalition that had its roots in the Unemployed Councils, the Communist Party, the "July Riot," and the Funsten Nut strike, and represented by a negotiating committee that included at least one communist (Sentner), one African American (Troy Lee), and one white woman (Hilda Marasche), the workers at Emerson held the plant for fifty-three days—the second-longest sit-down strike in the history of the nation—and won a new contract that included a substantial wage increase. In the teeth of the Depression, Black and white workers in St. Louis had created a radical alliance capable of exacting substantial concessions from both business interests and the city government.[53]

The Second World War transformed the economy of St. Louis. Ever since the development of the nineteenth-century lead smelters and military bases that supported the expansion of the American empire to the Pacific and beyond, St. Louis had boasted a strong military-industrial sector. As the US economy converted to war production, St.

Louis industrialists were at the forefront. On the eve of Pearl Harbor, there were no fewer than sixty thousand military contracts being fulfilled in St. Louis. Almost three hundred St. Louis firms were involved in wartime defense work, including the airplane manufacturer Curtiss-Wright, which was the second-largest recipient of defense contracts in the nation. By the end of the war, 75 percent of the industrial firms in the city were doing defense work—well above the national average.[54]

For factory owners, war production was easy money. War production contracts were generally on a cost-plus basis, with the government bearing the cost of plant conversions *plus* a guaranteed profit margin. In 1940, Atlas Powder became the nation's largest producer of TNT; the American Car Company and St. Louis Car Company switched over their streetcar production lines in order to build tanks. During the war, Emerson Electric grew from a regional supplier of small motors and consumer electronics into one of the largest industrial firms in the United States. The army's Office of Production Management built a 700,000-square-foot factory on the Emerson campus, where the company manufactured 40,000 gun turrets for the B-17 Flying Fortress bombers during the war. In the process, Emerson's annual revenue grew almost 200 percent between 1940 and 1944. The same company that had $4.8 million in sales in 1940 made $487 million in military contracts over the course of the war. With federal support, US Cartridge built the largest small arms ammunition plant in the world near Pine Lawn, and Mallinckrodt Chemical constructed the largest high-explosives plant in the nation in nearby Weldon Springs.[55]

Much of the practical work of building the atomic bombs that were eventually dropped on Hiroshima and Nagasaki was done in St. Louis. With government support, the Physics Department at Washington University built a particle accelerator to aid in the creation of weapons-grade plutonium, and scientists from Monsanto provided the plutonium for the first atomic bombs. Mallinckrodt Chemical processed sixty tons of uranium for the Manhattan Project, including the uranium that provided the raw material for the first sustained nuclear chain reaction in 1942—an aspect of the city's role in global history that continues to unfold in underground waste dumps and toxic groundwater across the region today.[56]

For African Americans, who had long been shut out of industrial jobs in St. Louis, sharing in the region's wartime economic gains required fighting for jobs. In St. Louis, that fight was led by the local office of the March on Washington Movement, one of the largest and most radical branches in the nation. After a threat from the Movement had forced President Franklin D. Roosevelt's 1941 Executive Order 8802 outlawing racial, gender, and religious discrimination in federal defense work, the organization's efforts focused on trying to get St. Louis companies to honor both the letter and the spirit of federal law. During the war, Black workers picketed Carter Carburetor and Bussman Manufacturing, protesting their whites-only hiring, and they also picketed US Steel and US Cartridge Company's massive "Small Arms" plant (as it was known), the largest plant of its kind in the world. Picketers demanded jobs for Black workers in general and Black women in particular, with signs reading, TWENTY THOUSAND WORKERS AT SMALL ARMS PLANT IN PRODUCTION—NOT ONE NEGRO, and 8,000 WOMEN EMPLOYED—NOT ONE NEGRO WOMAN. Hershel Walker gave a sense of the dangers faced by African American justice-seekers in those times: for the fifty or sixty Black protesters in the "march on the bullet plant," which employed tens of thousands of whites—rural Missouri whites who had come to St. Louis for war jobs they desperately needed—approaching that plant "was taking your life in your hands."[57]

The reality of high employment and the exigency of war production placed labor in a bargaining position that had been unimaginable in the lean years of the 1930s. For the most part, however, working people were forced to accept bargains made by political and organizational leaders: communists were instructed by the Comintern to support the war effort in accordance with the "Popular Front" strategy of postponing the struggle against capitalism until after the defeat of fascism, and the national unions (including the CIO unions) signed no-strike pledges. These agreements did not stop Black workers in St. Louis from staging wildcat strikes for better pay, better working conditions—including the integration of the production line—and the right to unionize at those plants where African Americans were employed, including Wagner Electric and, eventually, Small Arms. They were supported by the local chapters of the March on Washington and by William Sentner and District 9 of the Electrical Workers (in defiance of the position of the national CIO). In the fall of 1943, six hundred Black men walked off the job at General Steel Castings to protest the fact that the plant employed no Black women. Gradually, they made progress. Nine hundred Black workers, including two hundred machinists and three hundred women, were working at Small Arms by the end of 1942; by the end of the following year, more than four times that number worked at the plant, although, in deference to the racists working elsewhere in the plant, all of them were located in a single building, number 202. Neither the shame of East St. Louis nor the successes at Funsten Nut and Emerson Electric could convince some whites that they should make common cause with their fellows on the line.[58]

Almost as soon as Black workers won positions on the production lines, industry leaders began to worry about the economic wind-down that would come with the end of the war, which would require billions of dollars of capital to reconvert to peacetime production. Ten million soldiers would return, and they would need work. For many war workers, especially African American and female war workers, and most particularly African American female war workers, reconversion portended a disaster.

Even before the end of the war, production cuts began to bite. As government orders declined, plants cut overtime, which cut workers' take-home pay as much as 30 percent. Because they had been the last to be hired, African Americans were the first to be let go as military orders declined and wartime production lines were shut down. Thus were the discriminatory hiring practices of the early war years converted into unemployment and economic precarity in the years immediately following the war. In July 1943, US Cartridge cut production in building number 202, laying off an entire shift; in November, the company laid off one thousand more Black workers. The aircraft producer Curtiss-Wright laid off 50 percent of its Black workers in the same year. Carter Carburetor and McDonnell-Douglas soon followed, laying off Black workers as government orders declined. White workers were also threatened by the cutbacks and often responded with misguided aggression toward their Black coworkers. Beginning in the spring of 1944 at the General Cable Company, and lasting through the duration of the postwar reconversion, white industrial workers in St. Louis staged a series of hate strikes protesting the hiring of Black workers.[59]

Hate strikes were only one aspect of the social disorder that many feared would follow the inevitable postwar industrial contraction. The recent history of capitalism provided an indelible memory of what might happen if reconversion failed to provide jobs for ten million returning veterans: the hoboes and Hoovervilles of the Great Depression and, most pointedly, the 1932 Bonus Army of over forty thousand unemployed workers, many of them First World War veterans, who marched on Washington and camped in the city while demanding payment of wartime military bonuses (and who were eventually routed by the DC police and army units under the command of General Douglas MacArthur the younger). In St. Louis, Sentner and the CEO of Emerson Electric, Stuart Symington, joined a group of other local leaders—an Episcopal bishop, who sat at the head of the group, the CEO of Monsanto Chemical, and several lawyers—in what they termed the Serious Thinkers Club to work out a postwar settlement for the city. Symington and Sentner were profiled in *Fortune* magazine—"A Yale Man and a Communist"—as examples of what was possible (no strikes, the production of hundreds of thousands of gun turrets, the massive expansion of production and revenue) when the representatives of capital and labor trusted one another and pulled together. By the close of the war, Symington had been appointed by President Harry S. Truman to be the head of the government's Surplus Property Board, which was responsible for the conversion of war-related government property to the use of private enterprise.[60]

Nationally, the solution to the economic crisis of the end of war turned out to be simply not letting the war end. The continuation of a global fight for freedom, epitomized by the Marshall Plan for the reconstruction of Europe and the beginning of the Korean War in 1950, were the most obvious material manifestations. Both required continued government investment in the defense industry. Almost as soon as it had closed down, the US Cartridge production line that produced 30mm small-arms ammunition for the army in the Second World War reopened as a plant producing 105mm artillery shells for the US Army to use in Korea.

In St. Louis, Sentner and the UE (United Electrical, Radio, and Machine Workers) supported plans for a massive Missouri Valley Authority—a public works program on the model of the Tennessee Valley Authority—that would transform the Missouri River into a series of flood-controlled reservoirs that could be used by valley farmers for irrigation during the planting season. In 1944, they got a guarantee of union jobs in the enormous Pick-Sloan Missouri River Basin Project (not quite as enormous as the MVA, but still enormous) begun in 1944: five huge earthen dams intended to provide flood protection and water for irrigation to the Missouri Valley's agricultural settlers. As visionary as the scheme must have seemed to labor activists in St. Louis, it was framed by the same imperialist blinkers that had narrowed the vision of many of the nineteenth-century radicals. The Pick-Sloan dams flooded hundreds of thousands of acres of land on Lakota and Dakota reservations—Santee, Yankton, Rosebud, Lower Brule, Crow Creek, and Standing Rock—themselves vastly reduced from the size of the Great Sioux Nation established by the Fort Laramie Treaty of 1868. It was, according to historian Nick Estes, "a twentieth-century Indigenous apocalypse"—and one that foreshadowed a similar catastrophe along Mill Creek Valley in St. Louis a decade later.[61]

These postwar "bargains" marked the subordination of the radical alliance of communists and African Americans that had shaped the labor history of St. Louis in a new relationship between capital and labor. These new arrangements were subsidized by the US government and made under the Taft-Hartley Act (1947), which required union leaders to sign an oath attesting that they had never been communists and had never supported the overthrow of the US government. This requirement effectively sidelined the most radical of the unions, like Sentner's UE, which went from 600,000 active members in the years immediately after the war to 200,000 by 1953. Sentner himself was voted out of his leadership position in the UE in 1949 and convicted in 1952 under the 1940 Smith Act for having once advocated the violent overthrow of the United States—in other words, for having been a member of the Communist Party. Though his conviction was overturned in 1958, his career as an organizer was over.[62]

The Taft-Hartley Act also ignored the evident problems of discriminatory hiring and firing in the postwar economy and the question of seniority: how were Black workers, working women, and most especially Black working women, ever to attain enough seniority to gain priority within their union and avoid being the "first fired" during slack times, given that they were always, almost by definition, the "last hired" and had long been barred from many of the unions now given federal legal sanction as the representatives of "labor"?[63] The Black women and communists of the Unemployed Councils, the Funsten Nut strike, and the Emerson sit-down strike; the freedom fighters of the March on Washington Movement, the fight for fair employment, and the protests in front of Small Arms; even the dogged lawyers of the NAACP and the behind-the-scenes moral suasionists of the Urban League: all of these were left out of the postwar economic settlement between the US government, the corporations, and organized labor. This settlement amounted to a second counterrevolution of property that took and takes the shape of officially sanctioned dispossession and dispersal of Black people and government-subsidized employment and elevation of white people.

Within the city of St. Louis, a tacit bargain was struck to achieve a massive reconstruction of the city fabric in the name of jobs, progress, and property values: urban renewal. As elsewhere in the nation, and as in the case of the Pick-Sloan project and the Indians of the Missouri Valley, this was, in effect, a jobs program for white men that involved the destruction of the encircled homes of darker people, in this case the people who lived in Mill Creek Valley. It would not, however, be correct to term this massive project "previously unimaginable." As it turned out, city leaders had been imagining the destruction of large sections of Black (and radical) St. Louis for quite some time.

9 | "BLACK REMOVAL BY WHITE APPROVAL"

When white folks want you gone, you gone.

—JAMALA ROGERS, *Ferguson Is America*

THE 1907 CITY PLAN FOR ST. LOUIS WAS THE FIRST COMPRE-
hensive planning document produced by any city in the United States.
It proposed a network of parks and vistas of the Mississippi River that
would bind the city neighborhoods together, with a huge downtown
park devoted to the city's greatest geographic (and scenic) asset—the
Mississippi River. The plan recommended channeling industrial development into certain areas of the city, thereby minimizing the effects
of nuisance and pollution on the general population while enhancing
"property values" throughout the city. It was to be government action
taken on behalf of regulated economic development, public health,
and civic cultural and (white) racial cohesion. The plan specifically
mentioned the need to create connections and social harmony between
various ethnic enclaves in the city—Italian, German, Russian, Jewish,
"and so on." As for Black St. Louis, it recommended the "transformation" of Chestnut Valley into a public park.[1]

At the heart of the plan that lies at the root of the history of city planning in the United States was an expressed horror at the Black-owned and -operated nightclubs, saloons, and bordellos in the neighborhood along Chestnut Street between city hall and Union Station. And the same document proposed a solution that has shaped the history of St. Louis (and the United States) down to the present day: take it, tear it down, and bury the memory.

No single person's name has been as consistently associated with the destruction of the neighborhoods of Black St. Louis as Harland Bartholomew. Bartholomew, who began working for the city of St. Louis in 1916, was appointed city planning commissioner in 1919 and held that role until 1950. During that time, he was also the principal of Harland Bartholomew and Associates, which served as a consulting firm for over 150 American and Canadian cities, including Atlanta, Chicago, Honolulu, Indianapolis, Kansas City, Los Angeles, Memphis, New Orleans, New York City, Vancouver, and Washington, DC. Bartholomew was an early advocate of comprehensive planning, single-use zoning, and automobile-based transportation planning. He was appointed to various federal commissions, frequently testified before Congress, and capped his career as chairman of the National Capital Planning Commission, to which he was appointed by President Dwight D. Eisenhower. He has, with some justice, been called "the father of American urban planning."[2]

For Bartholomew, city planning, especially zoning, was an expansion of the "police power" of the state—the exercise of law in support of the general welfare. Along with Progressive-era city planners in New York and Chicago, Bartholomew outlined a vision in which "zoning is a justifiable use of the police power in the interests of health, safety, and the general welfare," with "general welfare" defined as enhancing property values in order to support a city's tax base. Although he was living in a city that had just passed a racial segregation ordinance based on the argument that Black "invaders" were destroying the property values in "white" neighborhoods, and across the river from a city in which white terrorists had driven thousands of Black people from their homes and into St. Louis, Bartholomew alluded only indirectly to the relation of racism and segregation to zoning and real estate in the tens of thousands of pages of city plans he produced over his career. About as close as he came in his plans for the city of St. Louis were his repeated uses of the phrase "the district east of Grand" in his 1919 plan, along with his observation that most of the areas of the city that he hoped to zone as "single-family residential" already had "restriction in the deeds" that protected the value of the properties from unwanted development.[3]

It was Bartholomew's particular malign genius (one historian has termed it a form of "administrative evil") to be able to translate the terms of existing institutional racism—the "segregation ordinance" and the "restrictive covenant"—into the notionally color-blind terms of liberal white supremacy—"property values" and "the public good." This was the role he had played as the chair of the Conference on Home Building and Home Ownership, a position he was appointed to by the floridly racist President Herbert Hoover in 1931 in recognition, according to the historian Richard Rothstein, of Bartholomew's skill in keeping St. Louis segregated even in the aftermath of the Supreme Court's 1916 decision in *Buchanan v. Warley*. Zoning, Bartholomew had written in defense of his 1919 plan for the city, was protection "against the day when private restrictions expire." Zoning, that is to say, was segregation by other means: "before decay sets in it seems absolutely necessary, logical, and reasonable to establish permanent restrictions which will continue to preserve those districts in their present condition." Necessary, logical, and reasonable—bywords of the man who, by 1931, would be the segregation and suburbanization czar of the United States, using St. Louis, by every account, as his laboratory.[4]

As his reputation and power in St. Louis grew in the years after the First World War, Bartholomew turned the city's attention to the warehouse district that had once been the administrative center of the American empire. A 1915 effort to replace the nightclubs and lean-to houses that stretched along Chestnut Valley had been defeated by a campaign centered on the message that, if "15,000 Negroes who now live in that district will be forced to find other quarter. Some of them may move in next door to you." But as the Depression deepened, more of the industrial capacity along the Mississippi was idled and the area along the riverfront became a refuge for the unemployed and unhoused (as well as an incubator of radical ideas and threatening solidarities). In 1928, Bartholomew proposed a new city plan centered on riverfront redevelopment, and over the next decade that plan guided the response of the city of St. Louis to the Depression: tearing down its actually existing history and replacing it with a (hoped-for) monument.[5]

Bartholomew had a powerful ally in Mayor Bernard Dickmann, a real estate developer by trade, who saw the potential of the riverfront— not the potential of rebuilding it, for there was no real plan to do that at first, but the potential of tearing it down. In 1935, in the teeth of the Depression, Dickmann presented city voters with a bond issue for redeveloping (read: bulldozing) the riverfront. The immediate benefit to the city was advertised to be five thousand jobs. The mayor and his guild also looked forward to a large taking: some of them through negotiating sweetheart deals with the city for the sale of property they owned in the targeted district, others through the anticipated windfall to those who owned industrial property and warehouses elsewhere in the city. There was more than five million square feet of industrial space in the buildings along the riverfront. All of what it contained would have to go somewhere: "The absorption of this large amount of space, together with the short period of time available for procuring new locations will temporarily, and perhaps permanently, increase real estate values in St. Louis." Led by the mayor, the real estate interest was putting the squeeze on business owners by downsizing the city, tearing down one neighborhood in order to increase the value of another. The lives and livelihoods of the people who lived and worked in the neighborhood were an acceptable cost.[6]

The idea of making the riverfront into a monument emerged only after the mayor and the landlords realized how much money could be made by tearing it down. If the area could be converted into a national monument, there might be federal money available for its reconstruction, and it was on the basis of a hastily agreed understanding with the president and the National Park Service that matching funds would (might?) be available for redevelopment that the mayor put the bond issue before the city in 1935. The bond issue, which was strongly supported by the realtors and the unions (especially the AFL-organized building trades, which, remember, were open only to whites in St. Louis), was presented to the city by a corveé mobilization of seven thousand city employees who were instructed by Mayor Dickmann to set aside whatever else they were doing to go door to door in support of the measure. "I hate to be a dictator," the mayor said at the time, "but . . . "[7]

The massive voter fraud revealed by the *St. Louis Post-Dispatch* in the aftermath of the vote makes it impossible to know what would have actually happened in an honest election, but as far as the mayor was concerned, the 1935 bond issue passed by a margin of nearly three-to-one. After a stare-down with the federal government about whether or not there had actually been any promise to match funds from the city, the mayor got his National Park Service money, and the bulldozers moved on the waterfront, beginning on October 9, 1939. "We have made every retail corner in the downtown area more valuable," crowed one of the city's developers in a letter written shortly after the approval of the bond issue.[8]

Beneath today's Gateway Arch National Park lies the memory of the thirty-seven square blocks of the historic riverfront. Two hundred apartment buildings and houses were among the four hundred or so buildings that were torn down in the fall of 1939, almost all of them occupied by renters, many of them Black. So, too, the cluster of bars, coffeehouses, and squats that had once been known as the "Greenwich Village of the West," the places where the poets and the radicals had met and conspired during the years of the Depression. It was almost as if Mayor Dickmann were revenging himself upon on the Black-communist-bohemian alliance that had so often demonstrated outside (and sometimes inside) his office in the 1930s.[9]

As many as five thousand people had jobs in the old riverfront district, at companies like Seller-Brown-Coffee, Federal Fur and Wool, and Prunty Seed and Grain—companies that reflected the city's history as the hub of the American empire. It was only after they came down that it became apparent that there was no real plan for the riverfront—only a plan to make a plan. And so for twenty-five years the city's planners and developer visionaries cycled through possible plans: maybe it could be a football stadium or an airport or a gigantic bomb shelter for all of the residents of the city's downtown. In the meantime, the city of St. Louis could boast that it had the largest municipal parking lot in the world. That was not quite the architectural homage to the city's imperial past that Bartholomew's 1928 plan had imagined, but at least it helped with the congestion.[10]

If St. Louis is today known for the Finnish-American architect Eero Saarinen's Arch, which was finally built on the riverfront beginning in 1964, the city is directly encountered on an everyday level according to the vision of Harland Bartholomew's 1947 *Comprehensive City Plan*. It was in this plan that Bartholomew outlined the network of expressways and arterial highways that channels the city's traffic to this day. (The city is the only place in the United States where four interstate highways converge.) The 1947 plan also provided the basic template for the city's zoning, separating single-family houses from apartment buildings and industrial development. Bartholomew's plan modeled for the nation a future of suburbs, automobiles, and airplanes; it was a first draft of the material fabric of our contemporary lives. And it relied on the extensive use of the city's "police power" in the form of zoning, as well as on novel forms of development-supporting tax abatement that Bartholomew himself had promoted and seen written into the revised state constitution in 1945.

The *Comprehensive City Plan* was based upon projections that the population of the city would reach one million by 1970 (and just as improbably, as it turned out, that the city and county would be administratively reunited); its thirty-one maps and fifteen tables tracked population patterns, traffic densities, and travel times and compared them to other US cities. The plan was designed around automobiles and motion: wide roads and ample parking for those commuters coming in from pleasant single-family homes in low-density neighborhoods to work in the city center, and thirty-five airports, including several heliports, to make it easy to get anywhere in the world from anywhere in the city. Bartholomew sought to reduce population density and increase access to sunlight by lowering the height of the city and expanding its limits—effectively by spreading it farther across the broad floodplain between the Mississippi and the Missouri—and to anchor its neighborhoods with parks, schools, and libraries, tying them together with a network of boulevards and scenic parkways. All in all, Bartholomew's 1947 *Comprehensive City Plan* provided a beginner's guide to building a racist city—incising and intensifying existing differences of race and class in the physical form of the built environment.[11]

Two of the three superhighways that would tie the downtown to the suburbs were to be routed through one of the city's principal Black neighborhoods: one, on the Northside, through Carr Square then alongside the northern boundary of Fairground Park; the other, on the Southside, straight up through the heart of Mill Creek Valley. Planning for the construction of the superhighways began in the fall of 1943, the year when, amid the growing anxiety about the increased unemployment that would come with the end of the war, the American concrete industry recommended that highways could "contribute in a substantial manner to the elimination of slum and deteriorated areas." While the route of the Mark Twain Expressway (Interstate 70) was eventually adjusted to take a slightly wider circuit around the Northside and thus destroy a slightly less densely populated Black neighborhood, the terms of the basic bargain remained the same when construction began in 1950: contracts for all-white contractors and jobs for all-white workers in all-white unions, subsidized access for whites to the segregated suburbs that were expanding west of the city,

and destruction and displacement for the residents of the neighborhoods that stood in the pathway of progress. Not even the dead could
escape civic progress: I-70 was built directly through the historically
Black Washington Cemetery, requiring the disinterment of thousands
whose graves were relocated to cemeteries all over the metropolitan
area, in a process so haphazard that the locations of many remain a
mystery today.[12]

As tragic as the destruction of these neighborhoods has seemed to
many subsequent observers, for Bartholomew it was less an acceptable
cost than a fortunate happenstance. For at the very heart of his plan
was a proposal to demolish most of Black St. Louis. Of course, Bartholomew did not say that. He did not need to. There was not a single
explicit reference to "Negroes" or "segregation" in the *Comprehensive
City Plan*. Instead, there were maps and tables that outlined the deplorable conditions of the slumlord rentier–owned neighborhoods east
of Grand: the density of habitation, the number of outdoor toilets, the
usage of buildings built before 1900, the proportion of "sub-standard"
(a term undefined) accommodations. Rather than seeing the poor
conditions as an index of racist exploitation in a segregated housing
market and trying to do something to build the neighborhoods up,
Bartholomew simply proposed tearing them down. In the 7 percent of
the area of the city he judged to be "obsolete," Bartholomew wanted
to tear everything down. That was an arc about ten blocks wide
around the downtown, an area of almost three thousand acres—three
times the size of Central Park in New York City, seven times the size
of the French Quarter in New Orleans, almost ten times the size of
the National Mall in Washington, DC, and thirty times the size of
Disneyland in Los Angeles. Moreover, Bartholomew declared one-
quarter of the remaining portion of the city—a gigantic arc around
the center of the city encompassing about half of the Northside and
a good deal of the Southside—to be "blighted" and proposed tearing
down large portions of it. That was eleven thousand acres of city land:
houses and apartment buildings and corner stores and insurance agen-

cies, places where people were born and lived and worked and laughed and loved and died. All told, Bartholomew was recommending the renovation by destruction of over twenty square miles.[13]

It was Bartholomew's view that the reconstruction of the city would pay for itself in the form of new investments and an improved revenue structure. During the Depression, he had employed workers from the Works Progress Administration to do a financial survey of all the city's neighborhoods; he concluded that many areas of the city were absorbing more in city spending than they were producing in tax revenue—to the tune of $4 million annually. New businesses would be encouraged to relocate in the cleared areas around the downtown with a new redevelopment tool that Bartholomew himself had designed and promoted to the state legislature—a tax abatement, which would be included in the Chapter 353 Urban Redevelopment Act. Available only to those who planned to build in "blighted" areas of the city, Chapter 353 abatements encouraged investment by defraying the risk of such investment with an offer to entrepreneurs of a twenty-five-year real estate tax abatement. By simply tearing down all these neighborhoods, Bartholomew concluded, the city would save the $4 million a year it was spending on maintaining infrastructure from which it received no revenue in return. It could then encourage the reconstruction of those buildings on terms favorable to businesses that would contribute to the city's economy and its revenue structure.[14]

It was vintage Bartholomew: necessary, logical, reasonable. Unless you slowed down to figure out what was really going on. Bartholomew had used white workers who were being paid by the federal government—white workers on the dole—to produce a report suggesting that their Black neighbors were living at the expense of white taxpayers (rather than that white intellectuals were living at the expense of Black people whose social life and economic plight formed the basis of their own federally subsidized salaries). From that unstable first principle, Bartholomew raced to reach what we must imagine was a foreordained conclusion: underperforming neighborhoods, virtually all of

One of the leading urban planners in the United States, Harland Bartholomew
had his greatest influence in St. Louis. His 1947 plan for the city recommended
the complete or substantial demolition of almost twenty square miles. (Washington University in St. Louis Special Collections)

them inhabited by Black people, should be torn down and replaced with
supposedly revenue-producing businesses that would be induced by tax
abatements (by the government forgoing the revenue they produced,
that is, but never mind . . .) to build in these "blighted" areas.

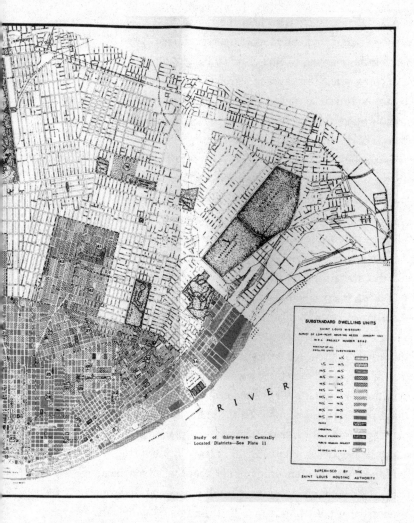

There was more to the story, it turned out, than that. More to
it than wanting to address the poor living conditions in the neighborhoods where Black St. Louisans rented (and much less frequently
owned) some of the oldest housing stock in the city, neighborhoods in
which Bartholomew's office workers had been paid to go around and
count the number of outdoor toilets—89 in Compton Hill, 1,066 in
Hyde Park, 3,190 in Soulard, and so on. There was more to it even than

a good-government effort to help the city of St. Louis maximize its revenue so that it could build more (segregated) parks and playgrounds for its sunshine-loving (white) citizens. Besides all this, there was the fear of contagion. "This cancerous growth may engulf the entire city if steps are not taken to prevent it," read the caption on Bartholomew's ostensibly scientific survey map of the "obsolete" and "blighted" neighborhoods of the city of St. Louis.[15]

Bartholomew's alarm was soon echoed in the press. In February 1948, the *St. Louis Post-Dispatch* published a map of the Mill Creek Valley neighborhood under the headline "Cancerous Slum District Eating Away at the Heart of the City." Two months later, the paper published a full-page photo spread that included images of dilapidated buildings and street scenes in Mill Creek Valley; the accompanying short article noted that the Anti-Slum Commission was considering a bond issue to tear down the neighborhood. The caption of one photo contrasts the broken-down condition of the buildings on the east side of Grand to the line of tall buildings fortifying the western side of Grand. Another photo simply shows three African American children—they look to be about eight years old—on the sidewalk in front of a group of rowhouses; one of them is riding a bike. The headline is "Marching Blight"—as if those three little kids produced the architecture of segregation and exploitation amid which they lived and were planning a mission out to some white neighborhood to see if they could ruin that too.[16]

If there was any remaining doubt about what Bartholomew was talking about—that is, *whom* he was talking about—he specified that it was of the utmost importance that the "good, comparatively new residential areas in the northern, western, and southern sections of St. Louis" be protected from the changes occurring elsewhere in the city. "The enactment of the much delayed revised zoning ordinance will be extremely beneficial to these areas. Supplementing the zoning, however, there should be encouragement for the formation of strong neighborhood associations interested in protecting their character and environment"—in other words, what you or I or any reader of the

Comprehensive City Plan who had even a glancing familiarity with the history and geography of St. Louis in 1947 would call "racial covenants." That was as close as Bartholomew ever got to saying it out loud: the basic premise of his plan for the future of St. Louis, the unarticulated imperative driving the entire venture, was residential segregation.

St. Louis never built the thirty-five airports and heliports Bartholomew asked for, but it did much of the rest of what the 1947 city plan called for. The city today is evidently shaped by the city Bartholomew imagined. The interstate highways are roughly where Bartholomew suggested they should be: Natural Bridge Road, Gravois, and Forest Park Parkway are the same superwide arteries connecting the suburbs and the downtown that he had used to scaffold his plan. The downtown is full of the parking lots and garages that he thought would be necessary to accommodate the quarter-million vehicles he imagined would be driving more than 2.4 billion miles annually in and out of downtown St. Louis by 1970. Following the 1947 plan, the city of St. Louis built the infrastructure of white exodus—much of it directly through Mill Creek Valley, the 471-acre area bounded by Grand to the west, Olive to the north, Twentieth to the east, and Scott and the railroad to the south. All of the one hundred square blocks—where almost twenty thousand people, 95 percent of them Black, lived in the years after the Second World War—that were marked for destruction in that sector of Bartholomew's plan were eventually destroyed.[17]

The city's adoption of Bartholomew's 1947 plan and the rumors of its imminent destruction that soon followed put Mill Creek Valley in a deep freeze. No one wanted to buy anything there or fix anything up because they were afraid that it might all soon be torn down. "Then the realty sharks would come in," remembered onetime resident Robert Riley. Real estate agents bought up property they knew the city would soon have to buy from them. "The technique was to come with a suitcase filled with money, new bills. Sit here, talk with you, offer you this cash money. Sign your name. They took advantage of people knowing they were going to have to move."[18] This doesn't sound that different from the treaties that William Clark made with the eastern tribes a century and a quarter earlier and six miles to the northwest: create a climate of fear based on an imminent threat of removal and offer a short-term induce-ment to move with a vague promise of resettlement. Gradually, those who could afford to leave the neighborhood, or who thought they could afford to leave the neighborhood, or who could be cajoled and deceived into believing they could afford to leave the neighborhood, did. They left behind those who were too poor or too old or too bound by their families or their homes or their jobs or even their own unrealistic hopes to leave.[19]

There was no real plan to help any of the residents of Mill Creek Valley find homes. In October 1948, the city's Race Relations Commis-sion, made up of community and faith leaders appointed by the mayor, distributed a report predicting that the city's existing plans would lead to a massive dislocation of Black residents. Noting that cities like Chi-cago had included relocation funds in their neighborhood-destroying bond issues, the commission suggested that the same be done in St. Louis, and in any event it demanded that the city make a moral "guar-antee" to support the relocation of Mill Creek Valley residents to the city's white neighborhoods. The city's Progressive Party followed up by writing to the League of Women Voters asking for help in cosponsor-ing a conference on the housing crisis, a letter that should be read as a plea from left-of-center white and Black progressives to centrist whites for help in averting a crisis in the Black community. The letter was passed between several of the leaders of the league, each of whom pen-ciled in possible responses before it reached the president. It sits today in a file folder housing the league's "Slum Clearance Correspondence" file, interleaved with chummy letters from St. Louis bankers who noted their financial support for the league and urged its leaders to support the city's effort to do something about "the sore spot at the center of our

Mayor Raymond Tucker (right) and Sidney Maestre look out over rowhouses in Mill Creek Valley. The displacement of over twenty thousand African Americans was justified as a way to reduce "blight" and replace it with "economic development." (Missouri Historical Society)

city." How did the president of the League of Women Voters respond to the Progressive Party's request for support in drawing attention to the plight of those who would be unhoused by the clearance plans? The penciled notation reads, "'No' is my answer to this letter."[20]

In truth, the division of labor that had defined the previous thirty years of Black and radical struggle in St. Louis left many of the existing organizations ill equipped to confront the removalism of real estate–speculative racial capitalism after the war. Labor radicals, including Black labor radicals, had long been focused on fighting for the rights of Black *workers*, and much less on thinking about the condition of Black lives outside the factory gates—which is what Hershel Walker meant when he suggested that the communists should have spent more time listening and less time talking in the neighborhoods where they recruited. The unions, even those that were not themselves segregated, were focused on supporting social policies that created jobs, and Bartholomew's plan certainly promised that, although almost all of these jobs would be in the (almost all-white) building trades. The Urban League had been decrying the condition of neighborhoods like Mill Creek Valley for more than a decade; it could hardly turn around and try to preserve it. And the NAACP, which had just won a huge victory against housing segregation in the city of St. Louis, was now faced with a plan that would ostensibly promote mixed-race neighborhoods, although no one could quite say how the people who were being displaced were going to be able to afford to live in them or overcome the white fear and violence that would be deployed to keep them out. None of the existing organizations were configured in a way that allowed them to understand and address the physical fabric of the city itself as a form of racial capitalist injustice.

The tradition of Black women's radicalism dating back to the Unemployed Councils and even earlier might have provided some leadership, but the movement that started with the 1932 food riot had long since been superseded by all of the others. In the end, much of the city's Black "leadership," including the editorial boards of both Black-owned newspapers in the city, the *St. Louis American* and the *St. Louis Argus*, supported the 1955 bond issue that led to the destruction of Mill Creek Valley. The most coherent opposition was mounted by the block committees of the Urban League—the street-level neighborhood organizations through which the league was trying to transform poor and migrant Black people into respectable workers and socially integrated city-dwellers. Only the block committees, in defiance of their organization's leadership, resisted the destruction of their neighborhoods.[21]

In the meantime, the business and political elite reorganized the structure of rule in the city around the imperatives of the land grab. Thirty of the CEOs of the city's leading firms formed an organization called Civic Progress, which orchestrated the campaign for the bond issue along with the unions, the churches, and the League of Women

Voters. The measure passed by a six-to-one margin. The city, crowed the *Post-Dispatch*, "had voted for the new and the clean—and against the outmoded and the dirty. For a moving, growing, advancing future—and against a blighting, killing past." The St. Louis Land Clearance for Redevelopment Authority, newly created in 1951, hired a firm headed by the real estate economist and land speculator Roy Wenzlick to provide a feasibility study of the redevelopment of the 471-acre tract of land. Wenzlick recommended tearing it all down, even while acknowledging that most of the current inhabitants of the neighborhood would not be able to afford to move back after the area was redeveloped, and that "there is practically no new housing available anywhere in the metropolitan area for Negro families." Notwithstanding the displacement of its residents, Wenzlick noted, the destruction of Mill Creek Valley would create a huge number of jobs for construction workers. And there were millions of dollars to be made—as much as $10 million from the sale of the cleared land alone.[22]

And so, beginning in February 1959, Mill Creek Valley structures fell before the wrecking ball: the People's Finance Building, where Black professionals had their offices; the Pine Street YMCA, which neighborhood residents thought had the best food in the city; City Hospital No. 2; Saint Malachy Church; the offices of the *Argus* and the *American*; the Booker T. Washington Hotel; the Star, the Strand, and the London, the three Black theaters in the neighborhood; and the ballpark on the corner of Compton and Laclede, where Cool Papa Bell had played for the Negro League champion St. Louis Stars in the twenties and thirties. Also razed were homes where almost twenty thousand people had lived, stored their memories, and saved up their hopes.[23]

It was in these very years that southern segregationists were advocating "massive resistance" to school integration in the aftermath of the *Brown* decision, removing their children from public schools, and enrolling them in the "segregation academies" and parochial schools of a network that continues to serve wealthy whites today. But in St. Louis the strategy was different. Instead of massive resistance, the historian

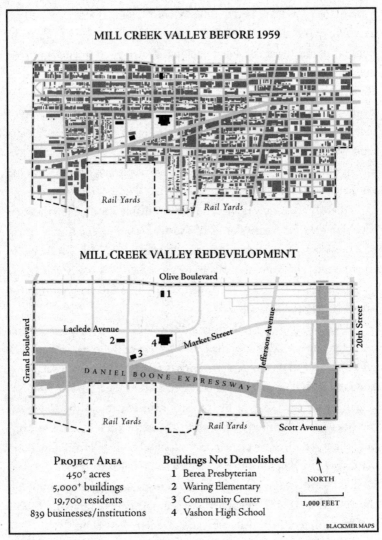

The buildings of Mill Creek Valley before and after demolition. (Blackmer Maps)

Clarence Lang has argued, there was massive redevelopment. Resistance to integration and redevelopment were not variant forms of plain and simple attitudinal bias, but variant forms of racial capitalism. In St. Louis, where the real estate interest held sway over the terms of racial governance, the order of the day was redevelopment and removal. This pattern, which had deep roots in the city's history and was gradually spreading out in every direction from its western crucible in St. Louis, was, as the St. Louis housing rights activist Ivory Perry said at the time, "Black removal by white approval."[24]

Mill Creek Valley was far from the only St. Louis neighborhood to be sacrificed to the dream of development through demolition. In the years after the Second World War, following upon the legacy of the destruction of Deep Morgan, Chestnut Valley, and the Riverfront, a host of St. Louis neighborhoods were torn down, their residents scattered in the name of the public good: Cochran Gardens (1952–1953); Darst-Webbe (1954); Kosciusko (1956–1958); DeSoto-Carr (repeatedly through the 1940s, '50s, and '60s). Indeed, the wrecking has continued down to the present day. Nor was Mill Creek Valley the only neighborhood in the nation to be sacrificed in the name of "urban renewal" in the postwar period. The bulldozer was the primary tool of postwar urban planning, especially after the federal Housing Acts of 1949 and 1954. But the wholesale destruction, population dispersion, and wanton speculation in the absence of any real plan pioneered on the St. Louis riverfront in 1939, taken to Washington by Harland Bartholomew, and epitomized in Mill Creek Valley stand out as evidence of the city's leading role in the history of urban planning and racial removal in the United States. Long after the focus of the federal government shifted from tearing neighborhoods down to trying to rebuild and rehabilitate them, urban planners, city leaders, and business interests in the city of St. Louis remained committed to development by demolition. Indeed, they remain so today.[25]

Not much ever became of the Mill Creek Valley redevelopment plans. St. Louis University built a new campus on part of the tract. The campus is named for General Daniel Frost, the Confederate who surrendered to General Nathaniel Lyon at the beginning of the Civil War—a statue commemorating Lyon was removed along with everything else in the neighborhood. Eventually, the long-planned

In the aftermath of the clearance of almost five hundred acres, St. Louis residents began to refer to Mill Creek Valley as "Hiroshima Flats." Much of the area remains undeveloped today. (Missouri Historical Society)

extension of Interstate 64 was built through the demolished neighborhood, providing truckers, travelers, and suburban commuters a bypass route through what the residents of the city of St. Louis came to call "Hiroshima Flats," the name bearing witness to an earlier act of violence on an unimaginable scale. As for the residents, there had been a rough working assumption that most would be rehoused in the gigantic Pruitt-Igoe housing complex being built on the Northside. In the end, however, fewer than 20 percent of those who had lived in Mill Creek Valley found places in Pruitt-Igoe. As for the rest of the erstwhile residents of Mill Creek Valley, it is hard for a historian to provide a general answer, because there was no contemporary administrative oversight of their relocation—nobody was keeping track. It was apparently enough to know that they were gone.

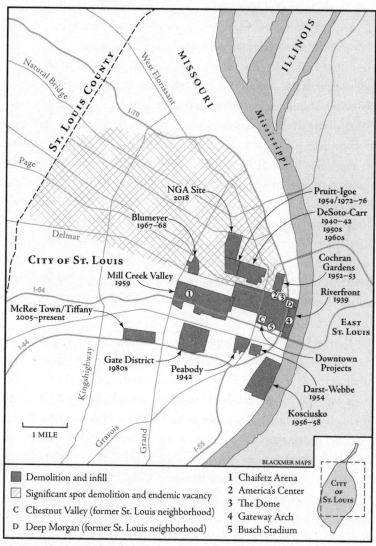

Demolition and development in the city of St. Louis, 1939–2019. (Blackmer Maps)

As the history of Black St. Louis disappeared into the dust, a new white world was built to the west—suburbs connected to the city and the world by roads that were quite literally built over the ruins of the old world. The decade after 1950 was the first in which the population of the city of St. Louis fell (from its high-water mark near 850,000), and it has continued to decline in every subsequent decade. Much of the city's population loss was attributable to a one-to-one gain in the white population of the county, which had begun to explode in the 1940s as rural Missourians moved to the metro area to take up wartime jobs in the plants. In 1940, the population of almost entirely white St. Louis County was about 250,000; by 1960, it was over 700,000. Whites were moving out of the city and to the county on Bartholomew's federally subsidized highways, taking with them their wealth and the potential tax revenue they provided. And because of the hard boundary established between city and county in 1876, there was no way for the city to follow them by expanding its limits to capture their taxes.

During the war, St. Louis had solidified its position in the defense and aerospace industries. Many of the residents of the county as well as some of those who lived in the city were among the thirty-five thousand who worked at McDonnell Aircraft (later McDonnell-Douglas), the nation's second-largest defense contractor and the world's largest producer of fighter planes through much of the Cold War. "There will be a demand for military aircraft so long as the necessity exists for the United States to police a disorderly world," said the company's chairman, James McDonnell, forging a link between what he saw as his company's boundless future and his city's imperial past. F-4 Phantoms, F-15s, and components of AWACs, Spartan missiles, and ABM missiles were all produced in St. Louis, and the planes were sold around the world (to Germany, Japan, South Korea, Greece, Turkey, Saudi Arabia, and Israel), as was McDonnell's DC-9, its most visible and least reliable civilian aircraft. Monsanto, headquartered in Creve Coeur, emerged as one of the largest chemical companies in these years, producing, one after the other, some of the most notorious products in human history: DDT, Agent Orange, and Roundup, the herbicide whose effects are only now coming to light. In the 1950s, the CEOs of Monsanto, Mallinckrodt, Ralston-Purina, and McDonnell-Douglas all served together on the board of trustees of Washington University—a tidy representation of the network of shared purpose that one historian has called "the military-industrial-academic complex."[26]

In 1965, when the television journalist Charles Kuralt went on the road in search of Cold War America, he found it in Webster Groves, Missouri. "Just below St. Louis, but above-average in every way," he put it with wry disapproval. Kuralt and his crew spent several days at the high school, where they administered a thirty-seven-page survey to the school's seven hundred or so sixteen-year-olds. The children of Webster Groves, Kuralt discovered, were greatly interested in getting good grades and achieving material success, but not much else. Only 13 percent of them were worried about being drafted (about the same number that were not planning to attend a four-year college, Kuralt pointed out); only 20 percent knew who North Vietnamese leader Ho Chi Minh was, a sad contrast to the 99 percent who could identify the actor Dick Van Dyke; and 93 percent worried habitually about their appearance, almost twice as many as the number of those who worried about the threat of nuclear war. From Mrs. Condon's Dance School to the Friendship Dance at the high school to golf at the country club and highballs at the Monday Club, from going steady to getting pinned, then engaged and married, and then moving from one house in Webster Groves to another house in Webster Groves—the lives of these suburban teens were shaped around a single categorical imperative: the social reproduction of Webster Groves. Get good grades to go to a good school to get a good job to have a good family and have children who get good grades . . . In the words of one almost animatronic teen explaining his goals: "I'd like to be financially a success, support my family handsomely, have two cars, have a two-story house, and have a high-status with my friends." Insular. Conventional.

Self-satisfied. Mediocre. "Sixteen in Webster Groves" Kuralt entitled his documentary.[27]

Kuralt was not the first to set out in search of America and end up in Webster Groves. In the mid-1950s, the Washington University anthropologist Jules Henry did research there as well, for the book that eventually became *Culture Against Man*. Henry found in Webster Groves an empty cavity at the heart of the American Dream. The community's values were expressed by "pecuniary philosophy, pecuniary history, pecuniary psychology, and pecuniary truth," which sentenced its children to the loneliness, shallowness, and materialism of foreshortened dreams. Henry's book, an early example of anthropologists' "studying up," was widely reviewed and fulsomely praised as an intellectual's guide to the suburbs. Kuralt's nationally televised beatdown three years later was the occasion for an extended national self-reckoning with "the America we are becoming." In the 1960s, Webster Groves, Missouri, was arguably the most famous suburb in the United States.[28]

Its residents bitterly resented Webster Groves being made into the archetype of the soulless suburb by Kuralt and CBS, both at the time and ever since. After the national television debut of the award-winning documentary, they demanded that Kuralt return to Webster Groves and make another documentary, this time portraying their frustration with the first documentary. The anchor on St. Louis's most popular morning television show even suggested, as was the style in the city in those days, that Kuralt's documentary had been part of a communist plot to undermine America. But the damage was done. Webster Groves had become a byword for suburban shallowness and materialism.[29]

In 1965, when Kuralt visited Webster Groves, the city was 96 percent white and fighting to stay that way. For Jules Henry, who was obsessed with advertising, the whiteness of Webster was apparently beside the point. Kuralt was more pointed. In spite of the incessant substitution of the word "community" for the words "white people" in the interviews—"nice community," "good community," "our community"—Kuralt did manage to break through several times. Having asked one of the stars of the football team whether he would go on a double date with his Black teammate, one of the very few African Americans in the school, he was told that the white boy's father would never let him, nor would he want to himself, though he couldn't quite say why. Asked by Kuralt whether he had ever been downtown, another boy, who stands out in the context of the film as comparatively worldly and curious, says that when he went downtown for an internship, he saw "people I'd never seen before in my life. They were from the slums . . . they were mentally retarded. . . . They have all these depressing problems." After asking a group of parents whether they would let their children participate in a civil rights demonstration, Kuralt was told by the fathers both that any child who did so "would not be able to sit down" for a week after getting punished upon returning home and that sixteen-year-olds in Webster Groves were not competent to make decisions about political matters because they "can't even change their diapers." The proximate images of butt-punishing and bowel movement would probably have delighted the Freudian Henry, but they were deployed to more straightforward purpose by Kuralt in "Sixteen in Webster Groves." His documentary revealed that the city of St. Louis, only two miles away on the map, was both unimaginable to the people of Webster Groves, and at the bottom of everything.

The insularity of Webster Groves was no accident. It was the deliberately engineered result of US government policy and municipal law: federally subsidized and locally enforced whiteness. In the years after the Second World War, and in a pattern that reflected developments nationwide, thousands, then tens of thousands, then literally hundreds of thousands of whites left behind the city of St. Louis for St. Louis County, as well as St. Charles and Franklin Counties. In so doing, they left behind houses soon occupied by Black residents, some of them displaced by the destruction of Mill Creek Valley and the construction of the interstates, whose unwanted proximity touched off still other waves of white migration. All of this movement was subsidized by the United

States of America. And all of it was money in the bank for white realtors, contractors, and construction workers—racial capitalism.[30]

Founded in 1934, the Federal Housing Administration observed a strictly segregationist policy in the provision of loan guarantees for qualifying home-buyers. The FHA provided its on-the-ground appraisers with a manual, first distributed in 1935, that advised them, "If a neighborhood is to retain stability it is necessary that properties shall continue to be occupied by the same social and racial classes," and cautioned them to guard against the "infiltration of inharmonious racial or nationality groups." When the St. Louis developer Charles Vatterot sought FHA funding to develop the suburb of St. Ann, built beginning in 1942 to house defense workers living near the airport in St. Louis County, his proposal included a requirement that "no lot or portion of a lot or building erected thereon shall be sold, leased, rented or occupied by any other than those of the Caucasian race." Following the Second World War, as the Veterans Administration extended Depression-era home loan guarantees to returning soldiers, it followed the same policy. Like the New Deal, the charter documents of postwar suburban America turn out to have had a whites-only codicil.[31]

To simplify their decision-making and improve their efficiency in responding to any given case, federal home loan specialists across the nation made maps of their cities, dividing the metropolitan area into color-coded blocks according to their racial composition and the supposed risk of lending in each of them. In St. Louis, the first maps were made in 1937, and they were colored red ("hazardous") along the riverfront and then westward into the center of the city; these were the same neighborhoods that Harland Bartholomew would target for razing and redevelopment: the Black neighborhoods. The categories attached to the colors seem to have been trying to capture and stabilize the process of the westward migration of the Black population within the city, and of the white population from the city to the county: red ("hazardous"), yellow ("definitely declining"), blue ("still desirable"), and green ("best"). Ladue, just to the northwest of Webster Groves, for example, was green-lined in 1940 because it contained, in the words of the federally employed researcher, "not a single foreigner or Negro." Between 1934 and 1960, the FHA insured over five times as many home loans in increasingly white St. Louis County as it did in the increasingly Black city of St. Louis. By the 1960s, only 3.3 percent of FHA-insured mortgages in the metro area (city and county) were held by African Americans; in the county, the rate was less than 1 percent. These were, remember, only loan guarantees, not loans: this was a public-private partnership. Indeed, because the FHA eventually shared the maps it had made with private bankers, who used them as proxy evaluations for loan applicants, federally sanctioned segregation had a decades-long afterlife subsequent to its supposed legal demise.[32]

Long after the Supreme Court's 1948 decision in *Shelley v. Kraemer*, realtors in St. Louis enforced the separation of white and Black neighborhoods. The National Association of Real Estate Boards code of ethics, adopted in 1924, had stated that "a Realtor should never be instrumental in introducing into a neighborhood . . . members of any race or nationality, or any individual whose presence will clearly be detrimental to property values in that neighborhood." This plank in the racial capitalist platform continued to control much of the real estate business in St. Louis through the 1970s and beyond, with varying degrees of legality. In barely concealed defiance of the US Supreme Court's decision in *Shelley v. Kraemer*, the Missouri Supreme Court ruled in 1949 that, although restrictive covenants could not be invoked in order to use state power to *evict* a Black family from a white-covenanted neighborhood, they could nevertheless be grounds for white parties to the covenant to file a civil suit claiming damages against those who sold their houses to Black buyers. Even when the US Supreme Court ruled these civil suits unconstitutional in 1953, realtors in St. Louis (and elsewhere in the United States) continued to include covenant language in the deeds of the houses they sold. Indeed, in spite of a 1972 Supreme Court ruling that the recording of such deeds was unconstitutional, deeds containing stipulations that forbid the sale of a given house to, for instance,

"Negroes or Malays," turn up at home-sale closings in both St. Louis and St. Louis County *to this very day*. To several generations of white home-buyers, they must have seemed (at best) a curious historical relic, but inevitably they remind unsuspecting minority home-buyers of the line they are about to cross.[33]

Well into the 1950s, realtors in St. Louis advertised home sales in a separate "for colored" section of newspapers for listings north of Delmar, east of Union, south of Natural Bridge, and west of Grand (the onetime western boundary of Black habitation). The St. Louis Real Estate Exchange continued to defend segregation well into the 1960s, directing Black clients to homes and apartments in Black neighborhoods and even advising sellers to pull their property off the market in response to letters of interest or offers from Black buyers. "We never sell to colored. When they ask for a specific house, we tell them there is already a contract," bragged a St. Louis realtor in 1969. Beginning in the 1970s, real estate agents played both sides against the middle, creating "block-busting" panic among white residents about a Black "invasion" by, say, hiring a Black woman to walk down the street pushing a baby carriage, and then earning commissions as the white owners sold their houses, one after the other. As recently as the early 1990s, realtors in University City admitted steering Black clients to one corner of the city, a practice that many believe persists up until the present day.[34]

African American families who were able to pull together enough cash or somehow secure a loan to buy a house in St. Louis sometimes faced violence if they tried to move into "white" neighborhoods. Black families who bought houses to the west of Grand on Market Avenue in the 1940s were targeted with stink bombs and drive-by threats, a pattern that was replicated block by block in many neighborhoods of the city as African Americans moved westward during the Second World War and after. Mr. and Mrs. Byron Boone, who became the first Black family on their Walnut Park block in 1965, were still facing harassment four years later: in December 1969, a forty-pound concrete block was heaved through their front window, the eighth such incident since they had moved in. Black families who moved into the county faced similar acts of intimidation and violence. In the fall of 1963, whites in Jennings staged a series of nighttime demonstrations outside the house of a Black family who had moved into the all-white North County suburb.[35]

Much of the resistance to Black home-buyers was organized by all-white homeowners and neighborhood associations, which transformed the formalized racketeering of the restrictive covenants into a form of white supremacist civil society. In April 1956, Dr. Howard Venable, an African American ophthalmologist who was the head of his department at Homer G. Phillips Hospital and an instructor at the St. Louis University School of Medicine, began construction on a house in Creve Coeur, an outer-ring suburb of the city of St. Louis. His existing house was in the pathway of the Daniel Boone Expressway being built to connect the city to its growing suburbs. Over the course of the next few months, Dr. Venable was approached several times by lawyers representing white citizens of Creve Coeur who had pooled money in the hope of buying the property before he moved in—a common tactic throughout the metropolitan area.

By June, the doctor had refused all offers, and the neighborhood association that had been trying to buy him out had reconstituted itself as an arm of the city government: a newly created "Citizens Advisory Committee on Parks." Before long, the new committee made its first proposal to the city—the proposal it had, in fact, been created to make: the city should use its police power to condemn and take any property for which a group of citizens was willing to donate one-half of the cost of turning it into a public park. Over the objection of the mayor, who feared that the city might go bankrupt if it bought the property out from under every Black family trying to move to Creve Coeur, the city council unanimously approved the proposal and gave Dr. Venable two weeks to agree to sell the property or face condemnation. Two weeks later, they sued the doctor to force him to surrender his property to the eminent domain of the city. And not long after that, the city elected a new mayor—John T. Beirne, one of the original members of the Citizens Advisory Committee on Parks.

Dr. Venable fought the city in the courts and continued to build his house, but in December 1959, the Missouri Court of Appeals ruled in the city's favor. The court's decision acknowledged the evidence of racial animus and a conspiracy to deprive Dr. Venable of his civil rights, as presented by the defense in its counterclaim against the city, but ruled that these issues were not relevant to the city's power to decide where it put its parks and how it got the property to put them there. Seeing the writing on the wall, Dr. Venable sold his house to the city and moved farther west, to Ballwin, where he started over. And Creve Coeur turned his land into a park, converting his single-story ranch-style house into a clubhouse for the city's white citizens. Today the park boasts a "half-mile paved trail, three tennis courts, and a soccer field." It is named for John T. Beirne, the man who rode Dr. Venable's dispossession into the mayor's office.[36]

Actions like those taken by the white citizens of Creve Coeur and countless others throughout the metro area inspired outrage among Black St. Louisans—particularly middle-class Black St. Louisans—and among many whites as well. In 1961, Black and white activists formed the Freedom of Residence Committee, which cataloged complaints, provided legal and limited financial support to Black home-buyers seeking homes in "white" areas, and ran informal undercover operations that sent white and Black members to inquire in turn about a given piece of property. In response to their efforts and those of many others, the city passed a fair housing ordinance in 1961, as did St. Louis County in 1964.

It was the Freedom of Residence Committee that in 1965 helped Joseph Lee and Barbara Jo Jones file suit against the Alfred H. Mayer Corporation, which had refused to sell the Joneses a house in the developer's newly constructed Paddock Woods neighborhood in Florissant, northwest of the city, because Joseph Jones was Black. Although *Shelley v. Kraemer* had ruled that state enforcement of restrictive covenants in the real estate market violated the Fourteenth Amendment, it had left open the question of whether or not private parties could continue to discriminate in the absence of state action (by simply agreeing to racist covenants and abiding by them, not allowing any Black golfers into the country club, and so on).[37]

In *Jones v. Mayer* (1968), the last case decided by the comparatively liberal Warren Court, the US Supreme Court set aside the question of state action and the Fourteenth Amendment in holding that racial discrimination of the type faced by the Joneses violated the *Thirteenth* Amendment, which had abolished slavery in the United States, and the 1866 Civil Rights Act, which had outlawed action perpetuating the "badges or incidents" of slavery—the various forms of racist wrong to which enslaved people had been subjected, including the violation of their freedom to choose to live where they wanted. It is this case that provides the legal foundation for the recent revival of the effort to claim reparations from the US government for its legal complicity in perpetuating the "badge" of slavery in the form of discriminatory policies and practices in the FHA, the GI Bill, and so on. The decision in *Jones v. Mayer* followed passage of the Civil Rights Act of 1964 and the Fair Housing Act of 1968, and it might have seemed to portend the end of housing discrimination in the United States.[38]

And yet, amid all this seeming change, the president of the St. Louis Real Estate Exchange assured clients who wanted to make sure that the neighborhoods in which they bought houses would remain all-white—so that they could send their children to all-white schools to prepare them to properly steward the legacy of all-whiteness that would be passed on to them along with their parents' property—that realtors in St. Louis had ways to "weed out the n—s." Among other things, he was counting on the fact that the Fair Housing Act had been methodically stripped of any enforcement provisions in advance of its passage, and that both the city and county governments lacked the resources (not to mention the will) to set about the massive task of desegregating the metro area.[39]

More than anything else, however, the president of the Real Estate Exchange was counting on zoning—that is, on the tools passed down to him by the patriarch of the St. Louis suburbs, Harland Bartholomew, and on the identification of police power with the protection of property values. As a trickle of Black people began to try to move to the county in the 1960s, then many more in the 1970s, they found all manner of obstacles still barring the way.[40]

In 1926, the US Supreme Court's decision in *Village of Euclid v. Ambler* (which originated in a suburb of Cleveland) added zoning to the police powers of cities, as Bartholomew had been urging since the time of the First World War. If cities were bound to try to foster their citizenry by maintaining the general welfare, the court reasoned, and if one dimension of general welfare was the protection of private property from the downward influence of proximity to undesirable neighbors, then cities had a legal interest in controlling development within their limits. In so doing, the Court created a legal framework for the same conflation of public order and property values that had underlain the segregation ordinances of the previous decade. This time, however, the language was color-blind, although some of the support behind the measure surely was not. As an *amicus curiae* brief in the case argued, zoning could be an effective tool in protecting middle-class homeowners from "disorderly, noisy, slovenly, blighted and slum-like districts": from you know who.[41]

In the 1940s and 1950s, as developers built outward into previously undeveloped areas of St. Louis County, zoning became the principal tool of racial capitalist real estate development. Inner-ring suburbs like Maplewood, Ladue, and Webster Groves were zoned to foster and protect the development of single-family residences on large lots in the years immediately following the Second World War. In much of the rest of the county, zoning followed the pattern of settlement. Small clusters of new homeowners in the county would organize a neighborhood association and then incorporate themselves as a city, the guiding

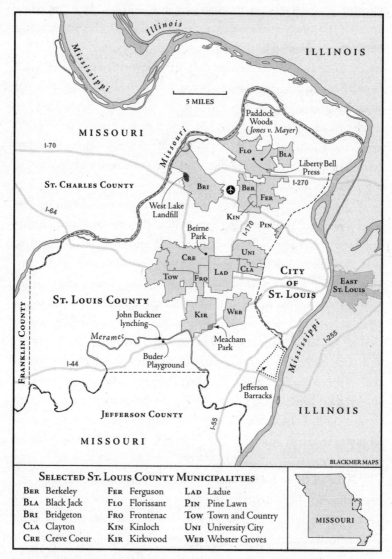

St. Louis County, showing locations mentioned in this book. (Blackmer Maps)

purpose of which was to zone their neighborhood and the surrounding area. Of the ninety-two municipalities in St. Louis County today, over half were established during the single-family suburban land rush between 1943 and 1954. Many of these new towns featured very small populations (the smallest was Champ, which had seven people) and absurdly large lot sizes—often as large as three acres (for instance, in much of Ladue), and very rarely less than five thousand square feet. In 1965, the government of St. Louis County rezoned ninety thousand acres into three-acre lots in order to create a vast land bank for future high-end development.[42]

Along with large lots, the exclusion of multi-unit dwellings was a principal tool of population regulation. The city of Ferguson first outlawed multi-family dwellings in 1932 and then again in 1956, when a cluster of duplexes was developed in one corner of the city. City planners in Webster Groves, claiming there was no demand for apartment buildings in the city, limited multi-family residences to the city's commercial district. Meanwhile, they tracked development in the self-declared "City of Fine Homes" on a map that identified several areas as "100% Negro or very close," and on which they noted their worry about a "developing ghetto" on the other side of the railroad tracks, labeled "the Great Divide." In 1960, there were 200,000 housing units in St. Louis County, only about 7 percent of which were in multiple-family residences, and almost all of those were duplexes rather than apartment buildings.[43]

None of these zoning codes were explicitly racial. And only occasionally did their underlying purpose spill into the public record. There were the indelicate notations on the planners' map from Webster Groves in 1963. And the city of Kirkwood's helpful suggestion that it would be much better for "all of the colored families to be grouped in one major section where they could be provided with their own school and recreational facilities, churches and stores." And the decision by the cities of Ferguson and Berkeley to close off all but one of the roads that connected them with the neighboring all-Black town of Kinloch.

And Ferguson's yearlong argument about building a ten-foot-high brick wall along the length of its mile-long border with Kinloch. That was in 1976. But even then, city officials claimed that their position was not racial—it was just that the inhabitants of Kinloch, whoever they were, seemed to include an inordinate number of people interested in stealing the hubcaps off cars parked in all-white Ferguson.[44]

Many in St. Louis County viewed the suburbs in the same way their forebears had viewed the West: as a "white man's country." But in time they learned not to say that out loud. For the most part, these years that saw the establishment of dozens of all- or almost-all-white towns through the cynical use of the tools of city planning were also years of officially sanctioned euphemism in St. Louis County. That poor white people were also unable to move into many of the new cities popping up along the horizon of white privilege was an acceptable cost—just another of the ways in which the excessive character of racial capitalism drags, disciplines, and diminishes poor white people along with the poor Black people who are its primary targets.

The *nudge-nudge, wink-wink* white supremacy of discriminatory zoning in the city of St. Louis reached a crossroads in the city of Black Jack. In the spring of 1970, the Inter-Religious Center for Urban Affairs, represented locally by St. Mark's United Methodist Church in Florissant, proposed the construction of Park View Heights Apartments, a 210-unit, mixed-income, racially integrated apartment complex in a North County neighborhood known for the type of oak trees that grew there. Its goals were simple: to provide comfortable homes for families who needed them, and to foster "cultural interchange" and understanding between people separated by history. The immediate reaction among many of the white residents of Black Jack was the same mixture of self-righteous outrage and hypertrophic fear typical of white settlers from Jamestown right down to the present. It would be an "abscess in the middle of the community," filled with the very people whom the residents of Black Jack (and nearby Spanish Lake) had just moved away from—people from Wellston and Walnut

Park, people who had been displaced by urban renewal, people who would not be able to get to work because there were no buses out in the suburbs, people who would clog up the roads if they had cars. People who had lots of children.[45]

Besides a few residents who insisted on speaking honestly—a man who told a reporter that he believed that people are just "happier with their own race," or an old lady who admitted she would be terrified if she walked out of her house and saw a Black person—the leaders of the neighborhood associations were able to keep their people mostly on script. They set about resisting the integration of their neighborhood by emphasizing the burden that the new residents would put on the surrounding Hazelwood School District. Never mind that what was really at stake was adding about one hundred new students to a district that already educated nineteen thousand students—an increase of just over one-half of 1 percent.[46]

The focus on the supposed number of children likely to be born to the hypothetical residents of a not-yet-built apartment building, and on schools as the site of the anticipated damage, calls our attention to the questions of gender and social reproduction in the suburban resistance movement. So, too, does the leading role taken by white women in Black Jack, represented by the "housewives march" in front of the St. Louis County Court Building in July 1970. This was not a simple struggle over whether or not Black people could be allowed to live in Black Jack: it was a fight over Black children being waged by white parents on behalf of their own children. At the bottom of the questions about school enrollments and property values was a set of calculations that mixed race, reproduction, and real estate into a cocktail of implacable animosity.[47]

Declaring themselves "ready for a street fight," the white resistance of Spanish Lake and Black Jack held community meetings at which they organized letter-writing campaigns (to local, state, and federal authorities as well as to various Methodists) and hectored and shouted down representatives of St. Mark's and the US Department of Housing and Urban Development, which had been created by the Fair Housing Act of 1968 to do things like build racially integrated low- and middle-income housing in St. Louis County. Most pointedly, however, the white resisters began to organize themselves as a city: the brand-new city of Black Jack, the formation of which was supported by a petition signed by over fourteen hundred of the area's two thousand inhabitants. The city of Black Jack was incorporated on August 6, 1970, and although it lacked most of the standard features of municipal government—it had no police department, for example, and no city collector capable of overseeing the taxation of its residents—it did have a zoning code. That code stipulated that the area in which St. Mark's United Methodist Church intended to build the Park View Heights Apartments was zoned for single-family residences with a minimum lot size of fifteen thousand square feet, or about one-third of an acre.[48]

In 1970, the United States sued Black Jack, and in arguing that the city's zoning code violated both the Fair Housing Act and the Supreme Court's holding in *Jones v. Mayer*, it effectively claimed that the city's prohibition on multiple-family dwellings was perpetuating the history of slavery. The city contended in response that its zoning code was simply meant to eliminate traffic, reduce pressure on the public schools, and protect property values, and that it had nothing to do with Black people per se. After all, the city argued, it was also discriminating against low- and moderate-income whites. In December 1974, the Eighth Circuit of the US Court of Appeals ruled in the federal government's favor, noting that the history of race and real estate in St. Louis County—not to mention the fact that Black Jack, like North County generally, was 99 percent white—made it obvious that the city's action was racially discriminatory. The court's ruling, for the first time in housing law, used the legal standard of "disparate impact"—the idea that plaintiffs did not need to prove that there was an *intention* to discriminate against them, only that the action taken by the defendant had the *effect* of racial discrimination.[49]

While several other federal circuit courts used the *United States of America v. City of Black Jack, Missouri* (1974) decision as precedent in housing discrimination cases, it was not until 2015, in *Texas Department of Housing and Community Affairs v. Inclusive Communities Project, Inc.*, that the Supreme Court took up the question of "disparate impact" and finally declared the standard constitutional, basing its decision on the government's reasoning in the *Black Jack* case. For the third time in the past seventy years, the struggle to integrate a St. Louis neighborhood defined the housing law for the entire nation.[50]

Despite the courage of those who were willing to move their families into hostile suburbs and send their children to all-white suburban schools—not to mention the courage of those children (and, indeed, the courage of their white supporters in organizations like the Freedom of Residence Committee and St. Mark's United Methodist Church, who faced ridicule and retaliation in their own neighborhoods)—and despite the efforts of the NAACP and the ACLU, which supported fair housing litigation both nationally and in St. Louis, in many neighborhoods white separatists and their allies in the real estate industry held the line. Long after the end of restrictive covenants and redlining, the pattern of racial discrimination remained structured into the transportation system (interstates everywhere, but no buses) and the single-family suburbs. Indeed, by the time of the *Black Jack* case, the attorneys for both the United States and the city of Black Jack agreed on one thing: material life in St. Louis County was so profoundly segregated that one did not have to speak actively of discrimination in order to further segregation. It was so deeply structured into the nature of things that it provided its own alibi—one could speak of the houses, the roads, and the schools without saying the words "Black" or "white" and be perfectly clear about the demographic implications. In 1950, the population of St. Louis County was about 1.9 percent Black; twenty years later—years during which hundreds of thousands of new houses were built in the county—the comparable figure was 4.8 percent.[51]

Through some combination of the influence of the defense industry (and the imperial past), the local history of a genuinely radical alliance of communists and Black radicals, and the hothouse atmosphere of the emerging suburbs, the white enclaves of St. Louis in these years nurtured some of the most prominent right-wing voices in the United States. These were voices that amplified the oscillating sense of entitlement and embattlement in the white resistance in the suburbs into extremist jeremiad. The Christian nationalist monthly *The Cross and the Flag*, published in St. Louis from 1942 until 1977, was edited by Gerald L. K. Smith, founder of the isolationist America First Party during the Second World War and erstwhile ally of Huey Long, Father Charles Coughlin, and Henry Ford, whom he credited with teaching him that "Communism is Jewish." Smith's final years were devoted to the construction of the seven-story Christ of the Ozarks statue in Eureka Springs, Arkansas, the centerpiece of the Holy Land Christian theme park he was planning at the time of his death in 1976.[52]

In the decades after the Second World War, Smith devoted most of his time to giving speeches at rallies across the country and editing his journal. Published out of an office on Grand Avenue, *The Cross and the Flag* promoted a ten-point code for Christian nationalists, including promoting "America as a Christian Nation" against the substitution of "Jewish Tradition for Christian Tradition"; fighting "mongrelization and all attempts being made to force the intermixture of the black and white races"; ending "Immigration in order that American jobs and American houses may be safeguarded for American citizens"; following "the George Washington foreign policy" of ending entangling alliances; and abolishing the Federal Reserve Bank.[53]

As well as *The Cross and the Flag*, St. Louis in the years of the Cold War was home to the Reverend John A. Stormer. Stormer came of political age under the guidance of the anticommunist and segregationist Oklahoma minister George Benson and was for many years the pastor of Heritage Baptist Church in suburban Florissant. In 1963, Stormer published *None Dare Call It Treason* under his own imprint, Liberty

Bell Press, PO Box 32, Florissant, Missouri, and sold this bottled lightning to a generation of right-wing Republicans and John Birchers who distrusted mainstream media and the publishing industry. Stormer's book sold a reported seven million copies in the years just before Barry Goldwater's 1964 presidential campaign and is often credited as having provided a good measure of the intellectual infrastructure for the far right wing of the Republican Party in the years that followed.

In Stormer's view, virtually every institution in the United States had been infiltrated and corrupted by communists, and sinister forces were at work trying to convince ordinary Americans that their traditions and cherished values were indecent and perhaps even insane. "Do you hold rigidly to 'outmoded' concepts of right and wrong? Do you reject Socialism? Do you oppose foreign aid waste? Do you object to letting African cannibals vote on how we should live under world government?" Stormer wrote, before suggesting that holding these positions in the United States of America could be grounds for involuntary commitment and forcible "mental health" treatment, including "electric shock treatments, chemotherapy, hypnosis, or conceivably, a frontal lobotomy." Four years before his death in 2018, Stormer warned that the uprising following the Michael Brown shooting in Ferguson, which shares a border and a school district with Florissant, was part of a communist conspiracy—"hundreds of people from all over the country," he insisted, had been brought to St. Louis "to bring about revolution."[54]

Also living in St. Louis in the early 1960s was the young Patrick Buchanan, an editor at the *St. Louis Globe-Democrat*, which spun together anticommunism, anti-elitism, suburban separatism, white resentment, and unwavering support for the police into one strand of the double helix of the Goldwater-Reagan-Buchanan-Trump wing of the Republican Party. Through those years, the *Globe-Democrat* editorialized, variously, in favor of the greater use of police dogs in the city of St. Louis; in favor of the immediate execution of Californian inmate Caryl Chessman in spite of the "maudlin" and "Communist" opposition to the death penalty; in favor of massive expansion of government funding for the Nike air defense missile program, but against federal support for local public transportation; in favor of mincemeat pie (an often neglected aspect of Anglo-Saxon cultural inheritance); in favor of military action against Cuba's Fidel Castro, before whom the United States had too long been "supine"; in favor of more and wider expressways connecting the city to the suburbs in metro St. Louis; against the formation of a civilian review board to oversee the St. Louis Police Department; in favor of missile sales to Israel; in favor of Nixon's program for "Black capitalism" ("Capitalism is not racist. It works equally well for all)"; in opposition to the "reverse racism" of the "slogan 'Black Power'"; and so on. Working up and down the scales of politics, the editorial page of the *Globe-Democrat* connected global anticommunism to local opposition to civil rights and unwavering support for the police.[55]

At the behest of Pat Buchanan, the *Globe-Democrat* was one of five newspapers in the United States to cooperate with the Federal Bureau of Investigation in a precursor to COINTELPRO (the "Counter-Intelligence Program" targeting African American activists), publishing planted stories designed to undermine Black activism in St. Louis and elsewhere. Beginning in late 1963, and in cooperation with J. Edgar Hoover's FBI, which provided the newspaper with classified documents, the *Globe-Democrat* ran a series of ten articles by the reporter Denny Walsh asserting that the Congress of Racial Equality (CORE) had been infiltrated by "pro-Communists" and "outside agitators." Walsh's reporting focused particularly on the ongoing employment protest at Jefferson Bank in downtown St. Louis, singling out the presence of onetime communists like Hershel Walker in order to try to associate a struggle to make it possible for Black people to get *wage-earning* jobs *in a bank* with communism. In June 1965, in an editorial defending the St. Louis Police Department from charges of police brutality and opposing calls for the appointment of a civilian review board, Buchanan's editorial page specifically named the activist Percy Green and called on the police to beat him up: "Police officers ought to put a knot in his head if he tries some monkey shines and interferes with police work."[56]

After supporting Goldwater in 1964, Buchanan left the *Globe-Democrat* to work for the 1968 Nixon campaign and eventually worked as an adviser and speechwriter in the White House until Nixon's resignation in 1974. It was Buchanan who coined the phrase "silent majority" as a tag for the (self-described) embattled, traditionalist, working-class, white Americans to whom he thought the Republican Party should address itself. Over the following decades, Buchanan held down the "traditionalist" (read: white nationalist) right wing of the Republican Party, running for president in 1992, 1996, and 2000, occasionally appearing with a pitchfork at campaign rallies in a gesture reminiscent of the South Carolina populist and white supremacist "Pitchfork" Ben Tillman. Of Buchanan's speech at the 1992 Republican Convention, the journalist Molly Ivins famously wrote, "It probably sounded better in the original German."[57]

Also living in the St. Louis metro area during the formative years in which the New Right emerged out of segregationist "massive resistance" and Cold War anticommunism was Phyllis Schlafly, who traces the historical thread of the other half of the double helix of Trumpism. In 1964, Schlafly published *A Choice Not an Echo*, which urged "grassroots Americans" to join her in supporting Barry Goldwater's presidential bid and opposing both leftist subversives within the government and the "phony Republicans" who let them get away with it. While Schlafly never mentioned "the Jews" (of the St. Louis extremists, she was unquestionably the most likely to be invited out in polite company), her book was full of dark innuendo about "secret kingmakers," "New York financiers," "Communists," J. Robert Oppenheimer, "Democrat Liberals," "hidden persuasion and psychological warfare techniques," "internationalists," A. O. Sulzberger of the *New York Times*, "mysterious financial support," "powerful but shadowy figures," "egghead reasoning," "the international power structure," "the Cosa Nostra, Black Muslims, and CORE," Eugene Mayer of the *Washington Post*, Lehman

Brothers, the Morgan banking group, and even the *Des Moines Register*. Her main suggestions were that the United States adopt a more isolationist foreign policy, which she termed "America First," and prepare for a global war against communism. Suitably edited, it all might have fit well in the pages of *The Cross and the Flag*, but Schlafly instead published the book independently. It very shortly sold three million copies, joining *None Dare Call It Treason* as one of the forgotten best-sellers of the rise of Goldwater and the so-called New Right.[58]

Schlafly sat out the 1968 and 1972 presidential campaigns. She respected Nixon's anticommunism, but thought him soft on school segregation and housing discrimination; in comparison to many of her St. Louis neighbors, he no doubt was indeed "soft"—it was, after all, the Nixon Justice Department that sued the city of Black Jack in 1970. The author of the *Phyllis Schlafly Report* reemerged in the mid-1970s as a self-declared antifeminist "housewife" (much like the women of Black Jack) opposed to the Equal Rights Amendment, reproductive rights, affirmative action, homosexuality, and, in later years, immigration. In a March 2016 rally in St. Louis, she endorsed Donald Trump for president, declaring that "Donald Trump is the one who has made immigration the big issue it really is . . . because Obama wants to change the character of our country." Four months later, Schlafly's *The Conservative Case for Trump* declared that "Christianity is under attack all over the world, most dramatically from Islamists, but also insidiously here at home." Later that fall, Donald Trump was the first to speak at Schlafly's memorial service, held at the St. Louis Cathedral. "With Phyllis, it was always America first," he said.[59]

The American Nazi Party was an insistent, if episodic, aspect of politics in St. Louis in the 1970s and even after. In March 1978, the party organized what it billed as the first legally permitted Nazi march in the United States since 1945, and a lead-up to their planned rally the following month in Skokie, Illinois. After a drawn-out struggle with the city of Florissant about gaining access to a public park for an outdoor rally, the Nazis finally obtained a court order allowing them to march in the city of St. Louis. Planned in coordination with the party's national meeting that spring, the march was to follow a path down Cherokee Street to party headquarters at 2808 Chippewa, on the city's Southside. The march was well publicized in advance, and on the morning of March 12 the forty-five or so Nazis assembled on Jefferson Avenue were vastly outnumbered by thousands of protesters lining Cherokee Street. Instead of marching through the hostile corridor, the marchers rode on the back of a flatbed truck, yelling "White Power!" while flanked by hundreds of policemen, some of them on horseback, others with dogs. As the onlookers threw snowballs at the passing Nazis, the police drove them back in what might in other circumstances have been referred to as a police riot. The Nazis themselves were evacuated to the Third District Police Station, where they were allowed to change out of their brown shirts before sneaking back out onto the street.[60]

Not all the white people in St. Louis or the county were like Schlafly or Stormer or Buchanan or the white separatist "housewives" of Black Jack or the namesake of Beirne Park. Far from it. Many whites in the St. Louis suburbs during these years probably grew up the way I did, living two hours to the west. They believed in "good schools," "nice neighborhoods," and "high property values," and dis-identified (if not always openly or, still less, courageously) with the overt racism of some of their neighbors. And that served them, as it did me, as an alibi for failing to connect the dots between their own privileged lives and the white supremacists out on patrol on the perimeter of their towns.[61]

Had they looked a little harder, they might have found inspiration and insight in the life of the Holocaust survivor and housing rights activist Hedy Epstein, who was a mainstay in the "freedom of residence" movement during these years. In later years, she was a fierce critic of Israel and the Occupation of the West Bank and Gaza, and she was arrested along with other protesters in Ferguson in August 2014 after the police killing of Michael Brown. Barry Commoner, founder of the Citizens' Party, a leader in the nuclear test ban movement, and America's most famous eco-socialist, was teaching at Washington University in these years, though he remained largely aloof from politics in the city. And Washington University was home to a lively and effective branch of Students for a Democratic Society (SDS), some of whom, most notably the merry prankster Eugene Tournour (and even the subsequent biographer of the activist Ivory Perry and the intellectual godfather of this book, George Lipsitz), became strongly involved in Black politics in the city.[62]

But the leading edge of white separatism in St. Louis was prominent and hard-edged. It was evident at the Grapevine Tavern, the Arsenal Street bar owned by John Larry Ray, brother of Martin Luther King assassin James Earl Ray, and frequented by the white supremacist Gordon Baum, who later became a member of the school board. In June 1970, an estimated forty-five thousand marchers—drawn, the *Post-Dispatch* declared, from "virtually every community within a fifty mile radius of St. Louis," and virtually all of them white—marched in one of the largest of that summer's national series of "Hard Hat" parades. Although it was generally and properly understood as a march in support of the Vietnam War, the stated purpose of the march was to "show that we honor the police"; a white women's auxiliary of the march pinned roses to the lapels of the officers stationed along the route. "There was a threat in the air, a sense of belligerence and intolerance," reported the *Post-Dispatch*. At various points along the four-mile route, marchers waded into the crowd and attacked counterprotesters, injuring dozens by the end of the day. A photo in the following day's *Post-Dispatch* depicted a young man curled in a fetal position on the ground while two marchers kicked him in the head. He had been holding a sign that read VIET NAM VETERAN AGAINST THE WAR, and he told the paper that he had only been out of the army for two days. The police stood by and watched the mayhem unfold, according to the paper, doing "little to ease the tension."[63]

So, it bears asking: From what—against whom—were all of these suburban warriors trying to defend themselves? What were they so scared of? One answer comes from Webster Groves. Provoked by one of Charles Kuralt's questions about civil rights, one of the Webster Groves fathers, a large, loud, and self-assured white man, perhaps a former Webster Groves football player, who sat for the camera with his legs crossed and his pant leg pulled up to reveal a large stretch of flesh between cuff and sock, was derisive, angry almost. "You remember when I sat Clark down during the Jefferson Bank demonstration?" he said, looking momentarily to his wife for confirmation, "and all any normal child had to do was look at the demonstration at Jefferson Bank, and a bunch of beatnik whites, Blacks, green, yellow, everything. And most of them filthy. They looked like they pulled them out of some wine jug or something and put them out to demonstrate." Something had spooked Clark's father. As far as he had burrowed into the all-white womb of suburban conservatism, he could not escape his fear of the city and the Black-beatnik insurgency he believed was unfolding there. To truly understand the reaction, we need to look to the radicalism: to the Jefferson Bank protest and the Black working-class movement it reignited in the city of St. Louis.[64]

10 | DEFENSIBLE SPACE

They don't need to break into an apartment and shoot you.
They can just leave you in North St. Louis to die.

—TEF POE, *This American Life*

THOUGH IT IS OFTEN DATED TO FEBRUARY 1960 IN GREENS-boro, North Carolina, the sit-in movement began in St. Louis in 1947, at the downtown lunch counters of the city's department stores. Using a strategy pioneered during the Funsten Nut and Emerson Electric strikes of the 1930s, Black and white women members of the Congress of Racial Equality would go downtown, sit at the lunch counters, and wait to be served. When they were not, they would wait until closing time, then make plans to come again another day. Mostly forgotten since, these St. Louis sit-ins were ignored (perhaps it would make more sense to say that they were "covered up") by the *St. Louis Post-Dispatch* for most of the six years they went on, but they were successful. By the summer of 1953, all of the downtown department stores had inte-grated lunch counters. And the following year most of the downtown theaters and hotels followed suit. When the city of St. Louis passed an ordinance integrating public accommodations in 1961, it was simply acknowledging what the activists had already achieved.[1]

In these years, the St. Louis CORE chapter was viewed as the leading chapter in the United States—it was organized, confrontational, and successful. The members were students and teachers from the local colleges—Stowe Teachers College, St. Louis University, Washington University—and even from a few of the high schools, including Vashon. They were women and men, Black and white, and they viewed the integrated character of their organization as an example of democratic practice for the world they were trying to bring into being. And they were mostly middle-class. Among the earliest and most prominent white members were Irving and Margaret Dagen; she was a teacher at Clayton High School, with a PhD in industrial and labor relations from Cornell, and he was a lawyer from Brooklyn with degrees from Columbia and St. Louis University. Charles Oldham, a white lawyer, and his wife, the former Marian O'Fallon, an African American social worker with degrees from Stowe and the University of Michigan, were other charter members.[2]

Over the next decade, the movement in St. Louis would be transformed and splintered by a cadre of younger activists—many of them working-class, most of them Black. This younger generation was less concerned with integration per se than with economic justice, a vision with deep roots in the radical history of the city, and one that represents a commonly overlooked aspect of the national African American freedom struggle. Overlooked by historians, that is to say, for during the same years that Webster Groves was being represented by Charles Kuralt as the emblematic American suburb, the massive Pruitt-Igoe apartment complex was becoming the most famous housing project in the world—a site of academic fascination and lurid public fantasy that continues to shape dominant notions of public housing, policing, and African American urban life. In St. Louis, the reaction to the radicalization of the civil rights struggle was fierce and enduring, conforming to the shape of the suburban reaction described in the last chapter, but also embodied in a counterinsurgent militarization of the police and the material fabric of the city that persists today.[3]

In the mid-1950s, with the struggle over public accommodations basically won, members of CORE, combined with the most radical and labor-oriented members of the NAACP—people like Margaret Bush Wilson, who would later lead the NAACP in St. Louis, and Ora Lee Malone, a union organizer in the garment industry who did much to focus the St. Louis NAACP on the struggles of working-class Black people—to form the Joint Opportunities Council (JOC), which renewed and refocused the struggle for jobs that had characterized the movement in St. Louis in the 1940s. The group began by taking up the wartime struggle to ensure that laws barring discrimination in military and other federal contract work were being enforced—St. Louis was still a defense industry town—but it soon broadened the struggle to include all sorts of employers in the region. In so doing, the JOC self-consciously built on the struggle begun by the Black women of the Colored Clerks' Circle in the early 1940s—"Don't Buy Where You Can't Work."[4]

Beginning with the Kroger and A&P grocery stores in 1957, the JOC staged demonstrations insisting that companies doing business in Black areas of the city begin to hire more Black people for better jobs—jobs as clerks and butchers and bakers as well as custodians. "Negroes Must Eat, Too (and Not Just Stew!)," Margaret Bush Wilson entitled a pamphlet supporting the protests. "The 'consumer dollars' of Negroes flowing into A&P cash registers are far from 'token dollars.' WHY THEN ARE NEGROES GIVEN ONLY TOKEN EMPLOYMENT????" The JOC won a series of concessions, first from A&P, then from Kroger, and then from the Famous-Barr department store and Taystee Bread. Often after coming to an agreement with the protesters, the businesses would temporize, sometimes they would backslide, and always progress was incremental—a couple dozen Black clerks and meat cutters were hired at Kroger, twenty-three cashiers at Famous-Barr. Victories that would once have seemed like parting the waters now seemed to some like barely wading into the edge of a sea of structural unemployment and endemic discrimination. White people were moving to the suburbs and taking the economy with them as companies like Emerson Electric, which had once been headquartered downtown, moved out to the suburbs along with their engineers and the bulk of their employees.[5]

The activist Percy Green would later refer to this period as the "tea and cookies" phase of Black struggle in the city of St. Louis. Born on the Southside, Green had graduated from Vashon and then taken night classes in electrical engineering at DeVry Institute of Technology while working as an orderly at Barnes Hospital. On graduation, he got a job at McDonnell Aircraft. He was drafted into the army in 1958 and received advanced electrical training there before returning to St. Louis and McDonnell, where he was the only Black engineer in a research-and-development department that employed six hundred people. He began going to CORE meetings in late 1962 at the urging of a white McDonnell coworker and fellow Machinists Union member, Joel Fischetti. Green and Fischetti regularly socialized in the bars around Gaslight Square, remnants of the city's bohemian 1930s.[6]

Green found something he had been looking for in CORE. "They were talking about the white power structure. . . . They described it as this invisible wall that Black men came up against. It was the first time I heard a rationale that explained all the things I'd seen. . . . There was a wall we had to break through." But he was perplexed by the approach taken by the organization's leadership and bargaining committee in the Kroger protest. "People had gone and talked to management, come back, and reported what the experience was like. Said they noticed changes in the mannerism . . . brought them tea and cookies. They were evaluating all this as noticeable change. Street-wise, can't you see that's bullshit . . . a stalling mechanism?" Along with others—mostly younger working-class African Americans, but also some radicalized whites—Green was becoming restive, suspicious about the goals and uncertain about the leadership of the existing civil rights organizations in the city. The issue would come to a head in front of Jefferson Bank in downtown St. Louis in the summer of 1963.[7]

Located on the corner of Washington and Jefferson, near the edge of Mill Creek Valley, Jefferson Bank had a large Black clientele, but no Black tellers. The protest was planned for Friday, August 30, 1963, two days after the March on Washington and Martin Luther King's famous "I Have a Dream" speech; those who had gone to Washington had just enough time to get back and head for Jefferson Avenue. On August 26, Charles Oldham, the white lawyer who was president of CORE, learned that Jefferson Bank was seeking an injunction forbidding the protesters from marching in front of the bank. On the afternoon of the thirtieth, in defiance of the resulting injunction, and over the objections of Oldham and other CORE leaders, hundreds marched on the bank. Even as the CORE leaders tried to keep the protest confined to a picket on the sidewalk in front of the bank, one group of demonstrators broke off and sat down on the steps in front and another group went around to the back, blocking the doors to the bank. As the police tried to move the demonstrators off the steps, the crowd pushed through the doors and into the lobby of the bank; some began to sing, and others sat down on the floor in front of the tellers' windows.[8]

Over the weekend, the police began to arrest the nine people who had been specifically named in the injunction—among them, Charles and Marian Oldham and future congressman William Clay, at that time a newly elected Northside alderman and an emerging political leader in the Black struggle. Like the Oldhams, most of those arrested had not been at the bank on August 30. Nevertheless, the governor of the state of Missouri warned of "anarchy" in the streets of St. Louis. Mayor Raymond Tucker, who had supported and signed the ordinance outlawing discrimination in the city's public accommodations, called for "law and order." Wayne Millsap, the bank's lawyer and a son-in-law of its president, was appointed special prosecutor in the cases of the nine demonstrators, several of whom, including Charles Oldham, remained in jail. The protests continued. Among those who walked the picket line in front of the bank were Hershel Walker, the onetime leader of the Communist Party in St. Louis, and Ora Lee Malone, the Mississippi-born shop steward of the Amalgamated Clothing and Textile Workers Union.[9]

On one day, African American professionals—the men wearing suits, the women in pearls—might march in front of the bank carrying signs with slogans such as "Respectable People Want Justice," or "Doctors Want Democracy." On another day, protesters might sit down in the middle of the street, blocking traffic and carrying signs demanding full employment. The difference between the two groups and their approaches reflected an emerging strain over the question of direct action among St. Louis activists. The protests in front of the bank continued through the fall. On October 7, when seven more protesters were arrested, hundreds of activists crowded into the lobby with single dollar bills in their hands, seeking change. Four more were arrested. Four days later, protesters blocked the street in front of the bank and lay down in the parking lot. Dozens were arrested, but when the police loaded them into a van to take them downtown, several others, including William Clay, sat down in front of the van, trapping it on the street. When the police arrested them as well, still others surrounded the van. Two weeks later, the judge in the first of the protest cases brought to trial by the special prosecutor issued sentences ranging from sixty days to a year in jail. The sentenced protesters went directly from his courtroom to the city "Workhouse" to begin serving the time.[10]

Even in the face of the draconian sentences, the protests continued. And the protesters began to follow the money, protesting agencies and businesses in the city that had money deposited in Jefferson Bank, tracing out a map of what Green called "the white power structure." On the morning of October 28, an estimated one thousand people gathered in front of city hall to demand that the city of St. Louis stop doing business with Jefferson Bank. That night they protested at St. Louis University. The next day they were at the St. Louis Land Clearance and Housing Authority, which had deposited the Mill Creek Valley "redevelopment" funds at the bank. The day after that, they were outside the mayor's office. In the first week of November, Percy Green staged an after-hours sit-in strike in the city treasurer's office and had to be carried out on a stretcher when he went limp in the arms of the officers sent to remove him. Nightly vigils were held at the Workhouse, where twenty-nine protesters were now imprisoned. In the middle of November, with the support of many of the city's Black ministers, CORE led a two-day boycott of downtown department stores. "No Jobs—No Money Today" read the handbills they passed out in front of the stores. As the old-line civil rights organizations—the Urban League and the NAACP—reiterated their opposition to these "counter-productive" disruptions, a breakaway faction in CORE discussed plans to disrupt Christmas in the downtown stores and the city's bicentennial celebration scheduled for the following spring.[11]

Step by step, from Jefferson Bank to city hall and from the agencies to the downtown department stores, the CORE demonstrations were power-mapping the city, probing the nexus of capitalism and white supremacy. When they got to the city's planned 1964 bicentennial, they reached its heart. The bicentennial was an occasion for the city's white elite, who gathered in and around the self-appointed leadership organization Civic Progress, to express imperial pride. Recall that Civic Progress had emerged at the time of the 1959 Mill Creek Valley clearance as a way for the city's business and political elite to muster its economic resources and political clout into a single shared agenda. Among its members were Mayor Raymond Tucker and the CEOs of McDonnell, Anheuser-Busch, Southwestern Bell, and Famous-Barr. It was what Percy Green would have called "the white power structure," or what a later historian might call a "racial capitalist political bloc," made material in the form of monthly meetings and a busy social calendar. And they were planning a party.[12]

GATEWAY TO WHAT? read one of the signs held by protesters outside the bicentennial gala held at the Chase Park Hotel at the beginning of 1964—a critique, perhaps, of the empty promises of Jefferson's "empire for liberty," launched on the western rivers nearby, where the

Gateway Arch was beginning to take shape on the city's waterfront. President Lyndon Johnson arrived in St. Louis two weeks later to kick off the bicentennial and check in on the progress being made on the Arch. Once again over the strenuous objections of the NAACP and others, CORE's new direct-action faction planned a protest. But the night before Johnson arrived, the faction's members were rounded up by the St. Louis police, who preemptively arrested eighty-six people they suspected (or had been informed?) were planning to demonstrate. While they were being held, Johnson met with NAACP member and civil rights attorney Frankie Muse Freeman, who had been responsible for the case that integrated the city's public housing projects in 1955. Nine years later, she was working for the city's Land Clearance and Housing Authority, and meeting privately with the president of the United States while the St. Louis police detained eighty-six people whom they thought might disrupt a black-tie event. Three weeks later, Johnson appointed Frankie Freeman to the US Commission on Civil Rights, the first Black woman to serve on the commission. There is a statue of Freeman in downtown St. Louis today, one of the very few memorials to Black history anywhere in the city.[13]

Six weeks later—and seven months and countless demonstrations after the Jefferson Bank protest had begun—Jefferson Bank gave in and hired five Black tellers. Fourteen other local banks followed suit, and soon there were several dozen Black tellers working across the St. Louis metro area. But the Jefferson Bank protest accomplished more than better jobs for Black workers. The Jefferson Bank protest marked a generational shift in the Black struggle in St. Louis. It developed a seasoned cadre of activists who had entered the movement through CORE but would leave the organization behind after losing a leadership struggle later that spring. Led by Percy Green, this group was impatient with the idea that well-behaved Black people making reasonable demands in closed-door meetings (or even in the nation's courts) were ever going to change the city enough, still less the state or the nation, to benefit the poor and working-class people whom they represented and with whom they identified—the "itty-bitty people" as Green, himself the son of a meat-cutter, termed them. In the spring of 1964, this group left CORE to found the Action Council to Improve Opportunities for Negroes (ACTION), taking with them much of the energy that had sustained CORE over the 1950s and early 1960s. What remained of the old guard began to drop away, and the remaining whites left the organization when it shifted toward Black nationalism in 1966 and fell for Nixon and his chimerical promise of "Black capitalism" in the late 1960s.[14]

A CTION's first demonstration was one of the most memorable in the history of the city of St. Louis. On July 14, 1964, Green and Richard Daly (not *the* Richard Daly of Chicago, but a white member of ACTION with the same name) climbed the Gateway Arch to protest the lack of Black construction workers being employed by Millstone Construction Company, which held the federal contract for the project. While Green and Daly hung on about halfway up the half-completed Arch—perhaps 150 feet in the air—and work on the site came to a complete standstill, ACTION members on the ground announced the group's demand that Black workers be hired to fill 10 percent of the jobs on the site, as well as one thousand other jobs in the notoriously segregated building trades throughout the city. When they climbed down at the end of the day, Green once again lay down on the ground and went limp, so that the police had to carry him on a stretcher to be arrested. Downtown, as planned, Daly spent the night in jail, but Green bonded out—they had timed the action so that he could work the night shift at McDonnell.[15]

Over the next fifteen years, ACTION pursued a strategy of non-violent confrontational direct action. Its membership remained both Black and white. As Green explained, "Some folks interpret 'Black Power' as 'we need to get rid of all the whites.' ACTION and my-self thought that was bad strategy. All those who wanted to support what we mandated were welcome." But the organization's leadership was all-Black. "We felt that Black folks need to make their own mistakes, same as anyone else," Green remembered, and that it would be "therapeutic" for whites (and even some Black radicals) to work under Black leadership. They socialized together at house parties or at the Pub in Laclede Town, the Glass Bar, or Regal Sports. They listened to Motown and "progressive" jazz by Marvin Gaye, Dave Brubeck, James Moody, George Shaw, and even Frank Sinatra. The organization's guiding imperative was as old-school as it was plainly necessary: "More and better jobs for Black men." It reflected the dominance of the theory, then current in social science (though since then discredited as racist, sexist, and heteronormative), that a male breadwinner was the keystone figure of healthy Black family life.[16]

More durable was the organization's class-based critique of the focus of the early generations of mostly middle-class Black activists on integrating homeownership and public accommodations (as well as the ongoing struggle over housing in St. Louis County): What good was the right to go see a movie at the Odeon if you didn't have the money to buy a ticket? Or, still less, what good was the right to build in Creve Coeur if you were stuck in Pruitt-Igoe? Although ACTION welcomed the communists who were shunned by many of the mainstream civil rights organizations, it never developed—never, in Green's formulation, paused to take time to develop—a philosophical critique of racial capitalism. "You can think about that once you are able to survive," he says today, comparing questions about whether the group's commitment to "more jobs" was a limiting condition of its ultimate vision of liberation to asking a starving man whether or not he believes in God: "If he can survive another day, you can ask him his philosophy." As for the Afrocentric cultural nationalism that was emerging in the late 1960s, Green remembered, "I wasn't going to stop trying to get jobs for folks in order to wear no damn dashiki."[17]

Green's brilliance was tactical—by turns confrontational, comical, and even scatological—but always rigorously researched, carefully organized, pointedly political, and action-oriented. For fifteen years, Green and ACTION kept up a rolling campaign against the largest employers in metro St. Louis: Southwestern Bell, Union Electric, Laclede Gas, McDonnell-Douglas. Green estimates that he went to jail four or five times a year between 1964 and 1979. Dressed in T-shirts bearing the legend ACTION Urban Guerrilla and black berets, members would pull up on crews from Southwestern Bell or Laclede Gas and block their work because the company had not met its commitment (nor, actually, even agreed to make a commitment) to making the workforce at every level of the company 10 percent Black. ACTION staged a "stick-in" at Laclede, pouring molasses in the lobby of the company headquarters on Pine Avenue downtown, because racism is sticky. Then they held a "stink-in," breaking into the company at night and smearing the walls with dog poop, because racism is stinky. They staged a "lock-in" at McDonnell's downtown headquarters, chaining the doors shut in the middle of the day, and a "stall-in" timed to coincide with a shift change at McDonnell's North County factory to protest Green's firing in the aftermath of the Arch protest and to demand 1,700 new jobs. When the Catholic Church in St. Louis refused to divulge its holdings and divest from the companies ACTION had targeted, Green threatened to send undercover agents to services in order to spit in the communion chalice.[18]

For Green and for ACTION, the white whale of the Black struggle in St. Louis was the Veiled Prophet—the elite secret organization that might be thought of as the cultural department of Civic Progress. The Veiled Prophet organization sponsored a yearly parade—the same parade that had been inaugurated in 1878 as a way for the city's white leaders to reassert control over the street in the aftermath of the 1877 General Strike—and a ball at which it crowned a "Queen of Love and Beauty" selected from a court of five local debutantes, daughters of the city's leading families. The Veiled Prophet himself, drawn from among the area's business and political leaders, presided over the parade and the ball, his identity concealed beneath a pointed hood that, to this day, many in Black St. Louis believe signals a secret (thinly veiled) affinity with the Ku Klux Klan. The idea of attacking the Veiled Prophet was to jam the organization's elitist messaging: to take local interest in the ball and the parade, which were televised throughout the region, and use it to, in Green's words, "follow the money and embarrass these people by . . . showing all the CEOs belong to this racist organization."[19]

In October 1965, as the parade traveled down Twelfth Street toward Kiel Auditorium and the Veiled Prophet ball, Green and two other members of ACTION—Loretta Hall and Dallas Jackson—stepped out into the street, blocked the float carrying the queen, and chained themselves to its frame. Over the next several years, protests forced the Veiled Prophet organization into a series of tactical retreats: first the parade was moved from the evening to the afternoon; then the route was changed to avoid downtown; then the queen stopped riding; and, finally, the Veiled Prophet himself stayed home and watched the parade on television from the suburbs, wondering along with the rest of St. Louis what the protesters were planning.[20]

The antic humor was an essential aspect of the ACTION strategy: every time Percy Green did something like climb the Arch or chase the Veiled Prophet from pillar to post, white fear looked a little more absurd. The self-serious self-celebration of the white ruling class of the city was undermined by the image of a Black boogeyman who might be just around the corner. ACTION seemed to be saying to white St. Louis, "Don't you want to laugh just a little? Isn't it all just a little bit funny?" Part of its goal was "to neutralize the adversary with a certain amount of humor . . . to create conversation among people who were used to just going along." People within the dominion of the Veiled Prophet began to collaborate with ACTION, secretly sharing intelligence about the organization to show that they got the joke even if they couldn't say so out loud. A tone of anxiety crept into the newspaper coverage leading up to the annual parade, and the name Percy Green became commonplace in white St. Louis. "Basically we were transmitting a message to the power structure that we had organization,

Percy Green, leader of ACTION, was prominent in the struggle for racial and economic justice in 1960s and 1970s St. Louis. In 1964, along with a white accomplice named Richard Daly, Green climbed the half-completed St. Louis Arch, blocking construction for several hours in order to call attention to the whites-only construction contracts on the massive federal project. (Missouri Historical Society)

know-how, execution, sustainability. You have control over the money, but we have control over how you are going to be seen in history."[21]

In 1972, ACTION finally caught the Prophet. Provided tickets to the ball by sources within the Veiled Prophet organization, ACTION sent two members, Gina Scott and Jane Sauer, white women dressed in ball gowns for the occasion, inside the auditorium in pursuit of the Prophet. Once inside, the women improvised a plan: they would go to opposite ends of the auditorium, and while Sauer created a distraction by raining leaflets down from the balcony, Scott would slide down a backstage rope and unveil the Veiled Prophet. But as Scott slid down the rope (still in her gown), the rope gave way, and she fell the last six or so feet to the floor. One of the Prophet's guards started toward her, but she waved him off as she staggered toward the Prophet, grabbed his mask, and threw it to the floor. There was a pause. Then the guard picked up the mask and placed it, cockeyed, on the Prophet's head, and the police moved in to arrest Scott and Sauer for . . . they weren't sure what . . . disturbing the peace? The next day both the *Post-Dispatch* and the *Globe-Democrat* reported on the incident, though in keeping with tradition (the tradition being white hegemony), they refused to name the Prophet. Only the left-leaning *St. Louis Journalism Review* did that, and, for the record, it was Tom K. Smith, a vice president at Monsanto and former member of the board of Civic Progress.[22]

A number of other organizations and individuals worked alongside ACTION in these years. In the Northside neighborhood that came to be known as Jeff-Vander-Lou (referring to the names of the streets that border and bisect it: Jefferson, Vandeventer, and St. Louis), the activist Macler Shepard led an effort to rebuild one of the city's oldest Black neighborhoods amid the dislocations and destruction of federally funded Mill Creek Valley–style urban renewal. Shepard, who had moved to St. Louis from Arkansas as a child and attended Vashon High School, was an upholsterer by trade. In 1966, having already been bulldozed out of two downtown homes, he decided to try to make a stand on the Northside by creating a community-based alternative to urban renewal. Rather than tearing down the old neighborhood, he would fix it up. "We roped off a city block and played a game called 'Trade-off,'" he explained. "We put different kinds of boxes around the block and asked people to choose whether they liked the boxes that stood for new houses, or high rises, or their old houses. They all seemed to want the older houses fixed up. So that's what we decided to do." It was as simple as that: he asked the people in his neighborhood what they wanted it to look like, and then he tried to make it happen.[23]

Out of all the places he looked for support, the most consequential response came from what must have seemed like one of the least likely sources: the plainspoken, earnest, peace-loving, white Anabaptists of the Mennonite Disaster Service, to whom, among many others, Shepard had applied for assistance. They stood out on the Northside, to be sure, with their cowboy boots and formal carriage, hands folded in front of them as they spoke, almost as if in prayer. But, like Shepard, they listened. And they learned. As Hubert Schwartzentruber wrote of attending his first protest march, of standing, fearfully and uncertainly at first, and then proudly with the people whom he had come to serve, "We may never keep people guessing as to whose side we are on. Nor can we wait till we have all the answers before we can walk with and stand beside those who are oppressed. The answers come while we are walking."[24]

All told, Shepard's Jeff-Vander-Lou, Inc. (JVL) built or rehabilitated over six hundred homes and apartments on the Northside. Then it rented and sold them to Black people on favorable terms. It built, for a time, a thriving neighborhood where there had only recently been a scattered population living in an array of broken-down and boarded-up brick buildings. At the heart of it, and existing to this day, was Bethesda Mennonite Church—a majority Black Mennonite congregation in the heart of the Northside.[25]

Also active in these years was Ivory Perry, a Korean War veteran who had moved to St. Louis from Arkansas as a young man. Although he was a member of ACTION, Perry served as a one-man strike force during the later 1960s in St. Louis, whether he was chaining himself to doors in support of the protests or simply walking out into the street, lying down, and stopping traffic. Pioneered in front of Jefferson Bank in 1963 and Southwestern Bell in 1964, this tactic was employed regularly by Perry, who became a rolling one-man traffic jam. Countless photos from the era show Perry, dressed in a coat and a tie and often wearing a hat, lying down in the road in front of a car. It was this tactic, first used by Perry and others in the 1960s, that resurfaced in Ferguson fifty years later and came to define the resistance of Black Lives Matter. More than any other voice in St. Louis, it was Perry who came to speak for those displaced by urban renewal and the construction of the interstate highway system. "Negro removal by white approval," he termed it.

Perry, too, became active in the housing struggle, serving as a coordinator for the Human Development Corporation, a local vehicle for the administration and distribution of federal community development block grants. At the Human Development Corporation (HDC), Perry sought to call attention to the health hazard of lead paint in the city's rental stock: extensively exposed to lead, Black children, on average, had levels of lead in their blood five times higher than those of white children who lived only a few miles away from them in the St. Louis area.[26]

In 1958, the Nation of Islam (NOI), a Black nationalist organization that emphasized personal discipline and community self-determination that had been founded in Detroit in the 1930s, established Temple No. 28 on Grand Avenue in St. Louis under the leadership of Clyde X. The Nation soon developed several businesses around the temple—a restaurant, a dry cleaner, a record store, a clothing shop, a grocery store—and the area became known as "Little Egypt." Through the 1960s, the Nation brought several leaders in the struggle to St. Louis. NOI's leader, the Honorable Elijah Muhammad, spoke to over three thousand people at Kiel Auditorium in 1961, and convert and heavyweight champion of the world Muhammad Ali visited the city in 1968. The Black radical university professor Angela Davis, who would later cite the historical influence of the communist Union Army colonel Joseph Weydemeyer in her pathbreaking book *Women, Race, and Class*, addressed the Nation in East St. Louis in 1971, declaring, "We must build a nation for ourselves."

In St. Louis, as elsewhere, the Nation was plagued by infighting. Questions about Clyde X's leadership and doubts about his accounting—he reportedly drove a late-model two-tone Mercury and lived in the Central West End—led to tension within the temple, and a breakaway faction founded an alternative temple on Union Boulevard in 1961. An October 1966 assassination attempt left Clyde X wounded and another man dead outside the Shabazz Restaurant on Grand. Several months later, Clyde X's home was firebombed. And two days after that, Andrew Hoffman and his wife, members of the Union Boulevard temple, were shot to death, while another member of the breakaway temple was beaten to death. No one was ever charged with the murders, which the *St. Louis Argus* reported as the "Black Muslim Revenge Killings."[27]

Although the Communist Party in St. Louis had mostly been busted up and driven out by the 1960s, there was a small, committed group that assembled as the DuBois Club, under the leadership of Eugene Tournour. Tournour was a white Washington University graduate who had grown up in St. Louis and the Catholic Church—at one time he had considered becoming a priest. But by the time of the Jefferson Bank protest, he had joined CORE, and it was he who suggested that activists clog the lobby of the bank with lines of people holding $1 bills, waiting for change. Tournour, along with several other Marxists, was theatrically read out of CORE in the aftermath of the 1963 *Globe-Democrat* exposé about communists in the movement, but he was welcomed as a member of ACTION and participated in many of that group's colorful (and sometimes flavorful) protests over the course of the decade. The DuBois Club retained a global and anti-imperialist outlook throughout the 1960s and connected the Black movement with anti–Vietnam War activists, both intellectually and operationally. But wherever Tournour went, the *Globe-Democrat* was sure to follow, insistent on establishing that the struggle against racism was really a front for the communist infiltration of the United States. The 1965 visit to St. Louis of the Marxist historian Herbert Aptheker was lavishly covered in the paper, complete with pop-up paparazzi at the airport and several embedded reporters who provided notes on Aptheker's lecture about W.E.B. Du Bois—"the leading man of the twentieth century"— for their outraged readers in Webster Groves and other white enclaves around the city.[28]

As we have seen, rather than fighting a block-by-block battle over segregation during the years after the Second World War, white people in general followed the Veiled Prophet parade and moved to more defensible space. They left behind the four hundred or so restrictive covenants they had drawn up, the grocery stores with the Black butchers, and the diners with the Black patrons and moved to the county. In St. Louis itself, city leaders began to rely on urban planning and "development" as a means of racial control—and of course, the police. Nowhere was this more clearly the case than in the massive Pruitt-Igoe housing project—thirty-three eleven-story buildings on the city's Northside.[29]

In the same years that Webster Groves was becoming the nation's emblematic suburb, Pruitt-Igoe, only nine miles away, became its most notorious housing project. Designed by the architect Minoru Yamasaki, who would later design the World Trade Center in New York, the federally sponsored project was completed in 1954. Originally, there were to have been two separate housing complexes on the fifty-seven-acre site. One, named for the African American World War II airman Wendell O. Pruitt, for African Americans, and the other, named for US congressman William Igoe, for whites. The 1955 decision of the US District Court for the Eastern District of Missouri in *Davis et al. v. St. Louis Housing Authority* (the case argued by Frankie Freeman), however, ended segregation in federal housing projects, and Igoe was opened to Black as well as white residents shortly after opening. Before long, the same pattern that took hold elsewhere in the United States took hold in St. Louis: federal money was used to subsidize white flight to the suburbs and the sequestration of Black urban-dwellers in housing projects—racially and spatially distinct approaches to urban "renewal" and economic "development." It was with Pruitt-Igoe in mind that the city had torn down Mill Creek Valley and other Black neighborhoods on the Southside and downtown. The housing complex was to be a vast receptacle for African Americans displaced by the economic development and renewal promised by the futuristic plans of city planner Harland Bartholomew. Indeed, in these years the city's Land Clearance and Redevelopment Authority and its Public Housing Authority were combined into a single agency, the Land Clearance and Housing Authority. Ivory Perry might have termed it the Department of Negro Removal.[30]

Although the planned population density in the project was to be greater than that of Mill Creek Valley, the initial responses of the new residents were positive, bordering on ecstatic. Regular and reliable hot water and fully equipped kitchens were a substantial improvement for many of those who had for too long lived at the mercy of their landlords. Fannie Mae Ralph, who was presented to the press as the "first resident" of Pruitt-Igoe, declared it "perfect . . . I'd never had a place—never seen any place as nice as Pruitt." A photo of Ralph and her children gazing out the window of their new apartment became the iconic image of the promise of Pruitt-Igoe. The almost uniformly positive memories among residents of the early years of Pruitt-Igoe (the complex reached its peak occupancy rate, 91 percent, in 1957) has occasioned a low-key debate among historians: Were the problems that emerged in the complex due to cost-cutting or design flaws? If properly maintained, would the complex have fulfilled the promise it seemed to offer its earliest residents?[31]

The positive initial responses are one data point in an ongoing debate about the design of the project, specifically about whether a project of this scale could ever have succeeded, especially given some of the shortcuts taken in the eventual construction, such as elevators that stopped only on every other floor, leaving some tenants feeling exposed in lonely stairwells, and no air conditioning, in a city where the temperature frequently reaches ninety degrees with high humidity in the summer. The project is famous in the history of design, which treats it as one of the greatest architectural failures of all time and a symbol of the shortcomings of massive modernist social design. Indeed, critics often refer to the demise of Pruitt-Igoe as marking "the end of modern architecture." The project's defenders, instead, often blame the tenants, poor Black people, whom they apparently think let down the building that housed them. Yamasaki has gone so far as to declare himself a victim of the project.[32]

But that is getting ahead of the story. Whatever might have happened had Pruitt-Igoe been properly maintained, we will never know, because it was not properly maintained. The federally imposed limits on living in Pruitt-Igoe were extreme. Because residents were means-tested, and because federal aid had been designed with the idea that Black America's problems boiled down to the problem of unwed mothers, many women in Pruitt-Igoe had to keep their husbands, lovers, and other male visitors hidden from inspectors, who would insist on raising their rent or removing them from the complex entirely if they thought the man in question represented another source of income. Residents were likewise tacitly forbidden to have telephones or televisions, both of which were looked upon by the inspectors and building management as suggesting a level of personal wealth incompatible with public housing.[33]

From the beginning, the complex was not only poorly maintained but understaffed. Built with federal funds, the complex was to be maintained by the city. But because the city housing authority shared a budget with the city land clearance authority, the money that might have been used to maintain and improve Pruitt-Igoe was the very same money that was being used by the planners and developers seeking to "revitalize" the downtown. The buildings soon began to fall into disrepair—one plumber, one carpenter, one welder, one electrician, and one glazier were employed for the entire complex. And there was only one watchman per building. Soon trash began to pile up in the hallways in front of chutes that had at first seemed like a modern convenience but turned out to be frequently jammed. There were no lights in the hallways. The roof began to leak. Poor conditions in the project and poor economic prospects for Black job-seekers combined to produce a criminogenic environment; some young people with too much time and too little hope turned to dealing and doing drugs. Residents began to fear the stairwells and galleries. Repairmen contracted to do work in the project began to insist on having protection from the already strained security staff. When conditions deteriorated even further, people began to move out. By 1965, the vacancy rate had risen to 25 percent. By 1969, it was 43 percent—the complex was almost half-empty. All of the empty apartments presented further maintenance and security problems. In the winter of 1970, pipes burst in vacant and unheated apartments all over the complex, and the massive icicles on the outsides of the buildings formed by the resulting floods of water became an enduring image of the failure of Pruitt-Igoe and of public housing in the United States more generally. "Every time I asked for more help, they hired another planner, another dreamer," remembered the exasperated head of maintenance for the St. Louis Housing Authority.[34]

By the late 1960s, there were more sociologists working in Pruitt-Igoe than dedicated maintenance workers. Between 1963 and 1969, a team of sociologists from Washington University conducted an extended ethnographic study of Black life inside the complex. The study was supported by the National Institutes of Health and received at least $1 million of federal money. In addition to several senior scholars, among them some of the most prominent sociologists in the United States—Lee Rainwater, the principal investigator, was joined by Alvin Gouldner, Jules Henry (who was finishing up his work in Webster Groves), and several others—the project employed eight full-time investigators for much of its run.[35]

The Washington University investigators were seeking to overthrow what they saw as the excessive "moralism" of existing studies of Black family life in the United States. They hoped also to probe the roots of Black anger, or as Rainwater put it in the preface to the resulting study, *Behind Ghetto Walls*, they wanted to bring attention to the "social and political responses which serve to sustain the individual in his punishing world but also generate aggressiveness towards the self and others which results in suffering directly inflicted by Negroes on themselves and on others." By drawing attention to the degrading *conditions* in Pruitt-Igoe and suggesting that these social ills were the first cause of people's self-destructive reactions, Rainwater and his team were trying to shift the field of sociology away from its ongoing obsession with the supposed insufficiency of Black family life and the "pathology" of Black culture. As Rainwater wrote in the conclusion of the book, which chronicles the history of Black removal and sequestration in St. Louis and elsewhere in the nation, "Federal programs show a line of development from slum clearance to public housing to urban renewal to urban rehabilitation to model cities. . . . They have succeeded in moving people from one place to another, but they have provided very few with good housing."[36]

Behind Ghetto Walls provided a scholarly foundation for the antiracist emphasis on poor social conditions (as opposed to cultural pathology) as a basis for federal policy in regard to cities and the people who lived in them. It shifted the blame for the political radicalization and supposed criminality of the Black and urban poor from the supposed cultural and psychological insufficiency of Black people for dealing with modern life to the social conditions that prevailed in the United States—that is, from racism to social criticism. The book was framed by the argument that poor conditions in the Pruitt-Igoe housing project were producing extreme personality types—people who were variously overzealous in their Christianity, extremist in their (antiwhite) politics, oversexualized, or just plain immoral. The solutions proposed by the sociologists— government programs providing for full employment, because "an equitable society should not require its families to achieve median income by forcing wives and children to enter the labor market"—could have been drawn from an ACTION policy paper: their proposals were pointedly critical of racial inequality, but written within the frame of the existing economic and patriarchal order.[37]

But, by emphasizing the socially pathogenic character of Pruitt-Igoe—by treating relentless religiosity and extreme political engagement as signs of social anomie when they might just as well have been treated as signs of social integration—the Washington University sociologists unwittingly participated in reinforcing the notion that the people in Pruitt-Igoe were damaged, angry, and disorderly. They framed their otherwise laudable proposals as a pragmatic response to urban pathology rather than as a simple principled response to extreme inequality. Their framing might be simply read as the perspective of sociologists: they looked for the larger social structures framing the lives, the problems, and the ideas of those whom they studied, and they justified their policy proposals in relationship to what they had found. But it turned out that the very character of the sociological discipline was being called into question from within the Pruitt-Igoe project, which, alongside Rainwater's book, produced Joyce Ladner's *Tomorrow's Tomorrow*. This landmark study transformed ("decolonized") academic method by adopting a new ethics of academic research, one focused on the lives, experiences, and, especially, the self-understanding of Black women.

Ladner came to St. Louis in the mid-1960s from Mississippi, where she had been active in the civil rights movement and a student of movement leaders Medgar Evers, Robert Moses, Fannie Lou Hamer, and Ella Baker. She entered Pruitt-Igoe, however, not as an activist, but as a social scientist, an objective observer equipped with a set of book-learned ideas about the social and cultural ills of the urban Black and poor. It was a posture that did not last long. "I went into the field equipped with a set of preconceived ideas and labels that I intended to apply to these women. . . . However, this role was difficult, if not impossible, for me to play because all of my life experience invalidated the deviant perspective." Confronted with the lives of the Black girls with whom she was spending time in Pruitt-Igoe, girls whom she had been taught to see as damaged—as "deviant"—Ladner began to question the entire edifice of her learning, her discipline, and the social sciences in general. Rather than sociology being a way to understand the effects of racial inequality, and thus a tool in service of its abolition, Ladner began to understand it as "the conceptual framework of oppression." *Tomorrow's Tomorrow* was arguably the first full-length effort to "decolonize" social scientific methodology—to produce academic knowledge that analyzed the world from the position of the oppressed rather than from that of the dominant and to begin, finally, to throw off the imperial intellectual legacy of the 1904 World's Fair.[38]

Ladner did not diminish the hard edge of life in Pruitt-Igoe. She wrote of crime and children exposed to hunger, sexual violence, and fear at a very early age. But rather than the social scientists' all-purpose answer for the impact of these conditions—"damaged self-esteem"—Ladner found "emotional precocity," "realism," and "resourcefulness." Expecting to find "inadequacy, worthlessness, and self-disparagement," she instead found that "many of the young ladies possessed an abundance of human resourcefulness and hope. . . . And the hatred, if present at all, was directed toward those individuals and institutions which inflict pain upon them, instead of being directed inward." The girls understood their poverty as a manifestation of their Blackness, but they were not ashamed: they thought the problem was with the rich white people. "I wouldn't want to be rich at all. I don't think it is fair for anyone to be rich and not help people, because if they think back they will realize that deep down inside they could have been the people that they see walking the street and looking like tramps," one of them told Ladner. Perhaps that is why the people in Webster Groves were so upset by the protest at Jefferson Bank, or why they were talking about building a wall in Ferguson. Perhaps the problem was on the inside of the wall rather than what was outside it. "It is only when the analysis of the oppressive forces which produce various forms of antisocial behavior has been conducted that we can reverse the conceptualization of pathology. *The society, instead of its members, [is] pathological.*"[39]

The girls with whom Ladner spoke viewed the police as an occupying force "whose duties are to punish rather than protect the community." Little wonder: the St. Louis police in the 1960s were notorious for random stops and racial harassment on the streets of the Northside. Sometimes the traffic stops had a pretext—a broken taillight, a crossed yellow line—and sometimes they just seemed to the children of Pruitt-Igoe like plain old power-tripping. Behind the harassment, however, was a deeper purpose. In these years, the city of St. Louis was the center of a federally sponsored pilot project to develop a model of predictive policing by applying the techniques of counterinsurgency in the terrain of an American city. The St. Louis Police Department made random stops all over the city, but particularly on the mostly Black Northside and around Pruitt-Igoe, and coded the information they gathered into a database that was used to map connections between individuals and to identify candidates for preemptive arrest: "If a youth persistently stays in a group of questionable purpose, charges of . . . loitering may be brought against him," read the departmental guidelines on the acceptable reasons for arresting people for doing nothing. "Civil rights is not my bag, but this stuff scares me," wrote an official in the Nixon White House in response. "What you have here is a compilation of policemen's opinions, without court tested evidence of proof, which turns people into suspects for future crimes." While the official's doubts may seem quaint today—so familiar has the notion of data-based predictive policing become—the parameters of the program in St. Louis leave little to the imagination about why kids in the projects might have hated the police. Arbitrary arrest was an accepted part of police practice in St. Louis; indeed, it was official policy.[40]

By the early 1960s, Pruitt-Igoe was viewed by the police as a territory apart. Inside the project, the visual logic that allowed the police to control the streets was reversed. They were the lonely pedestrians caught out in the open: targeted with bricks and bottles thrown from the windows above whenever they went into the project. There is even some agreement between accounts from police and former residents of refrigerators being launched from the roof, although the legend of snipers targeting police from the upper floors of the complex seems to trace back to an incident at the nearby Cochran Apartment Buildings, where police fired hundreds of shots at a "sniper" who may never have existed and then ransacked the apartments of project residents before taking into custody, and then quickly releasing, a fourteen-year-old boy.[41]

SUCCESSFUL in thwarting vandals at the Wohl Community Center were Patrolman Paul McCulloch and his dog Duke. Three boys, 8 to 11 years old, who had been throwing rocks at the building's windows, fled when challenged by the officer, but stopped immediately when he threatened to turn Duke loose.   —Globe-Democrat Photo

The St. Louis Police Department was among the first in the United States to employ police dogs. In the 1960s, officers took dogs with them whenever they entered the Pruitt-Igoe housing project. Canine officer Paul McCulloch was shot to death in Pruitt-Igoe in 1963. (Missouri Historical Society)

After 1957, the St. Louis police generally took dogs with them when they went into Pruitt-Igoe, which they referred to as "Korea," in reference to the war in which many of the officers had fought. The dogs had been trained by the British military and were made available to American police departments in 1956. St. Louis was one of the first cities to form a canine unit—along with Baltimore, and even before Bull Connor's Birmingham—and Pruitt-Igoe was one of the first sites of their regular deployment. Photos from the era show large crowds of Black children standing back from the dogs in the courtyards between the buildings, some terrified, some enchanted, some simply nonplussed. In 1964, canine officer Paul McCulloch was shot one time in the head inside the complex after having pursued a fleeing "robbery suspect," who was later convicted of first-degree murder. The officer left behind a wife and two sons, one of whom, Robert, would grow up to be the prosecuting attorney in St. Louis County. The McCulloch shooting was a touchstone event in the history of the St. Louis Police Department, commemorated as recently as the summer of 2014—a seeming emblem of the enduring antagonism between the police and the project.[42]

One would be hard-pressed to come to a different impression after reading the memoir of St. Louis Police Department officer William Leahy, who worked in the Fifth District, near Pruitt-Igoe on the Northside. It was a commonplace on the force, he remembers, to refer to Black migrants from the South as "Swamp Turkeys" and to Pruitt-Igoe as a "cesspool of humanity," a "living nightmare," "a combat zone," and, inevitably, "Fort Apache." His memoir is written in a tone of jocular sadism—"there was something special about the close quarters in the back of those old cruisers that encouraged dialogue . . . it has been said, but not confirmed, that sometimes when a [beaten or wounded] prisoner has not been forthright with critical information there is a corresponding difficulty with finding the driveway to the Hospital Emergency Entrance." Leahy's memoir is written, that is to say, in the tone of a dishonest police report: it sutures the observable facts together with stories so implausible that the cover-up itself takes on an edge of menace. Like Leahy's story of a badly beaten suspect whose condition was explained as the result of having "fallen down the stairs . . . several times." Like officer Paul McCulloch's story that his police dog had been unleashed on a man in Forest Park because the officer stumbled into a hole on the golf course.[43]

Like the countless number of fleeing "robbery suspects" shot by the St. Louis police in these years: "Fleeing Youth Shot to Death by Policeman"; "Youth, 19, Shot and Killed by Policeman"; "Suspect Wounded by Police Charged with Armed Robbery"; "Patrolman Shoots Youth Dismantling an Auto"; "Policeman Shoots Boy, 16, During Store Burglary"; "Killing of Youth by Police Held Justifiable"; "Police Shoot 'Pete' Herron Five Times"; "Woman Is Shot in Melee over Arrest of Sons"; "Man Shot by Policeman at Depot Dies"; "Witnesses Say Police Lied about Killing, Never Saw Nightstick in Victim's Hand"; "Boy, 16, Shot by Patrolman

During Chase"; "Police Shoot Youth Found in Shop"; "Charge of Beating Denied by Officers"; "Officer Shoots, Wounds Fleeing Robbery Suspect"; and "Suspect Shot in Chase." All of these headlines were collected by ACTION in a single year. Of the stories that accompanied them, that for "Policeman Shoots Boy, 16, During Store Burglary" can perhaps serve as representative: "A 16-year-old boy was shot and seriously wounded Sunday night when police reported catching him in an attempted burglary at the Gold Star Market, 2633 Glasgow Ave." Upon returning to the store, police discovered that nothing had been taken.[44]

ACTION's 1970 "blue paper" report on the St. Louis Police Department, entitled "Thugs in Blue Uniforms," documented thirty-five police killings in the years between 1965 and 1970, as well as twenty-three instances in which suspects were shot but not killed and fifty-two severe beatings. The report recommended that the St. Louis police be forbidden from shooting at fleeing suspects as well as from using hollow-point bullets, which were designed to "mushroom" upon impact, the soft lead folding back around the copper jacket and thus maximizing damage to muscle, bone, and tissue. (St. Louis was one of the few police departments in the nation that issued the bullets, which had been foresworn by the US military in a treaty signed at the Hague in 1907.) The report also recommended that policemen be required to live in the neighborhoods they patrolled, and that the department's director of community relations (who had recently replaced an officer who turned out to be a member of the avowedly segregationist John Birch Society) be forced to move into a majority-Black and poor neighborhood. Finally, it suggested that the police department form all-Black "goon squads" to patrol white neighborhoods as white "decoy squads" did in Black neighborhoods.[45]

Two police killings were singled out for special attention in ACTION's report. On June 12, 1965, eighteen-year-old Melvin Cravens was detained on "suspicion of robbery" by Officer Darrell Rommell. Handcuffed inside the Lucas Avenue Police Station, Cravens was shot in the back of the head and died on the floor of the booking room.

Rommell's claim that the handcuffed Cravens had attacked him and tried to take his gun was accepted by the Board of Police Commissioners (the state-appointed board that had overseen the St. Louis Police Department since it was created by proslavery Missourians hoping to wrest control of the city from the US Army in the early days of the Civil War), and Rommell was cleared of any wrongdoing. On July 2, 1965, ACTION staged a large rally in front of police headquarters downtown, and then another in the aftermath of the Board of Commissioners' decision later that month. The protests continued through the fall.

The following September, twenty-seven-year-old Russell Hayes was shot and killed outside the Central Police Station. Though Hayes was handcuffed and confined in the backseat of a police car, officers claimed that he had managed to lunge for one of their guns—to prove their case, they hired a contortionist to "reenact" the incident on live television in St. Louis by getting out of handcuffs while sitting on a park bench. Again, there were large protests across the city. On October 13, 1966, police in the Ninth District shot Timothy Walsh, a white teenager suspected in a shooting, claiming that he had escaped from a police station by diving through a window, running away, and jumping a six-foot fence, though he too was handcuffed at the time. It was the Walsh shooting that occasioned the organization of a joint protest march. When Black activists, including Macler Shepard and Ivory Perry (who was arrested during the march), marched from the downtown area and white activists marched from the West End to meet them, it was one of the moments in the history of St. Louis when it became clear to many white people that the city's architecture of control might have been created with Black people in mind, but that its unruly growth had come to endanger their children as well.[46]

B lack activists in St. Louis in these years faced an organized campaign of harassment from both local law enforcement and the FBI. Percy Green, who had been placed on an FBI watch list as a potential revolutionary "Black Messiah" to be arrested immediately in case of an urban insurrection, was the subject of a local harassment effort that included frequent calls to his home informing his wife, Betti, that she needed to come down to the city morgue to identify his body. Though the Greens remained friendly, Betti eventually took their young son and moved to a different home in the apartment complex where they lived, partly out of fear that the apartment in which Green continued to live would be bombed. It was in these years that the *Globe-Democrat* published the editorial naming Percy Green and calling on the St. Louis police to assault him. In the summer of 1966, Green was stopped by a policeman he later identified as Officer Dale Myers, who looked at the name on his license, put a "drop" gun to his head, and said, "So, you're *the* Percy Green." Warned by his partner that they were being watched from across the street, Myers arrested Green on a set of sixteen fabricated charges, including rolling up his window on the officer's arm and dragging him down the street; Green was later acquitted of all charges. By the late 1960s, Black organizations in St. Louis were full of informants; their presence corroded the trust necessary for organizational cohesion and made it impossible to do anything without the police knowing in advance. Still they persevered: Green remembered thinking, on the assumption that there were surely police informants in ACTION, "I was going to put the informants to work."[47]

While ACTION remained committed to militant nonviolence during these years, a group called Black Liberators emerged in 1968 to wage brief, but intense, armed struggle against the St. Louis police. Modeled on the Black Panther Party in Oakland and the Deacons of Defense in Mississippi and Louisiana, the Liberators were led by Charles Koen, a Black radical organizer who had come to St. Louis from Cairo, Illinois. Koen, who was also on the FBI's "Black Messiah" watch list, and the Liberators were committed to armed and revolutionary self-defense. The group emerged in the summer of 1968 in St. Louis; wearing black military-style uniforms, the Liberators patrolled the streets of North St. Louis in a black sedan embossed with

the legend THE BLACK LIBERATORS . . . THE BLACK PEOPLE'S PROTEC-
TORS and occasionally mounted armed patrols through those streets.
They were headquartered near the "Wall of Respect," a mural depict-
ing the heroes and martyrs of the Black struggle, including Malcolm
X and Martin Luther King Jr., on the side of a building at the corner
of Leffingwell and Franklin Avenues. At the top was a quotation from
Marcus Garvey: "Rise Up, You Mighty Black Race."[48]

The mostly young, mostly poor, entirely male Liberators were
guided by a Ten Point Program that included demands for land, jobs,
decent housing, and education; a commitment to working "side-by-
side" with Black women, backed by a paternalist promise to give them
"total care"; and a program for the reform, even partial abolition, of
the St. Louis Police Department. The police reforms they demanded
included an end to police killings of young Black men; an end to
police patrols in Black neighborhoods; public support of Black self-
policing and protection in Black neighborhoods; and the end of cash
bail. Though some at the time viewed the Liberators as a front organization for a scheme to extort protection money from white merchants
on Franklin Avenue (to whom the Liberators did extend an offer of a
protection contract, in keeping with the emphasis on Black enforcement in Black neighborhoods), and though their alignment with the
protection of white property in a Black neighborhood might seem a
somewhat inauspicious foundation, even a cynical observer could see
that the Liberators' Ten Point Program provided a model, however
short-lived, of a Black radical critique of racial capitalism.

Among the Black Liberators, the word "humanism" stood for this
revolutionary goal, though it was too small and too short-lived an organization to develop a fully revolutionary program. At least some of its
members hoped, however, to build collectively owned Black agricultural
cooperatives on abandoned land in North St. Louis and beyond. And
though they were an avowedly separatist organization, they were not
antiwhite in any simple sense. Their goal, one Liberator said, was not to
get rid of white people, but to educate them about the common sources

of the suffering of poor Black and poor white people: "to teach the white man how he's been screwed, and how his mind has been put in slavery." The Liberators had strong ties to white activists opposing the war in Vietnam, and they urged Black men to resist the draft, because the war was simply another manifestation of "the system." The Liberators' "humanism" was, in the formulation of one of the organization's lieutenants, distinct from both "human rights" and "communism"—it was a vision of Black-led, anticapitalist, anti-imperialist human emancipation.[49]

In the event, the Black Liberators had little time for big ideas, because their energy and finally their organization were consumed in a battle with the police. On August 17, 1968, Congressman Adam Clayton Powell of New York City visited St. Louis and gave a not particularly radical speech about the virtues of Black businessmen. But what caught the attention of many in the city, including the police, was the presence of openly armed Liberators providing the congressman's security. The police arrested two of the Liberators as they left the auditorium and held them on gun charges—nineteen-year-old Edward Baily for having a pistol "concealed" in his car, and nineteen-year-old Larone Thomas for having a sawed-off shotgun. Koen himself was arrested on September 4. The following night, someone fired shots into the windows of the Ninth District Police Station, and shots were also fired into the house of St. Louis police lieutenant Fred Grimes, a Black officer who was notoriously disdained in Black St. Louis. The same night a firebomb was thrown through the window of the house owned by real estate agent C. W. Gates, who was the first Black member of the state police board that governed the city police department and who was, if anything, even less popular than Lieutenant Grimes.

The police began rounding up the Liberators and held twenty-one of them overnight, before releasing them without charges. During the night, while the Liberators were being held, a group of men destroyed their undefended headquarters, turning over the drawers, breaking the furniture in the street, and burning the organization's car. Though the police attempted to cast the blame on a rival Black nationalist organization (the Zulu 1200s), witnesses at the scene were sure they had seen Lieutenant Grimes presiding over the mayhem. A photograph from the *Post-Dispatch* that summer depicts a white police officer brandishing a machine gun from the window of a squad car, and the caption reads, "Ready for action, near the Black Liberators' office."[50]

On September 13, city police officers stopped Koen and another Liberator, Leon Dent, for driving with a broken taillight. They took Koen and Dent to the basement of the Ninth District Police Station, where they beat them and left the men lying on the floor, bleeding from cuts made by blows to their heads, and with hands broken trying to defend themselves from the club-wielding officers. The police charged Dent with possession of a concealed weapon (a comb) and charged both men with resisting arrest and the destruction of city property—a chair that had been broken in the melee. The charges were later dropped, and an internal investigation resulted in suspensions of six Ninth District officers, including Detective Rudolph Oehlert. Suspended for a month, the longest suspension served by any of the officers, Oehlert was defending himself at the time in a wrongful death suit brought by the parents of Timothy Walsh, who had been shot outside the same police station two years earlier.[51]

The Liberators' case was taken up by, among others, Teamsters 688 leader Harold Gibbons, who at one time had been thought to be next in line for the organization's national leadership, and by Congressman William Clay, who wrote to US Attorney General Ramsay Clark to urge (unsuccessfully) that a civil rights investigation be opened. Along with Percy Green and a member of the Washington University SDS chapter, and supported by the ACLU, Koen filed suit against the St. Louis Police Department on October 10, 1968, seeking an injunction against further police harassment of St. Louis activists. Writing for the US District Court of the Eastern District of Missouri, Judge Roy W. Harper dismissed the activists' claims as an effort to "rock the boat," stating that "we live in a good city." He referred presumably to St. Louis, though Justice Harper himself lived in Ladue.[52]

For most of the Liberators, it was too late anyway; for all intents and purposes, the organization had been infiltrated and intimidated out of existence by the end of 1968. Charles Koen left St. Louis and returned to Cairo, where he and others fought a medium-intensity war against local police and white vigilantes that involved 140 documented shooting incidents over a two-year period between March 1969 and February 1971—a struggle memorialized by the pioneering jazz drummer Max Roach, who included a song dedicated to Koen and those who fought alongside him in Cairo on his 1971 album *Lift Every Voice and Sing*.[53]

From the military-trained police dogs to the machine guns to the invocations of "Fort Apache," "Korea," and North St. Louis as a "combat zone" to the specially trained and designated countersubversive units, there is little question that policing in the city of St. Louis in the postsegregation era took on many of the trappings of imperial counterinsurgency and military occupation. None of that, however, conveys the depth of the militarization of the landscape of racial control in St. Louis in the 1950s and 1960s as much as the US Army's secret radiological weapons experiments conducted on the city's unsuspecting population.[54]

I n 1949, the US Army Chemical Corps began to plan field tests of the airborne dissemination of aerosolized radiological weapons. Three North American cities—Winnipeg, Minneapolis, and St. Louis—were selected for the tests on the basis of their supposed physical similarity to Moscow and Leningrad in the Soviet Union. The bulk of the testing took place in St. Louis. Beginning in July 1953 and lasting well into 1954, unmarked vehicles crisscrossed several neighborhoods of the city, leaving a low-hanging iridescent fog in their wake. While the city government and the newspapers stuck to the cover story that the fog was a harmless composite designed to derange the vision of hypothetical Soviet long-range bombers, in fact the fog was zinc cadmium sulfide, which, according to the historian who has done the most to un-cover this history, was produced at Stanford University and was being sprayed across the city with local support from scientists from Washington University and Monsanto.[55]

In all, 163 chemical release experiments were conducted in the city during the first round of open-air tests, most of them in neighborhoods identified by the researchers as "densely populated slum districts" and "poorer sections" of the city, chosen because they were subject to greater "police surveillance." All in all, the test area mapped neatly onto the areas of the city targeted for destruction in Harland Bartholomew's 1947 city plan. And zinc cadmium sulfide was not harmless: it is, in fact, toxic in large doses, though the National Institutes of Health maintains that even the doses experienced in St. Louis, the highest doses on the continent, were not high enough to be dangerous. (The next-highest amount of zinc cadmium sulfide dispersed over a city during this round of experiments was just over thirteen pounds in Winnipeg, less than half of 1 percent of what was eventually sprayed on St. Louis.) The army has denied knowing at the time of the experiments that zinc cadmium sulfide was dangerous, but some remember that the crates in which the material was shipped from California were labeled with the word POISON. While these tests targeted Black neighborhoods, the very nature of the experiment highlighted the unpredictability of the exposure and provided a classic example of the unpredictable (actually, predictably unpredictable) overflows of violence distributed according to a racial template—in this case, into the immigrant and white working-class neighborhoods that abutted much of Black St. Louis.[56]

In May 1963, the government began a second round of radiological weapons tests in St. Louis, this time focusing on the city's public housing projects, especially Pruitt-Igoe, which was seen to be an architectural analog of the massive Kolpino housing complex in Leningrad. This round of tests lasted until March 1965 and involved the dispersion of over one ton of aerosolized chemicals from radio towers surrounding

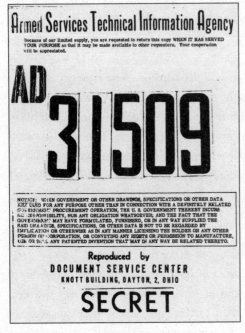

The US Army Chemical Corps conducted classified open-air tests of radiological weapons in the 1950s and 1960s in St. Louis. (US Army Chemical Corps, "Behavior of Aerosol Clouds," *Joint Quarterly Report* 3, January–March 1953)

the projects and from the roofs of the buildings in Pruitt-Igoe. Again, the US Army Chemical Corps claimed that the releases were limited to zinc cadmium sulfide, a claim bolstered by the material about the tests declassified by Secretary of Energy Hazel O'Leary in 1996. Much of the material pertaining to the Pruitt-Igoe tests, however, remains classified, including the results of a "special study" overseen by the same radiological weapons specialists responsible for the intentional exposure of US Army soldiers to radioactive fallout in 1957.[57]

In the St. Louis experiments, the United States of America converted the lives of poor and Black people, and especially poor Black people, into experimental raw material in the service of national "defense."[58]

A survey of baby teeth taken from the mouths of St. Louis children between 1961 and 1970 showed increasing rates of radioactive strontium 90 (a focus of the army's classified experiments) in children born over the course of the 1950s, with a radical break beginning in 1963: children born in St. Louis after 1963 had over fifty times the level of strontium 90 in their teeth as those born before 1950. The initial data from the "baby tooth survey" is generally credited with leading President John Kennedy to sign an international treaty banning the atmospheric testing of nuclear weapons on August 3, 1963, although the testing in Pruitt-Igoe continued unabated.[59]

The culminating struggle of the era took place in Pruitt-Igoe and the city's other public housing projects, where Black women organized one of the first rent strikes in the modern history of the United States. The strike built on several years of organizing by poor and working-class Black women in St. Louis, most notably the Darst project resident Jean King. They were supported by a white legal services lawyer, who would later go on to be one of the largest private developers of low-income housing in the United States. In August 1967, nine Black women had occupied the HDC demanding more and better jobs for Black women. When a sheriff's officer came in to warn them that they faced jail time if they refused to leave the premises, Birdie Lou Saine sent him away with the admonition, "Next time you come back with the contempt citation, bring some food with you." That November, public housing residents staged a large demonstration outside the office of the St. Louis Housing Authority, demanding better maintenance and more reliable policing, lower rents, and tenant representation on the board that governed the projects. The demonstrations, which continued through 1968, were organized and led by Black women, with members of ACTION and the Zulu 1200s serving as protest marshals.[60]

The rent strike began in early 1969, when the Housing Authority announced a sixfold rent increase. Residents in all five St. Louis housing projects stopped paying their rent; in four of them, the effort was led by Black women. The generational shift in the freedom struggle was starkly represented by the fact that they addressed their demands

Ora Lee Malone was a union member and leader in the NAACP who was active in the Jefferson Bank protests and the effort to prevent the closing of Homer G. Phillips Hospital. (Wiley Price/*St. Louis American*)

to Irvin Dagen, the onetime CORE member and supporter of the Freedom of Residence Committee in St. Louis County, who had become the chairman of the Housing Authority. The city was never going to provide the Housing Authority with enough money to properly run the projects, and since Dagen, however pure his intentions, had been pressed into the service of the city as a professional manager of racial discontent, it was now his job to run them anyway.

The tenants' demands were pointed and comprehensive: that their rent be calculated based on their income rather than on the size of their apartments; that tenants' board approval be required when the Housing Authority planned to sue residents for back payments; that there be mechanisms for the approval of partial payment of rent in exigent circumstances; that the Housing Authority advertise job openings to tenants before making them generally available; that space be set aside for cooperative groceries and businesses within the housing projects;

and that the Housing Authority provide better maintenance, better policing, and "due process" in the assessment of charges for property damages. They also demanded that tenants be appointed to the Housing Authority's Board of Commissioners. Until their demands were met, they refused to pay their rent.[61]

The more than one thousand tenants who participated in the strike represented around a quarter of those still living in the city's deteriorating housing projects. They were supported by virtually every Black activist organization in the city, including Ivory Perry's Metropolitan Tenants' Organization, the Zulu 1200s, and the Black Liberators. ACTION demonstrated in front of Irvin Dagen's suburban Clayton home, put a FOR SALE sign in his yard, and threatened to build a tent city in the middle of Clayton, reasoning that it was the impoverished public housing tenants who paid Dagen's salary, and hence his property taxes, and thus the city of Clayton was a direct beneficiary of their suffering. "ACTION plans to bring any evicted public housing tenant that volunteers to dramatize the human suffering and poverty of the urban public-housing concentration camps to [live in] the city of Clayton," read one of the organization's press releases. Facing bankruptcy, the chronically underfunded Housing Authority gave in to almost all of the tenants' demands on October 19, 1969.[62]

The anticommunism of the postwar era had foreshortened the demands of the civil rights movement in St. Louis and elsewhere—even the landmark struggles of the 1940s, 1950s, and 1960s were struggles over jobs in defense plants and banks. But the 1969 rent strike in St. Louis hearkened back to an earlier, more radical era. As in the unemployed marches of 1932, the rent strikers forced a recalculation of the social wage owed them by the state. And as in the nutpickers' strike of 1933, it provided the nation with an example of successful mass action under the leadership of Black women. In the fall of 1969, the tenants of Pruitt-Igoe, as well as of the other housing projects in the city, set about the hard work of building a self-determined and cooperative community in the nation's most notorious federally sponsored ghetto.

And then, in 1972, the federal government blew it up. Occupancy in Pruitt-Igoe had been falling almost from the day the first families moved in. By the end, fewer than one-third of the available apartments were occupied. Vacancy contributed to the physical deterioration of the complex, and the physical deterioration led to more vacancy. Vacancy provided space for all manner of wrongdoing. Over the course of the 1960s, older residents increasingly complained that empty apartments were being taken over by addicts and gang members whom the police refused to pursue into the project. During the rent strike, the Housing Authority closed sixteen of the Pruitt-Igoe buildings, boarding up the windows, welding the doors shut, and concentrating the declining population in the remaining seventeen buildings, a measure designed not only to cut costs but also, perhaps, to punish the recalcitrant residents for their temerity in withholding their rent. By that time, the project had become internationally notorious as a symbol of the "urban crisis," a fifty-seven-acre object lesson in the supposed failure of the social welfare policies of President Johnson's Great Society. In October 1971, George Romney, the Nixon administration's secretary of housing and urban development, ordered Pruitt-Igoe torn down.[63]

On March 16, 1972, the first of the thirty-three buildings was imploded on national television, yet another spectacularly violent episode in the city's long history of Black removal. The demolition was finally completed in 1975, after a failed effort by Macler Shepard to obtain the four remaining buildings for the purpose of setting up a self-governing Black community on the site.[64] Over the years the pieces of the demolished buildings were hauled away to a landfill in the county and trees began to grow on the site, where today a medium-density second-growth forest conceals the occasional stowaway streetlamp or illegal dumping site. Since 2016, the site has been controlled by St. Louis real estate developer Paul McKee, who bought it from the city, promising to build an office complex and hospital serving North St. Louis. But

The Pruitt-Igoe housing complex had been planned as a segregated project but was integrated shortly after completion in 1955. Most of the white tenants moved out early on, deepening further the pattern of white suburbanization and Black sequestration. In later years, the complex was plagued by poor maintenance and high vacancy rates. The implosion of large parts of the complex was nationally televised in 1972. (US Department of Housing and Urban Development)

to date, there is only a weather-beaten banner promising an urgent care center. In 2018, when the National Geospatial-Intelligence Agency (NGA) finalized plans to build a $2 billion global surveillance center in St. Louis, rather than building on the vacant Pruitt-Igoe site, it arranged with the city for the demolition of a ninety-seven-acre neighborhood directly across the street.

Out of the ruins of Pruitt-Igoe arose the career of another of the most influential urban planners of the late twentieth century. Oscar Newman's "defensible space" city planning dramatically reshaped the city of St. Louis, beginning in the 1970s, and contributed to both the gating-in of suburban neighborhoods and the privatization of public housing nationwide. Newman, who was a professor of architecture at Washington University in the mid-1960s, eventually developed an entire theory of city planning based upon his understanding of what had happened in Pruitt-Igoe. Like many who looked at the ruins of Pruitt-Igoe, Newman saw not a historical failure, or a structural failure, or even an institutional failure, but a design failure: too much public space. "Because all the grounds were common and disassociated from the units, residents could not identify with them," Newman wrote. He believed that this was why "the areas proved unsafe. . . . The mail-boxes on the ground floor were vandalized. The corridors, lobbies, elevators, and stairs were dangerous places to walk. They became covered with graffiti and littered with garbage and human waste. The elevators, laundry, and community rooms were vandalized, and garbage was stacked high around the choked garbage chutes." The residents, Newman concluded, lacked a sense of ownership—and thus a sense of personal responsibility.[65]

Looking for a way to foster that feeling, Newman found an example in the wealthy gated neighborhoods of the Central West End—the enclave communities that dated back to the heyday of the Big Cinch. "Also in St. Louis," he wrote, "I came upon a series of turn-of-the-century neighborhoods where homes are replicas of the small chateaux of France. They are the former palaces of St. Louis'

commercial barons—the rail, beef, and shipping kings." Newman noticed that he felt watched and confined when he walked purposelessly
(well, purposefully purposelessly) down these streets. "One knew that
one was intruding into a private world and that one's actions were under constant observation," he said of this feeling of inhibition, which
led him to wonder: could poor people be made to feel the same disquiet in their own neighborhoods that they felt in wealthy neighborhoods if their streets were blocked off and their neighborhoods were
similarly "gated"?[66]

Beginning in the 1970s and continuing through the 1990s, the
major tools of urban planning in St. Louis were the gate and bollards—
the huge concrete pots placed in the middle of the road, which are
known locally as "Schoemehl Pots" in cheeky homage to the city mayor
who began the program, Vincent Schoemehl. By the best contemporary estimate, 285 of the city's streets are closed off in this way, many
of these barriers simply reinforcing the boundary between the Black
and white neighborhoods of the city. Meanwhile, Newman's theory
was taken up by successive presidential administrations (Nixon, Ford,
Carter) as the basis for the future planning of public housing, public
schools, street patterns, and public transportation—all of which were
to be designed to foster a great degree of preemptive surveillance. Not
for the first time, the dilemmas of racial control in St. Louis produced
a solution that was later employed on a nationwide scale; in this case,
the solution was arguably the precursor of the "broken-windows" policing so powerfully associated with the rise of mass incarceration in
the 1990s.[67]

In the meantime, a group of former students of Newman's from
Washington University were formulating what became the most notorious city plan in the history of St. Louis, one that remains today a
byword for the abandonment of North St. Louis: Team 4. Drafted by
a group of young urban planners and submitted to the city, although
never officially implemented, the Team 4 plan was an exercise in urban
"triage." Recognizing the failures of the "urban renewal" policies of

the 1950s, the era of redevelopment by bulldozer, urban planners in the United States had turned by the 1970s to "rehabilitation"—the sort of rebuilding work that Macler Shepard and others had already been doing in Jeff-Vander-Lou (and others had been doing in neighborhoods around the country) since the mid-1960s. Contracted by then-mayor Alphonse Cervantes in 1973 in response to a RAND Corporation report that suggested that the city's best hope was to become a majority-Black suburb of Clayton, the business and administrative center of St. Louis County, the Team 4 plan was supposed to provide a guide to the sustainable rehabilitation of the city of St. Louis.[68]

But when they went out and looked at St. Louis, particularly North St. Louis, the urban planners at Team 4 felt overwhelmed. Of course, they did not put it that way. Instead, they simply stated that, given the existing resources, certain areas of the city were beyond repair. They accordingly recommended a tripartite division of the city. The city's first priority should be the support and enhancement of already thriving "conservation" areas, the "most successful" neighborhoods in the city, which would provide the foundation for future development. Surrounding many of these neighborhoods were "redevelopment areas" poised between "progress and decay." The report recommended strategic city investment in these areas, especially through the use of tax abatements to subsidize and encourage private investment. These areas of the city could be spot-zoned, repurposed according to the needs of emerging opportunities; spot-zoning would effectively allow private developers to become city planners in large sections of St. Louis. Listed in the final category in the Team 4 report were neighborhoods slated for "depletion." To wit: "areas of spotty City services and red lining—where large numbers of the unemployed, the elderly and the recipients of welfare are left to wait for assistance which does not seem to be forthcoming." The report recommended that the city postpone any new development in these areas; instead, the Land Redevelopment Authority could gradually aggregate properties through tax foreclosures and hold them for the foreseeable future—state-sponsored dispossession by debt not unlike the policy that Thomas Jefferson had recommended as a means of acquiring Indian lands. The report, that is to say, recommended gradually dispersing the population of North St. Louis and putting the area in a deep freeze until it could be properly redeveloped by a new population of presumably white settlers.[69]

The outcry among Black leaders on the Northside and across the city was immediate, and the city publicly distanced itself from the Team 4 document, which was never officially implemented. And yet many African Americans in St. Louis believe that, implemented or not, Team 4–style "triage" has driven planning in the city of St. Louis since the mid-1970s. And with good reason. One need look no further than the way the city allocates money to support public works. In St. Louis, money to maintain roads, streetlights and stoplights, and so on, is allocated according to population rather than need. Each ward is drawn to contain an equal number of people, and so each ward receives an equal budget for infrastructure and maintenance. But because the poorest areas of St. Louis are actually the least densely populated areas of the city, filled with abandoned houses and empty lots, they receive much less funding per square mile than do the wealthier, more densely populated areas. There is little about the material fabric of the city today—the extraordinary contrast between the gated enclaves along Union Boulevard near Forest Park and the broken-down buildings and empty lots on much of the North Side, or the neighborhoods in which you can look down a long straight street for five or ten blocks in the middle of the day and see no movement at all—that would lead one to believe that Team 4 was anything less than a master plan that holds the key to understanding the last forty years of the city's history. Or, for that matter, the history of the entire United States: the "triage" of selective investment, strategic redevelopment, and savage abandonment, set to a rolling score of Black removal and white-settler gentrification, seems increasingly to characterize the material lives of Americans.[70]

The struggle over the closing of Homer G. Phillips Hospital, first opened as the city's Black hospital in 1939, was the final act in the abandonment of the Northside. In January 1979, Mayor James Conway announced that the city was planning to shut down most operations at the hospital in order to close a $7 million budget gap. The hospital's staff and most of its functions were to be transferred to City Hospital on the Southside, where, in the 1930s, Black patients had been confined to the basement. Trying to spin the closing of one of the most prominent city institutions on the Northside as a final blow in the battle against "separate but equal," Conway said that Homer G. Phillips was "a monument to racism." At a meeting with Northside residents held the following week, city hospital commissioner Kenneth R. Smith explained that City Hospital had been chosen as the site of the consolidation rather than Phillips because of its superior location: "The access is better; it's easier to get there than having to drive all the way up here like we did tonight." In explaining how the city had balanced relative distance, social power, and the value of human life, Smith was expressing which lives a hospital should be best situated to save.[71]

Protests against the planned closing began within days of the announcement and continued through the spring and summer. Among those who wrote letters to the editor decrying the closing was Dr. Howard Venable, the hospital's onetime chief of ophthalmology who had been hounded out of Creve Coeur forty years before. The comedian Dick Gregory returned to his old neighborhood in North St. Louis and led several demonstrations against the closing, including one march that lasted for twenty-five straight hours and another that culminated with seventy arrests of demonstrators who had blocked traffic downtown, including Gregory himself, who spent the night in jail. The protesters singled out St. Louis University, for which City Hospital served as a teaching hospital, for pushing the closing in an effort to capture a supply of "indigent" patients upon whom its residents could practice, and, to a lesser extent, Washington University and Civic Progress, the invisible hand that orchestrated the city's politics.[72]

The week after the mayor's announcement, Third and Fifth Ward Alderpeople Freeman Bosley and Mary Ross led a sit-in in Conway's office, protesting the closing. US Congressman William Clay said that the proposal demonstrated once and for all that "the mayor is not the least bit concerned with the people in North St. Louis." In mid-April, ACTION announced plans for a citywide three-day work stoppage in the first week of May to protest the closing. The call was self-consciously modeled on the 1877 General Strike. The hope was to demonstrate the solidarity of the Black and white working class(es) in resisting the social austerity of the city government, as well as what many in the movement to save the hospital saw as the hidden hand of Civic Progress. While ACTION estimated that between thirteen thousand and fifteen thousand St. Louisans stayed home in solidarity with the stoppage, it would have taken ten times that number to shut down the city. Protesters passed out handbills calling "for the unity of Black and white working people against the closing of Phillips," and by the beginning of August they had barricaded the hospital's gate and were keeping up a round-the-clock vigil to ensure that nothing was moved out of the hospital.[73]

Early on the morning of August 16, 1979, the St. Louis police closed the hospital without notice. In what the newspapers referred to as a "massive show of force," 150 officers in riot gear, with a helicopter overhead and canine and mounted units held in reserve on the grounds of nearby Sumner High School, formed a line in front of the hospital and began the transfer of the sixty or so patients who remained inside. Over the course of the day they made at least seventeen arrests of protesters who tried to block the doors or sit in front of the ambulances and vans being used to move the patients. Journalists reported that several protesters were severely beaten at the edge of the protests, away from the television cameras that broadcast the events live on every channel in the city. By the middle of the day, the unannounced action—which had been planned for weeks in advance, complete with diagrams of the building and reconnaissance maps of the neighborhood distributed to the specially detailed officers—was complete. The hospital was empty. A doctor arriving for her afternoon shift was at first confused and then dismayed and then outraged to find only police left in the hospital. "Was this real? Was this a democracy?" she remembered thinking in an editorial she published in the *Post-Dispatch* days after the surprise closing.[74]

The closing of Homer G. Phillips Hospital left scars, most prominently on the Northside, where several generations of African Americans had brought their children into the world and seen their elders out, not to mention had their wounds bandaged and their illnesses treated, at the hospital affectionately known as "Homer G." The hospital had once been a symbol of Black excellence in the city—unmatched elsewhere in the United States, many would have argued, at the time of the Second World War—and now it was gone, just another symbol of economic decline and political disempowerment. Gradually, the Black resistance in St. Louis had been broken: demolished, divided, and dispersed; red-baited, gaslighted, and set up on charges; beat up, beaten down, driven out, and finally, for the moment at least, defeated. "The only thing we could have done is throw our bodies out there, and they threw out an army," said Ora Lee Malone, trade unionist, Jefferson Bank protester, and exemplar of the long tradition of working-class Black women's activism that dated back to the nutpickers' strike, and even before.[75]

As decades of dispossession were compounded by pointed disinvestment and straight-up destruction on the Northside, the city successfully applied in 1977 to participate as a demonstration site for the federal urban homesteading program, which aimed to provide guaranteed loans on low-priced terms to twentieth-century urban settlers. The program was self-consciously modeled on the Homestead Act of 1862, only this time it was Black neighborhoods rather than Indian lands that were being gathered for sale and distributed at low price. Two areas of the Northside were "targeted" for the effort, which was to begin with increased code enforcement supported by a special budget earmarked specifically for that purpose. Rather than using city money to help poor Black people maintain their homes, the city budgeted funds to drive them out. The program was open to

Black as well as white applicants, and the city included a long "equal opportunity" statement in its application. Also included, however, was an article about the program that pointedly separated the term "equal" from the term "opportunity" by declaring that "the typical St. Louis homesteader is 30 years old, with a Bachelor's degree and a working wife and a combined income of $16,200." Homesteading, the article continued, was difficult and expensive, and "to permit poor families to place all their hope and money into rehabilitating a vacant house . . . might be immoral and would serve little purpose. And it could intensify the poor homesteader's already considerable resentment to society." Declaring that "the frontiers have turned inward now," the city once again set about federally subsidized imperial conquest, this time of its own impoverished margins.[76]

The abandonment of North St. Louis, which continues to this day, coincided with a set of shifts in the global, national, and regional economies that, from the standpoint of production, increasingly rendered the working-class Black population of St. Louis surplus. Their labor was just not needed, at least not within the limits within which it was possible for them to travel, given the city's underfunded transportation network and, as we will see in the next chapter, the high costs of driving while Black in St. Louis. In the meantime, however, enterprising capitalists and ambitious local leaders pioneered novel ways of monetizing Black poverty—of extracting wealth from St. Louis's most precarious neighborhoods and poorest citizens.

11 | HOW LONG?

Everyone is polite. They speak in confidential tones of conquests.
Give each other gentled names. Nothing is as it seems.
Adventure means plunder. They are pirates turned captains
of industry.

— COLLEEN MCELROY, *A Long Way from St. Louie:
A Travel Memoir*

ON FEBRUARY 7, 2008, CHARLES "COOKIE" THORNTON AP-
proached Sergeant Bill Biggs on the sidewalk outside of the city hall of
the inner-ring suburb of Kirkwood and shot him dead. Thornton then
took Brigg's handgun and entered the building, where the city council was in session. Over the next one minute and thirteen seconds, he
shot and killed Kirkwood police officer Tom Ballman, council members
Connie Karr and Michael Lynch, and city public works director Ken
Yost. He also shot Mayor Mike Swoboda twice in the head; Swoboda
survived the shooting, but died a year and a half later from complica-
tions related to the injuries sustained in the shooting, combined with his
ongoing cancer treatment. Responding to the gunshots, Kirkwood officers ran across the street from the police station and up the stairs into

the council chambers, where they found Thornton and shot him dead. Lying nearby on the floor was a placard Thornton had been holding that referred to the city of Kirkwood as a "plantation."[1]

Thornton's invocation of Kirkwood as a plantation might, on the one hand, be seen as a rhetorical convention he used to represent both the historical character and the temporal anachronism of racial injustice in the United States—we know where this comes from, and shouldn't we be past it by now? But "plantation" also invokes the peculiarly economic dimension of that history: the extraction of white wealth from Black people. And behind Thornton's story, it turns out, there was a history of racial extraction and dispossession: the poor and the dispossessed of the city of St. Louis being driven from East St. Louis to Mill Creek Valley to Pruitt-Igoe, then dispersed throughout the declining neighborhoods of the Northside and a few foothold suburbs in St. Louis County, and then rendered up for a final round of extraction. That history tied the history of twentieth-century Kirkwood back to Team 4, through the various expropriations of urban "renewal," and also, arguably, to the era of Indian removal and the "white man's country." To anyone who might have been able to somehow see the future, that history could be traced forward in time to Ferguson—to the historical production of the conditions that framed the shooting of Michael Brown in 2014.

Cookie Thornton had grown up on the edge of Kirkwood, in Meacham Park, a small unincorporated Black enclave in St. Louis County that dated to the 1880s. Along with a small number of Black children from Meacham Park, Thornton had attended Kirkwood public schools, which were integrated by a municipal vote in 1954 following the *Brown* decision, and he graduated from the suburb's high school in 1975. He attended Northeast Missouri State University on a track scholarship and graduated with a degree in business administration. After college, Thornton returned to Meacham Park, where he founded Cookco, a small demolition, construction, and paving company he ran out of his home.[2]

Thornton was a community leader. In the aftermath of the murders, residents of Meacham Park remembered a man who had once walked around the neighborhood greeting passers-by with hearty calls of "Hallelujah!" and "Praise the Lord!" He had go-carts, and neighborhood kids would come to his house and race them around the track in his yard. He served as an unofficial mentor for young men in Meacham Park, hiring them to work alongside him on various jobs and teaching them the trade. By the mid-1990s, he was on the boards of the Kirkwood-Webster YMCA, the Kirkwood Historical Society, and the Kirkwood Housing Authority. Through Project 2000, one of several charitable organizations in which Thornton was active, he mentored children at a nearby elementary school. And in 1994, after Meacham Park was annexed by Kirkwood, he ran for a seat on the city council; even in defeat, he sounded optimistic: "I was just getting my feet wet," he said. "I just wanted to let folks know that there are qualified people from Meacham Park who are willing to participate in Kirkwood government."[3]

And then, sometime around the year 2000, things started to go sour. The city started ticketing Thornton: for parking his dump truck on his lawn, as he always had; for not properly posting work permits on jobs where he was working; for the type of signage he had on his property. As a neighborhood of the city of Kirkwood, Meacham Park was now subject to its municipal code. The fines started to add up, and by the end of 2001 Thornton owed the city over $12,000 in fines; in all, by 2008, he had received over 100 tickets, and owed almost $20,000—a total that is hard to understand as anything other than a massively disproportionate and punitive response to Thornton's claim (albeit a stubborn claim) of a long-standing customary right to do business in the way that he always had.[4]

Thornton began to attend city council meetings, speaking at length about the city's code enforcement and accusing city officials of racism. When the council passed an ordinance limiting citizens' comments to three minutes apiece, Thornton began to disrupt the meetings by walking past the microphone and addressing the council directly. When the council passed an ordinance confining the public behind a blue velvet rope placed at the front of the gallery, Thornton began to lie down in the aisle and bray like a donkey. When the council ordered him removed from the chambers, he went limp, forcing the city officers to pick him up off the ground and carry him out. In 2001, when Ken Yost, whom Thornton would kill in 2008, approached Thornton in his yard, Thornton threw some straw at him. Yost called the police, and Thornton was convicted of assault.[5]

In the aftermath of the massacre, many in Kirkwood thought Thornton had simply lost his mind. Thornton's brother saw it differently. In 2008, Thornton had once again been charged with assault, this time for tripping a man who had confronted him during a one-man demonstration outside a bar where the city attorney was known occasionally to have drinks. By that time, Thornton had lost his business and mortgaged his house in a long and unsuccessful legal battle with the city of Kirkwood and its racist fines. He thought he was out of legal options and likely to go to jail. "My brother went to war," said Gerald Thornton in the aftermath of the murders.[6]

Meacham Park became part of the city of Kirkwood in 1992, after voters in both polities approved the annexation by a margin of almost three-to-one. For voters in 97 percent Black Meacham Park, annexation came with the promise of better public services—many of the roads in the neighborhood were unpaved, and there were no streetlights—as well as better fire and police protection—five children had died in a house fire in Meacham Park when the impoverished fire district's truck would not start. For voters in 92 percent white Kirkwood, "the Queen of the Suburbs," where the average income was almost four times that in Meacham Park and the average home was worth almost three times as much, the annexation was publicly presented as an opportunity to do the right thing. But lingering in the background was the possibility of economic development. As the then-mayor of Kirkwood put it in 1994, "the citizens who voted for annexation voted for redevelopment." Of course, that left open several questions: What sort of redevelopment? With what sorts of benefits for what sorts of people? And with what sorts of costs for what sorts of people? Or as one of the residents of Meacham Park put it, "They annex us and then within two years they crawl into bed with [developers] and are ready to move us out of our community."[7]

The answer at the bottom of the chain of questions about Kirkwood's annexation of Meacham Park was a shopping mall. Bounded by an interstate on one side, a state highway on another, and a major east-west arterial street on still another, Meacham Park was a somewhat isolated place to live, as it was supposed to be, but it was a terrific place for a Walmart. When residents later expressed horror at the proposal for the shopping center that would eventually be built on the bulldozed remains of about half of their neighborhood, then-mayor Marge Schramm reminded them that she had always said "that development would be necessary to get the improvements to the neighborhood that were wanted." In fact, the city of Kirkwood was hoping to eventually draw as much as $3.5 million a year in tax revenue from paving over thirty-six acres of Meacham Park and signing a deal with the Opus Group of Minneapolis to build a shopping center—a deal so good that it later became apparent that the city had offered Opus all of Meacham Park, only to be told that half would be enough.[8]

There were promises made in return: $150 million in taxable business; seven hundred short-term construction jobs; six hundred permanent jobs; housing upgrades for residents who were able to stay in their homes; fair-market-value purchase of the homes of those who lived in the pathway of progress; new housing within the boundaries of Meacham Park at affordable prices for those who were displaced; and the transformation of the long-closed James Milton Turner School, named for the Reconstruction-era educational reformer, into a community center. It was enough to convince many of the residents of Meacham Park to cast their lot with Opus. Of course, it all turned out to be hogwash—or, if not hogwash, a sort of diluted runoff that still smelled like hogwash and was too dirty to wash away the wrong of it all. In the end, the mall project destroyed more than half of Meacham Park, taking at least ten more full blocks than in the original plan presented to the residents. A promised eighty-five new houses became six. The Turner School was never converted into a community center—on the site today sits a high-end rehabilitation facility that caters to professional athletes from across the continent. And on the day the city signed the final agreement with the developer, several of the residents who thought they were still in the middle of negotiations over the price they would get for their houses found condemnation notices taped to their front doors. For Opus, it was just business: "Obviously, we've got a schedule to meet, and we've got to give people a wake-up call," said a spokesman for the company.[9]

In Meacham Park, even those who had once been supporters of the project began to feel as if they had been taken. Bill Jones, who had accused those who opposed the mall of wanting "to throw Meacham Park back into the Dark Ages," said that he felt "sold down the river" by the condemnations: "What kind of plantation do they think they have out here?" The conflict over the condemned houses was enough to get Opus to pull out of the deal, but it was revived under the supervision of the DESCO Group, headquartered in Clayton, and construction began in 1995. On the site today sits Kirkwood Commons (the irony of the name is so obvious that it is hardly worth the words it would take to express it): 209,703 square feet of retail space, including Walmart, Lowe's, Target, Buffalo Wild Wings, Sonic, and White Castle, and almost three thousand parking places. Where there used to be several ways to get in or out of Meacham Park, now there are only two, the others having been closed off by the mall; one leads northward, onto Big Bend, and the other snakes around the back of the mall and then debouches in the far end of the parking lot.[10]

And yet, through it all, up until ground was broken, Cookie Thornton was a supporter. Neighbors remembered Thornton working on behalf of the developers, trying to convince resistant neighbors to negotiate terms of sale for their condemned houses. Virtually everyone in Meacham Park thought that Thornton had been promised work on the project in return for his support, including Thornton himself. Part of the pitch, after all, was that the mall project would bring seven hundred construction jobs to Kirkwood, and there were suggestions that priority would be given to Meacham Park residents in hiring. Indeed, Thornton claimed that he had been told by the mayor that he would be hired to do some of the demolition; she would later say, effectively, that she had just dangled the possibility without making a promise that would not be hers to keep. In any case, Thornton bought himself a new truck so as to be a credible candidate for the work he thought was coming his way—the very same truck that the city of Kirkwood began to ticket five years later, after it became clear that neither DESCO nor the city of Kirkwood was ever going to hire him to do anything. When the jobs were finally allocated and the contracts signed, Thornton was cut out of the work. As one of his neighbors remembered in the aftermath, "Cookie's biggest problem was he was one of the proponents of the annexation with Kirkwood. . . . Then they turn around, he don't get none of the contracts, he don't get none of the money."[11]

From the perspective of the Kirkwood city government and DESCO, it was simply business as usual: "I know we strongly urged that he be included in minority businesses—we did require a certain amount of work for minorities. But that's not just Cookie," said the mayor. Thornton had made a bet on "Black capitalism," on the promise of a piece of the action, and he had tried to sell his neighbors on the same promise. But when the time came to share the spoils, he was simply another Black cipher recorded on the page of a faraway account book—someone, a "minority" someone, who might be compared to other minority someones in a decision that came down to dollars and cents in the pockets of people who cared more about calculating the bottom line than taking the high road. It was then that Thornton began to split from the program and descend into the dark cycle of feelings of humiliation, betrayal, anger, and fear that led him to the city council chambers on that February night in 2008. "I think that Cookie was promised a lot and that he was lied to," remembered one of his neighbors, trying to make sense of things. "He was used and manipulated, and once he figured it out, he became irate, because he was hurt and disappointed. I think he really thought he could trust certain individuals and he just snapped." By the time he armed up and set out for city hall, he had lost his wife, his house, and a federal court case against the city of Kirkwood, which he had mortgaged his parents' house to pay for. He had nothing left to lose.[12]

According to the journalist who wrote with the most depth and sensitivity about the murders, white people in Kirkwood were shocked that such a thing could happen to them. People for whom the city wasn't "just a place, but a dream, a vision of how life should be," found themselves asking, "How could this happen here?" Their puzzlement was a distant echo of that experienced by the residents of Meacham Park when the annexation was first proposed: "When Kirkwood first came to annex us," remembered Harriet Patton, who ended up leading the effort to forestall the mall project, "we asked why do you want us?" After all, cities like (and including) Kirkwood had spent decades trying to keep Black people from settling within their city limits; for many years, the nicest thing that anyone in Kirkwood seemed to have to say about Meacham Park was that it should be torn down. But something had changed by the time of the annexation and the mall project— something that had politicians and developers all over St. Louis trying to figure out ways to leverage small and isolated populations of poor Black people into large economic gains. As an oft-repeated commonplace in Meacham Park had it, "Kirkwood pretty much ignored us, until it found a way to make money off us."[13]

S ince 1974, federal aid administered by the Department of Housing and Urban Development has been structured in the form of community development block grants. This program is based on the assumption that, rather than support specific projects—the destruction of the waterfront, for example, or the construction of Pruitt-Igoe—the federal government should allocate money to cities on the understanding that decisions about spending are best made on the local level. The block grant program emerged as a compromise between conservatives who could see it as part of President Gerald Ford's New Federalism, a way of diminishing federal involvement in state and local affairs, and liberals who could see it as a way of empowering community-based organizations by giving them control over their own lives and affairs. Unfortunately, in St. Louis, as elsewhere in the nation, city leaders often saw the program as a way of monetizing their population of poor and Black people to benefit their wealthier and whiter neighbors.[14]

Community development block grants were created with the stated purpose of supporting the economic development of low- to moderate-income residents of American cities. With a low degree of federal oversight (that was the point of the New Federalism) and a fairly high degree of local connivance, the CDBG program was soon transformed into a discretionary fund to support whatever type of economic development city governments thought might benefit their cities overall. In St. Louis, that meant focusing on the central corridor and skimping on the Northside as it devoted its efforts to building a city that was friendly to business rather than to Black people. In the first ten years of the program, the mayor's office allocated the same amount of federal money to the four wards between downtown and Forest Park as it did to the twelve wards on the city's Northside; at least 50 percent of the CDBG money spent in the city, according to the Association of Community Organizations for Reform Now (ACORN), was spent to subsidize either business owners or gentrification. Testifying before a federal court about segregation in the St. Louis schools in 1981, the political scientist Gary Orfield described the recent history of the city's disbursement of federal money through block grants as "yet another chapter in the long epic of federally-funded, locally administered residential segregation and re-segregation."[15]

By 1991, the city's inequitable CDBG spending had achieved a level of notoriety so great as to trigger a federal audit. The immediate cause was a $650,000 advertising campaign designed to lure new residents to the city—an expenditure that was not allowable under even the very broad and rarely enforced limits of the program. "We have no requirement that a community spend even one dollar on housing," said the local overseer of the federal program, so cities could waste all the money they wanted, as long as they were careful to "waste it away properly." Emblematically, the city's improper waste was a campaign to gentrify the Northside of the city by luring nonresidents to move there, complete with a brochure that papered over the poor and Black daily life of the Hyde Park neighborhood with a black-and-white photo of a white family having a picnic in Hyde Park in . . . maybe 1940?

Alongside the improper waste, the *St. Louis Post-Dispatch* followed up with a series of articles that documented an extraordinary level of proper waste—waste that was legally allowable but morally unconscionable: $8,000 to equip the mayor's niece and several of her coworkers, who were overseen by the mayor's sister, with car phones so that they could provide one another with up-to-the-minute information about the condition of vacant lots in the city; 101 subsidized house rehabilitations for homes that sold for an average price of $90,000 (about $175,000 in 2020 dollars, and thus well beyond the reach of low-income or even moderate-income St. Louisans); $330,000 to a home repair agency that employed more clerical workers than carpenters. In response to the question of whether someone in the city government should have walked around to check that grant recipients were spending money the way they were supposed to be spending it, St. Louis mayor Vincent Schoemehl replied that calls for that type of oversight represented a "nineteenth-century mentality."[16]

The underlying drift of the spending was apparent to anyone who walked around the wards of the city. Although the federal money had been justified largely by the Black poverty on the Northside, a majority of those funds were nevertheless being spent elsewhere in the city on—not to put too fine a point on it—white people. The largest single portion of federal grant money in the city of St. Louis, according to the *Post-Dispatch* investigation, was spent on the administration of federal grant money—almost 20 percent. The report further suggested that as much federal money was being spent in the city's wealthiest four wards as in its poorest twelve—and the latter, far from being distributed between those twelve wards, was concentrated in areas of the impoverished Northside adjacent to the wealthy Central West End. Moreover, most of the money directed toward actual bricks-and-mortar redevelopment of the city was spent in the city's *wealthiest* central-corridor neighborhoods. Meanwhile, spending on the city's poorest neighborhoods generally went to social programs—a disjuncture that some found akin to simultaneously investing in deepening structural racism while taking credit for addressing some of its most egregious surface symptoms.

Seen from the Northside, the spending of federal block grant funds seemed to follow the prescription of neighborhood triage outlined by Team 4 in 1979: invest in the wealthy neighborhoods, shore up the borders, and put the rest of the city in a deep freeze. The implication that the Team 4 plan had anything to do with the administration of the city in the 1990s was (and is) bitterly resented by Mayor Schoemehl, who explained his allocation of federal funds intended to support housing for low-income people to many of the wealthiest neighborhoods of the city instead in the following terms: "I just don't believe the city of St. Louis should become the region's final repository of all the poor, un-employed, and undereducated."[17]

The last decades of the twentieth century and the first decade of the twenty-first were unkind to the economy of St. Louis. The 1973 oil embargo and the 1979 recession (spurred by the mercilessly high interest rates maintained by Paul Volcker at the Federal Reserve in response to the inflation of the 1970s) led to the highest unemployment rate since the Great Depression—up to 20 percent for Black workers, according to government measures, a figure that is conventionally taken to measure only half of the actual level of unemployment. Because of its large role in the defense industry St. Louis was partly insulated from national trends by the Reagan-era defense buildup. Emerson Electric's company history describes these as lean years backstopped by increased orders for TOW missile launchers; McDonnell-Douglas in these years was in the early development stages for the A-12 Avenger, a long-range stealth bomber for the US Navy that would never be built, a failure that contributed to the company's later demise and eventual sale to Boeing.[18]

The 1980s was the era of deregulation and corporate raiding. Regional companies that had once thrived in St. Louis—Brown Shoe, the Stix, Baer & Fuller and Famous-Barr department stores—were gobbled up or displaced by larger super-regional competitors unleashed from the antitrust laws that had once protected against consolidation. Boatmen's Bank, which once claimed to be the oldest bank west of the Mississippi, was purchased by NationsBank in 1996, which was in turn acquired by Bank of America in 1998. (Jefferson Bank is still locally owned.) Transworld Airlines was acquired by Carl Icahn, the era's emblematic corporate raider, who first bought up Ozark Airlines, once hubbed in St. Louis, and then gradually stripped and sold off TWA until the airline that had once accounted for 80 percent of flights in and out of St. Louis and a full half of transatlantic flights to and from North America was run into the ground and bankrupted in 2001. With fewer and fewer flights at higher and higher prices, the city became harder to reach at the very moment when the global economy was being reordered around a few increasingly influential "global cities." McDonnell-Douglas, meanwhile, shed nineteen thousand employees between 1989 and 1996, when it was acquired by Boeing. When Boeing missed out on the contract for the Joint Strike Fighter in 2001, it laid off seven thousand more St. Louis workers.[19]

A final wave of acquisitions around the millennium and after resulted in the selling off of the city's heritage firms to global conglomerates. Longtime St. Louis stalwart Ralston-Purina was bought by the Swiss firm Nestlé in 2001, and in 2008 Anheuser-Busch, a company so synonymous with St. Louis that its television advertisements ended with the words "Anheuser-Busch, St. Louis, Missouri," became a wholly owned subsidiary of the Belgian firm InBev. Monsanto, perhaps the most notorious company in the world, held out the longest, producing herbicides and genetically modified crops across a global empire headquartered in Creve Coeur up until its purchase by Bayer in 2018. Among the landmarks in its corporate history were the artificial sweetener saccharine, the insecticide DDT, the pesticide Agent Orange, coolant PCBs, and the genetic modification of bovine growth hormones. Although the St. Louis metro region can boast of an unparalleled ground transportation network—four interstate highways supported by several interstate bypass routes converge in the city, a relic of Harland Bartholomew's soul-sucking influence over both regional and national development—it has struggled to compete in the increasingly deindustrialized, financialized, and globalized economy that has emerged over the past forty or fifty years. In 2006, the Ford Motor Company closed its Hazelwood plant in North County, which had employed around five thousand workers, and the exodus continues to this day. Among the largest employers remaining in the city today are the hospitals and Washington University—nonprofit institutions that pay no property taxes—and Peabody Coal, one of the nation's most notorious companies, a legacy firm that ties the city's economy back to its origins in the imperial extraction of Indian country.[20]

In Missouri, this global winnowing was accompanied (some might say exacerbated) by state-mandated fiscal austerity. As political leaders in the city and the county tried to make their region more appealing to increasingly mobile firms in an era of increasingly concentrated ownership, they had few tools at their disposal. Spurred by the example of California's passage of the tax-capping Proposition 13 in 1978, Missouri added an amendment to the state constitution that pegged future taxes in the state to the 1980s ratios of state revenue to aggregate state income and mandated that any future relative increases to local taxes be approved by full municipal referendum. The campaign for the amendment was led by future Missouri congressman Mel Hancock and his Taxpayer Survival Association, whose melodramatic name signals the appeal to white property owners that was central to Hancock's success. Under the Hancock Amendment, it is difficult for cities in Missouri to raise taxes on existing property-holders in order to provide the amenities necessary to draw new businesses (and hence new revenue) to the community. And hedged in by the hard boundary between county and city established in 1876, it is impossible for the city of St. Louis to capture revenue from adjacent areas through annexation and incorporation. Faced with these limitations on how it might raise revenue in a virtuous cycle with economic development, the city of St. Louis, along with municipalities all over the United States, has hit upon a seemingly paradoxical solution: rather than raising more money, they can simply give it away.[21]

In 1945, at the urging of municipal leaders and real estate developers looking forward to the clearance of Mill Creek Valley, and under the stewardship of Harland Bartholomew, the Missouri State Legislature passed the Chapter 353 Urban Redevelopment Act and the Chapter 99 Land Clearance Act. Chapter 353 provided tax abatements for those who developed "blighted" property in the city; for the first ten years that property would be taxed at its predevelopment, or "blighted," value, and for the next fifteen at one-half of its postdevelopment assessment; only after twenty-five years would its value come fully onto the books. Chapter 99 provided for the redevelopment of entire neighborhoods of the city by making them city property. The city often paid for substantial improvement and then leased the improved sites to new businesses, thus subsidizing the costs of customization while relieving those who built businesses on the redeveloped land of the obligation to pay property taxes and bearing much of the risk of failure.[22]

The original tax abatement laws defined "blight" as "that portion of the city within which the legislative authority of such city determines that by reason of age, obsolescence, inadequate or outmoded design or physical deterioration have become economic and social liabilities, and such conditions are conducive to ill health, transmission of disease, crime or inability to pay reasonable taxes." In the lexicon of urban politics in St. Louis, however, the word "blight" is a verb, usually in a sentence whose subject is a developer with a big idea and some friends in the city government and the object is a Black neighborhood. Thus, in 1959, after considering the reports from Harland Bartholomew and Roy Wenzlick & Company, the city of St. Louis blighted Mill Creek Valley. That is to say, the city declared that after the destruction of Mill Creek Valley, the area would be made available to developers on favorable terms. Through the 1960s and 1970s, much of the most notable development in the city was subsidized by Chapter 353 tax abatements, including the transformation of Laclede's Landing along the waterfront into an alternative downtown entertainment district more accessible by car than by foot from the actual downtown in 1966; the commercial redevelopment of the old Union Station, the onetime heart of Chestnut Valley, in 1974; and the building of the Washington University Medical Complex at the east end of Forest Park in the same year. All of this development, some of it successful and lasting, some of it not, had no short- or even medium-term impact on the city's real property taxes.[23]

In St. Louis, a great deal of the blighting was done near the Arch and in the long shadow of the 1904 World's Fair, the idea being that the city's pathway back to greatness was to become a destination city for tourists. In 1968, Mayor Alphonso Cervantes used Chapter 99 to blight much of what had once been Deep Morgan in order to relocate the Spanish Pavilion from the 1964 New York World's Fair to St. Louis, complete with a replica of Columbus's flagship, the *Santa Maria*. Shortly after the project was completed, the faux *Santa Maria* broke free from its moorings on the Mississippi during a storm and drifted out into the river, finally crashing into the shore, capsizing, and sinking amid the abandoned docks on the east side of the river. The relocated Spanish Pavilion met much the same fate, at least commercially speaking: it was shuttered in 1971.[24]

Much of the area was eventually developed into the TWA Dome—later the Edward A. Jones Dome and today the America's Center—under Chapter 100, a successor program that allowed the city to sell bonds in order to pay for the redevelopment of property that would then be leased to commercial tenants. In 1995, Mayor Freeman Bosley Jr., the city's first Black mayor (and son of the alderman who had fought for the hospital), used the promise of a downtown domed stadium owned by the city to lure the Los Angeles Rams to relocate to St. Louis—a deal that, at least for the week after the Rams won the Super Bowl in 2000, seemed like a coup. The underlying financial structure of the deal, however, suggested the circular downward flow of another sort of bowl—at least as far as the city of St. Louis was concerned. Because the facility was municipally owned, the city of St. Louis became responsible for its maintenance and improvement, and under its contract with the Rams the city was obligated to provide a stadium that was in the "top quarter" of NFL stadiums. For some period of time the Rams ownership "allowed" the city to simply make cash payments—amounting to around $70 million, all told—instead of improving the stadium. But eventually, in 2015, billionaire owner Stan Kroenke, heir by marriage to the vast fortune of Walmart founder Sam Walton, used the condition of the stadium as grounds to move the team back to Los Angeles, leaving the city of St. Louis as the owner of a 67,000-seat stadium in which to host horse shows and church conventions, as well as $144 million of debt still to be paid on the bonds that it had issued to pay for the stadium in the first place. In sports management circles, the deal Kroenke made with St. Louis is known as "possibly the most sweetheart lease of all time."[25]

Property tax abatement—whether through the municipal ownership of commercial property (Chapter 100) or through the negotiation of extended tax amnesty (Chapter 353)—was intended to be a way to raise revenue under the austere terms of the Hancock Amendment.

The city of St. Louis repeatedly agreed to forswear tax collection in the hope that this kind of subsidized development would provide other sorts of revenue or greater revenue down the line. The city, that is to say, pursued a paradoxical strategy structured by perverse incentives, starting with a long-term incentive toward gentrification, because in the absence of the ability to raise taxes, the best way to raise revenue was to raise property values. This is a problem (and solution) bedeviling many American cities today.

But in St. Louis, these long-term incentives have been mostly set aside by the short-term pursuit of increased revenue from sales and earnings taxes rather than from increased commercial activity and new jobs. As with other aspects of abatement-based development, even these revenue gains, when there are gains at all, come at a terrible price—a price that is much greater than the one-to-one calculation of dollar of property tax abated in return for a dollar of sales tax gained by which they are usually justified. Property taxes are progressive (thus falling more heavily on the rich) and are earmarked for schools, while sales taxes are regressive (thus falling comparatively more heavily upon the poor) and flow into the city's budget for general operating expenses. As the sociologist George Lipsitz put it, when the Rams defeated the Tennessee Titans in Super Bowl XXXIV, the people of St. Louis celebrated quarterback Kurt Warner, running back Marshall Faulk, wide receiver Isaac Bruce, and head coach Dick Vermeil—"the Greatest Show on Turf"—"but no one publicly recognized the contributions made by the 45,473 children enrolled in the St. Louis city school system."[26]

In the beginning, tax abatement under Chapters 99, 100, and 353 was used to accomplish the sort of "Negro removal" decried by Ivory Perry. Mill Creek Valley, the Maline Creek area of Kinloch, North Webster Groves, and Elmwood Park (near Olivette) were all Black areas of the St. Louis metro area that were "blighted and . . . eradicated" in the name of development between the 1950s and the 1990s, a process that continues all along the frontier of gentrification to this day.[27]

Meanwhile, on the other side of the frontier, poor homeowners are losing homes on which they cannot afford to pay the property taxes. As of this writing, the city's Land Reutilization Authority holds over twelve thousand properties in the city, the vast majority of them on the city's Northside, and the vast majority of them seized by the city in lieu of unpaid taxes. While many of the properties were undoubtedly abandoned for reasons other than their owners' inability to pay their real estate taxes, it is nevertheless profoundly ironic—malignantly ironic—that poor Black homeowners lose their houses over unpaid real estate taxes in a city where much of the commercial property held by wealthy firms is completely tax-exempt. And the irony deepens: the city itself is too broke to keep the property it has seized up to code—its own code—and so thousands of parcels of property sit boarded up, deteriorating, and abandoned while a large number of unhoused people sleep on the streets.[28]

Over the 1990s, the dialectic of economic development and Black removal that had arguably prevailed for most of the twentieth century was transformed into one in which developers used the proximity of Black people—some of them in pockets that remained in the wealthier neighborhoods and suburbs of the city, some of them refugees from previous waves of displacement and development—to justify the state subsidy of private development. Rather than concentrating on large projects like Mill Creek Valley or Laclede's Landing or the downtown stadium, developers began to pitch smaller projects located all over the city. And rather than the removal of Black people, these projects depended on their presence: small numbers of poor Black people living within a reasonable distance could be used to justify tax abatements—sometimes very large tax abatements—no matter whether or not the proposed projects would actually improve the overall condition of the area.

In a series of rulings in the 1970s, the Missouri Supreme Court had widened the definition of "blight" to include property that was not itself blighted but was near a blighted area included in the plans for redevelopment. That is to say, they made it possible to gain tax abatements over a span of parcels that joined together a large number of tracts with favorable commercial prospects and a sampling of "blighted" property. In the years between 1997 and 2008, Chapters 99, 100, and 353 were used to blight, abate, and develop over nine hundred parcels of property all over the city. During this period, almost one-third of the ordinances passed by the Board of Aldermen were enabling ordinances that spot-blighted this or that piece of property in an improvisational, developer-driven pattern that addressed inequality in the city in only the most cursory fashion.[29]

When you arrive in St. Louis today and drive east on I-70 from Lambert–St. Louis Airport to the downtown, one of the first sights you encounter is the massive Express Scripts campus. It sits on either side of the highway, within the boundaries of the Normandy School District, from which Michael Brown graduated in the spring of 2014. Until 2018, when it was purchased by Cigna, Express Scripts, a prescription medicine provider, was the highest-grossing corporation in Missouri, and its CEO was the highest-paid executive in the state. All told, the campus is 496,000 square feet, complete with two large parking lots to accommodate workers driving in on the interstate from the county and elsewhere; indeed, part of the construction for the project included building new access roads to make it easier for commuters to drive to and from work. Construction of the complex was subsidized by Chapter 100 and Chapter 353 tax abatements. According to a University of Missouri–St. Louis study published in 2014, the company received a total of $63 million in tax incentives related to its new headquarters.[30]

Noting that the payroll tax revenue that the state received from Express Script employees was far greater than the subsidy the company received, the study concluded that the subsidy had made sense from the perspective of the state of Missouri, and perhaps it had. But the project unquestionably represented a transfer of revenue from the Normandy schools to the Missouri State Legislature—a transfer, that is to say, to white Republicans (and ultimately rural whites) from a 97 percent Black school district that had an equal number of students eligible to receive free lunch and that lost its state accreditation the same year Michael Brown graduated from the high school. Though the Express Scripts campus sits within the boundaries of the Normandy schools' tax-catchment area (adjacent to the Ferguson-Florissant District), for Michael Brown and his fellow students, because of the abatements, the construction of the half-million-square-foot headquarters of a multibillion-dollar corporation (Cigna paid $69 billion for Express Scripts) in the neighborhood mattered not at all. Indeed, once the Normandy School District lost accreditation, its students were allowed, under state law, to transfer to schools in nearby suburban districts—provided that the Normandy School District paid those districts $20,000 per student, a good deal more than the Normandy district received per student in revenue. Thus, for the past five years, the Normandy School District, already cash-strapped, already struggling, has been subsidizing the schools in Clayton, Ladue, and other wealthy St. Louis County school districts.[31]

Since 1982, much of the subsidized development in the city of St. Louis has been supported by tax increment financing (TIF). Tax increment financing allows cities to sell bonds on behalf of developers. The bonds can be used to pay for feasibility studies and environmental impact studies and to assemble property, construct public works, rehabilitate or remodel old buildings, or even build new ones—to cover all of the costs of development. Property taxes in the TIF district are frozen for a period of time (twenty-five years in Missouri), and would-be property tax revenue above that zero-year threshold, the "increment" of revenue gained by development, is diverted into a fund to repay the bond. One-half of the sales and income taxes harvested from those who shop or work within the boundaries of the TIF are also diverted for that purpose, following a 1998 law. The theory is that the revenue produced by development will be great enough to cover the costs of the bond, and that the city and the state will eventually be able to gain revenue from the development they have financed on behalf of the developer.[32]

Like tax abatement, TIFs are justified as policy tools for addressing "blight" and as ways of encouraging investment in places where capitalists might otherwise be reluctant to take risks as well as harnessing the power of capitalist development to enhance the general welfare. The standard by which judgments were to be made as to whether existing buildings, neighborhoods, and even open land in the city were blighted was the "but for" clause—a required attestation that "but for" the state subsidy, the proposed investment would not occur. Leaving aside for a moment the philosophical imponderability of whether something would or would not happen in the absence of something that was already actually present as an inducement to its happening, it is perhaps enough to say that the "but for" clause has given developers in the St. Louis metro region (and the rest of Missouri) extraordinarily wide latitude in defining "blight" and gaining public subsidies for private development. The clause has also had the perverse effect of making "blight"—and thus Black people, the stereotypical signifiers of urban "blight"—valuable to developers. That's what happened in Kirkwood.[33]

The art of the TIF is in the drawing of the district. The more commercially vital the district, the better the result is likely to be for all of the principal actors: the developers, who are able to unload many of the sunk costs (and hence much of the risk of development) onto the city and state while still building in a location where they can make lots of money; and the city and state, which, in absorbing the risk of the development, are betting on its success. And so the drawing of TIF districts has come to resemble the practice of gerrymandering political districts. Enough blight must be included in order to meet the (admittedly very loose) legal standard, but the viability of the project is assessed by how much economic potential can be harnessed to the enabling blight. Recall the sentiment expressed in Meacham Park: "Kirkwood pretty much ignored us, until it found a way to make money off us." What was intended, or at least justified, as a project that would put the power of economic development behind community development has instead been turned inside out. Black populations—not Black communities, not Black people, not Black labor, but Black *populations*—have been conscripted to the cause of corporate subsidy. "Ain't nothing changed but the year," said one resident of Meacham Park after the annexation and the construction of the shopping mall. "It was more about the money, a tax bracket, and Kirkwood Commons. . . . To me that's all it was ever about," he said, "dirt roads . . . and dirt-road pimping," referring to the poor and unchanging conditions that continued in Meacham Park and had been used to justify the TIF.[34]

In theory, these incentives do not cost taxpayers any money. Cities issue the bonds feeling confident that the new businesses will generate more than enough revenue to pay the money back. The problem is that the amount the city must pay each year is locked in at the beginning of the bond issue. If the increased revenue is not as high as expected in any given year, the city finds itself in the red. Tax increment financing is a way of indenturing municipalities to their own hypothetical economic development. Actually, it's even worse than that. The municipal bonds issued by cities like St. Louis (and, we will see, Ferguson) are bundled and sold on a secondary market, in much the same way as the bundled subprime mortgages that figured so prominently in the financial crisis of 2008. The purchasers of these bonds then become, in effect, the creditors of the cities that have issued them. Municipal bonds are generally a good investment, for multiple reasons. First, under federal law, the interest they pay their holders is tax-exempt. Second, municipal bond-holders have the legal status of first-paid creditors: before a struggling city fixes its roads, or pays for the new park or the school on Main Street, it is legally obligated to pay the investors on Wall Street.

The result has been a catastrophic parody of the idea that the rising tide of economic development will lift all boats. Because of the constraints that cities face in raising revenue, TIFs have been disproportionately used to fund retail development, which at the very least provides cities with sales tax revenue (even if it comes at the expense of diverting revenue from schools to general operating funds). The most notorious example is perhaps the Des Peres Mall, built on the site of another West County mall in 2002. In spite of the fact that Des Peres had a median family income of over $100,000 at the time of the mall's construction, the existing mall was almost 100 percent occupied, and it was grossing over $1 million a year, the city of Des Peres created a $29 million TIF to subsidize the construction of a new mall, which, it should be pointed out in all fairness, would include *both* a Nordstrom and a Lord and Taylor.[35]

Perhaps Des Peres was worried about the Galleria Mall; built with TIF funding six miles away in Richmond Heights in 1984 and expanded with another TIF in 2016, the Galleria was wedged in between two of the metro area's most prosperous cities, Ladue and Clayton. There is no doubt that there was fierce competition between the malls to draw shoppers from the Orion Apartments, a building that was located in the city's prosperous Central West End, had been recently redeveloped with a $10 million TIF, and boasted "a rooftop saltwater pool, electric car charging stations, easy access garage parking, 24-[hour] concierge service, breathtaking city views, wi-fi thermostats, and customized closets." Today the building's website (the one they use to attract tenants, not the one they used to demonstrate the ways in which they were addressing blight), also boasts that nearby are "a Whole Foods Market and shopping plaza . . . Forest Park, St. Louis' biggest and most active park—home to the St. Louis Zoo, the Muny Amphitheatre, St. Louis Science Center, History Museum, Art Museum, World's Fair Pavilion, and . . . unique dining, entertainment, and nightlife in the bustling Maryland Plaza."[36]

Unsurprisingly, given the readily available evidence, TIFs have come to be seen by many as both inequitable and ineffective. A 2017 study by the Show-Me Institute estimated that around 80 percent of the roughly $700 million of TIF spending in the city of St. Louis over the past fifteen years had been spent south of Delmar Avenue, the city's long-standing racial dividing line. The *St. Louis Post-Dispatch* recently reported that, combined with other forms of tax abatement, TIFs cost the St. Louis city schools $31 million in 2018. Meanwhile, the *Riverfront Times* calculated, the city had forgone almost $1 million in taxes for each resident drawn to the city's central corridor (the already prosperous area of the city where almost two-thirds of the city's TIFs are located) over the first fifteen years of the new century.[37]

Of all the spot abatement done in the St. Louis metro area over the past decades, the most notorious has involved the developer Paul McKee, who has used tax increment financing to purchase hundreds of buildings on the city's Northside. A 2018 investigation by St. Louis Public Radio found that of the 154 buildings that the developer had specifically promised to rehabilitate in his 2009 application for tax increment financing, only two had actually been rebuilt, one of them to house the headquarters of McKee's corporation, Northside Regeneration. In the meantime, McKee had also benefited from the city's Land Assemblage Tax Credit Program, a $47 million program of which Northside Regeneration was the near-sole beneficiary, accounting for over 90 percent of the credits issued by the city. With little more than a broken-down sign advertising a promise of a three-bed urgent care facility on the Pruitt-Igoe site, which McKee purchased from the city in 2016, Northside Regeneration represents a huge land bank, accredited by the city of St. Louis and capitalized by the continued suffering of the poor Black population of the beleaguered Northside.[38]

McKee, however, is little more than a convenient villain. North St. Louis, which appears to the naked eye to be abandoned by investors, is, in fact, a site of plentiful, if minimal, investment: tens of thousands of houses unfit for human habitation are repositories of small stores of speculative capital, bought up by speculators willing to hold the property until something changes. Rather than the absence of investment, many of the decaying houses along the routes that children walk to school every day represent a particular form of land-banking speculative investment in poor neighborhoods across the nation: long-game bets on development and gentrification. For the children, however, the message is the same no matter who owns the dead-eyed houses with the trees growing out the top: someone here before you had hopes, and they came to this.[39]

By the fall of 2018, McKee's long game had gone on too long for even the city of St. Louis, which had allowed much of the Northside to lie fallow for almost forty years, and the city terminated its dealing with Northside Regeneration and condemned many of McKee's Northside properties. The immediate occasion was the discovery that McKee had inflated the value of several of the pieces of property for which he had received bespoke land assemblage tax credits. But lurking in the background was the largest urban land clearance since Mill Creek Valley: the condemnation through eminent domain of ninety-seven acres of land in North St. Louis—formerly the Greater Ville—in advance of the construction of the new headquarters of the National Geospatial-Intelligence Agency—the agency that provides the maps charting the pathways of US global interest, aspiration, and anxiety, uncanny digital descendants of the palimpsest map William Clark kept in his office just a few miles downtown. The NGA, of course, is a sovereign entity, part of the US government, and so it pays even less in property taxes than Paul McKee did. As with the tax subsidies provided to private developers, the case for the NGA has been based upon the idea that it will bring jobs to St. Louis. How many of those jobs—jobs in the building trades, which are to this day almost entirely white, and jobs in electrical engineering and data analysis—will go to the residents of the Northside, who suffer from decades of disinvestment in their schools and the sort of structural unemployment that can sap the energy of even the most dedicated job-seeker, remains to be seen.

If the impoverished—"blighted"—condition of Black St. Louis has provided a legal alibi for the distribution of corporate welfare through tax abatement, some have found even more direct ways to monetize their neighbors' poverty. Anyone who drives around St. Louis today, especially on the Northside, cannot help but be struck by the bright neon signs and welcoming storefronts of predatory lenders: Missouri Payday Loans, Planet Cash, Quik Cash, Community Quick Cash Advance and Payday Loans, ACE Cash Express, TitleMax, AAA1 Auto Title Loan, Title Loans Express, TitleBucks, and so on. Some of these firms are quite large—Quik Cash, the largest, headquartered in Overland Park, Kansas, has over one hundred stores across the state of Missouri—but the majority of lenders in the state represent companies with fewer than ten outlets. In one famous example, the members of a single suburban church in Kansas City pooled their money and started providing high-interest loans. Large or small, all of these predatory lenders make money by charging poor (and poorly banked or unbanked) people exorbitant rates of interest.[40]

Payday loans, which began to emerge on a large scale in St. Louis in the early 1990s, are the most familiar form of predatory lending. They work like this. Someone who needs money stops into a store and inquires at the counter. Perhaps they need $100. The clerk at the counter is friendly and informative and makes the requisite inquiries about wages. It often turns out that the loan applicant "qualifies" for an even larger loan than he or she had intended to take out, usually something just short of the amount of their biweekly paycheck. The terms of a loan for someone who makes $500 every two weeks might turn out to be something like $400 in cash at 500 percent annual interest, with payment due in two weeks, guaranteed in the form of a postdated check for $480. In two weeks' time, the loan begins to bite. The debtor cannot pay $480 and still get through the following month, but the lender turns out to be willing to accommodate: if the borrower can pay just the $80 interest, the borrower will roll the loan over for another two weeks; and then, for another $80, another two weeks; and so on. After several such cycles, someone who borrowed $300 might have paid the company $1,200 in interest and yet still owe the entire principal of $300. State laws that limit the number of renewals are easily evaded by reissuing a new loan to cover the old loan every six cycles. A 2002 Missouri state law that capped the rate of interest at 75 percent for short-term loans mattered even less: multiplied out, a two-week loan at 75 percent interest represents an annual rate of 1,950 percent, the highest allowable rate among the forty-three states that have set limits.[41]

During the year 2008, 2.8 million payday loans were made by 1,275 licensed lenders in the state of Missouri. That year, QC Financial, the largest loan company in the state, alone made 400,000 loans through its 100 outlets. The population of Missouri is just over six million people. In 2015, the activist Jamala Rogers calculated that there were twice as many payday loan stores in Missouri as there were McDonald's and Starbucks restaurants *combined*. The fact that payday lenders can now be found in every corner of the state (in 2006, nursing home owners in semi-rural Sikeston were found to be running an on-site payday loan company) suggests, once again, the ways in which extractive methods pioneered on the Black poor in urban areas can be generalized into practices that target poor and working-class people more generally.[42]

Although they have a lower annual percentage rate (APR)— generally around 270 percent in St. Louis—auto title lien loans are, if anything, even more dangerous for borrowers than payday loans. Automobiles are essential for many working-class people in cities like St. Louis that suffer from limited and unreliable public transportation, especially as one travels farther out into the county, where jobs are more plentiful. They are also the most substantial asset for many working-class and poor people, who spend much of their disposable income on rent and food. Auto lien loans thus pose an existential threat to those who enter the premises of any of the dozens of providers in the St. Louis metro area, disproportionately located in the poorer and Blacker areas of the city, where their shiny bright and welcoming appearance often contrasts jarringly with the surrounding economic devastation. In return for their auto title and a copy of the key to their car, customers receive high-interest loans that provide a bridge through acute crises but threaten to become chronic problems. In 2010, Beverly Brewer of St. Louis took out a $2,200 loan with Missouri Title Loans. Over the next two months, she made two payments of $550 apiece, knowing that if she did not, Missouri Title would declare her in default, seize her car, and resell it—no matter the payments she had already made. When she made the second payment, bringing the total amount she had paid on an initial loan of $2,200 to $1,100, she requested a statement of her account, which revealed a standing balance of $2,196.94. Her $1,100 had bought her six cents of principal.[43]

Although lawsuits like the one eventually brought by Brewer (who took her case against Missouri Title Loan Company all the way to the Supreme Court of the United States before settling when Missouri Title Loan agreed to forgive almost $250 million of debts it was holding) and reform at the federal level have curbed some of the abuses in the payday and title lien loan business, canny capitalist entrepreneurs have invented new ways to monetize their neighbors' desperation. Many St. Louis payday lenders have recently started offering "small loans," which have a term of six months at an APR of around 300 percent. For vulnerable people, the longer term increases the risk of events that will cause them to miss a payment and find themselves in default, such as a medical emergency, a job change, or a traffic ticket. Lenders of small loans often try to notify the borrower that the loan is in default, making what is known in court as a "good faith" effort but, in practice, is anything but; after tucking the loan away for a period of time, they pull it out of the drawer only to calculate the accruing interest. Then, after perhaps a year or so, they file suit against the borrower for the unpaid principal and accrued interest, a total that often dwarfs the amount of the initial loan. After she took out an initial loan of $100 in 2006, St. Louis resident Erica Hollins made one payment of $31 before ignoring several letters sent demanding payment of the rest. In 2009, Capital Solutions Investment filed suit against her, seeking payment for a loan on which they had been charging 199.7 percent; they obtained a judgment for $912.50. By 2015, Hollins was still so far behind on paying off her wildly exploding debt, which had grown to several thousand dollars, that CSI won a judgment to garnish her wages. But because the state of Missouri limits garnishment to 25 percent of total wages, Hollis's court-ordered payment plan leaves her falling ever further behind on her loan, which accrues faster than her garnished wages can pay it off—*she faces a 25 percent levy on all her lifetime earnings in service to what began as a $100 loan*. In St. Louis, as the essayist and social theorist James Baldwin wrote of the United States more generally, "it is extremely expensive to be poor."[44]

As in the rest of the nation, the 2008 subprime loan crisis wrought havoc in Black St. Louis, especially among homeowners who were trying to follow the infrastructure that had been built to subsidize white flight out to the suburbs. Many of the suburbs directly to the north of the city, Ferguson among them, had become majority-Black over the course of the 1990s, and quite a few of those migrants had become homeowners. Subprime loans accounted for almost half of loans made to Black home-buyers in the 1990s, and it became obvious in the aftermath of the crisis that as many as 60 percent of those buyers qualified for conventional mortgages but had been steered to more volatile (and more profitable for the banks) ones by their lenders. Around 2006 in St. Louis, the variable rate mortgages began to bite, and it became clear that banks like Countrywide had been using well-intended federal laws to entrap underinformed consumers in loans they could never pay—meanwhile, bundling those mortgages into packages and selling them on a speculative secondary market on Wall Street, where they made more money while spreading the risk of default far and wide through the economy.

When the bubble burst and the banks called the loans in, *more than half* the new homeowners—which is to say, the Black homeowners—in cities like Ferguson and areas of the city like Gravois Park found themselves underwater on their loans: the amount of money they owed was greater, in some cases far greater, than the value of their home. Many loans were foreclosed, and a Ferguson city council meeting in 2013—

before the murder of Michael Brown and the uprising—revealed a government struggling to figure out what to do about all of the foreclosed and abandoned properties within the city limits. All told, the 2008 crisis is said to have destroyed as much as one-half of the Black wealth in the United States—wiping out, in the process, the gains made in the wake of the 1968 Fair Housing Act, which had begun the process of prying open the suburbs.[45]

If you take the time to look carefully, the geography of metro St. Louis, like that of most American cities—indeed prefiguring that of most American cities—looks less like a series of scattered, unrelated buildings, some rising, gleaming and new, some slowly subsiding back into the earth, than it does a series of patterned and planned subterranean relationships. The decay enables the growth, whether that growth takes the form of subsidized shopping malls or legalized loan sharks. St. Louis, a national leader in both tax diversion and predatory lending, is once again a city on the frontier of the future, this time pioneering modes of extraction and dispossession by which people who have been deprived of just about everything else—neighborhoods, jobs, education, health care, safety—can be squeezed dry. And in St. Louis there are few places that represent all of these features, all of this history concentrated into a small space, as clearly as the city of Ferguson.[46]

On August 5, 2014, at its headquarters on West Florissant Avenue in Ferguson, Emerson Electric announced third-quarter sales of $6.3 billion, down about 1 percent from the second quarter, but undergirded by a record backlog of orders. A quarter-mile to the northeast, four days later, Officer Darren Wilson killed Michael Brown, who had been walking down the middle of a street near his grandmother's house. After a short scuffle in the street, Brown ran away. When Wilson shot him, several witnesses later asserted, Brown had his hands raised in the air. Wilson later claimed that Brown, whom he had already shot at least once, had turned around and run toward the officer, even as Wilson

Shortly after Ferguson police officer Darren Wilson shot unarmed Michael Brown on August 9, 2014, the child's stepfather, Louis Head, protested on the street in Ferguson. As Brown's body lay in the street for four hours, a crowd gathered, the beginning of several months of protest and police overreaction in St. Louis that touched off a national reckoning with police violence, mass incarceration, and racial injustice that has come to be known as the Black Lives Matter movement. (Associated Press)

kept shooting. FERGUSON POLICE JUST EXECUTED MY UNARMED SON, read the placard held by Brown's stepfather, Louis Head, as he stood near the scene. If you drew a straight line between the corporate head-quarters of Emerson and Canfield Drive, less than a half-mile's distance, it would cut through the lot behind ABC Cash Express.[47]

The protests in Ferguson transfixed the nation, providing indelible images of largely peaceful Black protesters under assault by militarized police and finally the US National Guard. The refusal that November of District Attorney Robert McCulloch (son of St. Louis police canine officer Paul McCulloch) to allow the case against Wilson to go to trial presented the nation with a lurid example of St. Louis–style police impunity. In the months that followed, anyone who cared to could have learned a lot about Ferguson. The white paper on the municipal courts in North St. Louis County prepared by the public interest lawyers ArchCity Defenders; Radley Balko's extraordinary reporting in the *Washington Post*; litigation in the Missouri courts against "policing-for-profit"; and finally, the March 2015 Justice Department report on the Ferguson Police Department—all helped to fill in a picture of the extraordinary climate of police harassment that culminated in the murder of Michael Brown. In Ferguson during the year 2013, 86 percent of traffic stops involved Black motorists, in spite of the fact that the population of the city was only 67 percent Black and its roads were driven by a high number of white commuters. After being stopped, Black drivers were twice as likely to be searched and twice as likely to be arrested as were whites, in spite of the fact that, when whites were searched, they proved to be two-thirds more likely to be caught with contraband. The initial citations in these cases and other similar municipal violations ranged from speeding and running red lights to driving without current registration or proof of insurance to having an unmowed lawn, putting out the trash in the wrong place at the wrong time, and jaywalking, known in the language of the Ferguson city code as improper "manner of walking in the roadway."[48]

The peculiar prominence of police stops for "manner of walking in the roadway," and the multiple occasions upon which they were followed by citations for "failure to comply," hint at something about the everyday terrain of policing in Ferguson in the years leading up to 2014. Indeed, similar citations were common in Meacham Park during the same period. "There were a couple of our kids that got tickets for walking in the streets," remembered one resident of Meacham Park. "We never had sidewalks around here until [we were] annexed, so a lot of people, especially the older people and like young people, they never walked on sidewalks, so it took a minute to adjust. But the officers were giving people tickets for walking in the street, not just warnings, but they were giving them tickets." Another resident remembered a similar set of public order offenses being extended over an empty lot where the men of Meacham Park had long gathered to socialize. Growing up, he said, "I aspired to get a job and retire and be able to pull my truck and my car up on the lot and be able to sit with the old men and drink my drink and sit by the fire. Grown men. Family men. . . . That's history, but the police and Kirkwood look at it as hanging out in the streets." And then there was Cookie Thornton, parking his truck where he had always parked it, hanging his sign the way he had always hung it, doing business the way he had always done it, but finding himself suddenly on the wrong side of the law.[49]

Code violations are characteristic offenses of the racial capitalism of the real estate market. In Meacham Park, they took the form of the policing of the neighborhood's erstwhile common spaces—roadways and lots that had served social purposes but were now subject to new value-protecting standards. In Ferguson, the social history was different, but the pattern of policing was similar: in 2012, the city of Ferguson issued two thousand tickets for property maintenance code violations. Like most of the rest of St. Louis County (including "Kirkwood proper"), mid-twentieth-century Ferguson had been defended by exclusionary zoning codes and whites-only collusion in the real estate market. In the 1960s, Ferguson was known as a "sundown" community: African Americans, mostly from neighboring Kinloch, came to work in the houses of wealthy whites in Ferguson during the day but were expected to be out of town by the time the sun set—an arrangement that was underscored by the effort of a large number of Ferguson residents to build a wall between the two cities in the mid-1970s. To this day, the adjacent cities are joined by only two through streets. If you have ever flown into the St. Louis airport, you have seen Kinloch up close. Over the past three decades, the vast majority of that city's Black residents have been displaced to accommodate the expansion of Lambert–Saint Louis Airport. Over the same period, a small number of African American homeowners and a much larger number of African American renters have gradually replaced whites in Ferguson. Almost entirely white in 1970, Ferguson today is majority-Black.[50]

An entire book could be written about the sensory aspects of white public order as enforced in St. Louis, whether the social setting is one of annexation (as in Kirkwood), Black migration (as in Ferguson), or gentrification (as in St. Louis neighborhoods like Benton Park, Botanical Heights, Tower Grove, and Shaw, where VonDerrit Myers Jr. was shot on October 8, 2014, by a St. Louis police officer who was detailing for a neighborhood watch group). Indeed, the political scientist Andrea Boyles's book about Kirkwood provides a brilliant exemplar of such a study. She details the ways in which the sounds of men drinking and boasting on an abandoned lot came to seem threatening; or kids standing together and talking on a corner came to seem suspicious; or braids and baggy pants and grills and tattoos came to be seen as signs of criminality rather than as the basic signs of accumulation available to people who don't own much other than themselves. "A lot of these boys that just be standing around are the sweetest boys if you knew them personally," Boyles quotes one Meacham Park resident as saying, "but in the police's eyes, it's like they are trying to stir up trouble." Rather than the advancing frontier of whiteness, as in Kirkwood or in any number of gentrifying neighborhoods across St. Louis or the United States where the police serve as public-order adjutants for the protection of white settler sensibilities and rising property values, in Ferguson the policing of public order represented a rearguard action taken on behalf of a declining white population by an almost entirely white city government.[51]

In some ways, Ferguson's pattern of racist policing is reminiscent of the "predictive" policing pioneered in St. Louis in the late 1960s and early 1970s. But where the random data-collecting stops on the Northside were framed by a logic of preemption—a theory that treated every young black man as a potential low-level offender and every low-level offender as a potential felon—policing in Ferguson (and many neighboring municipalities) seems to have been as focused on extracting revenue from an already impoverished community as it was on preventing hypothetical future crimes. "Ferguson's law enforcement practices are shaped by the City's focus on revenue rather than by public safety needs," the Justice Department concluded in its report on Ferguson's police department. The report found that the boundary between the fiscal and police functions of the city government of Ferguson had completely broken down. The city manager and the police chief had discussed using tickets to meet revenue benchmarks, and police officers were being evaluated on the basis of their ticket-pushing "productivity."[52]

In 2013, the city of Ferguson earned $2,635,400 from municipal court fines, which accounted for 20 percent of the city budget—the second-largest revenue share drawn from any single revenue source. "Absolutely, they don't want nothing but your money," the ArchCity Defenders' white paper quotes one defendant as saying. "It is ridiculous how these small municipalities make their lifeline off the blood of the people," said another. "It's an ordinance made up for them," said still another. "It's not a law. It's an ordinance." Following upon the initial citations from the years before 2014, the city issued over twelve thousand warrants for missed court appearances and unpaid fines. Citizens who failed to appear in court at the appointed time or to pay fines that were, according to the ArchCity Defenders, "sometime more than three times a person's monthly income," were liable to be jailed, sometimes for as much as three weeks, as they awaited a municipal court date. Those with outstanding warrants were likewise rendered ineligible for most forms of public assistance and government-provided social services.[53]

The city of Ferguson—with its white mayor, its majority-white city council, its almost totally white police force, and its white municipal court judge—was farming its poor and working-class black population for revenue. Cantoned according to the laws and practices of a white supremacist real estate market, the black inhabitants of Ferguson were summoned for a final round of extraction that threatened in many cases to dispossess them entirely, as excessive fines, exclusion from necessary social services, and exclusion from public housing combine to turn them out onto the streets. The murder of the jaywalking Michael Brown was an acute example of the chronic exploitation, harassment, debt bondage, and wanton bankrupting of the city of Ferguson's African American population.

In this, again, Ferguson is a pertinent example of the arc of our times. Over the past fifty years or so in the United States, discriminatory policing, selective enforcement, disparate rates of conviction, and wide variations in sentencing by race have combined to create a vast class of incarcerated and disenfranchised Black men. While African Americans account for 14 percent of the drug users in the United States, they yield up 35 percent of those arrested, 53 percent of those convicted, and 45 percent of those imprisoned for drug crimes. Where many see mass incarceration as a form of racial control—a "new Jim Crow"—Ruth Wilson Gilmore has importantly pointed to the role of prisons in creating and perpetuating opportunities for the accumulation of white wealth. The construction, maintenance, provision, and supervision of the vast US inland empire of incarceration has underwritten the economic development of entire communities—rural towns now compete to have prisons sited within their corporate limits—and the emergence of a new segment of the white middle class. In the post-industrial United States, the political economy of racial control is an emergent sector. Of the twenty-two state correctional facilities in Missouri, nineteen have been built since 1980, a period during which the state's prison population has increased by over 300 percent (to 859 per 10,000, well above the national average). Although the inmates in Missouri prisons are over four times as likely to be Black as white, almost all of the facilities are located in predominantly white rural areas—places such as Licking, Vandalia, Bowling Green, and Potosi—where they employ predominantly white construction workers, guards, and service workers and are often the leading sector of the local economy. The generalization of the economy of mass incarceration to a principle of municipal governance is evident in police practice in Ferguson.[54]

The Justice Department's *Investigation of the Ferguson Police Department* traced the revenue-farming in Ferguson back to a lack of training, supervision, and oversight, exacerbated by shoddy record-keeping and clear racial bias. The DoJ's report on the Ferguson police is almost unprecedented in its critical attention to systematically racist police practice in the United States. As such, it took what had long been the common sense about policing among poor and African American people across the country and briefly raised it to a principle of federal public policy. But the report stopped short of providing a *structural* analysis of racist policing in Ferguson. Put simply: how could the city government be reverting to medieval modes of revenue extraction at the same time that Emerson Electric was doing $24 billion a year of business out of its Ferguson headquarters? In Ferguson, the answer lay in the historical amalgam of white privilege, corporate welfare, fiscal conservatism, and misguided efforts to promote social equality through "economic development," which had guided municipal policy since the 1980s. Again, Ferguson, St. Louis, and Missouri are not unique in this so much as they are extreme: they provide an exemplary account of how state and local governments think about "economic development" and how corporations do business in the United States of America today.[55]

Take Emerson Electric. On July 27, 2009, Emerson opened a new $50 million flagship data center on its Ferguson campus. Subsequent press reports about the data center were filled with numbers: 100 dignitaries at the ribbon-cutting, including Missouri governor Jay Nixon; 35,000 square feet; 550 solar panels; $100,000 in annual energy savings for the company; ability to withstand an 8.0 magnitude earthquake. They noted how many people Emerson employed globally, nationally, and in the St. Louis metropolitan area, although the number of people who might eventually be employed in the new data center itself was hard to determine. In fact, a state-of-the-art data center might eventually employ about two dozen people, none of whom were guaranteed to live in (or anywhere near) Ferguson. The economic function of a data center, after all, is to eliminate clerical workers, not to provide them with jobs, and many of its operations can be performed remotely. But the most remarkable missing number of all was the amount of property tax revenue the county and city housing this state-of-the-art building would gain from its construction.[56]

In 2014, the assessed valuation of real and personal property on Emerson's entire 152-acre, seven-building campus was roughly $15 million. That value has gone up and down over the last several years as Emerson has sold off some buildings and built others, but it has hovered around $15 million in the period since the data center was completed. So, what happened to that brand-new $50 million building?[57]

In 2008, the St. Louis Economic Development Partnership announced that the data center was being built within a state-designated Enhanced Enterprise Zone, and Emerson subsequently received state tax abatements that were limited to corporations receiving local property tax abatements. Emerson, however, steadfastly denies that it received tax abatements to support the center's construction. According to company spokesman Mark Polzin, "None of our campus real estate is under abatement." Emerson has forgone tax abatements for which it is eligible, Polzin says, out of a concern for fairness. "We never availed ourselves of such. . . . We felt that our real property had already been being fairly assessed historically by St. Louis County." According to Emerson, the company is voluntarily paying more than required by law.[58]

It might seem improbable that a corporation with a fiduciary responsibility to its shareholders would forgo any tax break to which it was legally entitled. Emerson, after all, had petitioned the Board of Equalization for an adjustment of the assessed value of its personal property in the aftermath of the construction of the data center and been provided with a revised assessment that reduced its tax bill from the city of Ferguson by about $40,000, or 40 percent. Connecting the dots, one might conclude that Emerson did not need fancy Chapter 353 tax abatement because, when it objected to its tax bill, the Board of Equalization simply adjusted the assessment. At the very least, this raises important questions about the assessment value of property in St. Louis County.[59]

For tax purposes, Emerson's Ferguson campus is appraised according to its "fair market value." That means that a $50 million solar-powered data center is only worth what another firm would be willing to pay for it, a fact that the company, at least, blames on the city of Ferguson: "Our location in Ferguson affects the fair market value of the entire campus," Polzin explained. Never mind the absurdity of the argument that since there is not a ready buyer waiting on the corner of West Florissant and Ferguson Avenues with $50 million to spend on a data center, the value of that data center is effectively zero. On the twenty-five parcels Emerson owns all around St. Louis County, it paid the county $1.3 million in property taxes in 2014. Ferguson itself received far less. Even after a 2013 property tax increase (from $0.65 to the state maximum $1 per $100 of assessed value), Ferguson received at most $68,000 in property taxes from the corporate headquarters that occupies 152 acres of its tax base—not even enough to pay the municipal judge and his clerk to hand out the fines and sign the arrest warrants.[60]

St. Louis County does not just assess Emerson a low market value for its property. It then divides that number by three to make its final property value, for tax purposes, one-third of its already low appraised value. In some states, Ferguson would be able to offset this write-down by raising its own percentage tax rate. Voters would even be able to decide which services needed the most help and raise property taxes for specific reasons. But Missouri sets a limit for such levies: $1 per $100 of assessed property.[61]

Emerson Electric was not the only business on Ferguson's West Florissant Avenue in 2014. The street was also home to a number of big-box stores, including a Home Depot, a Walmart, and a Sam's Club, located at the city's northern limit. These companies all came to town in 1997, supported by tax increment financing. The TIF in Halls' Ferry (a neighborhood within the city limits of Ferguson) was originally valued at $8 million. Over the years before 2014, however, the revenue generated by the TIF district was not sufficient to cover the bond. The

TIF-specific deficits—$43,000 in 2012, for instance—had to be covered with taxpayer money. Like any other municipal bond, TIF bonds are ultimately secured by the ability of the issuer to raise revenue—in this case, by Ferguson's ability to tax its citizens in order to pay off the bonds it has issued. If the revenue falls short of projections, the debt has to be covered by local citizens—not by the banks (they're insulated because they have not loaned money directly to the underperforming retailers), and not by the retailers (they're protected because the city has paid for the capital improvements of the area, limiting their sunk-cost investment in the area). It's the taxpayers (and fine payers) who have to make up the difference.[62]

Not all TIFs fail to match projections. As it happens, there was also a successful TIF in Ferguson at the time of the uprising. Unfortunately, it demonstrates the ways in which the city's long shadow of segregation structures latter-day development projects aimed at—or at least justified by—reducing urban "blight." The South Florissant TIF was initiated in 2012 to build multi-use retail and residential space in Ferguson's downtown area. If, even before the post-uprising hit to the city's reputation, it was not entirely successful in the planning document's stated goal of establishing Ferguson as a "regional destination" along the lines of the Delmar Loop in University City, it nevertheless supported the emergence of the sort of photo-ready pleasantness illustrated in the planning documents. And it was in the black.[63]

So what's not to like? Ferguson's downtown TIF was self-consciously designed to provide a front door for the city's subsequent economic development—but it was not designed to improve life for existing residents. Its proponents envisioned an artery of retail and residential development that would connect the city (as well as the city of Cool Valley, which was also involved in the planning) to the campus of the University of Missouri at St. Louis and to the industrial development sprawling along I-70. The planning document mentioned that the new district would open downtown Ferguson to the employees of UMSL, Express Scripts, and Emerson. But that document never addressed the disconnection of South Florissant Road from West Florissant Road.

To get from the neighborhood where Michael Brown died to downtown Ferguson, one has to travel a long, undeveloped stretch of Ferguson Avenue and then make a near 180-degree turn under a railroad bridge to merge onto another street that leads to the downtown. There are no sidewalks bordering this stretch of road, and many of those who travel it do so by walking on the shoulder—a notable issue given the risk of being cited for "manner of walking in the roadway" faced by black pedestrians in Ferguson. The "two Fergusons" mentioned by many commentators at the time of the uprising are effectively connected by a back door.

All of this inverts the stated purpose of funding economic development through taxpayer dollars. As we have seen, under Missouri laws, TIF district plans are limited to areas that have been designated "blighted" by that municipality. They were designed to bring the benefits of capitalist development to areas that would otherwise be regarded as inhospitable to investment. Along with Chapter 353 tax abatements, similarly designed to target "blighted" areas, TIF bonds were designed to use the market economy to push forward the not-yet-realized project of racial equality in the United States. In the event, however, these tools have often been turned inside out: used to generalize the risk of investment to the entire population of a city while concentrating the financial benefits in small tracts of development.

The final twist in the story is an extraordinary one. Under the Hancock Amendment, municipalities can raise their *sales* tax without a local referendum in order to pay for the retirement of TIF bonds. And according to the Ferguson city budget, sales taxes accounted for the largest share of the city's revenues in the years before the uprising. Next came municipal court fines. And after that, franchise taxes—taxes on telecommunications, natural gas, and electricity usage. Only after that came revenue from property taxes. Taken together, regressive taxes account for almost 60 percent of the city's revenue. In contrast, property taxes account for just under 12 percent. The wealth of the city, scarcely taxed at all, was locked up in property that African Americans were prevented from buying for most of its history.[64]

"Economic development" in the United States turns out to have the bare meaning of "getting large businesses to locate their buildings within the city limits." And in St. Louis County, this race to the bottom has been turbo-charged by the postage-stamp pattern of municipal governance left over from the era of suburban segregation, which makes it astoundingly easy for businesses to pit municipalities against one another by threatening short-haul moves in search of the best possible deal. What does Walmart have to lose by moving four hundred yards down the road to a brand-new TIF district one town over?[65]

These factors—the drastic underassessment of corporate wealth, the indenture of municipal government to corporate development, the unequal allocation of risk and benefit between municipalities and the improvement districts they contain—are not unique to Ferguson. The legal constraints, the "development" tools they have spawned, and the negative consequences of their over-misapplication are present in many other cities in the United States: that is why I refer to them as aspects of the history of "structural" racism, rather than of "intentional" racism. They are the product of the misaligned incentives and priorities that characterize any effort to achieve social benefits through economic "development." The historical patterns of white privilege and black disadvantage, of residential segregation and police harassment, of municipal fealty and corporate subsidy, are old enough, deep enough, and entrenched enough to channel and subvert the actions of even the most well-meaning officials. History and the standing order have left those who seek to govern American cities with only bad choices.

To say that the recent history of Ferguson exemplifies the history of structural racism or the enhancement and defense of "the possessive investment in whiteness" is not necessarily to say that the Ferguson city government in the years before 2014 was especially craven in its poor decision-making or high degree of self-dealing. As it happens, however, the Ferguson city government in the years before 2014 *was* especially craven in its poor decision-making and high degree of self-dealing. Faced with only bad choices in the years leading up to 2014, the Ferguson city government repeatedly made disgraceful ones.

The Ferguson city budget for fiscal year 2013–2014 opened with a cautious note. The city, it warned, had not "recovered" from the loss of $1.5 million in annual tax revenue dating back to the financial crisis of 2008, which actually began in 2006 in St. Louis County. Or, in a more biblical mode: "The economic turbulence visited upon the city . . . has been unparalleled in recent memory." And yet the government of the city of Ferguson chose to respond to its straitened circumstances with a campaign of unparalleled spending on, well, the government of the city of Ferguson. In the two years before the uprising spawned by the killing of Michael Brown, the city of Ferguson built a new $8 million fire station, issued bonds to fund the portion of the $3.5 million renovation of the police station not being funded by the downtown TIF, and gave all municipal employees (almost half of whom worked for the police department) an 8 percent raise.[66]

The city's fiscal year 2013–2014 budget also earmarked half a million dollars for the replacement of all the city's marked police cars with brand-new Chevrolet Tahoes, presumably including the one that Officer Darren Wilson was driving when he confronted Michael Brown and then shot him with one of the sixty brand-new handguns the city purchased that year.[67]

So much spending on the infrastructure of municipal governance might have been appropriate in a city that was running a budget surplus, but as we have seen, the city of Ferguson was relying on municipal traffic fines to close the gap between its growing expenditures and its declining revenue. In addition to farming the population for revenue from municipal fines, however, the city of Ferguson was using almost a million dollars a year from its designated Parks Fund to cover bond payments and operating expenses. Like a junkie using his kids' lunch money to fund a bad habit, the city of Ferguson was raiding its parks to fund the overdevelopment of its police and fire departments.[68]

In a final twist, it turns out that the city of Ferguson used its downtown TIF bond to fund the renovation of the Ferguson Police Department and expansion of the municipal court complex. Now, the police station and the court complex are indeed located downtown, but they do not generate revenue, at least not of the sort that is earmarked for the repayment of the TIF bond. (Of course, if one counts the $2 million in municipal tickets annually issued from those buildings, they could be said to be likely to pay off.) The city used the structure of the TIF bond to move the renovations of the police department and the courts building to the front of the municipal queue. Rather than using money borrowed on security and provided by all of the citizens of Ferguson to double down on its police department, the city might have tried to use its TIF funds to link the downtown area to the rest of the city. Perhaps it could even have built a sidewalk alongside Ferguson Avenue—after all, as Officer Wilson surely reminded Michael Brown shortly before shooting him, in Ferguson jaywalking is illegal.

Understanding the recent history of St. Louis—from the shootings in Kirkwood to the murder of Michael Brown—requires understanding how business interests and municipal governments in the St. Louis metro region (as throughout the state of Missouri and the nation more generally) have tried, since the 1980s, to find ways to monetize a population of African Americans who were increasingly deemed surplus from the standpoint of capital. Whether one focuses on tax abatements justified by the inclusion of tranches of Black neighborhoods in the districts drawn on a map, the poverty parasitism of the payday loan industry, the for-profit policing of the segregated cities structured by St. Louis's past, or the political economy of mass incarceration, the recent economic history of the city provides a series of examples of how to extract wealth from people who have already been pushed to the precarious margin of survival.

One of the things about people who have little left to lose, of course, is that they have everything to gain. On August 9, 2014, the disinherited of St. Louis rose again to take control of their history. When the time came, they were ready—subjects of a history of serial dispossession and imperial violence so profound that it has been built into the very fabric and common sense of the city, yes, but also legatees of a history of Black radicalism and direct action as measurelessly implacable as the flow of the rivers. And still they rise.[69]

EPILOGUE: THE RIGHT PLACE
FOR ALL THE WRONG REASONS

Sitting on the veranda of the Boenker Hill Winery in St. Louis County, you can look out and see a slow-rolling image of the end of the world. The winery overlooks the West Lake Landfill, a former limestone quarry where a rogue contractor dumped Manhattan Project–era Mallinckrodt nuclear waste in the 1970s. For decades, radioactive waste leached into the groundwater surrounding the site—uranium-238, which has a half-life of four and a half billion years, and thorium-232, with a half-life of fourteen billion years—as well as into Coldwater Creek, which forms an arc through the northern part of the county. Children of my generation played on the banks of the creek and swam in it during the summertime. Not long ago, at a twentieth reunion at nearby McCluer North High School, a group of alumni realized how many of their classmates were already dead and began to wonder why. They created a Facebook page that now has over twenty thousand members. In the words of one of the investigative journalists who finally brought the contamination of the creek to light, it is an archive of "rare cancers, birth defects, multiple cases of conjoined twins and babies born with one ear and no eyeballs, and instances of infertility, multiple sclerosis and lymphoma, many of them in statistically impossible numbers." Today an underground trash fire in a landfill in nearby Bridgeton is burning its way toward the nuclear waste buried in West Lake Landfill. No one has figured out how to put it out.[1]

Many who live in the city today feel a sense of abandonment made more acute by the aftermath of the uprising in Ferguson. Once the television cameras and high-profile activists left the city, they found that little had changed. In September 2017, St. Louis was again rocked by protests against police misconduct, but this time few outside the city were listening. The nation had moved on to the serial melodrama of Trump's America—the gaffes, scandals, and outrages coming so quickly in succession that there was no time to press Pause and take notice of what was happening in the heart of the country.

The 2017 protests followed the acquittal of former St. Louis police officer Jason Stockley, who was accused of the 2011 murder of Anthony Lamar Smith. After an initial confrontation with Smith in a restaurant parking lot, in which Stockley wielded an AK-47 that he had brought with him to work, Smith fled in a car. During the car chase pursuit that followed, Stockley was recorded by the dashcam in his police cruiser saying, "We're going to kill this motherfucker," and minutes later he made good on his promise, firing five shots into Smith's vehicle after his partner had crashed into it on the street. Stockley was then captured on film searching through a personal duffel bag in the trunk of his cruiser, seemingly tucking something in the front of his pants, entering the car where Anthony Lamar Smith lay dead, and emerging seconds later with a handgun that he claimed to have found in the car but was later revealed to have only the officer's DNA upon its handgrip. In justifying his decision, the judge in the case noted that Stockley's promise to kill Smith was made in "the heat of the moment" and, therefore, could not be considered evidence of an intention to do something that he then went on to do minutes later, and that his own experience of thirty years on the bench had made him certain that the gun found in the car must belong to Smith because people like Smith ("urban heroin dealers") almost always had guns.[2]

The verdict spurred a monthlong series of protests that revealed more of the same police impunity: police officers sending one another texts looking forward to assaulting protesters under the cover of darkness ("it's gonna get IGNORANT tonight") and then heading out to indiscriminately surround and arrest crowds of people, some of them protesters, some journalists, some spectators, some of them simply passers-by, and one of them actually an undercover policeman; punitively and repeatedly Macing and pepper-spraying the same compliant and still-surrounded crowd as they kneeled on the ground, awaiting arrest; responding to peaceful protests with overwhelming force, riot police, snipers on the roofs, helicopters in the skies; trampling an elderly woman who was clearly confused by the orders being given by an advancing line of heavily armed, armored, and shield-bearing police; chanting, "Whose streets, Our streets!" in celebratory mockery of the protesters whose constitutional rights they were violating; mobilizing an auxiliary army of internet trolls and white supremacists by posting protesters' names and addresses online following their arrest and calling for the boycott of a pizza place owned by an actually pretty moderate man who dared to say some sympathetic things about the protesters.[3]

And yet for a month, as the protests went on and the police riot continued, the nation looked the other way. After his officers chanted, "Whose streets? Our Streets!" on the night of September 18, St. Louis interim police chief Lawrence O'Toole went on television to proclaim, "We owned tonight." St. Louis mayor Lyda Krewson's response to the out-of-control police rampaging through the city she allegedly governed was tepid at best. In response to the officers' chant, she said, "I wish they wouldn't have said that." Asked about O'Toole's response, she observed what was empirically true, that his comment was "inflammatory," before reiterating her "confidence in the chief" and canceling town hall events where she was scheduled to meet her supposed constituents. (O'Toole was a finalist for permanent appointment at the end of 2017, but was not hired.) The governor of Missouri, for his part, cheered on the police, posting an image at the top of his Twitter feed of a young man being hog-tied and carried away, facedown, by policemen holding his elbows behind his back. He turned out to be a student at a nearby university who had the temerity to stand between the police and a group of Black protesters when a commanding officer ordered the cops to charge the crowd. For Black protesters, their white allies, and anyone else unlucky enough to be standing nearby, St. Louis in the fall of 2017 represented a fearful image—part fulfillment, part portent—of the world according to Chief Justice Roger Taney: no rights that the white man was bound to respect. In St. Louis, the history of all the dead generations weighs like a nightmare upon the living.[4]

And yet I have never been to a more amazing, hopeful place in my life. St. Louis, as the onetime Washington University student radical, biographer of Ivory Perry, sociologist, and housing rights activist George Lipsitz says, is "the right place for all the wrong reasons." All over the city, people are finding new ways to live, to connect, to cultivate new sorts of spaces, to grow into new sorts of people. Perhaps they will be too late to change the course of our history. Or perhaps they will be just in time.

In the spring of 2017, St. Louis–based designer and organizer De Nichols collaborated with Chicago-based artists Amanda Williams and Andres Hernandez in a project designed to both honor the past and imagine the future in St. Louis. The site was an old brick warehouse at 3721 Washington Boulevard that was slated for demolition. In the weeks before it was torn down, they invited their friends, neighbors, and anyone else who wanted to come along, or who just stopped to look, to paint the building gold—to honor its past, and that of the city around it, before it was torn down. Once the demolition was complete, they took gold-painted bricks from the building and gave them out to organizations doing visionary work around the city: to the Art House Collective on the Northside, where artists gather to create as well as to provide mental health support and meals for neighborhood residents, and where the bricks were used to create a small event stage;

to Perennial, an organization dedicated to repurposing discarded objects and community education; to Solidarity Economy St. Louis and Citizen Carpentry, two organizations that are building and practicing small-scale networks of cooperation and mutual support—actually existing socialism—in the interstices of racial capitalism, which used the bricks to build a spiral pathway on "Tillie's Corner," the onetime site of a beloved neighborhood grocery; and to the Granite City Arts and Design Collective on the east side of the river, a group supporting urban gardening and sustainable agriculture.[5]

If you take the time to look, projects that are similarly visionary and humane can be found all around the city. Near the site of the original Jeff-Vander-Lou project, in among the abandoned houses and broken-down apartment buildings, near the Bethesda Mennonite Church where the pews are still filled on Sundays, Rosie Willis, a veteran of the original JVL project, and a local housing rights activist named Sal Martinez have planted a garden in an abandoned lot. As in most of the city's neighborhoods, the soil is contaminated, and so the gardeners have built boxes in which the flowers bloom. Martinez got married in the garden. Neighborhood activists use the garden as a place to resolve disputes between young people that might otherwise become violent.[6]

Nearby, in the Old North neighborhood, Sylvester Brown Jr. runs the Sweet Potato Project. Brown grew up in the city and got his first job at Laclede Gas—"Percy Green got me my first job," he says. After a career in journalism, he founded a nonprofit that turns vacant lots into urban farms planted, tended, and harvested by neighborhood children. They started with sweet potatoes, which are hard to kill and easy to harvest. With the help of a nutrition professor at St. Louis University, they make the potatoes into flour and bake them into cookies, which they package and sell throughout the city and online (http://sweetpotatoprojectstl.org/). "People say we're poor, but we're rich," Brown said. "Look at our children." Brown is one of the intellectual architects of the North City Food Hub, also supported by St. Louis University, a state-of-the-art industrial kitchen where

urban gardeners can sell their produce to cooks without a kitchen—
entry-level restaurateurs who use the common kitchen to make meals
for delivery, takeout, storefront service in a nearby dining room, or
food truck sales. Aspiring cooks can sign up to work food prep shifts
for pay and learn the trade.[7]

Not too far from the Pruitt-Igoe site and across the street from
where the National Geospatial-Intelligence Agency is building the
largest surveillance site on the continent, Lois Conley takes care of the
collection at the Griot Museum of Black History and Culture, which
she founded in 1997. Beginning with the slave trade and continuing
through the history of the city—Madame C. J. Walker, Josephine
Baker, Percy Green, Macler Shepard—the museum represents the history of Black St. Louis, which is almost completely unmemorialized
elsewhere in the city, through a series of wax figures beloved by St.
Louis schoolchildren. The museum is cash-strapped and a labor of love,
but it keeps up a schedule of cutting-edge rotating exhibits and events—
on displaced African American neighborhoods like Mill Creek Valley;
photography and the Ferguson uprising; or the little-known story of the
Black St. Louis teenager Robert Rayford, who was the first American
to contract the HIV virus (fifteen years before Patient Zero), and the
history of the racial representation (and misrepresentation) of AIDS.[8]

A little bit to the south of the Griot, in midcity, longtime organizer and writer Jamala Rogers—known as "Mama Jamala" among the
younger generation of activists to whom she has served as a model and
mentor—keeps up the fight at the Organization for Black Struggle.
OBS was among the first organizations on the ground in Ferguson. For
nearly forty years, OBS has been a training ground, helping to shape
many of the young people whose voices and vision influenced the uprising and remade America. In the years since Donald Trump was elected
president, Rogers has renewed connections with white activists in rural
Missouri that were first created during Jesse Jackson's 1988 presidential campaign. Where others see only differences, Rogers, like Macler
Shepard and the Mennonites in JVL, sees similarities: lives, urban and

rural, Black and white, made precarious by the disappearance of good
work and the inaccessibility of basic social support, the criminal neglect of young minds, and the imperial tragedy of hometowns where
military enlistment provides the most reliable road out of town.[9]

In the aftermath of the Ferguson uprising, when many of the out-
of-town activists left town to carry the struggle to larger stages, Tef Poe
stayed behind in St. Louis, where he and several other activists founded
Hands Up United. They created a "books and breakfast" program that
meets biweekly at various sites around the city, bringing together kids
and adults—mostly Black, but also a few whites—for food, fellowship,
and free books. Working on a shoestring, Poe is dedicated to increasing
the visibility of the artists of Black St. Louis: he cohosts an annual art
show, raises money to create a fellowship program for young photog-
raphers in the city, and supports the documentation and celebration of
the hard beauty of life in the city. Poe thinks that seeing their lives reflected back to them as art helps young people in St. Louis—the young
people who faced the riot police and got tear-gassed in Ferguson—to
feel less lonely, like they have not been forgotten. He dreams of taking
over an abandoned police station on the Northside and building an arts
collective where the artistic talent in the city will be celebrated and
supported, not squandered.[10]

Among those on the streets in Ferguson were two kids from Kirkwood, each shaped in his own way by the 2008 shootings at city hall,
and each committed to using art to visualize the history of St. Louis.
One is the young journalist and photographer Clark Randall; his work
documents the separation of Meacham Park and Kirkwood, and he
has turned his activist energy to the ongoing struggle to close the St.
Louis Workhouse, the central lockup and debtors' prison where those
too poor to pay bail await trial on often trivial charges, sometimes for
years. The other is Mark Loehrer, a white kid from Kirkwood who
creates photomontages that blur past and present, bringing back to life
the city that once was by superimposing historic images onto the street
scenes from Google Maps. He has colorized old photos of Mill Creek

Valley in the 1930s and '40s and can describe that neighborhood as if it were still there and he had walked its streets.[11]

Across the river, Larry Giles tends his museum of dismantled buildings—the National Building Arts Center. Along with the seven warehouses that hold the architectural history of St. Louis, he collects industrial periodicals documenting the best practices of a host of lost arts—*Iron Age*, *Brass Age*, and so on—and the fragile record of the history of radical St. Louis. The museum sits on low ground in Sauget, Illinois, the town once known as Monsanto, hard by the chemical plant and off a narrow strip of highway lined by gas stations and strip clubs. There, near the site of the ancient city of Cahokia, he curates a shadow city of forgotten designs and forsaken objects.[12]

Nearby, in Centreville, Illinois, two young Black woman lawyers, Kalila Jackson of the Equal Housing Opportunity Council (who grew up in Black Jack and remembers visiting the Griot as a child) and Nicole Nelson of Equity Legal Services in St. Clair County, Illinois, are beginning a battle to roll back decades of municipal disregard and corporate malfeasance that have culminated in chronic flooding and water and soil contamination. Situated in the low-lying bottomland near the Mississippi, Centreville spends several weeks underwater every year. Not just when the river floods and the rising waters make the national news, but whenever there is a heavy rain. The networks of ditches and pumping stations that once drained the city have fallen into disrepair, and so the mostly poor, mostly elderly, almost entirely Black residents' houses are gradually falling in, their foundations undermined by the water, their furnaces and water heaters shorted out by the floods. The stormwater interacts with the failing sewer system—some residents have small geysers of raw sewage running up into their yards twenty-four hours a day—to create toxic floods. Homes that the residents purchased for $25,000 or $30,000 in the 1980s and 1990s are now worth one-fifth of that—making it impossible for them to get home improvement loans to try to stem the tide, even if they thought they could, which they can't.

But beginning with the frustration of one of the residents, Walter Byrd, a former sewer worker himself, who uses a flatboat to help his neighbors move around during high water, the residents began to organize and eventually found their way to Jackson and Nelson. They've been joined in their work by a group of students who are trying to imagine a new way for universities to engage with the world. Instead of coming in with the same old peer-reviewed solutions that never work out as well on the street as they do in the seminar room, they are listening and trying to work in service and solidarity with the frontline actors and eyewitnesses in the city. Gradually Jackson and Nelson have built a coalition that is threatening to become a movement to try to roll back the toxic flood tide of racist neglect.[13]

Maybe these seem like small efforts—too insignificant to measure up against the creeping North County apocalypse, the murders, and the heavy pull of the violent history of empire and white supremacy. But look again and you will see that these ordinary people are doing something beautiful and profound. They are imagining new ways to live in the city, to connect with and care for one another, to be human. They are doing what marginal and radical people in St. Louis have always done: getting on with it and pointing the way forward for a nation that has not yet learned to listen.

On the track behind Normandy High School, Camille Curtis coaches the RC Striders track team, named for her father, Reverend Richard Curtis, who died in 1994. She remembers him as a man who lived for the kids in his neighborhood, taking them around to events in an old work van with the kids sitting on overturned buckets in the back. She started the team in 2008 as a memorial to him, a way of keeping his spirit alive. The runners are mostly kids from the Northside of the city and the North County suburbs near the high school. A lot of them have tough lives—drugs and guns in their neighborhoods, relatives in jail. The team doesn't go into the neighborhoods to recruit; the kids just start showing up one day and are welcomed, or they linger, watching from outside the chain-link fence for a while before accepting an invitation to join. Curtis's own son was shot to death by a police officer in January 2017. Even in the immediate aftermath of his death, she kept coaching the kids. "He should be breathing, and so with my every breath I try to put something positive into the air for these kids," she said. Of the fifty or so kids who form the core of the team, almost half qualified for the Junior Olympics in the summer of 2019. They fly around the track in the fading light, little kids taking impossibly long strides.[14]

CODA: STL 2020

There is only one thing we need to change, and that is everything.

—RUTH WILSON GILMORE, *Change Everything*

KARL MARX BEGAN THE PREFACE HE WROTE FOR THE SECOND edition of *The 18th Brumaire of Louis Bonaparte* with a tribute to his friend Joseph Weydemeyer, "the military commandant [*sic*] of the St. Louis District in the Civil War." It is *The 18th Brumaire* that includes Marx's famous dictum: "Men make their own history, but they do not make it just as they please; they do not make it under circumstances chosen by themselves, but under circumstances directly encountered, given and transmitted from the past. The tradition of all of the dead generations weighs like nightmare on the brain of the living." The book recounts the history of the defeat of the Revolution of 1848 in France and the process by which "the party of Order" took control of France in the name of "property, family, religion, order," and purged the body politic of "Socialism" and "Anarchism." The reaction first destroyed the revolutionary proletarians of Paris; protesting workers were shot down

443

in the streets. And then, Marx continued, "the Party of Order" turned upon its erstwhile liberal allies, castigating "every demand of the simplest bourgeois financial reform, of the most ordinary liberalism, of the formal republicanism, of the most shallow democracy as 'Socialism.'"[1]

In the end they made a mediocre man into a king. The Emperor Napoleon III was voted into a position of nearly unlimited power by a republic shrunk by the ceaseless tightening of the rule of "ever more exclusive interest." As the greedy self-dealing of the constantly diminishing circle of insiders turned on one group after another of former allies and enablers, the politics of France shifted from democracy to republic to kleptocracy to kakistocracy—and then finally to monarchy. The election and imperial elevation of the feckless and corrupt nephew of the first Emperor Napoleon was proof for Marx of the historical truism that history may not repeat itself, but it rhymes—staged for the first time as tragedy, it is replayed as farce.

It is with Marx's notion of farce in mind that we might turn to Mark and Patricia McCloskey on June 28, 2020, as they confronted a group of demonstrators in front of their house on Portland Place in St. Louis. He brandished a souped-up AR-15, she a bespoke .22. They were both shouting about their property rights and their lawn—or, as they would later term it, law and order. As much as the McCloskeys might have deserved it, the demonstrators were not there for them. They were merely passing by, part of a large crowd of St. Louisans who were cutting through Portland Place on their way to a demonstration in front of the nearby house of St. Louis mayor Lyda Krewson. Krewson had several days before used Facebook Live to read off the names and addresses of a dozen or so citizens who had presented her with letters suggesting that she close the city's notorious medium-security "Workhouse" and cut the budget of the city's police department. St. Louis is a city in which prominent protesters frequently receive death threats from the defenders of "order." And so Krewson's actions were seen—even by those who thought they were stupid rather than intentionally murderous—as reckless to the point of being dangerous.

The history that was passing through the McCloskeys' neighborhood on the way to Krewson's house was the local manifestation of the
uprising that was happening all over the United States in the summer of
2020—in Minneapolis, in Louisville, in New York, in Atlanta, in Al-
buquerque, in Los Angeles, in Seattle, in Portland. The list of protests
seemingly sought to match and uplift and atone for the never-ending
list of the dead—Ahmaud Arbery, George Floyd, Breonna Taylor,
Rayshard Brooks, and on and on. And in city after city, protesters were
met with a state-sanctioned police riot of the sort that St. Louis had
experienced in 2014 and then again in 2017—indiscriminate, brazen,
unpunished.[2]

When the June 28 crowd turned the corner onto Portland Place
on their way to the Mayor's, it passed through a small gate that limited
access to the private street from the city outside. The original gated
neighborhoods of St. Louis were laid out and populated in the late nineteenth and early twentieth centuries; Portland Place in 1888. W.E.B.
Du Bois referred to this era of US history as "the dictatorship of property." And so the gate through which the protesters marched was, in
essence, a marker of the history of imperial, racial, and class conflict
in St. Louis: behind this barrier protecting a sanctuary for whiteness
and privilege, the plunder of empire could be redefined as civilization.
Residents of early private streets like Portland Place were filtered with
exclusionary building standards, including steep minimum home values that made it all but impossible for any but the wealthiest residents
of the city to imagine building or buying there.[3]

The crowd coming through the gate, Mark McCloskey told a reporter, made him think that the "revolution" had come to Portland
Place. It was like the "storming of the Bastille." He was afraid the
protesters might "loot" his house and kill his dog. Though they did not
even so much as set foot on his lawn, once they set foot on Portland
Place, they might as well "have been in my living room." All of this
was so perfectly expressive of the politics of propertied entitlement and
white resentment that defined the reactionary politics of the United

States in the summer of 2020 that it was not long before the video of the McCloskeys went viral.[4]

As Mark McCloskey made the media rounds in the following days, he portrayed his wife and himself as "urban pioneers" who were forced to defend civilization from the barbarism that seemed to be closing in on them from every side. First the governor of Missouri, Mike Parson, then Missouri senator Josh Hawley, and finally the president of the United States of America expressed their support, the president declaring that, had they not defended themselves, the McCloskeys would have "been beat up badly, if they were lucky . . . and the house was going to be totally ransacked, probably burned down, like the way they burn down churches."[5] The pundits and the politicians reframed the McCloskeys' vigilantism as an aspect of the nation's frontier inheritance, "what generations of Americans have done" to defend home and hearth from the savagery at the edge of civilization.[6] Finally, in a prime-time star turn at the Republican National Convention in August, the McCloskeys darkly warned that, "What you saw happen to us could just as easily happen to any of you who are watching from quiet neighborhoods around our country." The nation, they cautioned, was being overtaken by "Marxist revolutionaries" and "criminals" who were seeking to destroy the "American Way of Life" in their quest to "abolish the suburbs altogether by ending single-family home zoning."[7]

Something was happening in St. Louis, but the McCloskeys did not know what it was. In St. Louis, the calls for racial justice—including for police reform and even abolition—that exploded into mainstream view on Portland Place had been taking shape since 2014 (not to mention since ACTION's 1970 report on the St. Louis Police Department, "Thugs in Blue Uniform"). In the intervening years, many of the Ferguson generation of radical activists in St. Louis had organized around the election of the activists-turned-state-legislators Bruce Franks Jr. (in 2016) and Rasheen Aldridge (in 2019); the "progressive" prosecutors Kimberly Gardner in the city (in 2016) and Wesley Bell in the county (where he was elected to replace former prosecuting attorney Robert

McCulloch in 2018); and, most notably the US congresswoman Cori Bush, a frontline veteran of the protests in Ferguson (in 2020). In 2018, a number of those who had been active in and energized by the protests in 2014 and 2017 had also organized the Close the Workhouse campaign, inaugurating the struggle that debouched on Portland Place in the summer of 2020.[8]

To the extent that the McCloskeys were able to keep the focus on their own aggrieved selves by connecting their struggle to anything that was actually happening in the city of St. Louis—their story had begun, after all, when they were bystanders watching a protest that had nothing at all to do with them or their home—it was by blaming St. Louis circuit attorney Kimberly Gardner for supporting "mob rule" in the city. One by one, Parson, Hawley, and Trump suggested that Gardner was undermining the rule of law by considering charges against the McCloskeys for brandishing their weapons at peaceful protesters (a threat that Gardner has in the meantime made good in the shape of indictments for the unlawful use of a weapon and tampering with evidence). Cast by the right as the leader of a left-wing mob, Gardner found herself being subjected to what she termed, in reference to white supremacist violence in the Reconstruction South, "a modern-day night ride"—a seemingly organized harassment campaign of threats and racist email that included a note on the windshield of her car reading: "I hope you hang from a tree."[9]

Sadly, the threats were nothing new for Gardner, who has frequently stated, prosecutor though she is, that the city needs "fewer police and fewer prisons." Early in 2018, Gardner indicted then–Missouri governor Eric Greitens, a Republican, for felony invasion of privacy in a case where he had allegedly tied up his half-naked lover and photographed her against her will in the basement of the house that he shared with his wife and children. Although Greitens was forced to resign from the governorship, the charges against him were eventually dropped—the photo that the victim remembered Greitens taking with his phone could not be proven to exist by the time the phone came into the custody of the prosecutor. In June 2019, after the charge against Greitens had been dropped, a local judge announced that he was appointing a special prosecutor to investigate the conduct of Gardner's office during the Greitens investigation. The request for the appointment of a special prosecutor with the power to subpoena and seize the records of the circuit attorney's office, it turned out, had been made by the St. Louis Police Department.[10]

Some in St. Louis connected the police department's interest in Gardner's conduct in the Greitens investigation (which was otherwise unconnected to the police) to the "exclusion list" maintained by her office. In 2018, Gardner had announced the existence of a list of twenty-two police officers with whom the prosecutor's office would not cooperate: officers whose cases they would not try, whose warrant requests they would not support, and whose testimony they would not use. (Many cities maintain such a list, and they are legally obligated to disclose the identities of the listed officers to those against whom those officers testify in court.) Following the 2019 public revelation of the disturbing level of involvement by officers of the St. Louis Police Department in posting online images that glorified police violence and derogated African Americans, Muslims, and Mexicans, dozens more officers were added to the list. The list, which has never been made public in its entirety, reportedly contained the names of at least seventy-five officers, or about 5 percent of those employed by the department. Gardner's attempt to reform the police by refusing to cooperate with "bad actors" has been denounced and resisted by the St. Louis Police Officers Association (SLPOA), which has noted that several former "officers of the year" are currently on the prosecutor's exclusion list.[11]

In January 2020, Gardner filed suit in federal court alleging that she had been targeted by a racist conspiracy to "thwart and impede her efforts to establish equal treatment under law for all St. Louis citizens." The SLPOA, the lawsuit alleges, conspired with Governor Greitens's criminal defense attorney and the special prosecutor—a high school friend and former law partner of the governor's lawyer—to mount a bogus investigation of the circuit attorney's office. That investigation, it further alleges, allowed the police to serve overbroad warrants and confiscate records from the circuit attorney, including information about as many as forty ongoing investigations of St. Louis police officers, twenty-five of which involved officers accused by citizens of using excessive force. As legal authority and historical reminder, the lawsuit invoked the 1871 Klan Act, which targeted the white supremacist takeover of governmental institutions in the Reconstruction South.[12]

According to the circuit attorney, the investigation of her office was a white supremacist effort to undermine the rule of law in St. Louis, prompted by the effort to bring one particularly high-profile suspect to trial and by the proposal of consequential but not really radical police reforms. Gardner's office, after all, had called for excluding "bad actors" from taking their cases to court, but not for firing or even suspending them, and it certainly was not proposing the "defunding" or "abolition" of the St. Louis Police Department. At the end of September, Gardner's suit was dismissed by a federal judge, who found no evidence of coordination between the parties named in the suit. Still, it was enough to make one wonder if there was hope at all of "reforming" the police. In the meantime, during a deadly pandemic, Gardner's office recommended the detention of dozens of citizens unable to pay bail as they awaited trial in courts where business had slowed, suggesting the limited effect of the election of "progressive" prosecutors.[13]

As the tension between the police and the prosecutor escalated, another controversy unfolded about the symbolism of the "thin blue line" and "Punisher" images as emblems of the reaction to the uprisings of 2020. In June 2019, the SLPOA urged its members to show solidarity with the officers on the exclusion list by replacing their social media avatars with the "Blue Line Punisher" symbol—a white skull overlaid on a blue-line American flag. The image combines the exhortation to excessive force of the Punisher symbol (drawn from a 1970s comic book whose central character is an ex-Marine who dispenses vigilante "curbstone" justice in New York City), the American flag, and the idea that the police form a "thin blue line" that, in the words of President Trump, "stands between civilization and total chaos."[14] As with so much of the history of St. Louis, the summer of 2020—combining as it did armed vigilantism, the incendiary posturing of Parson, Hawley, and Trump, and fears of a white supremacist insurgency being mounted from within the ranks of the police department—seemed to forecast the future that played out nationally in the January 6, 2021, attack on the nation's Capitol.

Slowing down a bit, however, and following the pathway of the "thin blue line" across the city, another, deeper pattern becomes apparent, one that lay behind the troubles in the city (and the nation) in the summer of 2020 and afterward: the structured inequality that the police were invented to protect; and the centuries-long social catastrophe that for much of 2020 lay hidden behind—beneath—the farcical preening of the president and his provincial epigones. The power of the police, Frantz Fanon wrote in *The Wretched of the Earth*, is "proportional to the marasmus"—that is, it is proportional to the inequality, or "social malnutrition." The "thin blue line" marks and defends the underlying boundary between plenty and poverty, and in St. Louis, as in much of the United States, that line is perilously close to the line between Black and white.[15]

On the bottom side of the "thin blue line," the city of St. Louis was in much the same condition that it had been for most of the twentieth century: most of its Black population remained spatially isolated, economically exploited, violently policed, and municipally abandoned; large portions of its poor and working-class white population continued to be disciplined by racialized threats and bought off with empty promises; and its ruling class was still holed up under police protection in comfortable suburbs and gated neighborhoods. And in 2020, as the McCloskeys and the rest of the ruling-class melodrama continued to dominate the headlines, the pandemic spread through St. Louis, tracing out as it did a ghostly map of the underlying tragedy of the history of the city at the heart of America.

As in the rest of the United States, the pattern of infection and mortality in St. Louis reflected the spatial and racial imprint of the city's long history of economic and social inequality: the history not just of discrimination but of systematic exploitation, exclusion, subordination, and predation. The first twelve people to die of COVID-19 in St. Louis were African American. As of this writing, the rate of COVID infection among African Americans in the city of St. Louis was just under two times the rate of infection among whites, and just over two times the rate among whites in St. Louis County. The death rates among those known to be infected (a statistic that probably understates both the total number of deaths from COVID and the disproportion between African Americans and whites) are similar: in St. Louis, African Americans are just over two times more likely to die of COVID than whites are, and in St. Louis County they are just under two times as likely to die.[16]

In St. Louis in 2020, as everywhere else in the United States, African Americans were overrepresented among frontline service workers, whose jobs require constant exposure to other people and whose commutes often require hours on public transportation. Because health care in our society is generally allocated according to employment, these same workers are less likely than those for whom they provide services to get medical care for themselves and their families—care is least available to those who need it most. Indeed, in St. Louis, African Americans are more than twice as likely as whites to be uninsured. The median income of African Americans in greater St. Louis is half of white median income, while rates of poverty and unemployment are three times greater for African Americans than for whites. Since 1980, by one estimate, the incomes of young black men in the city of St. Louis have fallen by 178 percent—to just over $11,000 a year.[17]

St. Louis today remains a divided city, bisected by Delmar Avenue. North of Delmar (where the population is roughly 95 percent African American), the housing stock has crumbled, economic opportunities have vanished, and public goods—especially schools—are scarce and deteriorating. African Americans in St. Louis are *twelve times* more likely than white residents to live in neighborhoods of concentrated poverty, which often contain environmental risks, including poor air or water quality, industrial toxins, and failed sanitary infrastructure. These are the sources of heightened rates of respiratory and other illnesses among African Americans. Such conditions compound other political, social, and economic disadvantages, which undermine access not just to economic opportunity but to adequate social services, decent schools, and nutritious food. The history of St. Louis—the history of white cupidity supported at every level of government and woven into the fabric of daily life—rendered up African Americans to the virus.[18]

It is with the jagged surface features of the city's long history of inequality in mind that we should return one final time to the McCloskeys and their gate. Though they were unable to grasp it, there was indeed a revolution beginning on their street, but not one that was concerned with their mansion, their lawn, or even their dog, at least not yet. The crowd on Portland Place represented a coalition in support of prison abolition that had grown directly out of the activism of the uprising in Ferguson. Some were veterans of the uprising. Others were former inmates, some of whom, unable to post bail, had spent months incarcerated as they awaited trial on inconsequential charges. Some were lawyers who had spent years trying to bring the conditions in the municipal court system and city prisons to light. They were Black and white, men and women, straight, queer, and trans, poor, working-class, and professional. Among them, with a bullhorn, was Cori Bush, veteran of the uprising in Ferguson and soon-to-be member of the US Congress.

Beneath the headlines, and behind the stage set of the farce on Portland Place, was an emerging struggle to remake the world in the image of the uprising that began in the summer of 2014. The initial target of the struggle was the closing of the St. Louis Workhouse, the outdated and costly symbol—and site—of racist mass incarceration. The money saved by the city would be used to establish a fund dedicated to abolishing the conditions that had produced the prison in the first place and kept it supplied with inmates ever since. "We've long held the belief that jails, prisons and police do not keep us safe— investment in people and communities does," said Inez Bordeaux, a leader of the Close the Workhouse campaign. More than the closing of a single notorious prison, the destruction of a symbol of white supremacy, or even the end of an era, the closing of the Workhouse was to mark the beginning of the process of dismantling the long history— "the tradition of all of the dead generations"—that had built it and kept it filled to capacity.[19]

On July 17, 2020, shortly after the march to the mayor's house, the city's board of aldermen voted to close the Workhouse. When, four months later, the city corrections commissioner and some of the lukewarm members of the board of aldermen temporized about meeting their democratic commitment, the activists prepared to hold them to their word. "It's incredibly frustrating that we have to fight to close the workhouse all over again," said Bordeaux. "But we will. We have no problem getting back in the streets if that's what it takes."[20]

ACKNOWLEDGMENTS

THIS BOOK, THE FRIENDS I MADE ALONG THE WAY IN WRITING it, and the city of St. Louis have brought so much good into my life that I scarcely know where to begin.

I started to see the city in a new way when I met Tef Poe, and I could not have come to know and love the city in the way I have, nor could I have written this book, without his friendship, his example, and his support. Tef introduced me to Percy Green and Jamala Rogers, and becoming friends with them has been one of the great honors of my life.

Also in (and from) St. Louis, Michael Allen, Jabari Asim, Iver Bernstein, Pam and Tony Berry, Brandon Bosley, Larry Briggs, Sylvester Brown Jr., Keona Ervin, Clarissa Hayward, Johari Jabir, Jonathan Karp, Rockwell Knuckles, Heidi Kolk, Clarence Lang, Aloha Misho, Clark Randall, Jodi Rios, Jay Stretch, Fresh Voice, and Timetria Watkins-Murphy helped me find my way. Mark Loehrer's knowledge and vision of the history of St. Louis have framed many pages of what I have written here; he has been more a historical guide to me than a research assistant. Miranda Rechtenwald at Washington University and Gwen Moore, Amanda Claunch, and Hattie Felton at the Missouri

Historical Society have helped out along the way. Sarah Coffin, Crosby Kemper, and Patrick Tuohey helped me understand the politics of tax abatement in Missouri, and Yoni Applebaum sharpened my first take on the topic.

At Harvard, Aabid Allibhai, Jacob Anbinder, Ione Barrows, Tim Barker, and Mycah Conner helped out with research and provided pointed and helpful comments.

George Lipsitz has been both muse and mentor to me at every step along the sidewalks of St. Louis, which I first came to think about historically through reading his work. Robin Kelley, Lisa Lowe, Nell Irvin Painter, Dan Rodgers, and David Roediger have pointed me toward the type of history that I am still trying to write.

Through the Commonwealth Project and its work in St. Louis, I have come to know José Constantine, Kalila Jackson, Nicole Nelson, and Sam Stragand—freedom fighters. As with John and Alicia Campbell, Justin Hansford, and Brendan Roediger—the other members of the League of Radical Lawyers—I have been blessed to be able to lend a hand in their work, although, truth be told, much of what I have done has been simply sending them brilliant and righteous young people to aid in the work—Che Applewhaite, Catriona Barr, Kale Catchings, Saul Glist, and the inexhaustible, irreplaceable, implacable Robin McDowell, who also helped out with the illustrations, the permissions, and the maps.

Teaching with Vincent Brown and Tommie Shelby has been both humbling and inspiring, as has been working with Brandon Terry and Elizabeth Hinton. I am very lucky to have the four of them, along with Kirsten Weld, my co-conspirator in many schemes, as friends and colleagues. I have learned enormously from Destin Jenkins, Manu Karuka, Justin Leroy, and K-Sue Park. Vivek Bald, Jason Beckfield, Larry Bobo, Evelyn Brooks-Higginbotham, Peggy Burns, Nancy Cott, Skip Gates, Claudine Gay, Roberto Gonzales, Mordecai Lyon, Tiya Miles, Marcie Morgan, and Khalil Muhammad have provided institutional support and intellectual company. Monnikue McCall,

Josh Mejia, Kimberly O'Hagan, Arthur Patton-Hock, Cory Paulsen, Flavia Perea, Jennifer Shepherd, and Abbie Wolf also deserve thanks; in ways small and large they have helped keep me from running off into the ditch when I lost track of the road right in front of me.

During the year that they were at the Charles Warren Center at Harvard, I was lucky to have the chance to sit with and learn from Garrett Felber, Julily Kohler-Hausman, Donna Murch, Micol Seigel, and Heather Thompson, as well as the other fellows in the Crime and Punishment Seminar. And the fellows in the Center's Global American Studies Program—Megan Black, Melissa Castillo-Garsow, Samantha Iyer, Allan Lumba, Elizabeth Mesok, Tejasvi Nagaraja, Juliet Nebolon, Stuart Schrader, and the aforementioned Jenkins and Leroy—have been a source of both pride and inspiration to me in the years I have directed it.

Samuel Moyn is from St. Louis, and his willingness to continue pretending to be amazed by the things I "discovered" about the city where he grew up was a frequent boost to me as I wrote. The influence of Stephanie Smallwood, also from St. Louis, is stamped on the face of everything I have written since I met her in . . . gee, when was it? . . . 1999? Jonathan Walton introduced me to both Habakkuk, which was never far from my mind as I wrote about St. Louis, and Micah 6:8, by which I have tried to guide my steps through the city and life more generally. And thanks to Andrew Baker, just because he's Andrew Baker.

Stephen Aron, Phil Deloria, Roxanne Dunbar-Ortiz, Keona Ervin, Nick Estes, Larry Giles, Peter Hudson, Kalila Jackson, Clarence Lang, Richard White, and Andrew Zimmerman have each read draft chapters and been patient with my mistakes (well, not Richard) and generous with their learning. Dan D'Oca, Priscilla Dowden-White, Keona Ervin, Rosemary Feuer, Colin Gordon, Kenneth Jolly, Clarence Lang, Sharon Romeo, and Lea VanderVelde, each of whom has written wonderfully about St. Louis and all of whom have taught me a great deal, have been generous in welcoming me to their territory. Likewise the two St. Louis history dissertation writers on whose committee I have served while writing the book, Laura Leigh Schmidt and Zachary Nowak.

Cynthia Buck, Dan Gerstle, Roger Labrie, Melissa Veronesi, and, especially, Brian Distelberg at Basic Books, as well as Elise Capron, Andrea Cavallo, and, especially, Sandy Dijkstra at the Dijkstra Literary Agency made this book happen and then made sure it would be readable. Kate Blackmer added wonderful maps.

There's just no way to really describe the friendship and intellectual company of Steven Kantrowitz and Adam Green. I have been extraordinarily lucky to share in their lives and the lives of their families for so many years.

Bobby and Elizabeth Findling and Al Fleig and Venus Masselam (as well as the cast of thousands on the Fleig-Masselam family reunion circuit) have provided good company and good conversation. David Fleig and Lauren Kleutsch are wonderful, beautiful, smart, and supportive in-laws, and they make me proud. And their Jeremiah has the most amazing smile.

George and Barb Johnson, my uncle and aunt, first introduced me to St. Louis. Their love inspires me, just as their generosity has supported me.

My relationship with my brother Willoughby Johnson has only deepened over the years I have written this book. From helping me understand municipal finance when I first started writing about the political economy of Ferguson in the fall of 2014 to reading and commenting on the final draft of the entire manuscript, he has been intellectually involved in every stage of this project. Thanks also to Christy Miller and to Zara and Wynn Johnson.

Giulia and Luca Johnson have grown into people with whom I can talk about history and politics during the years in which I have written this book. It is miraculous—like, literally miraculous, because I cannot take the credit for it—to see them growing into thoughtful and generous adults. Xander and Natalie-Susan Frank have never stopped being curious and asking hard questions, I have learned from their company, and I am enormously proud to be their (other) father. Felix Johnson, the capstone of our blended family, is everything his name suggests and more—a wholly undeserved joy-bringing, life-loving, hope-inspiring gift. In these mean times, I am daily reminded by my children why the world is worth fighting for.

Alison Frank Johnson's love has sustained me. She read every page of this book, and many of them two or three times. Her comments variously made me laugh out loud, bow my head in shame for what I had done, and nod my head in wise agreement, as if that was what I had meant to say in the first place. Just as she has made me a better person and made my life a better life, she made this book a better book. Her walk by my side is the greatest blessing of a lucky life. Her work on the book, I can say with some authority, has saved you, the reader, some frustration, although it might also have cost you a few laughs at my expense.

NOTES

PROLOGUE: MAPPING THE LOSS

1. The National Building Arts Center in Sauget, Illinois (http://web.national buildingarts.org/), is curated by the visionary archivist Larry Giles.

2. City of St. Louis, "Land Clearance for Redevelopment Authority," www .stlouis-mo.gov/government/departments/sldc/boards/Land-Clearance-for -Redevelopment-Authority.cfm; "Paul McKee's Northside Regeneration Accused of Tax Credit Fraud in Suit by Missouri Attorney General," *St. Louis Post-Dispatch*, June 14, 2018; "LRA Owns the 12,000 St. Louis Properties No One Wants. And It Can't Afford to Maintain Them," *St. Louis Post-Dispatch*, September 17, 2018.

3. 99% Invisible, "Dollhouses of St. Louis," November 7, 2017, https:// 99percentinvisible.org/episode/dollhouses-st-louis/.

4. Jason Purnell et al., "For the Sake of All: A Report on the Health and Well-Being of African Americans in St. Louis and Why It Matters to Everyone," Washington University, 2015, 27; Melia Robinson, Mike Nudelman, and Andy Kiersz, "The 25 Wealthiest Suburbs in America," *Business Insider*, November 4, 2014, www.businessinsider.com/richest-suburbs-in-america-2014-10.

5. One of the many extraordinary aspects of the history of St. Louis is the number of truly excellent books that have been written about the city. See, in particular, James Neal Primm, *Lion of the Valley: St. Louis Missouri, 1764–1980* (St. Louis: Missouri History Museum, 1981); Eric Sandweiss, *St. Louis: Evolution of an American Urban Landscape* (Philadelphia: Temple University Press, 2001); Colin Gordon, *Mapping Decline: St. Louis and the Fate of the American City* (Philadelphia: University of Pennsylvania Press, 2008); Clarence Lang, *Grassroots at the Gateway:*

Class Politics and Black Freedom Struggle in St. Louis, 1936–75 (Ann Arbor: University of Michigan Press, 2009); Adam Arenson, *The Great Heart of the Republic: St. Louis and the Cultural Civil War* (Cambridge, MA: Harvard University Press, 2010); Priscilla A. Dowden-White, *Groping Toward Democracy: African American Social Welfare Reform in St. Louis, 1910–1949* (Columbia: University of Missouri Press, 2011); Henry W. Berger, *St. Louis and Empire: 250 Years of Imperial Quest and Urban Crisis* (Carbondale: Southern Illinois University Press, 2015); Phillip Longman, "Why the Economic Fates of America's Cities Diverged," *Atlantic*, November 28, 2015, www.theatlantic.com/business/archive/2015/11/cities-economic-fates-diverge/417372/; Keona K. Ervin, *Gateway to Equality: Black Women and the Struggle for Economic Justice in St. Louis* (Lexington: University Press of Kentucky, 2017); Ryan Schuessler, ed., *The St. Louis Anthology* (Cleveland: Belt Publishing, 2019).

6. Although they are too often considered in isolation, the histories of empire and anti-Blackness have been productively intertwined in Ronald T. Takaki, *Iron Cages: Race and Culture in Nineteenth-Century America* (New York: Oxford University Press, 1979); Nell Irvin Painter, *Standing at Armageddon: A Grassroots History of the Progressive Era* (New York: W. W. Norton & Co., 1987); Alexander Saxton, *The Rise and Fall of the White Republic: Class Politics and Mass Culture in Nineteenth-Century America* (New York: Verso, 1990); Gail Bederman, *Manliness and Civilization: A Cultural History of Gender and Race in the United States, 1880–1917* (New York: Oxford University Press, 1995); Matthew Frye Jacobson, *Barbarian Virtues: The United States Encounters Foreign Peoples at Home and Abroad, 1876–1917* (New York: Hill and Wang, 2001); Laura Briggs, *Reproducing Empire: Race, Sex, Science, and US Empire in Puerto Rico* (Berkeley: University of California Press, 2003); Jodi A. Byrd, *The Transit of Empire: Indigenous Critiques of Colonialism* (Minneapolis: University of Minnesota Press, 2011); David R. Roediger and Elizabeth E. Esch, *The Production of Difference: Race and the Management of Labor in US History* (New York: Oxford University Press, 2012); Lisa Lowe, *The Intimacies of Four Continents* (Durham, NC: Duke University Press, 2015); Steven Hahn, *A Nation Without Borders: The United States and Its World in an Age of Civil Wars, 1830–1910* (New York: Penguin, 2016); Richard White, *The Republic for Which It Stands: The United States During Reconstruction and the Gilded Age, 1865–1896* (New York: Oxford University Press, 2017); Nikhil Pal Singh, *Race and America's Long War* (Berkeley: University of California Press, 2017); Manu Karuka, *Empire's Tracks: Indigenous Nations, Chinese Workers, and the Transcontinental Railroad* (Berkeley: University of California Press, 2019); K-Sue Park, "Self-Deportation Nation," *Harvard Law Review* 132 (May 10, 2019): 1878.

7. W. E. B. Du Bois, "The Souls of White Folk," in Du Bois, *Darkwater: Voices from Within the Veil* (New York: Harcourt, Brace, and Hale, 1920); Cedric J. Robinson, *Black Marxism: The Making of the Black Radical Tradition*, 2nd ed. (1983;

Chapel Hill: University of North Carolina Press, 2000). The usage, emerging as it does out of the history of the Black radical tradition, is terrifically pertinent, but not perfect: it must be stretched to fully encompass the history of US imperialism and Indian killing—"settler colonialism." For the state of the art, see Lowe, *The Intimacies of Four Continents*, 149–150.

8. Du Bois, "The Souls of White Folk"; David R. Roediger, *The Wages of Whiteness: Race and the Making of the American Working Class* (New York: Verso, 1991); George Lipsitz, *The Possessive Investment in Whiteness: How White People Profit from Identity Politics* (Philadelphia: Temple University Press, 2006); Karen E. Fields and Barbara J. Fields, *Racecraft: The Soul of Inequality in American Life* (New York: Verso, 2012); Robin D. G. Kelley, "Births of a Nation: Surveying Trumpland with Cedric Robinson," *Boston Review*, March 6, 2017.

9. Achille Mbembe, *Critique of Black Reason* (Durham, NC: Duke University Press, 2013); K-Sue Park, "Race, Innovation, and Financial Growth: The Example of Foreclosure," in *Histories of Racial Capitalism*, ed. Destin Jenkins and Justin Leroy (New York: Columbia University Press, forthcoming).

10. See Jonathan M. Metzl, *Dying of Whiteness: How the Politics of Racial Resentment Is Killing America's Heartland* (New York: Basic Books, 2019).

11. Patrick Wolfe, "Land, Labor, and Difference: Elementary Structures of Race," *American Historical Review* 106, no. 3 (2001): 866–905.

12. See Singh, *Race and America's Long War*; Karuka, *Empire's Tracks*; Park, "Self-Deportation Nation." My argument owes a great deal to Kelly Lytle Hernández, *City of Inmates: Conquest, Rebellion, and the Rise of Human Caging in Los Angeles, 1771–1965* (Chapel Hill: University of North Carolina Press, 2017), as well as to the mind-shaping friendship, scholarship, and mentorship of Adam Green and Stephanie Smallwood.

13. Lipsitz, *The Possessive Investment in Whiteness*; Fields and Fields, *Racecraft*; Sylvia Wynter, "Unsettling the Coloniality of Being/Power/Truth/Freedom: Towards the Human, After Man, Its Overrepresentation—an Argument," *New Centennial Review* 3, no. 3 (Fall 2003): 257–337.

14. US Department of Justice, Civil Rights Division, *Investigation of the Ferguson Police Department*, March 4, 2015, www.justice.gov/sites/default/files/opa/press-releases/attachments/2015/03/04/ferguson_police_department_report.pdf. The separate DoJ report on the murder of Michael Brown, on the other hand, is, at best, a legalistic restatement of the extraordinary latitude provided police officers who shoot unarmed people in the United States and, at worst, a complete misunderstanding of the full set of circumstances surrounding the shooting; see Khalil Gibran Muhammad, "The History of Lynching and the Present of Policing," *Nation*, May 17, 2018.

15. Walter Johnson, "Ferguson's Fortune 500 Company," *Atlantic*, April 26, 2015.

CHAPTER 1: WILLIAM CLARK'S MAP

1. See Daniel K. Richter, *Facing East from Indian Country: A Native History of Early America* (Cambridge, MA: Harvard University Press, 2001); Virginia Scharff, *Twenty Thousand Roads: Women, Movement, and the West* (Berkeley: University of California Press, 2003).

2. UNESCO, "Cahokia Mounds State Historic Site," https://whc.unesco.org/en/list/198; Joe Hollerman, "Spotlight: Last Indian Mound in St. Louis Still Deteriorating," *St. Louis Post-Dispatch*, October 4, 2015. See also Thomas E. Emerson, Brad H. Koldehoff, and Tamira K. Brennan, *Revealing Greater Cahokia, North America's First Native City: Rediscovery and Large-Scale Excavations of the East St. Louis Precinct*, Studies in Archaeology 12 (Urbana: Illinois State Archaeological Survey, University of Illinois, 2018).

3. Timothy R. Pauketat, *Cahokia: Ancient America's Great City on the Mississippi* (New York: Penguin, 2009), 2, 14–26; Timothy R. Pauketat, *Ancient Cahokia and the Mississippians* (Cambridge: Cambridge University Press, 2004), 67–95.

4. Pauketat, *Cahokia*, 69, 109; Pauketat, *Ancient Cahokia*, 78–80, 84–95; Blake de Pastino, "America's Largest Earthwork, Cahokia's Monks Mound, May Have Been Built in Only 20 Years, Study Says," *Western Digs*, September 17, 2015, http://westerndigs.org/americas-largest-earthwork-cahokias-monks-mound-may-have-been-built-in-only-20-years-study-says/.

5. Pauketat, *Cahokia*, 164–169.

6. Primm, *Lion of the Valley*, 7; Sarah E. Baires, "White Settlers Buried the Truth About the Midwest's Mysterious Mound Cities," *Smithsonian*, February 23, 2018.

7. Anne F. Hyde, *Empires, Nations, and Families: A New History of the American West, 1800–1860* (Lincoln: University of Nebraska Press, 2011), 240.

8. William E. Foley, *Wilderness Journey: The Life of William Clark* (Columbia: University of Missouri Press, 2004), 75–158; Landon Y. Jones, *William Clark and the Shaping of the West* (New York: Hill and Wang, 2004), 49–146, 145 (quotation).

9. Peter J. Kastor, *William Clark's World: Describing America in an Age of Unknowns* (New Haven, CT: Yale University Press, 2011), 101–159.

10. Nick Estes, *Our History Is the Future: Standing Rock Versus the Dakota Access Pipeline, and the Long Tradition of Indigenous Resistance* (New York: Verso, 2019), 72–74.

11. Charles McKenzie, "Charles McKenzie's Narratives," in *Early Fur Trade on the Northern Plains: Canadian Traders Among the Mandan and Hidatsa Indians, 1738–1818, the Narratives of John Macdonnell, David Thompson, François-Antoine Larocque, and Charles McKenzie*, ed. W. Raymond Wood and Thomas D. Thiessen (Norman: University of Oklahoma Press, 1985), 232.

12. Elizabeth A. Fenn, *Encounters at the Heart of the World: A History of the Mandan People* (New York: Hill and Wang, 2014); John Logan Allen, *Passage Through the Garden: Lewis and Clark and the Image of the American Northwest* (Ur-

bana: University of Illinois Press, 1975), 18, 19, 121, 143; Kastor, *William Clark's World*, 27–97.

13. Lewis quoted in Allen, *Passage Through the Garden*, 241–242; Reuben Gold Thwaites, *Original Journals of the Lewis and Clark Expedition: 1804–1806*, vol. 1, 50–51; Kastor, *William Clark's World*, 17, 151.

14. Scharff, *Twenty Thousand Roads*, 11–34; Fenn, *Encounters at the Heart of the World*, 214; Estes, *Our History Is the Future*, 79–81.

15. Fenn, *Encounters at the Heart of the World*, 216.

16. Foley, *Wilderness Journey*, 96, 102, 106–108, 110–111, 113, 116–118; Scharff, *Twenty Thousand Roads*, 11–34; Kastor, *William Clark's World*, 5, 196.

17. Fenn, *Encounters at the Heart of the World*, 216; William Clark to Toussaint Charbonneau, August 20, 1806, quoted in Jones, *William Clark and the Shaping of the West*, 146, 194 (see also 129); Scharff, *Twenty Thousand Roads*, 11–34.

18. Allen, *Passage Through the Garden*, 375; Kastor, *William Clark's World*, 160–190.

19. Jefferson quoted in Allen, *Passage Through the Garden*, 107; David J. Wishart, *The Fur Trade of the American West, 1807–1840* (Lincoln: University of Nebraska Press, 1979), 27, 19 (quotation).

20. Hyde, *Empires, Nations, and Families*, 7; Kathleen DuVal, *The Native Ground: Indians and Colonists in the Heart of the Continent* (Philadelphia: University of Pennsylvania Press, 2006), 1–12; Wishart, *The Fur Trade of the American West*, 64. DuVal's notion of "native ground" is an intended contrast to Richard White, *The Middle Ground: Indians, Empires, and Republics in the Great Lakes Region, 1650–1815* (Cambridge: Cambridge University Press, 1991).

21. Quoted in Wishart, *The Fur Trade of the American West*, 18, 81; Hyde, *Empires, Nations, and Families*, 41, 58.

22. DuVal, *The Native Ground*, 194, 183; Willard H. Rollings, *The Osage: An Ethnohistorical Study of Hegemony on the Prairie-Plains* (Columbia: University of Missouri Press, 1995); Jay Gitlin, *Bourgeois Frontier: French Towns, French Traders, and American Expansion* (New Haven, CT: Yale University Press, 2010), 73, 85, 88, 89–90, 128; Hyde, *Empires, Nations, and Families*, 31, passim.

23. Stephen Aron, *American Confluence: The Missouri Frontier from Borderland to Border State* (Bloomington: Indiana University Press, 2009); quoted in Jones, *William Clark and the Shaping of the West*, 218.

24. Alan Taylor, *The Civil War of 1812: American Citizens, British Subjects, Irish Rebels, and Indian Allies* (New York: Vintage, 2010); quoted in Jones, *William Clark and the Shaping of the West*, 151; Kastor, *William Clark's World*, 97–102.

25. Jones, *William Clark and the Shaping of the West*, 207 (quotation), 214; Primm, *Lion of the Valley*, 102–104; Hyde, *Empires, Nations, and Families*, 252–254.

26. Wishart, *The Fur Trade of the American West*, 45–46, 121.

27. Wishart, *The Fur Trade of the American West*, 45–46, 121; Aaron Robert Woodard, "William Ashley and Jedidiah Smith and the Arikara Battle of 1823,"

Journal of the West 51, no. 4 (Fall 2012): 76–77, 78; Hyde, *Empires, Nations, and Families*, 262–264; D. W. Meinig, *The Shaping of America: A Geographical Perspective on 500 Years of History*, vol. 2, *Continental America, 1800–1867* (New Haven, CT: Yale University Press, 1993), 71.

28. Hyde, *Empires, Nations, and Families*, 7, 59.

29. Aron, *American Confluence*; DuVal, *The Native Ground*, 232, 227–228; Jones, *William Clark and the Shaping of the West*, 310.

30. Jay H. Buckley, *William Clark: Indian Diplomat* (Norman: University of Oklahoma Press, 2008), 144–211.

31. Gitlin, *Bourgeois Frontier*, 73, 85, 88, 89–90, 128.

32. Jones, *William Clark and the Shaping of the West*, 331–334.

33. Hyde, *Empires, Nations, and Families*, 67; Primm, *Lion of the Valley*, 104. For the Lakota, see Estes, *Our History Is the Future*; Jeffrey Ostler, *The Lakotas and the Black Hills: The Struggle for Sacred Ground* (New York: Penguin Books, 2011); Pekka Hämäläinen, "Reconstructing the Great Plains: The Long Struggle for Sovereignty and Dominance in the Heart of the Continent," *Journal of the Civil War Era* 6, no. 4 (December 2016): 481–509.

34. Primm, *Lion of the Valley*, 108; Sandweiss, *St. Louis*, 38; Meinig, *The Shaping of America*, 77–78.

35. John Francis McDermott, ed., *The Western Journals of Washington Irving* (Norman: University of Oklahoma Press, 1944), 80–81; Wishart, *The Fur Trade of the American West*, 58; Kastor, *William Clark's World*, 233–244.

36. McDermott, *The Western Journals of Washington Irving*, 60, 82.

37. McDermott, *The Western Journals of Washington Irving*, 81–82.

38. Foley, *Wilderness Journey*, 75–158; Jones, *William Clark and the Shaping of the West*, 137.

39. William Clark to Jonathan Clark, July 21, November 22, and December 17, 1808, in *Dear Brother: Letters of William Clark to Jonathan Clark*, ed. James J. Homberg (New Haven, CT: Yale University Press, 2002), 144, 160, 167, 187.

40. McDermott, *The Western Journals of Washington Irving*, 82. I have standardized, just a bit, spellings and punctuation in the quotations from Irving's journal entries.

41. In *American Confluence*, Stephen Aron frames Clark's subsequent career as a repudiation of his debt to the Indians upon whom the success of the journey to the Pacific had depended.

42. Kastor, *William Clark's World*, 244–250.

CHAPTER 2: WAR TO THE ROPE

1. Elbert B. Smith, *Magnificent Missourian: The Life of Thomas Hart Benton* (Philadelphia: J. B. Lippincott Company, 1958), 19–21.

2. Smith, *Magnificent Missourian*, 41–42.

3. Smith, *Magnificent Missourian*, 46–48.

4. Gitlin, *Bourgeois Frontier*, 48 (quotation), 143–144; Sandweiss, *St. Louis*, 38–40, 43, 49, 66.

5. Aron, *American Confluence*, 111, 114; Gitlin, *Bourgeois Frontier*, 61.

6. Smith, *Magnificent Missourian*, 81 (quotation); Hyde, *Empires, Nations, and Families*, 257; Gitlin, *Bourgeois Frontier*, 67–73, 48 (quotation).

7. Smith, *Magnificent Missourian*, 59–64. "Indian money . . . treaty . . . lands and lastly their skins . . . must be our motto," wrote a fur trader quoted in Gitlin, *Bourgeois Frontier*, 67.

8. Register of the Debates in Congress (24 Cong., 2nd sess., 1836–1837), vol. 2, 748; Smith, *Magnificent Missourian*, 88–89.

9. Register of the Debates in Congress (21 Cong., 1st sess., 1829–1830), vol. 6, 24; Smith, *Magnificent Missourian*, 109; Samuel J. Watson, *Peacekeepers and Conquerors: The Army Officer Corps on the American Frontier, 1821–1846* (Lawrence: University of Kansas Press, 2013), 80, 122.

10. Smith, *Magnificent Missourian*, 93–94.

11. "Selections from Editorial Articles from the *St. Louis Enquirer* on Oregon and Texas, as Originally Published in That Paper, 1818–1819," Missouri Historical Society, quoted in Smith, *Magnificent Missourian*, 691; Takaki, *Iron Cages*, 155–156.

12. Quoted in Smith, *Magnificent Missourian*, 253.

13. Quoted in Smith, *Magnificent Missourian*, 253; Tom Chaffin, *Pathfinder: John Charles Frémont and the Course of American Empire* (Norman: University of Oklahoma Press, 2002).

14. Thomas Hart Benton, "To the Railroad Convention," October 16, 1849, in *The Senate, 1789–1989: Classic Speeches, 1830–1893*, ed. Robert C. Byrd (Washington, DC: US Government Printing Office, 1994), 219; Smith, *Magnificent Missourian*, 253; Theodore Roosevelt, *Life of Thomas Hart Benton* (Cambridge, MA: Riverside Press, 1886).

15. Benton, "To the Railroad Convention," 219; Smith, *Magnificent Missourian*, 255–256.

16. Aron, *American Confluence*, 209–210; Hyde, *Empires, Nations, and Families*, 284.

17. Francis Paul Prucha, *The Sword of the Republic: The United States Army on the Frontier, 1783–1846* (Lincoln: University of Nebraska Press, 1969), 75–77, 136–137, 324–353; Marc E. Kollbaum, *Gateway to the West: The History of Jefferson Barracks from 1826–1894*, vol. 1 (St. Louis: Friends of Jefferson Barracks, n.d.), 11.

18. Hyde, *Empires, Nations, and Families*, 235; Marc E. Kollbaum, *They Served at Jefferson Barracks: The Generals of the Civil War Who—at Some Point in Their Careers—Served at Jefferson Barracks* (St. Louis: Friends of Jefferson Barracks, n.d.), 59–62, 96; see also Kollbaum, *Gateway to the West*, 24–104.

19. Kollbaum, *Gateway to the West*, 161.

20. Watson, *Peacekeepers and Conquerors*, 52–54; Louis Gerteis, *Civil War St. Louis* (Lawrence: University Press of Kansas, 2001), 46.

21. Patrick J. Jung, *The Black Hawk War of 1832* (Norman: University of Oklahoma Press, 2007), 18–20.

22. Jung, *The Black Hawk War of 1832*, 20; Black Hawk, *Life of Black Hawk, of Mà-ka-tai-me-she-kià-kiàk, Dictated by Himself*, ed. Gerald Kennedy (1833; reprint, New York: Penguin Classics, 2008), 19.

23. Jones, *William Clark and the Shaping of the West*, 227.

24. Black Hawk, *Life of Black Hawk*, 53–55.

25. Black Hawk, *Life of Black Hawk*, 57.

26. Black Hawk, *Life of Black Hawk*, 56–59; Adam John Waterman, "The Corpse in the Kitchen: Black Hawk and the Poetics of Extraction" (forthcoming), manuscript chapter in author's possession.

27. Black Hawk, *Life of Black Hawk*, 60; Jung, *The Black Hawk War of 1832*, 49, 75–76.

28. Watson, *Peacekeepers and Conquerors*, 7.

29. Prucha, *The Sword of the Republic*, 27, 216 (quotation); Watson, *Peacekeepers and Conquerors*, 10.

30. Black Hawk, *Life of Black Hawk*, 74–75; see also Jung, *The Black Hawk War of 1832*, 88.

31. Jung, *The Black Hawk War of 1832*, 75, 77–78, 89.

32. Black Hawk, *Life of Black Hawk*, 78; Jung, *The Black Hawk War of 1832*, 90.

33. Jung, *The Black Hawk War of 1832*, 100, 119; quoted in Buckley, *William Clark*, 209.

34. Black Hawk, *Life of Black Hawk*, 79–82; Jung, *The Black Hawk War of 1832*, 150.

35. Black Hawk, *Life of Black Hawk*, 84.

36. Black Hawk, *Life of Black Hawk*, 85–86.

37. Black Hawk, *Life of Black Hawk*, 87.

38. Adam John Waterman, "The Anatomy of a Haunting: Black Hawk's Body and the Fabric of History," in *Phantom Pasts, Indigenous Presence: Native Ghosts in North American Culture and History*, ed. Colleen E. Boyd and Coll Thrush (Lincoln: University of Nebraska Press, 2011); George Catlin, *Letters and Notes on the Customs and Manners of the North American Indians*, vol. 2 (New York: Wiley and Putnam, 1842), 211.

39. Catlin, *Letters and Notes*, 211; Benita Eisler, *The Red Man's Bones: George Catlin, Artist and Showman* (New York: W. W. Norton and Co., 2013), 154–158. Catlin was allowed to set up a studio in the hospital at Jefferson Barracks and was given access to Black Hawk and several other captured Indians for "as long as he needed them to pose" (Eisler, *The Red Man's Bones*, 155).

40. *Missouri Republican*, February 28, 1825; Prucha, *The Sword of the Republic*, 234–235, 234; Pekka Hämäläinen, *The Comanche Empire* (New Haven, CT: Yale University Press, 2008).

41. Report of Secretary of War Eaton, Macomb to Eaton, January 4, 1830, in *American State Papers: Military Affairs*, vol. 4, 219; Jesup to A. H. Sevier, April 5, 1830, in *American State Papers: Military Affairs*, vol. 4, 371; Watson, *Peacekeepers and Conquerors*, 20–22; Prucha, *The Sword of the Republic*, 239.

42. Kollbaum, *They Served at Jefferson Barracks*, 47–51.

43. George Rollie Adams, *General William S. Harney: Prince of Dragoons* (Lincoln: University of Nebraska Press, 2001), 12–16.

44. Adams, *General William S. Harney*, 36, 37, 40–42.

45. Adams, *General William S. Harney*, 47–48, 51, 53.

46. Harney to Taylor, August 15, 1839, Office of the Adjutant General: Letters Received, M567, roll 189, quoted in Adams, *General William S. Harney*, 71–73.

47. *St. Augustine News*, January 1, 1841; Adams, *General William S. Harney*, 76–77; Cameron Strang, "Violence, Ethnicity, and Human Remains During the Second Seminole War," *Journal of American History* 100, no. 4 (March 2014): 973–994; Kenneth W. Porter, *The Black Seminoles: History of a Freedom-Seeking People* (Gainesville: University Press of Florida), 1996.

48. Adams, *General William S. Harney*, 80–85, 102–103.

49. Adams, *General William S. Harney*, 120–121, 131.

50. Adams, *General William S. Harney*, 131–133.

CHAPTER 3: NO RIGHTS THE WHITE MAN IS BOUND TO RESPECT

1. Abraham Lincoln, "Address by Abraham Lincoln Before the Young Men's Lyceum of Springfield, Illinois, as It Appeared in the *Sangamo Journal*, February 3, 1838," reprinted in *The Collected Works of Abraham Lincoln*, 8 vols., ed. Roy P. Basler (New Brunswick, NJ: Rutgers University Press, 1953), vol. 1, 108.

2. Theodore Dwight Weld, *American Slavery as It Is: Testimony of a Thousand Witnesses* (American Anti-Slavery Society, 1839), 157; Elijah P. Lovejoy, "Awful Murder and Savage Barbarity," *St. Louis Observer*, May 5, 1836; Lincoln, "Address by Abraham Lincoln Before the Young Men's Lyceum," 1:108–115; Gerteis, *Civil War St. Louis*, 8.

3. Gerteis, *Civil War St. Louis*, 8–9, 13, 31; Weld, *American Slavery as It Is*, 157.

4. John Quincy Adams quoted in introduction to Owen and Joseph C. Lovejoy, *Memoir of the Reverend Elijah P. Lovejoy* (New York: John S. Taylor, 1838), 12; Gerteis, *Civil War St. Louis*, 8–9, 31.

5. Lincoln, "Address by Abraham Lincoln Before the Young Men's Lyceum."

6. Weld, *American Slavery as It Is*, 157; Lea VanderVelde, *Mrs. Dred Scott: A Life on Slavery's Frontier* (New York: Oxford University Press, 2009), 132.

7. Richard Wade, *Slavery in the Cities: The South, 1820–1860* (New York: Oxford University Press, 1964), 15 (quotation), 16.

8. Quoted in Gerteis, *Civil War St. Louis*, 14 (emphasis in original).

9. Thomas Jefferson to John Holmes, April 22, 1820, in *Memoirs, Correspondence, and Private Papers of Thomas Jefferson*, vol. 4, ed. Thomas Jefferson Randolph (London: Shackell and Baylis, 1829), 323–333.

10. *Congressional Globe*, 15th Cong., 2nd sess., 1213 (1818).

11. *Philadelphia Register and National Recorder*, vol. 1 (Philadelphia: Little & Henry, 1819), 279.

12. Robert Pierce Forbes, *The Missouri Compromise and Its Aftermath: Slavery and the Meaning of America* (Chapel Hill: University of North Carolina Press, 2009), 40; Thomas Jefferson to John Holmes, April 22, 1820, in Randolph, *Memoirs, Correspondence, and Private Papers of Thomas Jefferson*, 323–333; *Annals of Congress*, US House of Representatives, 15th Cong., 2nd sess., 1204–1206. My framing of the historical meaning of the controversy owes much to Forbes's excellent book. See also Adam Rothman, *Slavery Country: American Expansion and the Origins of the Deep South* (Cambridge, MA: Harvard University Press, 2007); and Laura Ford Savarese, "Slavery's Battleground: Contesting the Status of Enslaved and Free Blacks in St. Louis Freedom Suits, from Statehood to the Civil War" (undergraduate thesis, Harvard University, 2013).

13. Everett S. Brown, ed., "Documents: The Senate Debate on the Breckinridge Bill for the Government of Louisiana, 1804," *American Historical Review* 22, no. 2 (January 1917): 354.

14. Forbes, *The Missouri Compromise and Its Aftermath*, 207, 99.

15. Missouri Constitution of 1820, article 3, sections 26–28. The same convention narrowly defeated a provision directing the state legislature to require any emancipated slave to "depart from the state and give security that he will never thereafter return thereto." See Donnie D. Bellamy, "Free Blacks in Antebellum Missouri, 1820–1860," *Missouri Historical Review* 67, no. 2 (1973): 198–199.

16. Cyprian Clamorgan, *The Colored Aristocracy of St. Louis* (St. Louis, 1858), 27; Aron, *American Confluence*; see also Aziz Rana, *The Two Faces of American Freedom* (Cambridge, MA: Harvard University Press, 2014), 2–175.

17. Harrison Traxler, *Slavery in Missouri, 1804–1865* (Baltimore: Johns Hopkins University Press, 1914), 226; Wade, *Slavery in the Cities*, 20; see W.E.B. Du Bois, *Black Reconstruction in America* (New York: Free Press, 1992), 19.

18. Missouri Constitution of 1820, article 3, sections 4, 6; Saxton, *The Rise and Fall of the White Republic*, 127–161; Du Bois, *Black Reconstruction in America*, 28.

19. Forbes, *The Missouri Compromise and Its Aftermath*, 110.

20. Forbes, *The Missouri Compromise and Its Aftermath*, 110.

21. "The Revised Statutes of the State of Missouri," vol. 2 (1856), 1101; Bellamy, "Free Blacks in Antebellum Missouri," 205; Elizabeth Lawson, *The Gentleman from Mississippi: Our First Negro Senator*, introduction by William L. Patterson (New York: Elizabeth Patterson, 1960), 9.

22. Clamorgan, *The Colored Aristocracy of St. Louis*, 32, 39, 32, 38, 42, 29, 36. For the history of Black barbers and barbershops, see Quincy T. Mills, *Cutting Along the Color Line: Black Barbers and Barber Shops in America* (Philadelphia: University of Pennsylvania Press, 2013).

23. James Thomas, *From Tennessee Slave to St. Louis Entrepreneur: The Autobiography of James Thomas*, ed. Loren Schweniger (Columbia: University of Missouri Press, 1984).

24. Thomas, *From Tennessee Slave to St. Louis Entrepreneur*, 74.

25. Thomas, *From Tennessee Slave to St. Louis Entrepreneur*, 73, 199, 143; see also 90.

26. Thomas, *From Tennessee Slave to St. Louis Entrepreneur*, 89–90, 87, 71, 158.

27. Thomas, *From Tennessee Slave to St. Louis Entrepreneur*, 115, 90, 87, 93.

28. Clamorgan, *The Colored Aristocracy of St. Louis*, 27.

29. Bellamy, "Free Blacks in Antebellum Missouri," 198–205.

30. Thomas, *From Tennessee Slave to St. Louis Entrepreneur*, 155, 158, 81; VanderVelde, *Mrs. Dred Scott*, 180.

31. William Wells Brown, *Narrative of William W. Brown, a Fugitive Slave* (Anti-Slavery Office, 1847), 27; Elizabeth Keckley, *Behind the Scenes, or, Thirty Years a Slave and Four Years in the White House* (G. W. Carleton & Co., 1868); Lucy A. Delaney, *From the Darkness Cometh the Light, or, Struggles for Freedom* (St. Louis: J. T. Smith Publishing House, [189–?]).

32. A. B. Chambers, *Trials and Confessions of Madison Henderson, Alias Blanchard, Alfred Amos Warrick, James W. Seward, and Charles Brown* (St. Louis: Chambers and Knapp, 1841), 34, 63, 75–76.

33. Chambers, *Trials and Confessions of Madison Henderson*, 13, 14. For the "Madison Henderson Gang" and the unruly world of enslaved and free people of color on the Mississippi River, see Thomas C. Buchanan's excellent *Black Life on the Mississippi: Slaves, Free Blacks, and the Western Steamboat World* (Chapel Hill: University of North Carolina Press, 2007); see also Walter Johnson, *Soul by Soul: Life Inside the Antebellum Slave Market* (Cambridge, MA: Harvard University Press, 1999).

34. Chambers, *Trials and Confessions of Madison Henderson*, 14–18, 23; Darrel Dexter, *Bondage in Egypt: Slavery in Southern Illinois* (Cape Girardeau: Center for Regional History, Southeast Missouri State University, 2011), 336–368. Dexter's book is a little-known gem treating a mostly forgotten and utterly fascinating corner of the history of slavery. See also John Brown, *Slave Life in Georgia: A Narrative of the Life, Sufferings, and Escape of John Brown, a Fugitive Slave*, ed. F. N. Boney (Savannah: Library of Georgia, 1991), 43–45; Walter Johnson, *River of*

Dark Dreams: Slavery and Empire in the Cotton Kingdom (Cambridge, MA: Belknap Press of Harvard University Press, 2013), 61–67.

35. Chambers, *Trials and Confessions of Madison Henderson*, 24–27, 29, 64–68, 70–72.

36. Dexter, *Bondage in Egypt*, 241–368.

37. Chambers, *Trials and Confessions of Madison Henderson*, 72–74, 42–43, 75.

38. Chambers, *Trials and Confessions of Madison Henderson*, 62.

39. Chambers, *Trials and Confessions of Madison Henderson*, 34, 62.

40. Chambers, *Trials and Confessions of Madison Henderson*, 34, 75–76.

41. Chambers, *Trials and Confessions of Madison Henderson*, 76, 46, 2, 35, 4, 76.

42. *Frank Leslie's Illustrated Newspaper*, June 27, 1857.

43. Lea VanderVelde, *Redemption Songs: Suing for Freedom Before Dred Scott* (New York: Oxford University Press, 2014), x, 128.

44. VanderVelde, *Redemption Songs*, 57–65, 61 (quotation).

45. VanderVelde, *Redemption Songs*, x, 128.

46. VanderVelde, *Mrs. Dred Scott.*

47. Scott v. Emerson, 15 Mo. 576, 583 (Mo. 1852); Gerteis, *Civil War St. Louis*, 27.

48. Dred Scott v. Sandford, 60 U.S. (19 How.) 393 (1857).

49. Thomas, *From Tennessee Slave to St. Louis Entrepreneur*, 93. For "grace," see Julie Jeanette Miller, "A History of the Person in America Before the Civil War" (PhD diss., Harvard University, 2017).

CHAPTER 4: EMPIRE AND THE LIMITS OF REVOLUTION

1. Arenson, *The Great Heart of the Republic.*

2. Benjamin Madley, *American Genocide: The United States and the California Indian Catastrophe* (New Haven, CT: Yale University Press, 2017), 45–47, 49–50; Chaffin, *Pathfinder*, 310–311.

3. The classic account is Eric Foner, *Free Soil, Free Labor, Free Man: The Ideology of the Republican Party Before the Civil War* (New York: Oxford University Press, 1995).

4. Galusha Anderson, *The Story of a Border City During the Civil War* (Boston: Little, Brown and Co., 1908), 72–74; Gerteis, *Civil War St. Louis*, 78, 80.

5. Gerteis, *Civil War St. Louis*, 79.

6. William Vocke, "Our German Soldiers, Paper Read Before the Commandery of the State of Illinois, Military Order of the Loyal Legion, April 9, 1896," in *Military Essays and Recollections* (Chicago, 1899), vol. 3, 340–371, quoted in Karl Obermann, *Joseph Weydemeyer: Pioneer of American Socialism* (New York: International Publishers, 1947), 118.

7. Adams, *General William S. Harney*, 220.

8. Adams, *General William S. Harney*, 221–227; Gerteis, *Civil War St. Louis*, 95–96.

9. Anderson, *The Story of a Border City*, 89–92; Gerteis, *Civil War St. Louis*, 98–100; Henry Boernstein, *Memoirs of a Nobody: The Missouri Years of an Austrian Radical, 1849–1866*, trans. Steven Rowan (St. Louis: Missouri Historical Society Press, 1997), 294.

10. Boernstein, *Memoirs of a Nobody*, 296; Anderson, *The Story of a Border City*, 84; Gerteis, *Civil War St. Louis*, 101–104.

11. James Neal Primm, "Missouri, St. Louis, and the Secession Crisis," in *Germans for a Free Missouri: Translations from the St. Louis Radical Press, 1857–1862*, ed. Stephen Rowan and James Neal Primm (Columbia: University of Missouri Press, 1983), 4; Gerteis, *Civil War St. Louis*, 43.

12. Andrew Zimmerman, "From the Rhine to the Mississippi: Property, Democracy, and Socialism in the American Civil War," *Journal of the Civil War Era* 5, no. 1 (March 2015): 7–10. On 1848 in Europe, see Eric Hobsbawm, *The Age of Revolution, 1789–1848* (1962; New York: Vintage, 1996); Jonathan Sperber, *Rhineland Radicals: The Democratic Movement and the Revolution of 1848–1849* (Princeton, NJ: Princeton University Press, 1991); Jonathan Sperber, *The European Revolutions, 1848–1851* (Cambridge: Cambridge University Press, 1995). On the postwar migration from Europe, including to the United States, although not St. Louis, see Helena Toth, *An Exiled Generation: German and Hungarian Refugees of Revolution, 1848–1871* (Cambridge: Cambridge University Press, 2014).

13. Boernstein, *Memoirs of a Nobody*, 203–210.

14. Frank Blair, "The Destiny of the Races of This Continent: An Address Delivered Before the Mercantile Library Association of Boston Massachusetts on the 26th of January, 1859" (Washington, DC: Buell & Richard, 1859), 4, 22, 7, 8, 16–18.

15. Blair, "The Destiny of the Races of This Continent," 23, 19. On Blair, see William E. Parrish, *Frank Blair: Lincoln's Conservative* (Columbia: University of Missouri Press, 1998).

16. "Speech of the Hon. B. Gratz Brown, of St. Louis, on the Subject of Gradual Emancipation in Missouri: Delivered in the House of Representatives, February 12, 1857," 5, 25.

17. Arenson, *The Great Heart of the Republic*, 65–66, 67, 71–79.

18. Arenson, *The Great Heart of the Republic*, 67–70, 80.

19. "Speech of the Hon. B. Gratz Brown," 5, 25.

20. Zimmerman, "From the Rhine to the Mississippi," 12, 13. See also Stephen D. Engle, *The Yankee Dutchman: The Life of Franz Sigel* (Fayetteville: University of Arkansas Press, 1993); "The Rising of the People [*Volksturm*]," *Westliche Post*, May 8, 1861, in Rowan and Primm, *Germans for a Free Missouri*, 202–203; Franz Sigel, untitled document, Saturday, March 28 [no year], "Gegen Heinzen

und Marx—Gegen Kinkel: Andere Aphorismen: Aphorismen: März 1852," unpaginated, translation by Alison Frank Johnson, Franz Sigel Papers, folder 10, Missouri History Museum Library and Research Center.

21. Sigel, "Gegen Heinzen und Marx."

22. Zimmerman, "From the Rhine to the Mississippi," 11, 13; see also Engle, *The Yankee Dutchman.*

23. Daniel Hertle, *Die Deutschen in Nordamerika und der Freiheitskampf in Missouri* (Chicago: Staatszeitung, 1865), 59–60.

24. Kristen Layne Anderson, *Abolitionizing Missouri: German Immigrants and Racial Ideology in Nineteenth-Century America* (Baton Rouge: Louisiana State University Press, 2016), 43–79.

25. *Daily Alta California*, May 28, 1850, 2, quoted in Madley, *American Genocide*, 128–130, 130 (quotation).

26. As we reflect on the politics of memorialization, on the question of which history of the Civil War will be commemorated in the public squares and parks of the United States, we would do well to remember that many of the men who fought to free the slaves, even the most passionately radical among them, had been Indian killers before the war—and would be again in its aftermath.

27. Anderson, *The Story of a Border City*, 100–101; Gerteis, *Civil War St. Louis*, 101, 103.

28. Gerteis, *Civil War St. Louis*, 99, 104–105, 108–110.

29. Boernstein, *Memoirs of a Nobody*, 297–298, 309–311; "Important from St. Louis; Capture of Secessionists at Camp Jackson. Trouble Between the Mob and the United States Troops," *New York Times*, May 12, 1861; Gerteis, *Civil War St. Louis*, 109–111; Adams, *General William S. Harney*, 230.

30. Anderson, *The Story of a Border City*, 106–115; "Important from St. Louis," *New York Times*, May 12, 1861.

31. Boernstein, *Memoirs of a Nobody*, 300–303; Heinrich Börnstein, *Fünfundsiebzig Jahre in der Alten und Neuen Welt: Memoiren eines Unbedeutenden*, vol. 2 (Leipzig: Otto Wigand, 1881), 289–290.

32. Boernstein, *Memoirs of a Nobody*, 304.

33. Adams, *General William S. Harney*, 233–238.

34. Boernstein, *Memoirs of a Nobody*, 312, 315; Gerteis, *Civil War St. Louis*, 120, 123–124.

35. "Die Flüchtigen Rebellen-Sklaven," *Westliche Post*, June 19, 1861, quoted in Zimmerman, "From the Rhine to the Mississippi," 18.

36. Boernstein, *Memoirs of a Nobody*, 322, 324; *Anzeiger des Westens*, June 20, 1861, quoted in Rowan and Primm, *Germans for a Free Missouri*, 265–266.

37. Zimmerman, "From the Rhine to the Mississippi," 22–23.

38. Du Bois, *Black Reconstruction in America*, 55.

39. *Anzeiger des Westens*, August 28, 1861, in Rowan and Primm, *Germans for a Free Missouri*, 279.

40. Philip S. Foner and David R. Roediger, "Die Achtstundenbewegung: Artikel Joseph Weydemeyers in der 'Westlichen Post' (St. Louis)," *Marx-Engels-Jahrbuch* 7 (1984): 321; Angela Y. Davis, *Women, Race, and Class*, 2nd ed. (New York: Vintage Books, 1983), 149; Obermann, *Joseph Weydemeyer*, 7–19, 74, 92, 106.

41. David R. Roediger, *Joseph Weydemeyer: Articles on the Eight Hour Movement* (Chicago: Greenleaf Press, 1978), 1; Obermann, *Joseph Weydemeyer*, 84, 89–94, 118–119.

42. *Anzeiger des Westens*, September 4 and 18, 1861, in Rowan and Primm, *Germans for a Free Missouri*, 284–285; Chaffin, *Pathfinder*, 460; Gerteis, *Civil War St. Louis*, 146, 154; Anderson, *The Story of a Border City*, 204–206.

43. "Proclamation by the Commander of the Western Department," St. Louis, August 30, 1861, in "Die Flüchtigen Rebellen-Sklaven," *Westliche Post*, June 19, 1861, quoted in Zimmerman, "From the Rhine to the Mississippi," 18, 416n (Lincoln's response).

44. *Anzeiger des Westens*, November 13, 1861, in Rowan and Primm, *Germans for a Free Missouri*, 290; Gerteis, *Civil War St. Louis*, 153–156; Chaffin, *Pathfinder*, 467 (quotation); Gerteis, *Civil War St. Louis*, 151 (quotation, emphasis in original). For the conventional wisdom about Frémont, see Gerteis, *Civil War St. Louis*. For an account that positively emphasizes the revolutionary potential of Frémont's actions (and those of his subordinates), see Zimmerman, "From the Rhine to the Mississippi," 22–23.

45. *Anzeiger des Westens*, December 4, 1861, in Rowan and Primm, *Germans for a Free Missouri*, 291.

46. John F. Marszalek, *Commander of All Lincoln's Armies: A Life of General Henry W. Halleck* (Cambridge, MA: Belknap Press of Harvard University Press, 2004), 4–66; Madley, *American Genocide*, 128–130; "Miscellaneous Documents of the House of Representatives for the 2nd Session of the 52nd Congress" (Washington, DC: US Government Printing Office, 1893), series 1, vol. 3, 93–94; H. W. Halleck, Lieutenant of Engineers and Secretary of State for California, "Circular to Indian Agents and Others," in *California Star*, September 18, 1847, quoted in Madley, *American Genocide*, 148.

47. Ira Berlin, Barbara J. Fields, Thavolia Glymph, Joseph P. Reidy, and Leslie S. Rowland, eds., *Freedom: A Documentary History of Emancipation, 1861–1867*, series 1, vol. 1, 399, 401; "Commander of a Brigade in the Army of the West to the Headquarters of the Western Department," Boonville, MO, October 6, 1861; "Order by the Commander of the Department of the Missouri," St. Louis, MO, November 20, 1860; "Missouri Former Soldier to the Secretary of War," Rolla, MO, December 1, 1861; "Circular by the Commander of the 4th Division of the Department of Missouri," Rolla, MO, December 18, 1861; "Commander of the Frémont Hussars to the Commander of the 4th Division of the Department of Missouri," December 19, 1861; "Commander of the Department of Missouri to the Commander of the 4th Division of the Department," St. Louis, MO,

December 26, 1861; all in Berlin et al., *Freedom*, 416, 417, 420, 421–422, 423, passim; Sharon Romeo, *Gender and Jubilee: Black Freedom and the Reconstruction of Citizenship in Civil War Missouri* (Athens: University of Georgia Press, 2016), 39–56; *Anzeiger des Westens*, December 4, 1861, in Rowan and Primm, *Germans for a Free Missouri*, 291; Zimmerman, "From the Rhine to the Mississippi," 3, 21.

48. Kristen Layne Anderson, *Abolitionizing Missouri: German Immigrants and Racial Ideology in Nineteenth-Century America* (Baton Rouge: Louisiana State University Press, 2016), 112, 131–132, 137–140.

CHAPTER 5: BLACK RECONSTRUCTION AND THE COUNTERREVOLUTION OF PROPERTY

1. The reading of the "counterrevolution of property" as imperial and Western that follows is deeply indebted to Karuka, *Empire's Tracks*, and Lowe, *The Intimacies of Four Continents*, 170–171.

2. Mark E. Neely, *The Fate of Liberty: Abraham Lincoln and Civil Liberties* (New York: Oxford University Press, 1991), 34; Anderson, *The Story of a Border City*, 214–216, 192, 234–237.

3. Neely, *The Fate of Liberty*, 34; Anderson, *The Story of a Border City*, 234–237, 245.

4. Anderson, *The Story of a Border City*, 251, 262–263, 263–267. For slaveholders locking up enslaved people's shoes and coats during the night, see Berlin et al., *Freedom*, 410; Romeo, *Gender and Jubilee*, 33; Anderson, *Abolitionizing Missouri*, 144.

5. Romeo, *Gender and Jubilee*, 80–84.

6. US Department of War, *The War of the Rebellion: A Compilation of the Official Records of the Union and Confederate Armies*, series 2, vol. 4 (Washington, DC, 1880–1901), 72–73, 94–95, 171, 260, 295–298; J. G. Forman, *The Western Sanitary Commission: A Sketch* . . . (St. Louis, MO: R. P. Studley & Co., 1864), 134; Gerteis, *Civil War St. Louis*, 282; Berlin et al., *Freedom*, 410; Romeo, *Gender and Jubilee*, 34–36, 73–93; William Wells Brown, *The Negro in the American Rebellion: His Heroism and His Fidelity* (Boston: Lee and Shepherd, 1867), 157 (with thanks to Johari Jabir, who alerted me to the existence of "Give Us a Flag"). See also Mycah Lynn Conner, "'On This Bare Ground': The Ordeal and the Aftermath of 'Contraband Camps' and the Making of Emancipation in the Civil War West" (PhD diss., Harvard University, forthcoming).

7. US Department of War, *The War of the Rebellion*, 72–73; Gerteis, *Civil War St. Louis*, 224–225, 231; US Department of War, *The War of the Rebellion*, 295–298. "No traitor is too good to be killed by a Negro, nor has any traitor a right to insist on being killed by a white man," said Missouri Republican Charles Drake at the time. Gerteis, *Civil War St. Louis*, 282.

8. Anderson, *Abolitionizing Missouri*, 150–151.

9. Anderson, *Abolitionizing Missouri*, 153.

10. Anderson, *Abolitionizing Missouri*, 155; Gary R. Kremer, *James Milton Turner and the Promise of America: The Public Life of a Post–Civil War Black Leader* (Columbia: University of Missouri Press, 1991), 13–18; John Kaag, "America's Hands-On Hegelian," *Chronicle Review*, March 20, 2016; Anderson, *Abolitionizing Missouri*, 158; Liat Spiro, "Drawing Capital: Depiction, Machine Tools, and the Political Economy of Industrial Knowledge, 1824–1914" (PhD diss., Harvard University, 2019), chap. 4; Laura Leigh Schmidt, "Subject-Object Lessons: Social Science in the St. Louis Style, 1866–1917" (PhD diss., Harvard University, 2018).

11. Kremer, *James Milton Turner*, 19–24; Du Bois, *Black Reconstruction in America*, 667.

12. Anderson, *The Story of a Border City*, 251, 253–255, 261.

13. Joseph Weydemeyer, "The Eight Hour Movement," *Saint Louis Daily Press*, August 8, 1866 (*Westliche Post*, July 16, 1866), in Roediger, *Joseph Weydemeyer*, 5.

14. Joseph Weydemeyer, "The Eight Hour Movement—IV," *Saint Louis Daily Press*, August 19, 1866 (*Westliche Post*, July 24, 1866), in Roediger, *Joseph Weydemeyer*, 19; Anderson, *Abolitionizing Missouri*, 154.

15. Missouri State Constitution of 1865, article II, section 18 (Jefferson City: E. S. Forester, Printer, 1865).

16. Missouri State Constitution of 1865, article II, sections 3–14, 23, 24; Gerteis, *Civil War St. Louis*, 330–332.

17. Gerteis, *Civil War St. Louis*, 322; Hans L. Trefousse, *Carl Schurz: A Biography* (New York: Fordham University Press, 1998), 15–38, 126–175.

18. Trefousse, *Carl Schurz*, 15–38, 126–175; Anderson, *Abolitionizing Missouri*, 135–137, 181–192.

19. Parrish, *Frank Blair*, 254–256; Stewart Mitchell, *Horatio Seymour of New York* (Cambridge, MA: Harvard University Press, 1938), 23.

20. Eric Foner, *Reconstruction: America's Unfinished Revolution, 1863–1877* (New York: Harper Perennial, 1989), 546–586.

21. Philip S. Foner, *The Great Labor Uprising of 1877* (New York: Pathfinder, 1977), 43–210.

22. Foner, *The Great Labor Uprising of 1877*, 216, 217–222.

23. Foner, *The Great Labor Uprising of 1877*, 224, 228; Anderson, *Abolitionizing Missouri*, 163–164.

24. Madley, *American Genocide*, 22; Singh, *Race and America's Long War*.

25. Foner, *The Great Labor Uprising of 1877*, 233, 235, 238.

26. Foner, *The Great Labor Uprising of 1877*, 211, 238–239, 242.

27. Foner, *The Great Labor Uprising of 1877*, 244, 245.

28. Foner, *The Great Labor Uprising of 1877*, 214–215, 222, 229, 248, 249, 252, 266, 290.

29. *St. Louis Evening Post*, October 9, 1878, 5, quoted in Thomas M. Spencer, *The St. Louis Veiled Prophet Celebration, 1877–1995* (Columbia: University of Missouri Press, 2000), 19. Spencer notes that the newspapers differed about the outfit worn by the prophet; my account is based on the woodcut that ran in the *St. Louis Republican* on October 6, 1878.

30. Primm, *Lion of the Valley*, 299–306.

31. Du Bois, *Black Reconstruction in America*, 148–149; James D. Richardson, *The Messages and Papers of the President, 1789–1897* (New York: Bureau of National Literature, 1902), 127; *Complete Works of Abraham Lincoln*, vol. 8, 97.

32. Roxanne Dunbar-Ortiz, *An Indigenous People's History of the United States* (Boston: Beacon Press, 2014), 140–142.

33. Estes, *Our History Is the Future*, 101–102; Heidi Kiiwetinepinesiik Stark, "Criminal Empire: The Making of the Savage in a Lawless Land," *Theory and Event* 19, no. 4 (2016).

34. Dunbar-Ortiz, *An Indigenous People's History of the United States*, 137–138; Estes, *Our History Is the Future*, 101–102, 105; Ari Kelman, *A Misplaced Massacre: Struggling over the Memory of Sand Creek* (Cambridge, MA: Harvard University Press, 2015); Mark Grimsley, "'Rebels' and 'Redskins': US Military Conduct Toward White Southerners and Native Americans in Comparative Perspective," in *Civilians in the Path of War*, ed. Mark Grimsley and Clifford J. Rogers (Lincoln: University of Nebraska Press, 2002); Elliot West, "Reconstructing Race," *Western Historical Quarterly* 34, no. 1 (2003); Khal Schneider, "Distinctions That Must Be Preserved: On the Civil War, American Indians, and the West," *Civil War History* 62, no. 1 (2016).

35. Estes, *Our History Is the Future*, 108–109, 169.

36. Karuka, *Empire's Tracks*, 69–79; Meghan Black, *The Global Interior: Mineral Frontiers and American Power* (Cambridge, MA: Harvard University Press, 2018), 26–29; Dunbar-Ortiz, *An Indigenous People's History of the United States*, 9–10.

37. White, *The Republic for Which It Stands*; Karuka, *Empire's Tracks*; Richard White, *Railroaded: The Transcontinentals and the Making of Modern America* (New York: W. W. Norton and Co., 2012).

38. Quintard Taylor, *In Search of the Racial Frontier: African Americans in the American West, 1528–1990* (New York: W. W. Norton & Co., 1999), 85, 154, 165–191; Lowe, *The Intimacies of Four Continents*, 63; see also William H. Leckie, *The Buffalo Soldiers: A Narrative of the Negro Cavalry in the West* (New York: Bantam Doubleday Dell, 1967); and David Krueger, "To Hold What the US Has Taken in Conquest: The United States Army and Colonial Ethnic Forces, 1866–1914" (PhD diss., Harvard University, 2020).

39. Black, *The Global Interior*, 16–28; Hans Trefousse, "Carl Schurz and the Indians," *Great Plains Quarterly* 4, no. 2 (1984): 115.

40. Nick Estes, "On William Henry Pratt," *High Country News* 5, no. 17 (October 14, 2019).

41. Trefousse, "Carl Schurz and the Indians," 116. See, generally, Frederick E. Hoxie, *A Final Promise: The Campaign to Assimilate the Indians, 1880–1920* (Lincoln: University of Nebraska Press, 1984); Dunbar-Ortiz, *An Indigenous People's History of the United States*, 139, 149, 157–161.

42. L. U. Reavis, *Saint Louis: The Future Great City of the World* (St. Louis: Gray, Baker & Company, 1870), 6; Primm, *Lion of the Valley*, 274–275, 289.

43. Primm, *Lion of the Valley*, 274–275; Arenson, *The Great Heart of the Republic*, 178–198, 184 (quotations).

44. Manu Karuka, "Remembering the Golden Spike Ceremony," *Boston Review*, May 10, 2019.

45. Primm, *Lion of the Valley*, 286–290.

46. Primm, *Lion of the Valley*, 292, 294; White, *Railroaded*.

47. "The Opening of the Great Southwest" (St. Louis: MKT, 1970), 10–11.

48. Berger, *St. Louis and Empire*, 46, 47–49, 52; Joshua Specht, *Red Meat Republic: A Hoof-to-Table History of How Beef Changed America* (Princeton, NJ: Princeton University Press, 2019).

49. Berger, *St. Louis and Empire*, 57.

50. Berger, *St. Louis and Empire*, 62, 90–91.

51. Berger, *St. Louis and Empire*, 66, 87, 98–109. On the revolution generally, see John Womack Jr., *Zapata and the Mexican Revolution* (New York: Vintage Books, 1968). See also Painter, *Standing at Armageddon*.

52. Berger, *St. Louis and Empire*, 71.

53. Berger, *St. Louis and Empire*, 77, 81–83; Theodore Roosevelt, *Thomas Hart Benton* (Boston: Houghton Mifflin, 1889).

54. Eric Love, *Race over Empire: Racism and US Imperialism, 1865–1900* (Chapel Hill: University of North Carolina Press, 2004), 104–105, 182–183; Berger, *St. Louis and Empire*, 76–77; see also Painter, *Standing at Armageddon*.

55. Berger, *St. Louis and Empire*, 346–347; Leo A. Landau, *The Big Cinch* (St. Louis: Franklin Co., 1910); Du Bois, *Black Reconstruction in America*, 584, 585, 634; Painter, *Standing at Armageddon*.

56. Du Bois, *Black Reconstruction in America*, 634.

57. Primm, *Lion of the Valley*, 358–359, 274 (quotation).

58. "Three Killed and Fourteen Wounded; Statement Regarding Sunday's Shooting," *St. Louis Post-Dispatch*, June 11, 1900.

59. "Three Killed and Fourteen Wounded; Statement Regarding Sunday's Shooting," *St. Louis Post-Dispatch*, June 11, 1900; "An Old Man Was Shot Dead," *St. Louis Post-Dispatch*, June 11, 1900.

60. "Inquest on Riot Victims Today," "Recruits for the Posse," "Southern Electric Cars to Run," and "Six Fined in Police Court," *St. Louis Post-Dispatch*, June 12, 1900; "Civil War Veterans to Serve on Posse," *St. Louis Post-Dispatch*, June 13, 1900.

61. Primm, *Lion of the Valley*, 264, 274, 360.

CHAPTER 6: THE BABYLON OF THE NEW WORLD

1. Primm, *Lion of the Valley*, 274, 358.

2. W. C. Handy, *Father of the Blues: An Autobiography* (New York: Macmillan, 1941), 26.

3. Theodore Dreiser, *Newspaper Days: An Autobiography*, ed. T. D. Nostwich (Santa Rosa, CA: Black Sparrow Press, 2000), 229, 231, 267–268; see also Cecil Brown, *Stagolee Shot Billy* (Cambridge, MA: Harvard University Press, 2003), 91.

4. Dreiser, *Newspaper Days*, 348–350.

5. Dreiser, *Newspaper Days*, 405, 388; see especially Kevin J. Mumford's indispensable *Interzones: Black/White Sex Districts in Chicago and New York in the Early Twentieth Century* (New York: Columbia University Press, 1997).

6. Dreiser, *Newspaper Days*, 101–103, 128, 198, 292–295, 321–324. On this and all that follows, see Gail Bederman, *Manliness and Civilization: A Cultural History of Gender and Race in the United States, 1880–1917* (Chicago: University of Chicago Press, 1996); and Matthew Frye Jacobson, *Barbarian Virtues: The United States Encounters Foreign People at Home and Abroad, 1876–1917* (New York: Hill and Wang, 2001).

7. Kate Chopin, *The Awakening* (Chicago: Herbert S. Stone & Co., 1899). On Chopin in St. Louis, see George Lipsitz, *Sidewalks of St. Louis: Places, People, and Politics in an American City* (Columbia: University of Missouri Press, 1991), 61–64. On the turn-of-the-century coverup of the fact that white women were attracted to Black men, see Ida B. Wells-Barnett, "Southern Horrors: Lynch Law in All Its Phases," *New York Age*, June 25, 1892.

8. Stephen Longstreet, ed., *Nell Kimball: Her Life as an American Madam: By Herself* (New York: Macmillan, 1970), 72–73. *Nell Kimball* is a complicated source of uncertain provenance. It is partially plagiarized and almost certainly ghostwritten (or perhaps even entirely written) by the man who claimed to be its editor. Nevertheless, the terrific amount of information it contains about St. Louis in the 1870s that can be verified from other sources suggests that it was written by or with someone with a good deal of knowledge about the city. I have thus treated it as a compilation of street stories—a gathering of many otherwise unheard voices into the voice of an autobiographical avatar.

9. Dreiser, *Newspaper Days*, 395, 413–414.

10. *St. Louis Republic*, January 18, 1894.

11. Dreiser, *Newspaper Days*, 399–400.

12. Dreiser, *Newspaper Days*, 235, 402.

13. Dreiser, *Newspaper Days*, 402. On the history of ragtime generally, see Edward A. Berlin, *King of Ragtime: Scott Joplin and His Era*, 2nd ed. (New York: Oxford University Press, 2016); Edward A. Berlin, *Ragtime: A Musical and Cul-*

NOTES TO CHAPTER 6

tural History (Berkeley: University of California Press, 1980); John Edward Hasse, *Ragtime: Its History, Composers, and Music* (New York: Schirmer Books, 1985); Mary Collins Barile and Christine Montgomery, *Merit, Not Sympathy, Wins: The Life and Times of Blind Boone* (Kirksville, MO: Truman State University Press, 2012); Thomas C. Holt, *Children of Fire: A History of African Americans* (New York: Hill & Wang, 2011), 208–210.

14. Brown, *Stagolee Shot Billy*, 1–15. There are many versions of the song, and the elements I itemize do not appear in all of them, nor do they always appear in the same guise—in some versions, for example, Billy Lyons has two children and in some versions he has three. All of this and much more can be learned from Brown's book, which is painstaking, fascinating, and indispensable.

15. Brown, *Stagolee Shot Billy*, 23–25, 37, 91. My reconstruction of Lee's outfit is based on Brown (23) and on Dreiser, *Newspaper Days*, 403–404.

16. Nathan B. Young, excerpt from *Your St. Louis and Mine*, in *"Ain't but a Place": An Anthology of African American Writings About St. Louis*, ed. Gerald Early (St. Louis: Missouri Historical Museum Press, 1998), 345–346; Berlin, *King of Ragtime*, 112; Brown, *Stagolee Shot Billy*, 65; see also Arna Bontemps, *God Sends Sunday* (New York: Harcourt Brace Jovanovich, 1931).

17. Brown, *Stagolee Shot Billy*, 75–84.

18. Allen E. Wagner, *Good Order and Safety: A History of the St. Louis Metropolitan Police Department, 1861–1906* (St. Louis: Missouri History Museum, 2008), 100–108, 301; see also Dreiser, *Newspaper Days*, 130 ("Gambling and prostitution were never so rampant as now [1893]").

19. "Report of the Committee of the General Assembly Appointed to Investigate the Police Department of the City of St. Louis" (St. Louis: Missouri Democrat Book and Job Printing House, 1868), vi–xi (series 1), viii–xi (series 2) (with thanks to Garrett Felber); Wagner, *Good Order and Safety*, 161, 212, 218.

20. Wagner, *Good Order and Safety*, xvii, 161, 212, 218, 182–183; Dreiser, *Newspaper Days*, 141–143, 233; Handy, *Father of the Blues*, 27; Longstreet, *Nell Kimball*, 31.

21. Wagner, *Good Order and Safety*, 291–292; Handy, *Father of the Blues*, 27.

22. Longstreet, *Nell Kimball*, 8; Wagner, *Good Order and Safety*, 303. On minstrel shows, see Eric Lott, *Love and Theft: Blackface Minstrelsy and the American Working Class* (New York: Oxford University Press, 1995); Rhae Lynn Barnes, *Darkology: When the American Dream Wore Blackface* (New York: W. W. Norton & Co., forthcoming). On Joplin in St. Louis, see Lipsitz, *Sidewalks of St. Louis*, 68–72.

23. Berlin, *King of Ragtime*, 8, 44–46.

24. Berlin, *King of Ragtime*, 112–113.

25. Handy, *Father of the Blues*, 26–28; Berlin, *King of Ragtime*, 10, 50, 145, 199, 253, 295, 301, 309–311, 326.

26. Elsa Barkley Brown, "Polyrhythms and Improvisation: Lessons for Women's History," *History Workshop* 31 (Spring 1991): 85–90.

27. Brown, *Stagolee Shot Billy*, 41. For an earlier example of a similar process, see Elizabeth Blackmar, *Manhattan for Rent, 1785–1850* (Ithaca, NY: Cornell University Press, 1989).

28. Lincoln Steffens, *The Shame of the Cities* (New York: McClure, Phillips, and Co., 1904), 29–62, 101–146.

29. Steffens, *The Shame of the Cities*, 213, 23, 29, 31, 34.

30. Steffens, *The Shame of the Cities*, 23.

31. Steffens, *The Shame of the Cities*, 29, 54–59.

32. Edward McPherson, *The History of the Future: American Essays* (Minneapolis: Coffee House Press, 2017), 62; William R. Everdell, *The First Moderns: Profiles in the Origins of Twentieth-Century Thought* (Chicago: University of Chicago Press, 1997), 207, 226; James Gilbert, *Whose Fair? Experience, Memory, and the History of the Great St. Louis Exposition* (Chicago: University of Chicago Press, 2009), 20.

33. McPherson, *The History of the Future*, 62; Gilbert, *Whose Fair?*, 14; Everdell, *The First Moderns*, 207.

34. McPherson, *The History of the Future*, 65; Gilbert, *Whose Fair?*, 63, 76, 138; Everdell, *The First Moderns*, 210; Lee Gaskins, "At the Fair," https://atthefair.homestead.com/1904Fair.html (accessed June 11, 2018); Robert W. Rydell, *All the World's a Fair: Visions of Empire at the American International Expositions, 1876–1916* (Chicago: University of Chicago Press, 1984), 156.

35. Everdell, *The First Moderns*, 220–225.

36. Rydell, *All the World's a Fair*, 154, 159–160.

37. Pamela Newkirk, *Spectacle: The Astonishing Life of Ota Benga* (New York: Amistad, 2015), 129; Rydell, *All the World's a Fair*, 163; Everdell, *The First Moderns*, 215; Gilbert, *Whose Fair?*, 39; see also Sadia Qureshi, *Peoples on Parade: Exhibitions, Empire, and Anthropology in Nineteenth-Century Britain* (Chicago: University of Chicago Press, 2011).

38. Newkirk, *Spectacle*, 3–17, 79–139, 236–240.

39. Walter Benjamin, "Theses on the Philosophy of History," in *Illuminations*, ed. Hannah Arendt (New York: Schocken Books, 1969), no. 7.

40. Rydell, *All the World's a Fair*, 167, 170–172; Gilbert, *Whose Fair?*, 58, 139; Paul A. Kramer, *The Blood of Government: Race, Empire, the United States, and the Philippines* (Chapel Hill: University of North Carolina Press, 2006), 230–284; Roediger and Esch, *The Production of Difference*, 123–129; Painter, *Standing at Armageddon*.

41. Rydell, *All the World's a Fair*, 171; Roediger and Esch, *The Production of Difference*, 127.

42. Roediger and Esch, *The Production of Difference*, 128; Gilbert, *Whose Fair?*, 31; Rydell, *All the World's a Fair*, 163.

43. Rydell, *All the World's a Fair*, 162.

44. Gilbert, *Whose Fair?*, 137; Nikhil Pal Singh, *Race and America's Long War* (Berkeley: University of California Press, 2017), 49; Roediger and Esch, *The Production of Difference*, 126.

45. See Dowden-White, *Groping Toward Democracy*, 27; Gilbert, *Whose Fair?*, 131–152; McPherson, *The History of the Future*, 65; Gaskins, "At the Fair," https://atthefair.homestead.com/1904Fair.html (accessed June 12, 2018); see also Brown, "Polyrhythms and Improvisation."

46. McPherson, *The History of the Future*, 76–77; Rydell, *All the World's a Fair*, 160.

47. See Matthew Frye Jacobson, *Whiteness of a Different Color: European Immigrants and the Alchemy of Race* (Cambridge, MA: Harvard University Press, 1999); Nell Irvin Painter, *The History of White People* (New York: W. W. Norton & Co., 2011); David R. Roediger, *Working Toward Whiteness: How America's Immigrants Became White: The Strange Journey from Ellis Island to the Suburbs* (New York: Basic Books, 2018); Everdell, *The First Moderns*, 208; Rydell, *All the World's a Fair*, 155, 159.

48. Rydell, *All the World's a Fair*, 172.

49. Gilbert, *Whose Fair?*, 123–152.

50. Laura Wexler, *Tender Violence: Domestic Visions in an Age of US Imperialism* (Chapel Hill: University of North Carolina Press, 2000), 262–290.

51. "Filipinos Become a Fad with Foolish Girls," *St. Louis Post-Dispatch*, July 3, 1904; "Scouts Lose First Battle with Marines," *St. Louis Post-Dispatch*, July 7, 1904; Gilbert, *Whose Fair?*, 150–151; Rydell, *All the World's a Fair*, 176–177.

CHAPTER 7: THE SHAPE OF FEAR

1. Ida B. Wells-Barnett, *The East St. Louis Massacre: The Greatest Outrage of the Century* (Chicago: Negro Fellowship Herald Press, 1917), 3.

2. Elliott M. Rudwick, *Race Riot at East St. Louis: July 2, 1917* (Edwardsville: Southern Illinois University Press, 1964); Andrew J. Theising and Debra H. Moore, *Made in USA: East St. Louis: The Rise and Fall of an Industrial River Town* (St. Louis: Virginia Publishing, 2003); Malcolm McLaughlin, *Power, Community, and Racial Killing in East St. Louis* (New York: Palgrave Macmillan, 2005); Charles L. Lumpkins, *American Pogrom: The East St. Louis Race Riot and Black Politics* (Athens: Ohio University Press, 2008).

3. Wells-Barnett, *The East St. Louis Massacre*, 4.

4. Theising and Moore, *Made in USA: East St. Louis*, 94–103.

5. Excerpt from Miles Davis, with Quincy Troupe, *Miles: The Autobiography* (New York: Simon & Schuster, 1990), in Early, *Ain't but a Place*, 213.

6. Theising and Moore, *Made in USA: East St. Louis*, 103, 111–112, 118; W.E.B. Du Bois, "Of Work and Wealth," in Du Bois, *Darkwater*, 42; McLaughlin, *Power, Community, and Racial Killing*, 31.

7. Rudwick, *Race Riot at East St. Louis*, 177–178, 187; Theising and Moore, *Made in USA: East St. Louis*, 134, 137.

8. Rudwick, *Race Riot at East St. Louis*, 193.

9. Rudwick, *Race Riot at East St. Louis*, 190, 192–193; Theising and Moore, *Made in USA: East St. Louis*, 140 (Anderson quotation).

10. McLaughlin, *Power, Community, and Racial Killing*, 197–210.

11. Rudwick, *Race Riot at East St. Louis*, 197–210; Du Bois, "Of Work and Wealth," 30; Du Bois, *Black Reconstruction in America*, 30.

12. McLaughlin, *Power, Community, and Racial Killing*, 11; see James N. Gregory, *The Southern Diaspora: How the Great Migrations of Black and White Southerners Transformed America* (Chapel Hill: University of North Carolina Press, 2005); Isabel Wilkerson, *The Warmth of Other Suns: The Epic Story of America's Great Migration* (New York: Vintage, 2011).

13. McLaughlin, *Power, Community, and Racial Killing*, 35, 15–17; see also Roediger and Esch, *The Production of Difference*.

14. McLaughlin, *Power, Community, and Racial Killing*, 38, 45; Rudwick, *Race Riot at East St. Louis*, 24.

15. McLaughlin, *Power, Community, and Racial Killing*, 45; Rudwick, *Race Riot at East St. Louis*, 24. For this strain of white supremacy, see Nicholas Guyatt, *Bind Us Apart: How Enlightened Americans Invented Racial Segregation* (New York: Basic Books, 2016); Hernández, *City of Inmates*; Ikuko Asaka, *Tropical Freedom: Climate, Settler Colonialism, and Black Exclusion in the Age of Emancipation* (Durham, NC: Duke University Press, 2017). See also W.E.B. Du Bois, "The African Roots of War," *Atlantic*, May 1915, 707–714.

16. Berger, *St. Louis and Empire*, 114–115; Theising and Moore, *Made in USA: East St. Louis*, 118; Rudolf Alexander Clemen, *The American Livestock and Meat Industry* (New York: Ronald Press Co., 1923), 473 (with special thanks to Joshua Specht).

17. Rudwick, *Race Riot at East St. Louis*, 166.

18. US House of Representatives, Select Committee to Investigate the Race Riots in East St. Louis (1917), "Statement of Ben Beard (Colored) of East St. Louis, Laborer at Aluminum Ore," vol. 2, 342, and "Statement of Earl Jimerson, Financial Secretary, Amalgamated Meat Cutters and Butcher Workmen of North America," vol. 10, 2045, 2057–2058.

19. US House of Representatives, Select Committee to Investigate the Race Riots in East St. Louis (1917), "Statement of Henry Kerr, District Organizer, AFL," vol. 9, 1869–1870, 1939; "Statement of Earl Jimerson, Financial Secretary, Amalgamated Meat Cutters and Butcher Workmen of North America," vol. 10, 2024–2025; Rudwick, *Race Riot at East St. Louis*, 13, 158–159, 161, 168–169;

McLaughlin, *Power, Community, and Racial Killing*, 47–52; Lumpkins, *American Pogrom*; Rudwick, *Race Riot at East St. Louis*, 13. On ethnic cleansing and democracy, see Michael Mann, *The Dark Side of Democracy: Explaining Ethnic Cleansing* (Cambridge: Cambridge University Press, 2004).

20. McLaughlin, *Power, Community, and Racial Killing*, 52; "Statement of Henry Kerr," vol. 9, 1869–70; Rudwick, *Race Riot at East St. Louis*, 214.

21. W.E.B. Du Bois, "The Shape of Fear," *North American Review* 223 (June 1925): 291–304. The passage reappeared, unaltered, in the sixteenth chapter of *Black Reconstruction in America* (1935), where Du Bois introduced the notion of the "wages of whiteness"; see Du Bois, *Black Reconstruction in America*, 573–574. See also Roediger, *The Wages of Whiteness*; Cheryl I. Harris, "Whiteness as Property," *Harvard Law Review* 106, no. 8 (1993); and Lipsitz, *The Possessive Investment in Whiteness*.

22. McLaughlin, *Power, Community, and Racial Killing*, 39.

23. McLaughlin, *Power, Community, and Racial Killing*, 116; Du Bois, *Black Reconstruction in America*, 25.

24. Rudwick, *Race Riot at East St. Louis*, 145, 152–153; McLaughlin, *Power, Community, and Racial Killing*, 39–40; Du Bois, "Of Work and Wealth," 46.

25. McLaughlin, *Power, Community, and Racial Killing*, 96–97.

26. McLaughlin, *Power, Community, and Racial Killing*, 19, 100–103.

27. McLaughlin, *Power, Community, and Racial Killing*, 107, 171–172.

28. Rudwick, *Race Riot at East St. Louis*, 27–28.

29. Rudwick, *Race Riot at East St. Louis*, 29–30.

30. Rudwick, *Race Riot at East St. Louis*, 30–31.

31. McLaughlin, *Power, Community, and Racial Killing*, 98; Rudwick, *Race Riot at East St. Louis*, 149.

32. Rudwick, *Race Riot at East St. Louis*, 38–40.

33. US House of Representatives, Select Committee to Investigate the Race Riots in East St. Louis (1917), "Statement of Paul Y. Anderson," vol. 2, 252; "Statement of G. E. Popkess," vol. 2, 492; W.E.B. Du Bois and Martha Gruening, "The Massacre of East St. Louis: An Investigation by the NAACP," *The Crisis* (September 1917): 219–222, 232, 235; Wells-Barnett, *The East St. Louis Massacre*, 7; Rudwick, *Race Riot at East St. Louis*, 41–65; McLaughlin, *Power, Community, and Racial Killing*, 125–162.

34. Rudwick, *Race Riot at East St. Louis*, 53–55; McLaughlin, *Power, Community, and Racial Killing*, 163–177; Du Bois, "Of Work and Wealth," 42.

35. Du Bois and Gruening, "The Massacre of East St. Louis," 219–222, 232, 235; Wells-Barnett, *The East St. Louis Massacre*, 6, 7; Rudwick, *Race Riot at East St. Louis*, 41–65; McLaughlin, *Power, Community, and Racial Killing*, 125–162; US House of Representatives, Select Committee to Investigate the Race Riots in East St. Louis (1917), "Statement of Charles Roger," vol. 1, 107.

36. Carlos F. Hurd, "Post-Dispatch Man, an Eye Witness, Describes Massacre of Negroes," *St. Louis Post-Dispatch*, July 3, 1917.

37. Wells-Barnett, *The East St. Louis Massacre*, 4–7.

38. Du Bois and Gruening, "The Massacre of East St. Louis," 226–227, 231; US House of Representatives, Select Committee to Investigate the Race Riots in East St. Louis (1917), "Statement of Thomas Hunter," vol. 5, 1073–1080.

39. Wells-Barnett, *The East St. Louis Massacre*, 4–5.

40. Du Bois and Gruening, "The Massacre of East St. Louis," 235.

41. Rudwick, *Race Riot at East St. Louis*, 46, 67; Marcus Garvey speech, July 11, 1917, reprinted in Early, *Ain't but a Place*, 305.

42. Rudwick, *Race Riot at East St. Louis*, 111–131.

43. US House of Representatives, Select Committee to Investigate the Race Riots in East St. Louis (1917).

44. W.E.B. Du Bois, "The Black Man and the Unions," *The Crisis* (March 1918).

45. Du Bois, "The Souls of White Folk," 16, 21, 22. My reading of Du Bois owes everything to Robinson, *Black Marxism*; to the work of Robin D. G. Kelley, especially *Hammer and Hoe: Alabama Communists During the Great Depression* (Chapel Hill: University of North Carolina Press, 1990); and to "What Is Racial Capitalism and Why Does It Matter?," a lecture given by Kelley at the University of Washington on November 18, 2017, www.youtube.com/watch?v=--gim7W _jQQ. See also Destin Jenkins and Justin Leroy, eds., *The Old History of Capitalism* (New York: Columbia University Press, forthcoming). Finally, I must express my gratitude to my colleague Tommie Shelby, who allowed me to horn in on his franchise and coteach our course on "Reading Du Bois," and to all of the terrific students we have had in the class over the years we have taught it together.

46. Du Bois, "Of Work and Wealth," 48, 42.

47. Du Bois, "Of Work and Wealth," 44.

48. Du Bois, "The Souls of White Folk," 24.

49. Du Bois, "Of Work and Wealth," 44.

50. Wells-Barnett, *The East St. Louis Massacre*, 5.

CHAPTER 8: NOT POOR, JUST BROKE

1. "One-Way Ticket: Jacob Lawrence's Great Migration Series and Other Visions of the Great Movement North," www.moma.org/interactives/exhibitions /2015/onewayticket/; Selwyn K. Troen and Glen E. Holt, eds., *St. Louis* (New York: New Viewpoints, 1977), 211.

2. "United Welfare Association Explains Its Attitude on Question of Segregation," *St. Louis Post-Dispatch*, February 16, 1916; see also "Negro Leaders' Needless Alarm," *St. Louis Post-Dispatch*, September 25, 1915; Dowden-White, *Groping Toward Democracy*, 77 80.

3. Buchanan v. Warley, 245 U.S. 60 (1916); Shelley v. Kraemer, 334 U.S. 1 (1948); Dowden-White, *Groping Toward Democracy*, 34.

4. Wayne E. Wheeling, secretary, United Welfare Association, "In Defense of Race Segregation," letter to the editor of the *St. Louis Post-Dispatch*, August 27, 1915.

5. Harland Bartholomew, *Comprehensive City Plan: St. Louis, Missouri* (St. Louis: City Plan Commission, 1947), 15; Richard Wright, *Twelve Million Black Voices: A Folk History of the Negro in the United States* (1941; New York: Basic Books, 2002), 91–140; Dick Gregory, *N****r: An Autobiography*, with Robert Lipsyte (New York: Pocket Books, 1964), 34.

6. Richard Rothstein, *The Color of Law: A Forgotten History of How Our Government Segregated America* (New York: Liveright Publishing, 2017), 172–173.

7. Gregory, *N****r*, 3–4.

8. Gregory, *N****r*, 8, 11, 15, 17, 29, 30, 49–50; see also excerpt from *Any Boy Can: The Archie Moore Story*, reprinted in Early, *Ain't but a Place*, 81–92.

9. Earl Lewis, *In Their Own Interests: Race, Class, and Power in Twentieth-Century Norfolk, Virginia* (Berkeley: University of California Press, 1993).

10. Gregory, *N****r*, 25, 26, 28, 55, 59, 77. For dozens of similar neighborhood stories about Mill Creek Valley, see Ron Fagerstrom, *Mill Creek Valley: A Soul of St. Louis* (St. Louis: author, 2000).

11. Fagerstrom, *Mill Creek Valley*. For the rich history of Black St. Louis in these years, see Early, *Ain't but a Place*.

12. Early, *Ain't but a Place*, 81–120, 152–243.

13. James W. Endersby and William T. Horner, *Lloyd Gaines and the Fight to End Segregation* (Columbia: University of Missouri Press, 2016).

14. Missouri ex rel. Gaines v. Canada, 305 U.S. 337 (1938); Chad Garrison, "The Mystery of Lloyd Gaines," *St. Louis Riverfront Times*, April 4, 2007.

15. See excerpt from *Standing Fast: The Autobiography of Roy Wilkins*, and Langston Hughes, "In Racial Matters in St. Louis 'De Sun Do Move,'" both in Early, *Ain't but a Place*, 65, 348; see also Zachary Bostwick Nowak, "The State in the Station: The Nineteenth-Century American Train Station and State Power" (PhD diss., Harvard University, 2018). For these struggles as well as their underlying class character, see Dowden-White, *Groping Toward Democracy*; and Lang, *Grassroots at the Gateway*, 14, 17–42.

16. St. Louis Urban League, *Annual Report for 1944*, 2, 9–10; see also St. Louis Urban League, *Annual Report for 1939*, 6.

17. Clara Germani, "J. D. and Ethel Shelley Celebrating the People Behind the Landmark *Shelley v. Kraemer* Case," master's thesis (Washington University, 2019), 62; *Shelley v. Kraemer*. See Lang, *Grassroots at the Gateway*, 12, 78, 81, 141, 142, 191.

18. Phillip O'Conner, "Pool Riot Pivotal in Race Relations: City's Decision in '49 to Integrate Pools Sparked Violence That Triggered Change," *St. Louis Post-Dispatch*, June 21, 2009; Jamala Rogers, "Reflections on a Racist Ambush," *St. Louis American*, June 25, 2009.

19. O'Conner, "Pool Riot Pivotal in Race Relations"; Rogers, "Reflections on a Racist Ambush."

20. O'Conner, "Pool Riot Pivotal in Race Relations"; Rogers, "Reflections on a Racist Ambush."

21. Theodore Rosengarten, *All God's Dangers: The Life of Nate Shaw* (New York: Alfred A. Knopf, 1974); Kelley, *Hammer and Hoe*; Hosea Hudson and Nell Irvin Painter, *The Narrative of Hosea Hudson: The Life and Times of a Black Radical* (New York: W. W. Norton & Co., 1993); Glenda Elizabeth Gilmore, *Defying Dixie: The Radical Roots of Civil Rights, 1919–1950* (New York: W. W. Norton & Co., 2009). For St. Louis in particular, see Lang, *Grassroots at the Gateway*, and Ervin, *Gateway to Equality*.

22. Larry Giles, National Building Arts Center, interview with the author, January 8, 2019; Emma Goldman, *Living My Life* (New York: Dover Publishing, 1970), vol. 1, 452–453, 477; vol. 2, chap. 47.

23. Giles, interview with the author, January 8, 2019; see also Alice Martin Turner, *The Tempest Maker: The Story of Harry Turner* (New York: Exposition Press, 1955); Jack Conroy, *A World to Win* (New York: Covici Friede, 1935); Douglas Wixson, *Worker-Writer in America: Jack Conroy and the Tradition of Midwestern Literary Radicalism, 1898–1990* (Champaign: University of Illinois Press, 1994); James R. Green, *Grassroots Socialism: Radical Movements in the Southwest, 1895–1943* (Baton Rouge: Louisiana State University Press, 1978), 136, 221.

24. Conroy, *A World to Win*, 154, 165, 295; "'Hooverville' and 'Merryland,' New 'Subdivisions Along Riverfront Here'," *St. Louis Star and Times*, August 15, 1931; "Hooverville Will Decide Whether It Wants a New Mayor," *St. Louis Star and Times*, January 22, 1932; "Hooverville to Have Its Brightest Christmas," *St. Louis Post-Dispatch*, December 24, 1933; "Shot to Death by Rival in Row About a Woman," *St. Louis Post-Dispatch*, December 1, 1933.

25. Dowden-White, *Groping Toward Democracy*, 36–38.

26. Adam Kloppe, "New Insights from an Old Panorama," Missouri Historical Society, February 21, 2018, https://mohistory.org/blog/new-insights-from-an-old-panorama/.

27. "1,500 in Parade to City Hall Seek Food for Needy," *St. Louis Post-Dispatch*, July 9, 1932.

28. "1,500 in Parade to City Hall Seek Food for Needy," *St. Louis Post-Dispatch*, July 9, 1932.

29. "Police Drive 3,000 Led by Communists from City Hall with Tear Gas," *St. Louis Post-Dispatch*, July 11, 1932; see also "Four Shot in Riot at St. Louis," *Moberly Monitor-Index*, July 11, 1932.

30. "Police Drive 3,000 Led by Communists from City Hall with Tear Gas," *St. Louis Post-Dispatch*, July 11, 1932.

31. "Police Drive 3,000 Led by Communists from City Hall with Tear Gas," *St. Louis Post-Dispatch*, July 11, 1932.

32. "Police Drive 3,000 Led by Communists from City Hall with Tear Gas," *St. Louis Post-Dispatch*, July 11, 1932; "Police Seeking Warrants for 13 Charging Rioting," *St. Louis Post-Dispatch*, July 13, 1932.

33. "Directs Police to Stop Meetings of Communists," *St. Louis Post-Dispatch*, July 11, 1932; "Court Postpones Hearing for 35 in City Hall Rioting," *St. Louis Post-Dispatch*, July 14, 1932.

34. "Charges Police Beat Suspects in City Hall Riot," *St. Louis Post-Dispatch*, July 24, 1932.

35. "Alderman Brock Explains Plan to Establish Free Food Depots," *St. Louis Star and Times*, July 14, 1932; "Hung Jury at Trial of Alleged Red Rioter," *St. Louis Post-Dispatch*, September 23, 1932; Lang, *Grassroots at the Gateway*, 27–28.

36. Myrna Fichtenbaum, *The Funsten Nut Strike* (New York: International Publishers, 1991), 14.

37. Fichtenbaum, *The Funsten Nut Strike*, 6–8, 15; excerpt from Julius Hunter, *Kingsbury Place: The First Two Hundred Years*, in Early, *Ain't but a Place*, 391–401.

38. Fichtenbaum, *The Funsten Nut Strike*, 15–18.

39. "500 Negro Women Go on Strike for 'Living Wage,'" *St. Louis Post-Dispatch*, May 1, 1933; "Women Nut Pickers' Strike Continues; Factories Closed," *St. Louis Post-Dispatch*, May 17, 1933; Fichtenbaum, *The Funsten Nut Strike*, 15–18.

40. Ervin, *Gateway to Equality*, 34; "Frees Woman Beaten by Police," *St. Louis Post-Dispatch*, October 17, 1933; "68 Freed on Peace Charges in Strike of Nut Pickers," *St. Louis Post-Dispatch*, October 23, 1933.

41. "Mayor Hears Wage Protest of Nutpickers," *St. Louis Star and Times*, May 23, 1933; Mayor's Group Takes Up Strike of Nut Pickers," *St. Louis Post-Dispatch*, May 23, 1933; Lang, *Grassroots at the Gateway*, 30, 32.

42. "Nut Pickers to Return to Jobs at Double Pay," *St. Louis Post-Dispatch*, May 24, 1933; "Mayor's Arbiters Settle Strike of 1,200 Nut Pickers," *St. Louis Post-Dispatch*, May 25, 1933.

43. Ervin, *Gateway to Equality*, 33, 39–40; Trade Union Unity League, "To the Workers of St. Louis," reproduced in full in Fichtenbaum, *The Funsten Nut Strike*, 68.

44. Ervin, *Gateway to Equality*, 35.

45. "Communist Party Oral Histories: Hershel Walker," posted July 25, 2017, Tamiment Library, New York University, https://wp.nyu.edu/tamimentcpusa/hershel-walker/; see also Lang, *Grassroots at the Gateway*, 32.

46. "Communist Party Oral Histories: Hershel Walker," posted July 25, 2017, Tamiment Library, New York University, https://wp.nyu.edu/tamimentcpusa/hershel-walker/. For the March on Washington Movement, see Lang, *Grassroots at the Gateway*. For the PMEW, see Gerald Horne, *Facing the Rising Sun: African Americans, Japan, and the Rise of Afro-Asian Solidarity* (New York: New York University Press, 2018).

47. Angela Y. Davis, *Women, Race, and Class* (New York: Random House, 1981), 158; William H. Patterson, "Sikeston: Hitlerite Crime Against America" (St. Louis: Communist Party of Missouri, 1942); Rosemary Feurer, *Radical Unionism in the Midwest, 1900–1950* (Urbana: University of Illinois Press, 2006), 65–68; "Communist Party Oral Histories: Hershel Walker," posted July 25, 2017, Tamiment Library, New York University, https://wp.nyu.edu/tamimentcpusa/hershel-walker/. In the years immediately following, Herbert Aptheker sexually abused his young daughter, who told her story in Bettina F. Aptheker, *Intimate Politics: How I Grew Up Red, Fought for Free Speech, and Became a Feminist Rebel* (New York: Seal Press, 2006).

48. "Communist Party Oral Histories: Hershel Walker," posted July 25, 2017, Tamiment Library, New York University, https://wp.nyu.edu/tamimentcpusa/hershel-walker/.

49. Ervin, *Gateway to Equality*, 42–45; Fichtenbaum, *The Funsten Nut Strike*, 45.

50. Ervin, *Gateway to Equality*, 53–69.

51. On the mainstream civil rights movement seeing economic injustice as a key issue only in the late 1960s, see Taylor Branch, *At Canaan's Edge: America in the King Years, 1965–68* (New York: Simon & Schuster, 2006); on the movement outside the South, see Thomas J. Sugrue, *Sweet Land of Liberty: The Forgotten Struggle for Civil Rights in the North* (New York: Random House, 2009).

52. Ervin, *Gateway to Equality*, 79–95. The skepticism expressed by the St. Louis Urban League about the actions of the working-class Black women of the CCC seems an uncanny premonition of Oprah Winfrey's 2015 criticism of the protests in the aftermath of the murder of Michael Brown. "I'm looking for leadership," she said of a movement full of leaders.

53. *St. Louis Post-Dispatch*, March 2, 8, 9, 16, and 22, April 1, 19, and 29, and May 16, 1937; *St. Louis Star and Times*, March 22, 1937. On the Emerson strike, see Feurer, *Radical Unionism*, 65–68; "A Yale Man and a Communist," *Fortune* 28, no. 5 (November 1943): 147.

54. Lang, *Grassroots at the Gateway*, 44–49; George Lipsitz, *Rainbow at Midnight: Labor and Culture in the 1940s* (Urbana: University of Illinois Press, 1994), 58; "A Yale Man and a Communist," *Fortune* 28, no. 5 (November 1943): 218; see also Nelson Lichtenstein, *The Most Dangerous Man in Detroit: Walter Reuther and the Fate of American Labor* (New York: Basic Books, 1995); Ruth Milkman, *Gender at Work: The Dynamics of Job Segregation by Sex During World War II* (Champaign-Urbana: University of Illinois Press, 1986).

55. Berger, *St. Louis and Empire*, 175.

56. Berger, *St. Louis and Empire*, 160–161; Denise Degarmo, *The Disposal of Radioactive Wastes in the Metropolitan St. Louis Area: The Environmental and Health Legacy of the Mallinckrodt Chemical Works* (Lewiston, NY: Edwin Mellen Press, 2006).

57. Ervin, *Gateway to Equality*, 97; "Communist Party Oral Histories: Hershel Walker," posted July 25, 2017, Tamiment Library, New York University, https://wp.nyu.edu/tamimentcpusa/hershel-walker/; Ervin, *Gateway to Equality*, 97–112.

58. Ervin, *Gateway to Equality*, 97–112. See also Lipsitz, *Rainbow at Midnight*, 50; Michael Denning, *The Cultural Front: The Laboring of American Culture in the Twentieth Century* (New York: Verso, 2011).

59. Lipsitz, *Rainbow at Midnight*, 99.

60. Lipsitz, *Rainbow at Midnight*, 47, 48, 55; "A Yale Man and a Communist," *Fortune* 28, no. 5 (November 1943).

61. Feurer, *Radical Unionism*, 163–176; Lipsitz, *Rainbow at Midnight*, 99–135; Michael L. Lawson, *Dammed Indians: The Pick-Sloan Plan and the Missouri River Sioux, 1944–1980* (Lincoln: University of Nebraska Press, 1994).

62. William Sentner v. United States of America, US Court of Appeals for the Eighth Circuit, 253 F.2d 310 (1958).

63. Lipsitz, *Rainbow at Midnight*, 157–181; Robert H. Zieger, *The CIO: 1935–1955* (Chapel Hill: University of North Carolina Press, 1995); Nelson Lichtenstein, *Labor's War at Home: The CIO in World War II* (Cambridge: Cambridge University Press, 1982); Karl E. Klare, "Judicial Deradicalization of the Wagner Act and the Origins of Modern Legal Consciousness, 1937–1941," *Minnesota Law Review* 62 (1977–1978): 265.

CHAPTER 9: "BLACK REMOVAL BY WHITE APPROVAL"

1. Mark Abbott, "A Document That Changed America: The 1907 *A City Plan for St. Louis*," in Mark Tranel, ed., *St. Louis Plans: The Ideal and the Real St. Louis* (St. Louis: Missouri Historical Society Press, 2007), 17–53, 49 (quotation); Michael R. Allen, "The Evolution of the Gateway Mall (Part 2): The Civic Center," Preservation Research Office, January 6, 2012, http://preservationresearch.com/downtown/the-evolution-of-the-gateway-mall-part-2-the-civic-center/.

2. Harland Bartholomew and Associates, series 1–7 ("City Planning Reports"), Harland Bartholomew and Associates Collection, University Archives, Washington University, St. Louis; Norman J. Johnson, "Harland Bartholomew: Precedent for the Profession," *Journal of the American Institute of Planners* 39, no. 2 (1973): 115–124.

3. Harland Bartholomew, "Zoning for St. Louis: A Fundamental Part of the City Plan" (St. Louis: Nixon-Jones Printing Co., 1918), 16–17; Harland Bartholomew, "The Zone Plan: City Plan Commission" (St. Louis: Nixon-Jones Printing Co., 1919), 11, 30.

4. Roediger and Esch, *The Production of Difference*, 115–120; Rothstein, *The Color of Law*, 60–62, 82–88; Bartholomew, "The Zone Plan," 30.

5. Tracy Campbell, *The Gateway Arch: A Biography* (New Haven, CT: Yale University Press, 2013), 21–23.

6. Campbell, *The Gateway Arch*, 35.

7. Campbell, *The Gateway Arch*, 32–33 (quotation).

8. Campbell, *The Gateway Arch*, 37–43, 37 (quotation).

9. Campbell, *The Gateway Arch*, 27, 36, 46.

10. Campbell, *The Gateway Arch*, 27, 36, 45–52; Mark Tranel, "From Dreams to Reality: The Arch as a Metaphor for St. Louis Plans," in Tranel, *St. Louis Plans*, 1–13.

11. Bartholomew, *Comprehensive City Plan*.

12. "3 Superhighways Planned for Postwar St. Louis," *Saint Louis Post-Dispatch*, October 3, 1943; Rothstein, *The Color of Law*, 128; http://omeka.wustl.edu/omeka/exhibits/show/washington-park/about-cemetery. For the highways in St. Louis and throughout the nation, as well as the overall vision of race, space, and economy that frames this chapter, see Lipsitz, *The Possessive Investment in Whiteness*; see also Thomas J. Sugrue, *The Origins of the Urban Crisis: Race and Inequality in Postwar Detroit* (Princeton, NJ: Princeton University Press, 1996); Robert O. Self, *American Babylon: Race and the Struggle for Postwar Oakland* (Princeton, NJ: Princeton University Press, 2003); Ira D. Katznelson, *When Affirmative Action Was White: An Untold History of Racial Inequality in Twentieth-Century America* (New York: W. W. Norton and Co., 2006); Painter, *The History of White People*.

13. Bartholomew, *Comprehensive City Plan*, 28, plates 11, 12, and 13; Mark Abbott, "The 1947 *Comprehensive City Plan* and Harland Bartholomew's St. Louis," in Tranel, *St. Louis Plans*, 125.

14. Bartholomew, *Comprehensive City Plan*, 29; Abbott, "The 1947 *Comprehensive City Plan* and Harland Bartholomew's St. Louis," 125.

15. Bartholomew, *Comprehensive City Plan*, 28, plates 11 and 13.

16. "Map of 'Cancerous Slum District Eating Away at the Heart of the City,'" and "Marching Blight," *St. Louis Post-Dispatch*, February 12 and April 4, 1948.

17. Bartholomew, *Comprehensive City Plan*, 35; Abbott, "The 1947 *Comprehensive City Plan*," 135–138.

18. Fagerstrom, *Mill Creek Valley*, 62.

19. Park, "Self-Deportation Nation."

20. Jas. L. Ford (First National Bank) to "Dear Edna" (League of Women Voters), February 2, 1948; Jas. L. Ford to "Dear Addie" (League of Women Voters), March 11, 1948; Special Committee, St. Louis Race Relations Commission, October 7, 1948; Katherine Shryven (Progressive Party) to "Mrs. L. Matthew Werner" (League of Women Voters), December 28, 1948; all in box 107 ("Slum Clearance Bond Issue"), folder 1351 ("League of Women Voters Addenda, 1916–1977"), State Historical Society of Missouri, St. Louis.

21. Ervin, *Gateway to Equality*, 154; Lang, *Grassroots at the Gateway*, 103–109.

22. Roy Wenzlick and Co., *Market Analysis and Reuse Appraisal, Mill Creek Valley Redevelopment Project, St. Louis, Missouri*, submitted to the Land Clearance for Redevelopment Authority, October 1, 1956, 12, 36, 56.

23. Fagerstrom, *Mill Creek Valley*, 20; Early, *Ain't but a Place*, 79, 101.

24. Lang, *Grassroots at the Gateway*, 103; George Lipsitz, *A Life in the Struggle: Ivory Perry and the Culture of Opposition*, rev. ed. (Philadelphia: Temple University Press, 1995), 212.

25. Francesca Ressello Ammon, *Bulldozer: Demolition and Clearance of the Postwar Landscape* (New Haven, CT: Yale University Press, 2016); see also Mindy Thompson Fullilove, *Rootshock: How Tearing Up Neighborhoods Hurts America, and What We Can Do About It* (New York: Random House, 2004).

26. Berger, *St. Louis and Empire*, 179–190, 180 (quotation).

27. "Sixteen in Webster Groves" aired on CBS on February 25, 1966; it is clear from footage that includes a football game and the roasting of a turkey that it was shot the preceding fall of 1965.

28. Henry called the city in his study "Rome," but evidence in the Jules Henry Papers in the Washington University Archives (series 5, box 5), including student survey answers in which the respondents self-identify as students at Webster Groves High School, demonstrates that his research was in Webster Groves.

29. "56 in Webster Groves," *Riverfront Times*, March 1, 2006.

30. Kenneth T. Jackson, *Crabgrass Frontier: The Suburbanization of the United States* (New York: Oxford University Press, 1987); Lipsitz, *The Possessive Investment in Whiteness*; Kevin M. Kruse, *White Flight: Atlanta and the Making of Modern Conservatism* (Princeton, NJ: Princeton University Press, 2007); Beryl Satter, *Family Properties: How the Struggle over Race and Real Estate Transformed Chicago and Urban America* (New York: Picador, 2010); Rothstein, *The Color of Law*.

31. Rothstein, *The Color of Law*, 65 (quotation), 85.

32. Colin Gordon, *Mapping Decline: St. Louis and the Fate of the American City* (Philadelphia: University of Pennsylvania Press, 2008), 96–97; Rothstein, *The Color of Law*, 64–65; University of Richmond, "Mapping Inequality: Redlining in New Deal America," https://dsl.richmond.edu/panorama/redlining/#loc=4/36.71/-96.93&opacity=0.\8. On the importance of remembering the racial capitalist mechanism that the federal government was subsidizing, see Destin Jenkins, "Who Segregated America?," *Public Books*, December 21, 2017.

33. Rothstein, *The Color of Law*, 89–91, 91 (quotation). The deed quoted is from a home sale in Pasadena Hills.

34. Gordon, *Mapping Decline*, 87.

35. Gordon, *Mapping Decline*, 83–88, 97; "Windows Smashed at Negro Home," *St. Louis Post-Dispatch*, December 19, 1969; Lang, *Grassroots at the Gateway*, 177.

36. Jim Singer, "Beirne Park: The Shame of Creve Coeur," unpublished paper in my possession; see also City of Creve Coeur, "Parks & Rec," www.creve-coeur.org/284/Parks; Rothstein, *The Color of Law*, 125.

37. Freedom of Residence Committee Papers, 1962–1969, S0438, State Historical Society of Missouri.

38. Rothstein, *The Color of Law*, ix–xi.

39. Quoted in Gordon, *Mapping Decline*, 87. In this case, the "clients" were reporting to the Freedom of Residence Committee.

40. Jamala Rogers, *Ferguson Is America: Roots of Rebellion* (St. Louis: Mira Digital Publishing, 2015), 18–19.

41. Village of Euclid v. Ambler Realty Co., 272 U.S. 365 (1926); Gordon, *Mapping Decline*, 114, 136, 143.

42. Gordon, *Mapping Decline*, 129–136.

43. Gordon, *Mapping Decline*, 137–145, 147.

44. Gordon, *Mapping Decline*, 147; "Ferguson Again Considers Fence as Crime Deterrent," *St. Louis Post-Dispatch*, January 25, 1976; see also "Ferguson Council on the Fence for Barrier," *St. Louis Post-Dispatch*, April 24, 1975; "Ferguson Fence," *St. Louis Post-Dispatch*, April 25, 1975; "Ferguson to Seek Insurance Bids," *St. Louis Post-Dispatch*, May 14, 1975.

45. "Church-Sponsored Housing Project Is Under Attack," *St. Louis Post-Dispatch*, April 8, 1970.

46. "Church-Sponsored Housing Project Is Under Attack," *St. Louis Post-Dispatch*, April 8, 1970; "Political Figures Voice Opposition to Housing Project," *St. Louis Post-Dispatch*, April 10, 1970.

47. "Housewives March," *St. Louis Post-Dispatch*, July 22, 1970.

48. "'I'm Ready for a Street Fight,' Says Opponent of Church Homes," *St. Louis Post-Dispatch*, August 21, 1970; "Move to Incorporate Black Jack Advances," *St. Louis Post-Dispatch*, February 26, 1970.

49. United States of America v. City of Black Jack, Missouri, 508 F.2d 1179 (1974).

50. Texas Department of Housing and Community Affairs v. Inclusive Communities Project, Inc., 576 U.S. ___ (2015).

51. US Census Bureau, "Census of Population and Housing," 1950 data, vol. 2, Missouri, 76, www.census.gov/prod/www/decennial.html; Social Explorer and US Census Bureau, "Census 1970" (St. Louis County, Missouri), www.socialexplorer.com/tables/C1970/R12366530. On the role of federal mortgage subsidies in disciplining the white working class, see Keeanga-Yamahtta Taylor, *From #BlackLivesMatter to Black Liberation* (New York: Haymarket Books, 2016).

52. "The Great Passion Play," www.greatpassionplay.org/holy-land.html.

53. "Christian Nationalism Defined," *The Cross and the Flag* 11, no. 4 (July 1952). *The Cross and the Flag* is often cataloged by librarians as having been published in Detroit, where Smith lived, but it accepted submissions to a St. Louis post office box and stated in every issue that it was "Published at 1533 S. Grand, St. Louis Mo." See also "The Great Passion Play," www.greatpassionplay.org/holy-land.html.

54. John A. Stormer, *None Dare Call It Treason* (Florissant, MO: Liberty Bell Press, 1963), 158–159; "John Stormer, Whose 'None Dare Call It Treason' Was a Landmark of Conspiracy Literature, Dies at 90," *Washington Post*, July 16, 2018.

55. *St. Louis Globe-Democrat*, February 17, 19, 21, 23, 25, and 26, 1960, June 23, 1965, October 1, 1962, July 13, 1967, and July 30, 1968; see also "What's the Purpose Behind the *Globe-Democrat's* Military Expert's Sociopolitical 'Riot' Column," *St. Louis American*, February 19, 1967.

56. Lang, *Grassroots at the Gateway*, 176, 221–222; "Ultimatum of Percy Green," *St. Louis Globe-Democrat*, June 23, 1965; see also "Police Brutality," *St. Louis Globe-Democrat*, September 24, 1965.

57. Molly Ivins, *Nothin' but Good Times Ahead* (New York: Random House, 1993), 136.

58. Phyllis Schlafly, *A Choice Not an Echo* (Alton, IL: Pere Marquette Press, 1964), 16, 25, 56, 63, 67, 79, 99, 107, 111, 121.

59. Jill Lepore, *These Truths: A History of the United States*, 617, 655, 658–671, 662, 664, 668, 768, 777–778.

60. "Hostile Crowd Blocks Nazi March, Rally," *St. Louis Post-Dispatch*, March 12, 1978; see also "Nazis Get Permit for Protest to Go Through South St. Louis," *St. Louis Post-Dispatch*, February 3, 1978; "No Evidence to Link Hinckley to St. Louis Nazis," *St. Louis Globe-Democrat*, April 1, 1981.

61. Jonathan Franzen, *The Discomfort Zone: A Personal History* (New York: Picador, 2006).

62. "Hedy Epstein, Rights Activist and Holocaust Survivor, Dies at 91," *New York Times*, March 28, 2016; "Paul Revere of Ecology," *Time*, February 2, 1970; Barry Commoner, *The Closing Circle: Nature, Man, and Technology* (New York: Alfred A. Knopf, 1971); Barry Commoner, *The Poverty of Power: Energy and the Economic Crisis* (New York: Alfred A. Knopf, 1972).

63. "100,000 to Take Part in Parade of 'Hard Hats,'" *St. Louis Post-Dispatch*, June 7, 1970; "Some Violence at March Backing War," *St. Louis Post-Dispatch*, June 8, 1970; "Some Who Watched Parade Were Just Visitors from Park," *St. Louis Post-Dispatch*, June 8, 1970; "The Hard Hats in Lindell," *St. Louis Post-Dispatch*, June 9, 1970; see also Jefferson Cowie, *Stayin' Alive: The 1970s and the Last Days of the Working Class* (New York: New Press, 2010), 135, 178, 347.

64. A separate essay could be written on the indispensable role of the colors green and purple in proving that white people are not racist ("Sixteen in Webster Groves").

CHAPTER 10: DEFENSIBLE SPACE

1. Kenneth S. Jolly, *Black Liberation in the Midwest: The Struggle in St. Louis, Missouri, 1964–1970* (New York: Routledge, 2006), 18–28; Lang, *Grassroots at the Gateway*, 97.

2. Jolly, *Black Liberation in the Midwest*, 19–21.

3. See Clarence Lang, "Locating the Civil Rights Movement: An Essay on the Deep South, Midwest, and Border South in Black Freedom Studies," *Journal*

of Social History 47, no. 2 (2013): 371–400. Lang's argument for both the particularity and importance of the civil rights history of St. Louis provides the polestar of my analysis.

4. Lang, *Grassroots at the Gateway*, 112–114.

5. Lang, *Grassroots at the Gateway*, 112–134, 113 (quotations).

6. Percy Green, interview with the author, St. Louis, Missouri, March 7, 2018.

7. Lang, *Grassroots at the Gateway*, 158; Percy Green, interview with the author, St. Louis, Missouri, March 7, 2018.

8. Lang, *Grassroots at the Gateway*, 162.

9. Lang, *Grassroots at the Gateway*, 162–163.

10. See *St. Louis Post-Dispatch* photos dated October 10, 1963, and Jefferson Bank Collection, St. Louis Mercantile Library Collection, University of Missouri–St. Louis; "August 30, 1963: Protests at Jefferson Bank Lead to Major Changes in Hiring Practices in St. Louis," *St. Louis Post-Dispatch*, August 30, 2016; Lang, *Grassroots at the Gateway*, 166.

11. Lang, *Grassroots at the Gateway*, 166–177.

12. Lang, *Grassroots at the Gateway*, 103–109. Civic Progress is still around; see www.civicprogressstl.org/.

13. Lang, *Grassroots at the Gateway*, 178–179.

14. Percy Green, interview with the author, St. Louis, Missouri, March 7 and 8, 2018; "Put Capitalism to Work in Ghettos," *St. Louis Globe-Democrat*, July 30, 1968.

15. Percy Green, interview with the author, St. Louis, Missouri, March 8, 2018. Green described the surreal sensation of walking into his otherwise entirely white department at McDonnell and greeting coworkers who had seen him perched on the Arch on television that afternoon and evening.

16. Percy Green, interview with the author, St. Louis, Missouri, March 8, 2018.

17. Percy Green, interview with the author, St. Louis, Missouri, March 8, 2018.

18. Percy Green, interview with the author, St. Louis, Missouri, March 8, 2018; Lang, *Grassroots at the Gateway*, 194, 199, 200, 209, 212, 213, 220, 224, 234, 242, 246; McDonnell-Douglas Corp. v. Green, 411 U.S. 792 (1973); Chuck Henson, "Title VII Works—That's Why We Don't Like It," *University of Miami Race & Social Justice Law Review* 41 (2012); Chuck Henson, "In Defense of McDonnell Douglas: The Domination of Title VII by the At-Will Employment Doctrine," *St. John's Law Review* 89, no. 2 (Fall 2015): 551–596.

19. Percy Green, interview with the author, St. Louis, Missouri, March 8, 2018.

20. Percy Green, interview with the author, St. Louis, Missouri, March 8, 2018; Lang, *Grassroots at the Gateway*, 201.

21. Percy Green, interview with the author, St. Louis, Missouri, March 8, 2018.

22. Percy Green, interview with the author, St. Louis, Missouri, March 8, 2018; Lang, *Grassroots at the Gateway*, 241; Lucy Ferris, *Unveiling the Prophet: The Misadventures of a Reluctant Debutante* (Columbia: University of Missouri Press, 1975).

23. "Fading St. Louis Area Has Partial Revival," *New York Times*, December 9, 1979.

24. Hubert Schwartzentruber, *Jesus in the Back Alleys: The Story and Reflections of a Contemporary Prophet* (Teleford, PA: Dreamseeker Books, 2002), 39.

25. "Fading St. Louis Area Has Partial Revival," *New York Times*, December 9, 1979"; Cecil Miller, interview with the author, St. Louis, Missouri, September 25, 2018. Miller remembered "Mr. Shepard" as a man whose "definition of an educated person was someone who could go anywhere in the society, from the top to the bottom, without embarrassing themselves or embarrassing anyone else" ("Fading St. Louis Area Has Partial Revival"). See also Michael R. Allen, "The Vernacular as Repossession Project: Jeff-Vander-Lou in St. Louis," unpublished paper in author's possession. On everything JVL, see Mark Loehrer's forthcoming master's thesis, University of Missouri–St. Louis.

26. Ivory Perry, interview from "A Strong Seed Planted," in Early, *Ain't but a Place*, 357–358.

27. Jolly, *Black Liberation in the Midwest*, 89–91; Angela Y. Davis, *Women, Race, and Class*, 2nd ed. (New York: Vintage Books, 1983), 149.

28. Jolly, *Black Liberation*, 87–88. Also during these years, Curt Flood, the talented St. Louis Cardinals center fielder, challenged Major League Baseball's "reserve rule," arguing in court that it violated the Thirteenth Amendment. Though unsuccessful, Flood's suit paved the way for free agency in baseball. See Curt Flood, *The Way It Is*, in Early, *Ain't but a Place*, 121–133.

29. Lang, *Grassroots at the Gateway*, 103.

30. Bob Hansman, *Pruitt-Igoe* (Charleston, SC: Arcadia Publishing, 2018), 7–22. *Davis et al. v. St. Louis Housing Authority*, the case in which Frankie Muse Freeman was the lead counsel, seems to have been unreported.

31. Hansman, *Pruitt-Igoe*, 20–21, 33.

32. Colin Marshall, "Pruitt-Igoe: The Troubled High-Rise That Came to Define Urban America," *Guardian*, April 22, 2015.

33. See Chad Friedrichs's extraordinary 2010 film *The Pruitt-Igoe Myth*.

34. Hansman, *Pruitt-Igoe*, 48, 65, 67, 68, 69, 80. One place where the image of the icicles cascading out of the windows of the complex appeared was on the cover of Lee Rainwater's *Behind Ghetto Walls: Black Families in a Federal Slum* (Chicago: Aldine, 1970).

35. Rainwater, *Behind Ghetto Walls*, ix, 9; see also Evan Stark, "Talking Sociology: A Sixties Fragment," in *Radical Sociologists and the Movement: Experiences, Lessons, and Legacies*, ed. Martin Oppenheim, Martin Murray, and Rhonda F. Levin (Philadelphia: Temple University Press, 1991).

36. Rainwater, *Behind Ghetto Walls*, 524.

37. Rainwater, *Behind Ghetto Walls*, xv, 520, passim. That Joyce Ladner (about whom more soon) was part of both the Washington University Pruitt-Igoe project and the social world of ACTION suggests at least some interchange. See the photo of Joyce Ladner and her sister Dorie at ACTION's Afro-Bougaloo Festival, *St. Louis American*, March 5, 1968; Percy Green, interview with the author, St. Louis, Missouri, March 8, 2018.

38. Joyce A. Ladner, *Tomorrow's Tomorrow: The Black Woman* (1971; Lincoln: University of Nebraska Press, 1995), xxi, xxv–xxvii.

39. Ladner, *Tomorrow's Tomorrow*, 52–53, 65, 78, 84, 97, 101.

40. William B. Helmreich, *The Black Crusaders: A Case Study of a Black Militant Organization* (New York: Harper & Row, 1973), 43–44; Elizabeth Hinton, *From the War on Poverty to the War on Crime: The Making of Mass Incarceration in America* (Cambridge, MA: Harvard University Press, 2016), 23–24, 44, 46, 47, 91, 137. See also Jabari Asim's fictionalized memoir of the Northside, *A Taste of Honey: Stories* (New York: Broadway Books, 2010), which begins with a story about a police killing.

41. "Abuse Greets Foot Patrols," *St. Louis Post-Dispatch*, November 10, 1969; "Night Patrol," *St. Louis Post-Dispatch*, December 7, 1969; "Police Car Set on Fire in Pruitt-Igoe," *St. Louis Post-Dispatch*, August 30, 1969; ACTION, "Thugs in Blue Uniform" (1970), vii–viii.

42. Nikhil Pal Singh, *Race and America's Long War* (Berkeley: University of California Press, 2017), 51; Hansman, *Pruitt-Igoe*, 34, 43; Peter Hudson, "Who Killed Robert McCulloch's Father," *Los Angeles Review of Books*, September 18, 2014.

43. William Leahy, *Curbstone Justice: A Collection of True Cop Stories from the Fifties and Sixties* (St. Louis: self-pub., 2010), 46, 52, 63, 74, 198, 212; "Police Dog Nips Piece of T-Shirt in Losing Chase," *St. Louis Post-Dispatch*, June 14, 1962.

44. ACTION, *1968–69 Picture Magazine*, unpaginated.

45. ACTION, "Thugs in Blue Uniform" (1970), iv–xiii.

46. ACTION, "Thugs in Blue Uniform" (1970), unpaginated.

47. Jolly, *Black Liberation in the Midwest*, 151, 154–159; Percy Green, interview with the author, St. Louis, Missouri, March 8, 2018.

48. Jolly, *Black Liberation in the Midwest*, 96.

49. Helmreich, *The Black Crusaders*, 85, 98, 110; Jolly, *Black Liberation in the Midwest*, 58, 73, 76, 78, 82, 89, 96, 105, 158–159, 163–167.

50. Jolly, *Black Liberation in the Midwest*, 164; Lang, *Grassroots at the Gateway*, photo between pages 126 and 172. Percy Green maintains that the Liberators did not have the operational capacity to target Grimes at his home; he believes that white officers shot into the house, hoping to provoke the volatile Lieutenant Grimes to attack the Liberators. Percy Green, interview with the author, St. Louis, Missouri, March 8, 2018; ACTION, *1968–69 Picture Magazine*, unpaginated.

51. Jolly, *Black Liberation in the Midwest*, 164–165. Missouri Court of Appeals, St. Louis District, Second Division, Walsh v. Rudolph Oehlert, et al., 508 S.W.2d 222 (1974).

52. Jolly, *Black Liberation in the Midwest*, 165–167; "Roy W. Harper, 88; Was Longtime Federal Judge," *St. Louis Post-Dispatch*, February 15, 1994.

53. J. Anthony Lukas, "Bad Day at Cairo, Illinois," *New York Times*, February 21, 1971; Civil Rights Crusader Dr. Charles Koen Dies at 72," *Chicago Crusader*, July 26, 2018. The violence in Cairo is the subject of my forthcoming book, *The River City Race War*.

54. Singh, *Race and America's Long War*, xiv–xv, 6–13; Leahy, *Curbstone Justice*, 224.

55. Lisa Martino-Taylor, *Behind the Fog: How the US Cold War Radiological Weapons Program Exposed Innocent Americans* (New York: Routledge, 2018), 74–77, 81.

56. Martino-Taylor, *Behind the Fog*, 74–77, 81; National Research Council, US Committee on Toxicology, *Toxicologic Assessment of the Army's Zinc Cadmium Sulfide Dispersion Tests: Answers to Commonly Asked Questions* (Washington, DC: National Academies Press, 1997), www.ncbi.nlm.nih.gov/books/NBK233549/.

57. Martino-Taylor, *Behind the Fog*, 73, 95–102.

58. Martino-Taylor, *Behind the Fog*, 110.

59. Martino-Taylor, *Behind the Fog*, 110; Jeffrey Tomich, "Decades Later, Baby Tooth Legacy Survey Lives On," *St. Louis Post-Dispatch*, August 1, 2013.

60. Ervin, *Gateway to Equality*, 181–183.

61. Ervin, *Gateway to Equality*, 183.

62. Ervin, *Gateway to Equality*, 180, 184; *St. Louis Post-Dispatch*, April 14, 1969; Percy Green, interview with the author, St. Louis, Missouri, March 8, 2018.

63. Hansman, *Pruitt-Igoe*, 86–95.

64. Hansman, *Pruitt-Igoe*, 102–113; Allen, "The Vernacular as Repossession Project"; see also "Jeff-Vander-Lou, Inc. and the Ministers Union of Greater St. Louis Meeting on the Redevelopment of the Pruitt-Igoe Site," Missouri Historical Society, May 5, 1983.

65. Oscar Newman, "Creating Defensible Space" (1972; US Department of Housing and Urban Development, 1996), 10.

66. Newman, "Creating Defensible Space," 13.

67. Christopher G. Prener, Taylor Harris Braswell, Kyle Miller, and Joel P. Jennings, "Closing the Gateway: Street Closures, Bisected Geography, and Crime in St. Louis, MO," February 21, 2019, https://osf.io/preprints/socarxiv/2wext/; Michael R. Allen, "The City Body at War with Itself: Street Blockages in St. Louis," *NextSTL*, October 16, 2014, https://nextstl.com/2014/10/city-body-war-street-blockages-st-louis-2/; Leah Thorsen, "To Make St. Louis Safer, Hundreds of City Streets Were Closed Off. What if It Was a Mistake?," *St. Louis*

Post-Dispatch, February 25, 2019; Hinton, *From the War on Poverty to the War on Crime*, 288–289.

68. Patrick Cooper-McCann, "The Trap of Triage: Lessons from the 'Team 4 Plan,'" *Journal of Planning History* 15, no. 2 (2016): 149–156; Rogers, *Ferguson Is America*, 11–12.

69. Team Four, Inc., *Citywide Implementation Strategies* (1975), 7–15; Cooper-McCann, "The Trap of Triage: Lessons from the 'Team 4 Plan,'" 156.

70. Sylvester Brown, interview with the author, St. Louis, March 28, 2018.

71. "Special Panel Is Considering Consolidation of City Hospitals," and "Violence Hinted over Closing Phillips," *St. Louis Post-Dispatch*, February 9, 1979; Durrie Bouscaren, "Homer G. Phillips Hospital: 'They Were Not Going to Be Treated as Second-Class Citizens,'" *St. Louis Public Radio*, February 21, 2017, https://news.stlpublicradio.org/post/homer-g-phillips-hospital-they-were-not -going-be-treated-second-class-citizens.

72. "Letter to the Editor," *St. Louis Post-Dispatch*, October 3, 1979: "Gregory May Fast in Phillips Protest," *St. Louis Post-Dispatch*, August 31, 1979; "Phillips Protest Is No Joke to Dick Gregory," *St. Louis Post-Dispatch*, September 2, 1979; "Phillips Backers Threaten Boycott," *St. Louis Post-Dispatch*, August 18, 1979.

73. "Hospital," *St. Louis Post-Dispatch*, January 29, 1979; "Hospital Defenders Vow to Continue Protest," *St. Louis Post-Dispatch*, February 2, 1970; "Private Group No Longer Interested in Phillips," *St. Louis Post-Dispatch*, April 21, 1979; "Clay Blasts Conway Decision to Reduce Phillips Service," *St. Louis Post-Dispatch*, April 26, 1979; "Homer Phillips Backers Sit-in, Sleep-in to Protest Against Move," *St. Louis Post-Dispatch*, August 1, 1979; "Blockade at Phillips," *St. Louis Post-Dispatch*, August 1, 1970; "Phillips Nurse Arrested in Scuffle with Guards," *St. Louis Post-Dispatch*, August 4, 1979.

74. "Massed Policemen Shield Phillips Transfer," *St. Louis Post-Dispatch*, August 17, 1979; "Police Show of Force, Feints Effective in Phillips Shift," *St. Louis Post-Dispatch*, August 19, 1979; "Phillips Doors Closed," *St. Louis Post-Dispatch*, August 19, 1979.

75. "Black Leaders Analyze Fizzle of Phillips Picket," *St. Louis Post-Dispatch*, August 21, 1979.

76. City of St. Louis, "A Proposal by the City of St. Louis to the Department of Housing and Urban Development for Participation in Section 810 Urban Homesteading Demonstration," St. Louis City Data Collection Addenda, Publications, 1902–1985, State Historical Society of Missouri; Don Crinklaw, "What This Guy Needs Is Some Good $1 Houses," undated magazine article included in City of St. Louis, "A Proposal by the City of St. Louis to the Department of Housing and Urban Development . . . ," 25–45; see also Estes, *Our History Is the Future*, 189.

CHAPTER 11: HOW LONG?

1. Jeanette Cooperman, "The Kirkwood Shootings: Why Did Cookie Thornton Kill?" *St. Louis Magazine*, April 24, 2008; Andrea S. Boyles, *Race, Place, and Suburban Policing: Too Close for Comfort* (Berkeley: University of California Press, 2015), 150. The manuscript of this book was at the publisher by the time Colin Gordon's *Citizen Brown: Race, Democracy, and Inequality in the St. Louis Suburbs* (Chicago: University of Chicago Press, 2019) came out. Readers wishing to look further into the issues discussed here would do well to begin there.

2. Kevin Murphy, "He Couldn't Be Consoled," *South County Times*, February 15, 2008.

3. Murphy, "He Couldn't Be Consoled," *South County Times*, February 15, 2008.

4. Cooperman, "The Kirkwood Shootings: Why Did Cookie Thornton Kill?"; Boyles, *Race, Place, and Suburban Policing*, 155.

5. Cooperman, "The Kirkwood Shootings: Why Did Cookie Thornton Kill?"

6. Cooperman, "The Kirkwood Shootings: Why Did Cookie Thornton Kill?"

7. "Revoltin' Redevelopment," *Riverfront Times*, December 7–13, 1994; Boyles, *Race, Place, and Suburban Policing*, 12; Carla McGown, quoted in *Webster-Kirkwood Times*, August 13–18, 1994.

8. "Meacham Group Calls Development a Double Cross," *Webster-Kirkwood Times*, August 13–18, 1994; Tony Di Martino and Suzanne Langlos, "The Taking of Meacham Park," *Riverfront Times*, August 24–30, 1994.

9. Cooperman, "The Kirkwood Shooting: Kirkwood, Meacham Park, and the Racial Divide," *St. Louis Magazine*, April 24, 2008; *Webster-Kirkwood Times*, March 17–23, 1995.

10. Cooperman, "The Kirkwood Shooting: Kirkwood, Meacham Park, and the Racial Divide"; *Webster-Kirkwood Times*, March 17–23, 1995; Di Martino and Langlos, "The Taking of Meacham Park," *Webster-Kirkwood Times*, March 17–23, 1995; "Undone Deal," *Riverfront Times*, April 19–25, 1995; see also the Kirkwood Commons website at www.regencycenters.com/property/detail/60543/Kirkwood-Commons.

11. Cooperman, "The Kirkwood Shootings: Why Did Cookie Thornton Kill?"; Boyles, *Race, Place, and Suburban Policing*, 72, 138.

12. Boyles, *Race, Place, and Suburban Policing*, 140.

13. Cooperman, "The Kirkwood Shootings: Why Did Cookie Thornton Kill?"; "Meacham Group Calls Development a Double Cross," *Webster-Kirkwood Times*, August 13–18, 1994; Di Martino and Langlos, "The Taking of Meacham Park."

14. Hinton, *From the War on Poverty to the War on Crime*, 14, 187, 197; Gordon, *Mapping Decline*, 103, 178–180, 202.

15. Gordon, *Mapping Decline*, 178–180, 103 (quotation).

16. "Spending the Block Grant: Spent Effort," and "Brightside Car Phones Cost $8,000," *St. Louis Post-Dispatch*, December 9, 1991.

17. "Spending the Block Grant: Opportunity Denied," *St. Louis Post-Dispatch*, December 8, 1991.

18. Tim Barker, "Other People's Blood: On Paul Volcker," *n + 1*, February 26, 2019; *Emerson Electric Co.: A Century of Manufacturing, 1890–1990* (Ferguson, MO: Emerson Electric Co., 1989), 19.

19. Saskia Sassen, *The Global City: New York, London, Tokyo* (Princeton, NJ: Princeton University Press, 2001); Berger, *St. Louis and Empire*, 213.

20. Marie-Monique Robin, *The World According to Monsanto: Pollution, Corruption, and the Control of the World's Food Supply* (New York: New Press, 2010); Berger, *St. Louis and Empire*, 213, 216.

21. Gordon, *Mapping Decline*, 56, 202.

22. Gordon, *Mapping Decline*, 161–163.

23. Missouri Department of Economic Development, "Chapter 353 Tax Abatement," https://ded.mo.gov/programs/community/chapter-353-tax-abatement; Gordon, *Mapping Decline*, 164–167.

24. Gordon, *Mapping Decline*, 155.

25. Gordon, *Mapping Decline*, 155; "With Rams Gone, St. Louis Still Stuck with Stadium Debt," Reuters, February 3, 2016; Neil deMause, "Pay-to-Play Is the Stadium Grift That Keeps on Giving," *Deadspin*, April 29, 2019, https://deadspin .com/pay-to-play-is-the-stadium-grift-that-keeps-on-giving-1834338811.

26. George Lipsitz, *How Racism Takes Place* (Philadelphia: Temple University Press, 2011), 73.

27. Gordon, *Mapping Decline*, 171.

28. Celeste Bott and Jacob Barker, "LRA Owns the 12,000 St. Louis Properties No One Wants. And It Can't Afford to Maintain Them," *St. Louis Post-Dispatch*, September 17, 2018.

29. Parking Systems, Inc. v. Kansas City Downtown Redevelopment Corporation, 518 S.W.2d 119 (1974); Maryland Plaza Redevelopment Corporation v. Greenberg, 594 S.W.2d 284 (1979); Gordon, *Mapping Decline*, 167.

30. Edward C. Lawrence, Ellen N. Briskin, and Jane Qing-Jiang Qu, "A Review of State Tax Incentive Programs for Creating Jobs," *Journal of State Taxation* 118, no. 3 (2013): 25–32.

31. Paric, "Express Scripts Headquarters," www.paric.com/project/express -scripts-headquarters/; Armstrong Teasdale, "New Headquarters for Express Scripts," http://web.archive.org/web/20150923230942/https://www.armstrongteasdale .com/New-Headquarters-for-Express-Scripts/; Kase Wickman, "Express Scripts Inc. to Add New Building to Headquarters," *Riverfront Times*, December 10, 2017; Tim Bryant, "Express Scripts to Add Building," *St. Louis Post-Dispatch*, December 17, 2017; Lawrence et al., "The Economic Impact of Express Scripts on

St. Louis and Missouri"; Blythe Bernhard, "Students 'Were the Victims': End of the Transfer Program Highlights Inequality in St. Louis Area Schools," *St. Louis Post-Dispatch*, August 5, 2019, www.stltoday.com/news/local/metro/students-were -the-victims-end-of-the-transfer-program-highlights/article_c007f390-268c -51d6-ad48-675186f33292.html.

32. Missouri Department of Economic Development, "Local Incentive Programs: Tax Increment Financing," https://ded.mo.gov/community/local-programs #LocalTIF; Missouri Department of Economic Development, "State Supplemental Tax Increment Financing (TIF)," https://ded.mo.gov/programs /community/state-supplemental-tax-increment-financing; Gordon, *Mapping Decline*, 181.

33. Gordon, *Mapping Decline*, 181. The law providing for the additional diversion of state revenue toward the repayment of TIF bonds stipulates that, to be eligible, a TIF district must include at least one building that is fifty years old and it must also have experienced over the previous twenty years "generally declining" population and property tax revenue. See Missouri Department of Economic Development, "State Supplemental Tax Increment Financing."

34. Quoted in Boyles, *Race, Place, and Suburban Policing*, 63, 68.

35. Greg LeRoy, "TIF, Greenfields, and Sprawl: How an Incentive Created to Alleviate Slums Has Come to Subsidize Upscale Malls and New Urbanist Developments," *Planning and Environmental Law* 60, no. 2 (2008): 3.

36. "To TIF or Not to TIF?," *St. Louis Business Journal*, August 18, 1996; "Richmond Heights Approves TIF for Boulevard Expansion," *St. Louis Business Journal*, October 4, 2016; Oasis Corporate Housing, "Property #6050: The Orion Apartments," https://oasiscorporatehousing.com/Property-Details/6050; Patrick Tuohey and Michael Highsmith, "Tax-Increment Financing in St. Louis," Show-Me Institute Working Paper, September 22, 2017, https://showmeinstitute .org/publication/subsidies/tax-increment-financing-saint-louis.

37. Jacob Barker, "Tax Abatement Cost St. Louis, Schools $31 Million in Uncollected Revenue Last Year," *St. Louis Post-Dispatch*, January 22, 2019; see also Tim Logan, "As City's TIF Tab Grows, More Are Asking for Limits, *St. Louis Post-Dispatch*, January 4, 2014; Sarah Fenske, "St. Louis Gave Away $950K in Tax Incentives for Every New Central Corridor Resident," *Riverfront Times*, October 31, 2016.

38. Kae M. Petrin, "Once Promised for Rehab, Vacant Buildings Owned by Developer Paul McKee Now Scar City's North Side," *St. Louis Public Radio*, December 30, 2018; Jacob Barker, "McKee Got $2.5 Million in Tax Credits for a St. Louis Building He Didn't Pay For," *St. Louis Post-Dispatch*, May 16, 2018.

39. It is indicative of the dimensions of the issue that on the very day I wrote this paragraph, St. Louis County executive Steve Stenger was indicted on federal charges for a pay-to-play scandal, with a piece of land-banked property in impoverished Wellston at its core. See Jacob Barker, "Stenger Influenced Wellston Land

Sale to Donor, Former Partnership Employee Alleges," *St. Louis Post-Dispatch*, December 29, 2018; Jacob Barker, "Key Events Detailed in the Federal Indictment of St. Louis County Executive Steve Stenger," *St. Louis Post-Dispatch*, April 30, 2019.

40. Robert H. Teuscher, "The Payday Loan Industry in Missouri: A Study of the Laws, the Lenders, the Borrowers, and the Legislation," Better Business Bureau, July 2009, www.stlouisfed.org/~/media/files/pdfs/community %20development/paydayloanreport09color.pdf.

41. See "Debt, Inc.: Lending and Collecting in America" (series), *ProPublica*, www.propublica.org/series/debt-inc.

42. Richard Weaver, State of Missouri Division of Finance, letter to Governor Jay Dixon, January 14, 2009, https://finance.mo.gov/Contribute%20Documents /2009PaydayLendersSurvey.pdf; Woods v. QC Fin. Servs., Inc., 280 S.W.3d 90 (2009); Teuscher, "The Payday Loan Industry in Missouri"; Rogers, *Ferguson Is America*, 2.

43. Brewer v. Missouri Title Loans, 364 S.W.3d 486 (2012).

44. Hollins v. Capital Sols. Investments, Inc., 477 S.W.3d 19, 21 (Mo. Ct. App. 2015).

45. Richard Rothstein, "The Making of Ferguson: Public Policies at the Root of Its Troubles," Economic Policy Institute, October 15, 2014; Mary Delach Leonard, "The Great Recession: 10 Year Later," *St. Louis Public Radio*, May 23, 2018; Caitlin Lee and Clark Randall, "Foreclosures Devastated South St. Louis. Nathan Cooper Saw Opportunity," *Riverfront Times*, July 26, 2017. Keeanga-Yamahtta Taylor's *Race for Profits: How Banks and the Real Estate Industry Undermined Black Homeownership* (Chapel Hill: University of North Carolina Press, 2019) arrived while my own book was in production; it will surely be the new starting point for the discussion of this aspect of racial capitalist dispossession.

46. Rogers, *Ferguson Is America*; Gordon, *Citizen Brown*.

47. www.emerson.com/en-US/newsroom/news-releases/emerson-financial -news/Pages/Emerson-Reports-Q3Y14-Earnings.aspx.

48. Thomas Harvey, John McAnnar, Michael-John Voss, Megan Conn, Sean Janda, and Sophia Keskey, "ArchCity Defenders: Municipal Courts White Paper," updated November 23, 2014, 12, www.archcitydefenders.org/wp-content /uploads/2019/03/ArchCity-Defenders-Municipal-Courts-Whitepaper.pdf; Radley Balko, "How Municipalities in St. Louis County, Mo. Profit from Poverty," *Washington Post*, September 3, 2014.

49. For "driving while Black," see Boyles, *Race, Place, and Suburban Policing*, 18, 36, 37, 84, 88, 112, 115, 129.

50. City of Ferguson, Missouri, *Annual Operating Budget, Fiscal Year 2013– 2014*, www.fergusoncity.com/DocumentCenter/View/1609/2014-COFM-Budget -Final?bidId=page iii.

51. Christine Byers, "No Charges Against St. Louis Officer Who Killed VonDerrit Myers," *St. Louis Post-Dispatch*, May 18, 2015; Boyles, *Race, Place, and*

Suburban Policing, 101–103. See also Gerald Early, from *Daughters: On Family and Fatherhood*, in Early, *Ain't but a Place*, 244–255.

52. On this and all that follows, see Jodi Rios, "Racial States of Municipal Governance: Policing Bodies and Space for Revenue in North St. Louis County, MO," *Law and Inequality: A Journal of Theory and Practice* 37, no. 2 (June 2019); and Jodi Rios "Everyday Racialization: Contesting Space and Identity in Suburban St. Louis," in *Making Suburbia: New Histories of Everyday America*, ed. John Archer, Paul Sandul, and Kate Solomonson (Minneapolis: University of Minnesota Press, 2015), 185–207.

53. "Ferguson Sets Broad Changes for City Courts," *New York Times*, September 8, 2014; Harvey et al., "ArchCity Defenders: Municipal Courts White Paper," 7, 16–17, 24, 31.

54. Loïc Wacquant, *Deadly Symbiosis: Race and the Rise of Neoliberal Penalty* (Cambridge: Polity Press, 2009); Michelle Alexander, *The New Jim Crow: Mass Incarceration in the Age of Colorblindness* (New York: New Press, 2010); Fields and Fields, *Racecraft*, 265; Ruth Wilson Gilmore, *Golden Gulag: Prisons, Surplus, Crisis, and Opposition in Globalizing California* (Berkeley: University of California Press, 2007); Missouri Department of Corrections, "Institution Facilities," https://doc.mo.gov/facilities/adult-institutions/address-listing; Prison Policy Initiative, "Missouri Profile," www.prisonpolicy.org/profiles/MO.html.

55. US Department of Justice, Civil Rights Division, *Investigation of the Ferguson Police Department*, March 4, 2015, www.justice.gov/sites/default/files/opa/press-releases/attachments/2015/03/04/ferguson_police_department_report.pdf.

56. See, for example, "Emerson Opens New Corporate Data Center in St. Louis," *Data Center Dynamics*, July 25, 2009.

57. St. Louis County, GIS Service Center, "Property Lookup," http://maps.stlouisco.com/propertyview/. Emerson Electric's Ferguson campus is tract 12H320060; Emerson's personal property taxes are coded with that identifier.

58. Mark Polzin, personal communication with the author, March 30, 2015.

59. City of Ferguson, Missouri, *Annual Operating Budget, Fiscal Year 2013–2014*.

60. Mark Polzin, personal communication with the author, March 30, 2015; St. Louis County, GIS Service Center, "Property Lookup"; Mark Polzin, personal communication with the author, March 30, 2015; Harvey et al., "ArchCity Defenders: Municipal Courts White Paper," 32. The city does not publicly report Judge Ronald C. Brockmeyer's salary, but the budget for thirty-six sessions of court staffed by three full-time and three part-time employees is $318,300.

61. I am indebted to Sarah Coffin at St. Louis University's Center for Sustainability for helping me understand tax increment financing and for answering many elementary questions about a field in which she has long been doing advanced work.

62. City of Ferguson, Missouri, *Annual Operating Budget for 2013–2014*, 40, 102.

63. Urban Land Institute St. Louis, "Panel Recommendations to the Cities of Ferguson and Cool Valley," November 2012, www.fergusoncity.com/document center/view/1087, 3.

64. City of Ferguson, Missouri, *Annual Operating Budget for 2013–2014*.

65. I am particularly grateful to Gerald Frug for helping me think through the limitations of this commonsense notion of "economic development."

66. City of Ferguson, Missouri, *Annual Operating Budget for 2013–2014*, i, 24, 25, CIP-24, vi, 13. The raises were 2 percent in fiscal year 2012–2013 and 6 percent in fiscal year 2013–2014—slightly over 8 percent over the course of the two years.

67. City of Ferguson, Missouri, *Annual Operating Budget for 2013–2014*, CIP-10. These acquisitions were in addition to the fantastic array of federal-surplus military hardware deployed on West Florissant Avenue in the aftermath of the shooting to "keep the peace."

68. City of Ferguson, Missouri, *Annual Operating Budget for 2013–2014*, 87, 110. Parks are funded by sales tax revenue legally designated for that purpose. The city has budgeted between $250,000 and $500,000 a year from this designated Parks Fund to actually spend on the parks, an amount that was enhanced in 2014 by a pair of onetime grants from St. Louis County.

69. Rogers, *Ferguson Is America*; Taylor, *From #BlackLivesMatter to Black Liberation*; Wesley Lowery, *They Can't Kill Us All: The Story of Black Lives Matter* (New York: Penguin, 2017); Tef Poe, *Rebel to America* (New York: W. W. Norton and Co., forthcoming).

EPILOGUE: THE RIGHT PLACE FOR ALL THE WRONG REASONS

1. Ray Hartman, "We Wrote About Poisons in Coldwater Creek Thirty-Seven Years Ago. Guess What the Feds Just Confirmed?," *Riverfront Times*, May 15, 2019; "*Post-Dispatch* Coverage of the West Lake and Bridgeton Landfills," *St. Louis Post-Dispatch*, January 7, 2019, www.stltoday.com/news/archives /post-dispatch-coverage-of-the-west-lake-and-bridgeton-landfills/collection _f524db66-ffa9-54df-a131-b759a94ec3dd.html#utm_source=stltoday.com &utm_medium=web&utm_campaign=login_blueconic_incognito.

2. "Read the Verdict in the Jason Stockley Murder Case," *St. Louis Post-Dispatch*, September 15, 2017. Stockley, as was his right under Missouri law, had requested that his case be tried before a single judge rather than a jury.

3. Danny Wicentowski, "4 St. Louis Officers Charged in Undercover Officer's Beating During Jason Stockley Protests," *Riverfront Times*, November 29, 2018.

4. Brenden O'Brien, "After Protests, St. Louis Mayor Says Address Racism," Reuters, September 19, 2017.

5. "A Way, Away (Listen While I Say)," www.awayaway.site/.

6. City of St. Louis, "Rosie Willis," www.stlouis-mo.gov/government /departments/sldc/project-connect/nga/history/interviews/rosie-willis.cfm.

7. Sylvester Brown, interview with the author, March 28, 2018; North City Food Hub, www.northcityfoodhub.com.

8. Griot Museum of Black History and Culture, www.thegriotmuseum.com/.

9. Organization for Black Struggle, www.obs-stl.org/.

10. Hands Up United, www.handsupunited.org.

11. Close the Workhouse, "What Is Close the Workhouse?," www.close theworkhouse.org/.

12. National Building Arts Center, http://web.nationalbuildingarts.org/.

13. St. Louis Equal Housing and Opportunity Council, https://ehocstl.org/; Equity Legal Services, Inc., www.equitylegalservices.org/; Harvard University, Charles Warren Center for Studies in American History, "The Commonwealth Project," https://warrencenter.fas.harvard.edu/commonwealth-project.

14. Camille Curtis, interview with the author, Normandy High School, St. Louis, Missouri, July 8, 2019.

CODA: STL 2020

1. Karl Marx, *The Eighteenth Brumaire of Louis Bonaparte* (New York: International Publishers, 1963), 5, 15. For an excellent account of Weydemeyer's radicalism, see Abbet Sebastien, "Joseph Weydemeyer: A German American for Socialism and Black Rights," Historisches Seminar, University of Zurich, Fall 2016.

2. David Carson, Erin Heffernan, and Taylor Tiamoyo Harris, "Protesters Block St. Louis Interstate for Hours Before Gunshots Disperse Crowd; 1 Killed When Struck by Tractor-Trailer," *St. Louis Post-Dispatch*, May 30, 2020; Rachel Rice, Sarah Teague, and Taylor Tiamoyo Harris, "Protesters and Police Dispute Facts After 17 Arrests Sunday in Florissant," *St. Louis Post-Dispatch*, July 7, 2020; see also Colter Peterson, "Photos: ExpectUs Marches through the Central West End," *St. Louis Post-Dispatch*, July 4, 2020.

3. Walter Johnson, "The Revolution at the Gate," *Boston Review*, June 7, 2020.

4. Jeremy Kohler, "The St. Louis Couple Charged with Waving Guns at Protesters Have a Long History of Not Backing Down," *St. Louis Post-Dispatch*, August 19, 2020.

5. "Tucker Carlson Interviews St. Louis Gun Toter Mark McCloskey," July 1, 2020, www.youtube.com/watch?v=_xMsb5Vxp2w; Meagan Flynn, Tom Jackman, and Ben Guarino, "'A Modern-Day Night Ride': St. Louis Prosecutor Receives Death Threats as Trump Defends Couple Who Pointed Gun at Protesters," *Washington Post*, July 15, 2020.

6. Flynn, Jackman, and Guarino, "'A Modern-Day Night Ride.'"

7. "Raw: Mark and Patricia McCloskey Full Speech at RNC," August 25, 2020, www.youtube.com/watch?v=afDfBQR3eGY.

8. ACTION, "Thugs in Blue Uniform" (1970).

9. Flynn, Jackman, and Guarino, "'A Modern-Day Night Ride.'"

10. Robert Cohen, "Key Dates Leading to the Indictment of Missouri's Governor," *St. Louis Post-Dispatch*, February 22, 2018; "Tisaby Indictment Rooted in Gardner's Mistrust of Police," *St. Louis American*, June 19, 2019, www.stlamerican.com/news/editorials/tisaby-indictment-rooted-in-gardner-s-public-distrust-of-police/article_115dc4b6-92b6-11e9-95a5-eb1b65216c87.html. While Gardner herself was not indicted in the matter, the investigator, a former FBI agent, was, and is awaiting trial as of this writing.

11. Plain View Project, "Complete Collection," last updated June 20, 2019, www.plainviewproject.org/data?city=st_louis; "Another 15 St. Louis Police Officers Added to Top Prosecutor's Exclusion List," *St. Louis Post-Dispatch*, September 26, 2020; Christine Byers, "St. Louis Prosecutor Adds More Officers to Exclusion List," www.ksdk.com/article/news/crime/byers-beat/byers-beat-st-louis-officer-exclusion-list-fallout/63-32d6f685-22b6-4f2b-b5a0-ffccbe835b0a/.

12. Tony Messenger, "Read the Lawsuit Kim Gardner Filed Alleging Racist Conspiracy," *St. Louis Post-Dispatch*, January 13, 2020, www.stltoday.com/read-the-lawsuit-kim-gardner-filed-alleging-racist-conspiracy/pdf_43333b30-6f60-5b51-8d61-8d776ca99538.html.

13. Robert Patrick and Joel Currier, "Federal Judge Dismisses St. Louis Prosecutor's Lawsuit Alleging Racist Conspiracy against Her," *St. Louis Post-Dispatch*, September 30, 2020; *David Dixon v. City of St. Louis*, No. 19-2254 (8th Cir. 2020).

14. Christine Byers, "St. Louis Police Union Urges Members to Post Controversial Symbol on Social Media Pages," *St. Louis Post-Dispatch*, July 11, 2019; Maurice Chammah and Cary Aspinwall, "The Short, Fraught History of the 'Thin Blue Line' American Flag," The Marshall Project, June 8, 2020, www.themarshallproject.org/2020/06/08/the-short-fraught-history-of-the-thin-blue-line-american-flag.

15. Frantz Fanon, *The Wretched of the Earth*, trans. Richard Philcox (New York: Grove Press, 2004), 117. Two extraordinary books have illuminated the connections between overpolicing and inequality in St. Louis in the time since I completed work on this book: Colin Gordon, *Citizen Brown: Race, Democracy, and Inequality in the St. Louis Suburbs* (Chicago: University of Chicago Press, 2019); and Jody Rios, *Black Lives and Spatial Matters: Policing Blackness and Practicing Freedom in Suburban St. Louis* (Ithaca, NY: Cornell University Press, 2020).

16. Robert Samuels, Aaron Williams, Tracy Jan, and Jose A. Del Real, "'This Is What Happens to Us': How US Cities Lost Precious Time to Protect Black Citizens from the Coronavirus," *Washington Post*, June 3, 2020; Christopher Prener and Tim Wiemken, "Tracking COVID-19 in Missouri," https://slu-opengis.github.io/covid_daily_viz/index.html (accessed October 31, 2020).

17. Hye Jin Rho, Hayley Brown, and Shawn Fremstad, "A Basic Demographic Profile of Workers in Frontline Industries," Center for Economic and Policy Research, April 7, 2020, https://cepr.net/a-basic-demographic-profile-of-work ers-in-frontline-industries/; Dan Hutti, John Posey, and Mary Rocchio, "Where We Stand: The Strategic Assessment of the St. Louis Region," 8th ed., East-West Gateway Council of Governments, 2018, www.ewgateway.org/research-center /where-we-stand/; Sean Joe and Robert Motley, "Social Mobility: The Necessary Focus of St. Louis Investment in Black Males," Race and Opportunity Lab, Brown School at Washington University, February 2019, https://cpb-us-w2.wpmucdn .com/sites.wustl.edu/dist/a/1625/files/2018/06/Social-Mobility_-The-Necessary -Focus-of-St.-Louis-Investment-in-B-2olhe9m.pdf. This paragraph and the two that follow are based on Colin Gordon, Walter Johnson, Jason Q. Purnell, and Jamala Rogers, "COVID-19 and the Color Line," *Boston Review*, May 1, 2020. I am beyond grateful to my colleagues for allowing me to repurpose our collectively authored piece and present it under my own name here. See also Colin Gordon, *Mapping Decline: St. Louis and the Fate of the American City* (Philadelphia: University of Pennsylvania Press, 2009); Gordon, *Citizen Brown*; Jason Q. Purnell, Gabriela J. Camberos, and Robert P. Fields, eds., "For the Sake of All: A Report on the Health and Well-being of African Americans in St. Louis—And Why It Matters for Everyone," Washington University in St. Louis and Saint Louis University, revised July 31, 2015; and Jamala Rogers, *Ferguson Is America: Roots of Rebellion* (St. Louis: Organization of Black Struggle, 2015).

18. Hutti et al., "Where We Stand"; Eli Chen (St. Louis Public Radio), "St. Louis Communities with Polluted Air Are More Vulnerable to the Coronavirus," *St. Louis American*, April 21, 2020; Walter Johnson, "American Bottom," *Boston Review*, January 23, 2020; Michele Munz, "A Plea for Help: Centreville's Sewage and Drainage Problems Pose Health, Safety Risks," *St. Louis Post-Dispatch*, February 23, 2020; Nancy Cambria, Paul Fehler, Jason Q. Purnell, and Brian Schmidt, *Segregation in St. Louis: Dismantling the Divide*, Washington University in St. Louis, 2018; see also the goals and reports available at Forward Through Ferguson, "The Work—Forward Through Ferguson," https://forwardthroughferguson .org/implementation-2/.

19. Close the Workhouse, "The Campaign to Close the Workhouse," www .closetheworkhouse.org/.

20. Tony Messenger, "Krewson Administration, Aldermen Backtrack on Close the Workhouse Plan," *St. Louis Post-Dispatch*, October 9, 2020.

INDEX

ALISON FRANK JOHNSON

WALTER JOHNSON is Winthrop Professor of History and professor of African and African American Studies at Harvard University. A Missouri native and author of the award-winning *Soul by Soul* and the critically acclaimed *River of Dark Dreams,* he lives in Arlington, Massachusetts.